FIFTH EDITION

Focus on
Grammar 4

Marjorie Fuchs
Margaret Bonner

with Jane Curtis

Focus on Grammar 4: An Integrated Skills Approach, Fifth Edition

Pearson Education, 221 River Street, Hoboken, NJ 07030

Staff credits: The people who made up the *Focus on Grammar 4, Fifth Edition* team, representing content creation, design, manufacturing, marketing, multimedia, project management, publishing, rights management, and testing, are Pietro Alongi, Rhea Banker, Elizabeth Barker, Stephanie Bullard, Jennifer Castro, Tracey Cataldo, Aerin Csigay, Mindy DePalma, Dave Dickey, Warren Fischbach, Pam Fishman, Nancy Flaggman, Lester Holmes, Gosia Jaros-White, Leslie Johnson, Barry Katzen, Amy McCormick, Julie Molnar, Brian Panker, Stuart Radcliffe, Jennifer Raspiller, Lindsay Richman, Robert Ruvo, Alexandra Suarez, Paula Van Ells, and Joseph Vella.

Text design and layout: Don Williams
Composition: Page Designs International
Project supervision: Bernard Seal
Contributing editors: Françoise Leffler and Bernard Seal

Cover image: Andy Roberts / Getty Images

Library of Congress Cataloging-in-Publication Data

A catalog record for the print edition is available from the Library of Congress.

Printed in the United States of America

ISBN 10: 0-13-458330-2
ISBN 13: 978-0-13-458330-3

11 2019

Contents

Contents (continued)

WELCOME TO
FOCUS ON GRAMMAR
FIFTH EDITION

BUILDING ON THE SUCCESS of previous editions, *Focus on Grammar* continues to provide an integrated-skills approach to engage students and help them understand, practice, and use English grammar. Centered on thematic instruction, *Focus on Grammar* combines comprehensive grammar coverage with abundant practice, critical thinking skills, and ongoing assessment, helping students accomplish their goals of communicating confidently, accurately, and fluently in everyday situations.

New in the Fifth Edition

New and Updated Content
Focus on Grammar continues to offer engaging and motivating content that appeals to learners from various cultural backgrounds. Many readings and activities have been replaced or updated to include topics that are of high interest to today's learners.

Updated Charts and Redesigned Notes
Clear, corpus-informed grammar presentations reflect real and natural language usage and allow students to grasp the most important aspects of the grammar. Clear signposting draws attention to common usage, the difference between written and spoken registers, and common errors.

Additional Communicative Activities
The new edition of *Focus on Grammar* has been expanded with additional communicative activities that encourage collaboration and the application of the target grammar in a variety of settings.

Expanded Writing Practice
Each unit in *Focus on Grammar* now ends with a structured "From Grammar to Writing" section. Supported by pre-writing and editing tasks, students engage in activities that allow them to apply the target grammar in writing.

New Assessment Program
The new edition of *Focus on Grammar* features a variety of new assessment tools, including course diagnostic tests, formative and summative assessments, and a flexible gradebook. The assessments are closely aligned with unit learning outcomes to inform instruction and measure student progress.

Revised MyEnglishLab
The updated MyEnglishLab offers students engaging practice and video grammar presentations anywhere, anytime. Immediate feedback and remediation tasks offer additional opportunities for successful mastery of content and help promote accuracy. Instructors receive instant access to digital content and diagnostic tools that allow them to customize the learning environment to meet the needs of their students.

The *Focus on Grammar* Approach

At the heart of the *Focus on Grammar* series is its unique and successful four-step approach that lets learners move from comprehension to communication within a clear and consistent structure. The books provide an abundance of scaffolded exercises to bridge the gap between identifying grammatical structures and using them with confidence and accuracy. The integration of the four skills allows students to learn grammar holistically, which in turn prepares them to understand and use English more effectively.

STEP 1: Grammar in Context integrates grammar and vocabulary in natural contexts such as articles, stories, dialogues, and blog posts. Students engage with the unit reading and theme and get exposure to grammar as it is used in real life.

STEP 2: Grammar Presentation presents the structures in clear and accessible grammar charts and notes with multiple examples of form and meaning. Corpus-informed explanations and examples reflect natural usage of the target forms, differentiate between written and conversational registers whenever appropriate, and highlight common errors to help students avoid typical pitfalls in both speaking and writing.

STEP 3: Focused Practice provides numerous and varied contextualized exercises for both the form and meaning of the new structures. Controlled practice ensures students' understanding of the target grammar and leads to mastery of form, meaning, and use.

STEP 4: Communication Practice provides practice with the structures in listening exercises as well as in communicative, open-ended speaking activities. These engaging activities provide ample opportunities for personalization and build students' confidence in using English. Students also develop their critical thinking skills through problem-solving activities and discussions.

Each unit now culminates with the **From Grammar to Writing** section. Students learn about common errors in writing and how to recognize them in their own work. Engaging and motivating writing activities encourage students to apply grammar in writing through structured tasks from pre-writing to editing.

Recycling

Underpinning the scope and sequence of the *Focus on Grammar* series is practice that allows students to use target structures and vocabulary many times, in different contexts. New grammar and vocabulary are recycled throughout the book. Students have maximum exposure, leading them to become confident in using the language in speech and in writing.

Assessment

Extensive testing informs instruction and allows teachers and students to measure progress.

- **Unit Reviews** at the end of every unit assess students' understanding of the grammar and allow students to monitor their own progress.

- **Diagnostic Tests** provide teachers with a valid and reliable means to determine how well students know the material they are going to study and to target instruction based on students' needs.

- **Unit Review Tests, Mid- and End-of-Term Review Tests, and Final Exams** measure students' ability to demonstrate mastery of skills taught in the course.

- The **Placement Test** is designed to help teachers place students into one of the five levels of the *Focus on Grammar* course.

The Importance of Context

A key element of *Focus on Grammar* is presenting important grammatical structures in context. The contexts selected are most relevant to the grammatical forms being introduced. Contextualized grammar practice also plays a key role in improving fluent use of grammar in communicative contexts. It helps learners to develop consistent and correct usage of target structures during all productive practice.

The Role of Corpus

The most important goal of *Focus on Grammar* has always been to present grammar structures using natural language. To that end, *Focus on Grammar* has incorporated the findings of corpus linguistics,* while never losing sight of what is pedagogically sound and useful. By taking this approach, *Focus on Grammar* ensures that:

- the language presented reflects real, natural usage
- themes and topics provide a good fit with the grammar point and elicit the target grammar naturally
- findings of the corpus research are reflected in the syllabus, readings, charts, grammar notes, and practice activities
- examples illustrate differences between spoken and written registers, and formal and informal language
- students are exposed to common errors in usage and learn how to recognize and avoid errors in their own speech and writing

Focus on Grammar Efficacy

The fifth edition of *Focus on Grammar* reflects an important efficacy initiative for Pearson courses—to be able to demonstrate that all teaching materials have a positive impact on student learning. To support this, *Focus on Grammar* has been updated and aligned to the **Global Scale of English** and the **Common European Framework** (CEFR) to provide granular insight into the objectives of the course, the progression of learning, and the expected outcomes a learner will be able to demonstrate upon successful completion.

To learn more about the Global Scale of English, visit www.English.com.

Components

Student Books with Essential Online Resources include access codes to the course audio, video, and self-assessment.

Student Books with MyEnglishLab offer a blended approach with integration of print and online content.

Workbooks contain additional contextualized practice in print format.

Digital Teacher's Resources include printable teaching notes, GSE mapping documents, answer keys, audio scripts, and downloadable tests. Access to the digital copy of the student books allows teachers to project the pages for whole-class instruction.

***FOG Go* app** allows users to access the student book audio on their mobile devices.

* A principal resource has been Douglas Biber et al, *Longman Grammar of Spoken and Written English*, Harlow: Pearson Education Ltd., 1999.

The *Focus on Grammar* Unit

Focus on Grammar introduces grammar structures in the context of unified themes. All units follow a four-step approach, taking learners from grammar in context to communicative practice. Thematic units add a layer to learning so that by the end of the unit students will be able to discuss the content using the grammar points they have just studied.

STEP 1   GRAMMAR IN CONTEXT

Before You Read activities create interest and elicit students' knowledge about the topic.

Vocabulary exercises help students improve their command of English.

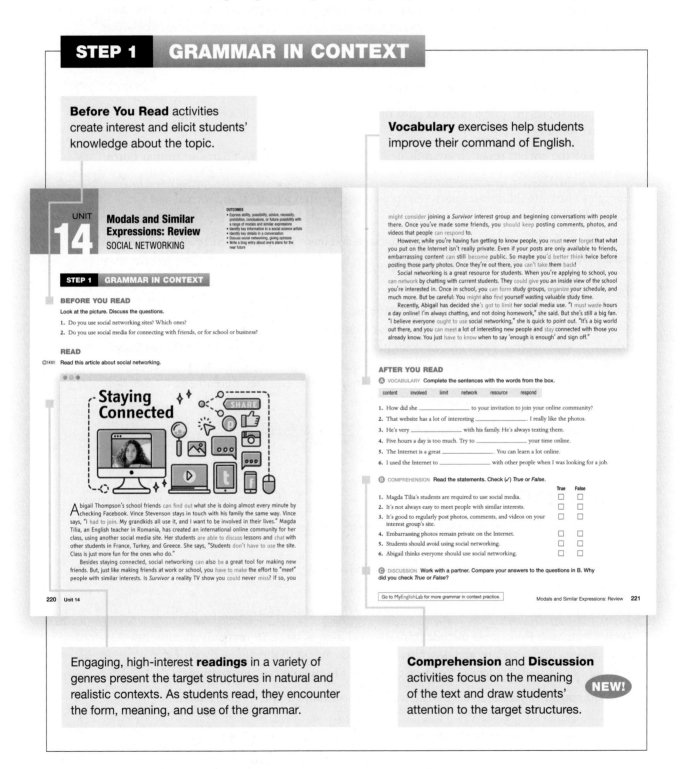

Engaging, high-interest **readings** in a variety of genres present the target structures in natural and realistic contexts. As students read, they encounter the form, meaning, and use of the grammar.

Comprehension and **Discussion** activities focus on the meaning of the text and draw students' attention to the target structures.

NEW!

Grammar Charts present the structures in a clear, easy-to-read format.

NEW!

The newly designed **Grammar Notes** highlight the main point of each note, making navigation and review easier. Simple corpus-informed **explanations** and **examples** ensure students' understanding.

STEP 2 GRAMMAR PRESENTATION

FUTURE

Affirmative Statements

We **are going to take**	
We **will take**	the airship at 9:00.
We **are taking**	
We **take**	

Negative Statements

We **are not going to take**	
We **will not take**	the airship at 10:00.
We **are not taking**	
We **don't take**	

Yes/No Questions

Is she **going to take**	
Will she **take**	the airship at 9:00?
Is she **taking**	
Does she **take**	

Short Answers

	Affirmative		Negative
	she **is.**		she **isn't.**
Yes,	she **will.**	No,	she **won't.**
	she **is.**		she **isn't.**
	she **does.**		she **doesn't.**

Wh- Questions

When is she **going to take**	
When **will** she **take**	the airship?
When is she **taking**	
When **does** she **take**	

FUTURE PROGRESSIVE

Statements

Subject	Be (not) going to/ Will (not)	Be + Base Form + -ing	
People	**are (not) going to will (not)**	**be traveling**	to Mars by 2050.

Yes/No Questions

Be/Will	Subject	Going to	Be + Base Form + -ing	
Are	they	going to	**be traveling**	to Mars?
Will				

Short Answers

Affirmative		Negative
they **are.**		they're **not.**
Yes, they **will.**	No,	they **won't.**

Wh- Questions

Wh- Word	Be/Will	Subject	Going to	Be + Base Form + -ing	
When	are will	they	going to	**be traveling**	to Mars?

GRAMMAR NOTES

1 Simple Present

Use the **simple present** to show that something **happens regularly** or for **unchanging facts**.

- **happens regularly**
  (always, usually, often, sometimes, rarely)

  Past ——— Now ——— Future
  People always call him Joe.

  People **always call** him Joe.
  We **usually prefer** first names.
  Dusya **sometimes uses** nicknames.

- **unchanging facts**

  She **comes** from Moscow. It's the capital.

BE CAREFUL! Remember to add *-s* or *-es* to third-person singular (*he, she, it*) of simple present verbs. Use *do/does* in questions and *do not/does not* in negative sentences.

Dusya **lives** in Toronto. She **doesn't live** in Ottawa.
NOT Dusya ~~live~~ in Toronto. She ~~don't live~~ in Ottawa.

USAGE NOTE We often use adverbs of frequency (*always, usually*, etc.) with verbs in the simple present. The adverb usually goes **before the verb**. If the verb is *be*, the adverb goes **after** *be*.
Sometimes and *usually* can also go at the **beginning** of the sentence.

Dusya **always gets** home at 7:00 p.m.
She **usually finishes** her work on time.
She **is never** late for class.

We **sometimes eat** lunch together.
Sometimes we **eat** lunch together.

2 Present Progressive

Use the present progressive to show that something is **happening now** or in a **longer present time**.

- **happening now**
  (right now, at the moment)

  Past ——— Now ——— Future
  She's studying.

  A: What's Dusya doing?
  B: **Right now**, she's **studying** in the library.

- **happening in a longer present time, but perhaps not at this exact moment**
  (this month, this year, these days)

  Past ——— Now ——— Future
  He's working.

  A: What's Jorge **doing** *these days*?
  B: He's **working** on a new project.

BE CAREFUL! Use *am, is*, and *are* with *-ing* for the present progressive. Do not forget to add *-ing* to the verb.

Dusya **is working** in Canada this year.
NOT Dusya ~~is work~~ in Canada this year.

USAGE NOTE We often use time expressions (*right now, this month, these days*, etc.) with verbs in the present progressive. The time expression can go at the **beginning** or **end** of the sentence. *Now* can also go **after** *be*.

These days, Dusya **is looking** for a new job.
Dusya **is looking** for a new job *these days*.

Now, she **is preparing** for a job interview.
She **is preparing** for a job interview *now*.
She **is** *now* **preparing** for a job interview.

NEW!

Clear signposting provides corpus-informed notes about common usage, differences between spoken and written registers, and common errors.

Pronunciation Notes are now included with the grammar presentation to highlight relevant pronunciation aspects of the target structures and to help students understand authentic spoken English.

NEW!

PRONUNCIATION NOTE

Intonation of Tag Questions

In tag questions, our **voice rises** at the end when we expect another person to give us **information**.	A: You're not moving, **are you?** B: Yes, I'm returning to Berlin.
Our **voice falls** at the end when we are making a comment and expect the other person to **agree**.	A: Seoul is interesting, **isn't it?** B: Yes, it is.

Go to MyEnglishLab to watch the grammar presentation.

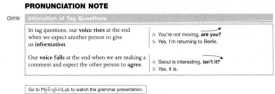

Discover the Grammar activities develop students' recognition and understanding of the target structures before they are asked to produce them.

Controlled practice activities lead students to master form, meaning, and use of the target grammar.

STEP 3   FOCUSED PRACTICE

EXERCISE 1   DISCOVER THE GRAMMAR

GRAMMAR NOTES 1–4   Read the statements. Check (✔) *Active* or *Passive*.

	Active	Passive
1. The first *National Geographic* magazine was published in October 1888.	☐	☑
2. Today, millions of people read the magazine.	☐	☐
3. The magazine is translated from English into forty other languages.	☐	☐
4. My cousin reads the Russian edition.	☐	☐
5. Some of the articles are written by famous writers.	☐	☐
6. *Young Explorer*, another publication, is written for kids.	☐	☐
7. The publication is known for its wonderful photography.	☐	☐
8. A *National Geographic* photographer took the first underwater color photos.	☐	☐
9. Photographers are sent all over the world.	☐	☐
10. The articles show a lot of respect for nature.	☐	☐
11. That picture was taken by Reza Deghati.	☐	☐
12. *National Geographic* is sold at newsstands.	☐	☐

EXERCISE 2   ACTIVE OR PASSIVE

GRAMMAR NOTES 1–4   The chart shows some of the forty language editions that *National Geographic* publishes. Use the chart to complete the sentences. Some sentences will be active; some will be passive.

Language	Number of Speakers*
Arabic	240
Chinese (all varieties)	1,200
English	340
Japanese	130
Korean	77
Russian	110
Spanish	410
Turkish	71

* first-language speakers in millions

1. Spanish *is spoken by 410 million people* .
2. Around 110 million people *speak Russian* .
3. Arabic _____ .
4. _____ Chinese.

EXERCISE 2   RELATIVE PRONOUNS AND VERBS

GRAMMAR NOTES 3–6   Complete the statements in the personality quiz. Circle the correct words. (In Exercise 9, you will take the quiz.)

Personality Quiz

Do you agree with the following statements? Check (✔) *True* or *False*.

	TRUE	FALSE
1. People who / which talk a lot tire me.	☐	☐
2. On a plane, I always talk to the stranger who take / takes the seat next to me.	☐	☐
3. I'm the kind of person that / which needs time to recover after a social event.	☐	☐
4. My best friend, that / who talks a lot, is just like me.	☐	☐
5. I prefer to have conversations which focus / focuses on feelings and ideas.	☐	☐
6. I am someone whose favorite activities include / includes reading and doing yoga.	☐	☐
7. People whose / their personalities are completely different can be close friends.	☐	☐
8. I'm someone that always see / sees the glass as half full, not half empty.	☐	☐
9. Difficult situations are often the ones that provide / provides the best opportunities.	☐	☐
10. Introverts, that / who are quiet, sensitive, and creative, are perfect friends.	☐	☐

EXERCISE 3   IDENTIFYING ADJECTIVE CLAUSES

Ⓐ GRAMMAR NOTES 1–4, 6   We often use identifying adjective clauses to define words. First, match the words on the left with the descriptions on the right.

_h_	1. difficulty	a.	This situation gives you a chance to experience something good.
___	2. extrovert	b.	This attitude shows your ideas about your future.
___	3. introvert	c.	This ability makes you able to produce new ideas.
___	4. opportunity	d.	This person usually sees the bright side of situations.
___	5. opposites	e.	This person requires a lot of time alone.
___	6. optimist	f.	This money was unexpected.
___	7. outlook	g.	This person usually sees the dark side of situations.
___	8. pessimist	h.	This problem is hard to solve.
___	9. creativity	i.	These people have completely different personalities.
___	10. windfall	j.	This person requires a lot of time with others.

A **variety of exercise types** engage students and guide them from recognition and understanding to accurate production of the grammar structures.

Editing exercises allow students to identify and correct typical mistakes.

EXERCISE 5   EDITING

GRAMMAR NOTES 1–7   Read this post to a travelers' website. There are ten mistakes in the use of embedded questions. The first mistake is already corrected. Find and correct nine more. Don't forget to check punctuation.

WORLDWIDE TRAVEL

Email this page to someone!   New Topic   Post a Poll   Post Reply

Subject: **Tipping at the Hair Salon in Italy**
Posted April 10 by Jenna Thompson

    if or whether
I wonder ~~if~~ you can help clarify some tipping situations for me. I never know what doing at the

hair salon. I don't know if I should tip the person who washes my hair? What about the person

who cuts it, and the person who colors it? And what happens if the person is the owner.

Do you know do I still need to tip him or her? That doesn't seem logical. (And often I'm not

even sure who is the owner!) Then I never know how much to tip or where should I leave

the tip? Do I leave it on the counter or in the person's hands? What if somebody's hands are

wet or have hair color on them? Can I just put the tip in his or her pocket? It all seems so

complicated! I can't imagine how do customers figure all this out? What's the custom? I really

need to find out what to do—and FAST! My hair is getting very long and dirty.

Listenings in a variety of genres allow students to hear the grammar in natural contexts.

STEP 4   COMMUNICATION PRACTICE

EXERCISE 6   LISTENING

🔊 20·03 **Ⓐ** Claudia Leggett and her son, Pietro, are flying from Los Angeles to Hong Kong. Listen to the announcements they hear in the airport and aboard the plane. Read the statements. Then listen again and check (✓) *True* or *False*.

	True	False
Announcement 1: Claudia has two pieces of carry-on luggage, and Pietro has one. They can take them all on the plane.	☐	☑
Announcement 2: Look at their boarding passes. They can board now.	☐	☐

	True	False
Announcement 3: Look at their boarding passes again. They can board now.	☐	☐
Announcement 4: Pietro is only ten years old. Claudia should put his oxygen mask on first.	☐	☐
Announcement 5: Claudia is sitting in a left-hand window seat. She can see the lights of Tokyo.	☐	☐
Announcement 6: Passengers who are taking connecting flights can get this information on the plane.	☐	☐

🔊 20·03 **Ⓑ** Work with a partner. Listen again to the announcements. Discuss your answers.

EXAMPLE: A: OK. So, why is the answer to number 1 *False*?
         B: The announcement says if you have more than one piece of carry-on luggage, you must check the extra pieces at the gate.
         A: Right. And they have three pieces, so they can't take them all on the plane with them. Now, what did you choose for number 2?

Passengers on Flight 396 to Hong Kong

In the **listening activities**, students practice a range of listening skills. A **new step** has been added in which partners complete an activity that relates to the listening and uses the target grammar. **NEW!**

Engaging **communicative activities** (conversations, discussions, presentations, surveys, and games) help students synthesize the grammar, develop fluency, and build their problem-solving skills.

EXERCISE 7   WHAT ABOUT YOU?

CONVERSATION   Work in a group. Talk about your hobbies and interests. What did you do in the past with your hobby? What have you been doing lately? Find out about other people's hobbies.

EXAMPLE: A: Do you have any hobbies, Ben?
         B: Yes. Since I was in high school, my hobby has been running. . . . Recently, I've been training for a marathon. What about you? Do you have a hobby?
         C: I collect sneakers. I got my first pair of Nikes when I was ten, and I've been collecting different kinds of sneakers ever since. . . .

EXERCISE 8   DONE, DONE, NOT DONE

Ⓐ INTERVIEW   What did you plan to do last month to develop your hobbies and personal interests? Make a list. Include things you did and things that you still haven't done. Do not check (✓) any of the items. Exchange lists with a partner.

Buy a new pair of running shoes.
Research healthy snacks for marathon runners.

Ⓑ Now ask questions about your partner's list. Check (✓) the things that your partner has already done. Answer your partner's questions about your list. When you finish, find out if the information that you recorded on your partner's list is correct.

EXAMPLE: A: Have you bought your new running shoes yet?
         B: Yes, I have. I bought them last week.
         A: And what about the research on healthy snacks?
         B: I haven't done it yet.
         A: OK. I think we've talked about everything on our lists. Let's make sure our answers are correct.

FROM GRAMMAR TO WRITING

A **From Grammar to Writing** section, now in every unit, helps students confidently apply the unit's grammar to their own writing.

NEW!

FROM GRAMMAR TO WRITING

Ⓐ BEFORE YOUR WRITE Diplomats are people who officially represent their country in a foreign country. Imagine that you are going to attend a school for future diplomats. Complete the information about some of the features of your ideal school.

Courses required: _____

Language(s) spoken: _____

Living quarters provided: _____

Food offered: _____

Trips taken: _____

Electronic devices provided: _____

Ⓑ WRITE Use your information to write one or two paragraphs about your ideal school for diplomacy. Use the passive with modals and similar expressions. Try to avoid some of the common mistakes in the chart.

EXAMPLE: I think the ideal school for diplomacy should teach a lot about cross-cultural understanding. Courses should be required in . . . More than one official language should be spoken. Classes could be offered in . . .

Common Mistakes in Using the Passive with Modals and Similar Expressions

Use *be* + past participle after the modal. Do not leave out *be*.	Language classes **should *be* required**. NOT Language classes should required.
Use the **past participle after *be***. Do not use the base form of the verb after *be*.	A lot **could be *learned***. NOT A lot could be learn.

Ⓒ CHECK YOUR WORK Read your paragraph(s). Underline the passive with modals and similar expressions. Use the Editing Checklist to check your work.

Editing Checklist

Did you use . . . ?

☐ *be* + past participle to form the passive after modals or similar expressions

☐ *will* or *be going to* for certainty in the future

☐ *can* for present ability

☐ *could* for past ability or future possibility

☐ *may*, *might*, and *can't* for future possibility or impossibility

☐ *should*, *ought to*, and *had better* for advice

☐ *must* and *have (got) to* for necessity

Ⓓ REVISE YOUR WORK Read your paragraph(s) again. Can you improve your writing? Make changes if necessary. Give your writing a title.

Go to MyEnglishLab for more writing practice.   The Passive with Modals and Similar Expressions   **299**

The **Before You Write** task helps students generate ideas for their writing assignment.

In the **Write** task, students are given a writing assignment and guided to use the target grammar and avoid common mistakes.

Check Your Work includes an Editing Checklist that allows students to proofread and edit their compositions.

In **Revise Your Work**, students are given a final opportunity to improve their writing.

UNIT REVIEW

Unit Reviews give students the opportunity to check their understanding of the target structures. Students can check their answers against the Answer Key at the end of the book. They can also complete the Review on MyEnglishLab.

UNIT 21 REVIEW

Test yourself on the grammar of the unit.

Ⓐ Match each condition with its result.

Condition	Result
_____ 1. If it rains,	a. you might have good luck.
_____ 2. Unless you study,	b. I could pay you back tomorrow.
_____ 3. If you cross your fingers,	c. I may not buy it.
_____ 4. Unless they lower the price,	d. I'll take an umbrella.
_____ 5. If you lend me $10,	e. you could rent one.
_____ 6. If you don't own a car,	f. you won't pass.

Ⓑ Complete the future real conditional sentences in these conversations with the correct form of the verbs in parentheses.

1. A: Are you going to take the bus?

   B: No. If I _____ the bus, I _____ late.
   a. (take)   b. (be)

2. A: What _____ you _____ if you _____ the job?
   a. (do)   b. (not get)

   B: I _____ in school unless I _____ the job.
   c. (stay)   d. (get)

3. A: If I _____ the test, I _____ .
   a. (pass)   b. (celebrate)

   B: Good luck, but I'm sure you'll pass. You've studied really hard for it.

   A: Thanks!

Ⓒ Find and correct six mistakes. Remember to check punctuation.

It's been a hard week, and I'm looking forward to the weekend. If the weather will be nice tomorrow Marco and I are going to go to the beach. The ocean is usually too cold

MyEnglishLab

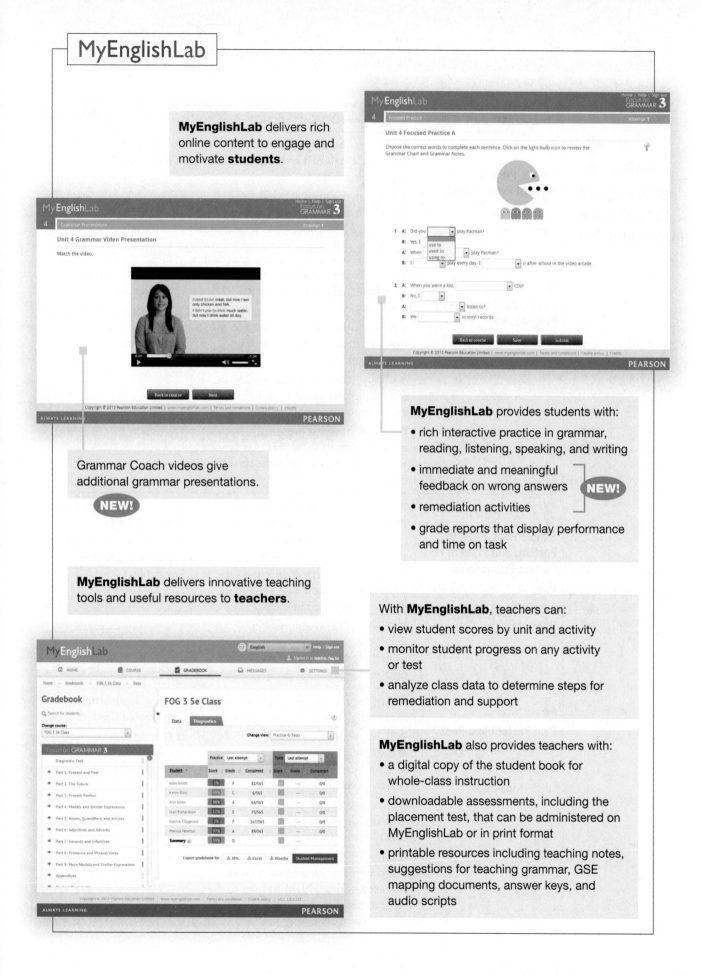

MyEnglishLab delivers rich online content to engage and motivate **students**.

Unit 4 Grammar Video Presentation

Watch the video.

I used to eat meat, but now I eat only chicken and fish.
I didn't use to drink much water, but now I drink water all day.

Back to course   Next

Grammar Coach videos give additional grammar presentations.

NEW!

Unit 4 Focused Practice A

Choose the correct words to complete each sentence. Click on the light bulb icon to review the Grammar Chart and Grammar Notes.

1 A: Did you [ ] play Pacman?
  B: Yes, I [use to / used to / using to]
  A: When [ ] play Pacman?
  B: I [ ] play every day. I [ ] it after school in the video arcade.

2 A: When you were a kid, [ ] CDs?
  B: No, I [ ]
  A: [ ] listen to?
  B: We [ ] to vinyl records.

Back to course   Save   Submit

MyEnglishLab provides students with:

- rich interactive practice in grammar, reading, listening, speaking, and writing
- immediate and meaningful feedback on wrong answers **NEW!**
- remediation activities
- grade reports that display performance and time on task

MyEnglishLab delivers innovative teaching tools and useful resources to **teachers**.

Gradebook

Search for students

Change course:
FOG 3 5e Class

FOCUS on GRAMMAR 3

Diagnostic Test
Part 1: Present and Past
Part 2: The Future
Part 3: Present Perfect
Part 4: Modals and Similar Expressions
Part 5: Nouns, Quantifiers, and Articles
Part 6: Adjectives and Adverbs
Part 7: Gerunds and Infinitives
Part 8: Pronouns and Phrasal Verbs
Part 9: More Modals and Similar Expressions
Appendices

FOG 3 5e Class

Data   Diagnostics

Change view: Practice & Tests

Student	Practice Last attempt			Tests Last attempt		
	Score	Grade	Completed	Score	Grade	Completed
John Smith	2%	F	81/565		...	0/0
Karen Ross	49%	C	6/565		...	0/0
Ann Jones	88%	A	64/565		...	0/0
Ivan Richardson	12%	E	73/565		...	0/0
Patrick Fitzgerald	2%	F	167/565		...	0/0
Monica Newton	57%	A	89/565		...	0/0
Summary	53%	D			...	

Export gradebook for   XML   Excel   Moodle   Student Management

With **MyEnglishLab**, teachers can:

- view student scores by unit and activity
- monitor student progress on any activity or test
- analyze class data to determine steps for remediation and support

MyEnglishLab also provides teachers with:

- a digital copy of the student book for whole-class instruction
- downloadable assessments, including the placement test, that can be administered on MyEnglishLab or in print format
- printable resources including teaching notes, suggestions for teaching grammar, GSE mapping documents, answer keys, and audio scripts

Scope and Sequence

PART **1**

Present and Past: Review and Expansion

LISTENING	SPEAKING	WRITING	VOCABULARY
A conversation about people ▣ Can identify people, based on descriptions in a conversation	▣ Can ask people for personal details and introduce them to others ▣ Can narrate a video, describing what people are doing ▣ Can discuss naming customs in different countries	▣ Can write a detailed paragraph about oneself	adjustment **AWL** consist of **AWL** convince **AWL** identity **AWL** in style **AWL** provide
A personal narrative ▣ Can identify the order of events in a recorded description	▣ Can describe one's first meeting with someone ▣ Can ask and answer questions about important life events ▣ Can create a story and present it to the class	▣ Can write two paragraphs describing past events in an important relationship	accomplish cover (v) influential pursue **AWL** recover **AWL** research (n) **AWL**
A conversation about hobbies ▣ Can recognize key ideas and details in a discussion about hobbies and personal interests	▣ Can talk about hobbies and personal interests ▣ Can discuss routine accomplishments ▣ Can research an interesting hobby and present findings to the class	▣ Can write a detailed paragraph about a recent trend	alternative (n) **AWL** experiment (v) motivation **AWL** passion survive **AWL** trend (n) **AWL**
An interview on a radio show ▣ Can understand the order of events in a radio program about career and life choices	▣ Can ask and answer questions about past events and personal achievements ▣ Can discuss one's schedule for the previous day ▣ Can research a famous child prodigy and present findings to the class ▣ Can compare two similar scenes and discuss differences	▣ Can write two paragraphs about a famous person's career and personal life	conduct (v) **AWL** contract (n) **AWL** ethnic **AWL** inspire participate **AWL** transform **AWL**

AWL = Academic Word List item

UNIT	GRAMMAR	READING

PART 2

Future: Review and Expansion

5

Future and Future Progressive

Page 68

THEME Life in the Future

- ■ Can use *will* or *be going to* to discuss future facts and predictions
- ■ Can use *will* when making quick decisions, offers, and promises, and *be going to* or the present progressive when making plans
- ■ Can use the simple present to discuss future scheduled events
- ■ Can use the future progressive to describe an action that will be in progress at a specific time in the future
- ■ Can use the simple present or the present progressive in future time clauses

Information Article: *Cities of the Future*

- ■ Can understand important points and details in a lengthy article about a scientific topic

6

Future Perfect and Future Perfect Progressive

Page 86

THEME Goals

- ■ Can use the future perfect to show that something will happen before a specific time in the future
- ■ Can use the future perfect progressive to show that something will be in progress until a specific time in the future
- ■ Can use the future perfect (progressive) with the simple present to show the time order between two future events
- ■ Can use adverbs such as *already* and *yet* to emphasize the first event, and expressions with *by* to refer to the second event

Business Article: *Young Entrepreneur Looks Toward the Future*

- ■ Can scan a text about a business topic in order to find specific information

PART 3

Negative and Tag Questions, Additions and Responses

7

Negative *Yes/No* Questions and Tag Questions

Page 102

THEME Places to Live

- ■ Can use a range of negative *yes/no* questions and tag questions to check information or comment on a situation
- ■ Can answer negative *yes/no* questions and tag questions

PRONUNCIATION Intonation of tag questions

Interview Transcripts: *It's a Great Place to Live, Isn't It?*

- ■ Can scan interview transcripts for key information

8

Additions and Responses: *So, Too, Neither, Not either,* and *But*

Page 118

THEME Similarities and Differences

- ■ Can use additions with *so, too, neither,* or *not either* to express similarity
- ■ Can use additions with *but* to express difference
- ■ Can use short responses with *so, too, neither,* or *not either* to express agreement
- ■ Can use short responses with *but* to express disagreement

Scientific Article: *The Twin Question: Nature or Nurture?*

- ■ Can extract specific information from a long, linguistically complex text on a scientific topic

LISTENING	SPEAKING	WRITING	VOCABULARY
A discussion about a conference ■ Can follow a group discussion, identifying important details such as the speakers' schedules and plans	■ Can discuss schedules, reaching agreement on plans ■ Can offer a detailed opinion about a controversial topic relating to technology	■ Can write two paragraphs about a hypothetical scenario that is set in the future	challenge (n) AWL individual (n) AWL innovative AWL technology AWL vehicle AWL vertical (adj)
A conversation about entrepreneurship ■ Can follow a fast-paced conversation about professional aspirations, identifying key details	■ Can talk about someone's future goals and accomplishments ■ Can discuss personal long-term goals and how to achieve them	■ Can write a detailed paragraph about a classmate's future goals and what that person is doing to achieve these goals	affordable convert (v) AWL corporate (adj) AWL initiative AWL meanwhile status AWL
On-the-street conversations ■ Can identify important details from fast-paced conversations	■ Can interview a classmate, asking questions and checking information ■ Can discuss details about cities around the world, asking questions and checking information	■ Can write an interview transcript about a classmate's home city, commenting on and checking information	attracted (adj) constant (adj) AWL extremely originally structure (n) AWL supply (v)
A first-date conversation ■ Can identify key details about people in a conversation	■ Can discuss similarities and differences between two people ■ Can conduct online research about twins separated at birth and report findings ■ Can discuss the controversial topic of nature vs. nurture and give own opinion	■ Can write two paragraphs about the similarities and differences between two people	complex (adj) AWL factor (n) AWL identical AWL image AWL investigate AWL reserved (adj)

AWL = Academic Word List item

LISTENING	SPEAKING	WRITING	VOCABULARY
A conversation about school food services ■ Can identify key details in a conversation	■ Can complete a questionnaire and discuss results ■ Can make cross-cultural comparisons about a familiar topic ■ Can conduct online research on fast food and report findings	■ Can write two paragraphs describing plusses and minuses of a certain type of food	appealing (adj) consequence AWL convenience globe AWL objection reliability AWL
A conversation between a student and a teacher ■ Can recognize how one speaker influences the other and gets that person do something	■ Can describe how someone has influenced one's life ■ Can contribute to a group discussion about a controversial topic	■ Can write three paragraphs about a controversial topic, giving arguments for and against and stating one's personal opinion	cruel former humane physical AWL rebel (v) reinforcement AWL
A phone conversation with a telemarketer ■ Can identify key details in a conversation	■ Can justify and sustain views clearly by providing relevant explanations and arguments ■ Can analyze and discuss advertisements	■ Can write two paragraphs describing a personal experience and what one learned from the experience	authorities AWL eliminate AWL equivalent AWL feature (n) AWL firmly tactic
A conversation between friends at a high-school reunion ■ Can identify the people described in a conversation	■ Can take a personality quiz and discuss the results ■ Can give an opinion and examples in response to a literary quote or an international proverb ■ Can complete a questionnaire and discuss the answers	■ Can write two paragraphs describing the ideal friend and one's best friend	contradict AWL require AWL sensitive tendency trait unique AWL
A description of a childhood room ■ Can follow a personal narrative well enough to identify specific details	■ Can conduct online research about a successful immigrant and report findings ■ Can give an opinion and examples in response to a literary quote	■ Can write a description of a place from one's childhood and why the place was important	compelling (adj) encounter (v) AWL generation AWL issue (n) AWL poverty struggle (v)

AWL = Academic Word List item

LISTENING	SPEAKING	WRITING	VOCABULARY
A conversation about Facebook ■ Can identify key details in a conversation	■ Can discuss social networking websites, giving opinions ■ Can take a quiz and compare answers with classmates ■ Can discuss the advantages and disadvantages of social networking	■ Can write a blog entry about plans and events in the near future	content (n) involved (adj) AWL limit (v) network (v) AWL resource AWL respond AWL
A personal narrative about regrets ■ Can follow a personal narrative well enough to identify specific details	■ Can take a survey and discuss the results ■ Can discuss a situation, examining people's actions and giving opinions as to what the people should have done	■ Can write three paragraphs describing a past problem and evaluating what should or shouldn't have been done	examine exhausted (adj) paralyzed (adj) perceive AWL strategy AWL unrealistic
Conversations between archaeology students ■ Can identify key details in conversations and match each conversation with a picture	■ Can discuss ancient objects, speculating on what they are and what they might have been used for ■ Can discuss and speculate on new facts found about the Iceman	■ Can write a detailed paragraph speculating about an unsolved mystery	assume AWL decade AWL indicate AWL preserve (v) speculation victim
An academic lecture about Haiti ■ Can follow an academic lecture well enough to identify key details and complete notes	■ Can discuss and interpret an international proverb ■ Can engage in an extended conversation about geographical locations and resources found there ■ Can take a quiz and compare answers with classmates	■ Can write an essay about a country one knows well	edition AWL explorer inhabitant mission publication AWL respect (n)
Conversations from a science-fiction movie dialog ■ Can follow conversations well enough to identify key details	■ Can discuss rules for group living in close quarters ■ Can make recommendations for improvement of one's environment ■ Can discuss the pros and cons of investing money in space projects	■ Can write one or two paragraphs describing the ideal school for diplomacy	assemble AWL benefit (v) AWL concern (n) cooperate AWL perspective AWL undertaking AWL

AWL = Academic Word List item

UNIT	GRAMMAR	READING
▼ PART **7** CONTINUED		
19 **The Passive Causative** Page 301 THEME Personal Services	■ Can use the passive causative to describe services people arrange for someone to do for them ■ Can use the passive causative with *by* + agent when the agent is new or important information	**Fashion Magazine Article:** *Body Art* ■ Can identify specific information in an article on a familiar topic
20 **Present Real Conditional Sentences** Page 316 THEME Shopping	■ Can use present real conditional sentences with *if/when* to describe real conditions and results that are certain, such as general truths and habits ■ Can use modals or similar expressions in the result clause to express possibility, advice, or necessity ■ Can use an imperative in the result clause to express instructions, commands, or invitations	**Information Article:** *Pick and Click: Shopping@Home* ■ Can identify specific information in an article on a familiar topic
21 **Future Real Conditional Sentences** Page 331 THEME Cause and Effect	■ Can use future real conditional sentences with *if/unless* to describe real conditions and results that are certain ■ Can use modals or similar expressions in the result clause to express possibility, advice, or necessity	**Magazine Article:** *Knock on Wood!* ■ Can identify specific information in an article on a familiar topic
22 **Present and Future Unreal Conditional Sentences** Page 344 THEME Wishes	■ Can use present and future unreal conditional sentences to describe unreal conditions and results that are untrue, imagined, or impossible ■ Can use *might* or *could* in the result clause to express possibility ■ Can give advice using *If I were you* ■ Can use *wish* to express wishes related to the present or future	**Fairy Tale:** *The Fisherman and His Wife* ■ Can identify specific information in a story
23 **Past Unreal Conditional Sentences** Page 359 THEME Alternate Histories	■ Can use past unreal conditional sentences to describe past unreal conditions and results that are untrue, imagined, or impossible ■ Can use *might have* or *could have* in the result clause to express possibility ■ Can use *wish* + past perfect to express regret or sadness	**Information Article:** *What if . . . ?* ■ Can extract specific information from a linguistically complex article

PART **8**
Conditional Sentences

LISTENING	SPEAKING	WRITING	VOCABULARY
A conversation between father and daughter ■ Can identify key details in a conversation about tasks on a To Do list	■ Can talk about plans and preparations for a trip to another country ■ Can compare *Before* and *After* pictures of a person and discuss changes in appearance ■ Can discuss steps people from different cultures take to improve their appearance	■ Can write one or two paragraphs describing preparations for a future event	caution (n) expand AWL option AWL permanent (adj) risk (n) temporary (adj) AWL
Announcements in an airport and aboard a plane ■ Can infer correct information from public announcements	■ Can discuss and complete an online order form ■ Can discuss shopping in different places ■ Can compare the advantages and disadvantages of shopping in stores and shopping online	■ Can write a short article describing things to do and see in one's city or town	consumer AWL dispute (v) policy AWL precaution secure (adj) AWL site (n) AWL
An interview with a candidate for student council president ■ Can follow an animated conversation well enough to identify details	■ Can discuss common problems and possible solutions ■ Can discuss superstitions, giving opinions and making cross-cultural comparisons	■ Can write a short speech about what one will do if elected class or school president	anticipate AWL attitude AWL confident insight AWL percent AWL widespread AWL
A modern fairy tale ■ Can follow a recorded story well enough to identify key details	■ Can discuss common problems and give advice ■ Can discuss hypothetical questions and wishes	■ Can write a detailed paragraph describing a wish one has for oneself or society, and what might happen if it came true	consent (v) AWL embarrassed (adj) enchanted (adj) furious grant (v) AWL regular (adj)
Conversations about past events ■ Can follow animated conversations well enough to identify key information about past events	■ Can speculate about past events or hypothetical situations ■ Can analyze past situations and evaluate the decisions made ■ Can talk about a past decision one regrets and about what one wishes had happened and why	■ Can write one or two paragraphs speculating about what would have happened if an important event hadn't taken place	alternate (adj) AWL dominate AWL occur AWL outcome AWL parallel (adj) AWL version AWL

AWL = Academic Word List item

LISTENING	SPEAKING	WRITING	VOCABULARY
Conversations between friends and coworkers ■ Can follow animated conversations well enough to identify key details	■ Can have a discussion about lying ■ Can give an opinion and examples in response to a literary quote or international proverb ■ Can complete a questionnaire and compare answers with classmates	■ Can write one or two paragraphs about a past conversation, reporting what was said using direct and indirect speech	aware AWL justify AWL majority AWL nevertheless AWL reveal (v) AWL survey (n) AWL
A conversation about a recent weather report ■ Can identify key details in a discussion about a weather report	■ Can conduct a simple interview and report the other person's answers ■ Can do an online search about an extreme weather event and report findings	■ Can write two paragraphs about an extreme weather event, reporting another person's experience	devastation exceed AWL extreme inevitable AWL shelter (n) whereas AWL
A conversation about a visit to a headache clinic ■ Can identify key details in a conversation about medical advice	■ Can discuss health problems and possible home remedies ■ Can report on how someone followed instructions	■ Can write one or two paragraphs describing a health problem one had and reporting the advice one received	astonishing fatigue (n) interfere monitor (v) AWL persist AWL remedy (n)
A conversation about a job interview ■ Can identify key details in a conversation about a job interview	■ Can role-play a job interview and discuss with classmates ■ Can talk about a personal experience with a job interview ■ Can complete a questionnaire about work values, discuss answers, and report conversations	■ Can write a report on a job interview	appropriate (adj) AWL candidate evaluation AWL handle (v) potential (adj) AWL pressure (n)
A call-in radio show about tipping ■ Can understand a call-in radio program well enough to identify information	■ Can discuss tipping around the world, giving opinions ■ Can talk about problems encountered during first-time experiences ■ Can role-play a conversation between a hotel clerk and a guest asking for information	■ Can write a detailed paragraph about a confusing or surprising situation	clarify AWL custom depend on logical AWL ordinary ultimate AWL

AWL = Academic Word List item

About the Authors

Marjorie Fuchs has taught ESL at New York City Technical College and LaGuardia Community College of the City University of New York and EFL at Sprachstudio Lingua Nova in Munich, Germany. She has a master's degree in Applied English Linguistics and a certificate in TESOL from the University of Wisconsin-Madison. She has authored and co-authored many widely used books and multimedia materials, notably *Crossroads 4*; *Top Twenty ESL Word Games: Beginning Vocabulary Development*; *Families: Ten Card Games for Language Learners*; *Focus on Grammar 3* and *4* (editions 1–5); *Focus on Grammar 3* and *4, CD-ROM*; *Longman English Interactive 3* and *4*; *Grammar Express Basic*; *Grammar Express Basic CD-ROM*; *Grammar Express Intermediate*; *Future 1: English for Results*; *OPD Workplace Skills Builder*; workbooks for *Crossroads 1–4*; *The Oxford Picture Dictionary High Beginning* and *Low Intermediate*, (editions 1–3); *Focus on Grammar 3* and *4* (editions 1–5); and *Grammar Express Basic*.

Margaret Bonner has taught ESL at Hunter College and the Borough of Manhattan Community College of the City University of New York, at Taiwan National University in Taipei, and at Virginia Commonwealth University in Richmond. She holds a master's degree in library science from Columbia University, and she has done work toward a PhD in English literature at the Graduate Center of the City University of New York. She has authored and co-authored numerous ESL and EFL print and multimedia materials, including textbooks for the national school system of Oman; *Step into Writing: A Basic Writing Text*; *Focus on Grammar 3* and *4* (editions 1–5); *Focus on Grammar 4 Workbook* (editions 1–5); *Grammar Express Basic*; *Grammar Express Basic CD-ROM*; *Grammar Express Basic Workbook*; *Grammar Express Intermediate*; *Focus on Grammar 3* and *4, CD-ROM*; *Longman English Interactive 4*; and *The Oxford Picture Dictionary Low Intermediate Workbook* (editions 1–3).

Jane Curtis teaches in the English Language Program at Roosevelt University in Chicago. She has also taught at the Universitat de Barcelona in Barcelona, Spain, and at Wuhan University in Wuhan, China. She holds a master's degree in Spanish from the University of Illinois at Urbana-Champaign and a master's degree in Applied Linguistics from Northeastern Illinois University. She has authored materials for *Longman Academic Writing Series 3: Paragraphs to Essays*, Fourth Edition; *Future 4: English for Results*; and the workbook for *Focus on Grammar 4* (editions 3 and 4).

Acknowledgments

Before acknowledging the many people who have contributed to the fifth edition of *Focus on Grammar*, we wish to express our gratitude to the following people who worked on the previous editions and whose influence is still present in the new work: **Joanne Dresner**, who initiated the project and helped conceptualize the general approach of *Focus on Grammar*; our editors for the first four editions: **Nancy Perry**, **Penny Laporte**, **Louisa Hellegers**, **Joan Saslow**, **Laura LeDrean**, **Debbie Sistino**, and **Françoise Leffler**; and **Sharon Hilles**, our grammar consultant for the first edition.

In the fifth edition, *Focus on Grammar* has continued to evolve as we update materials and respond to valuable feedback from teachers and students who use the series. We are grateful to the following editors and colleagues:

- **Gosia Jaros-White** for overseeing with skill and sensitivity a complex series while never losing sight of the individual components or people involved in the project. She offered concrete and practical advice and was always mindful of learners' needs.

- **Bernard Seal**, of Page Designs International, who joined the *Focus on Grammar* team with a great deal of experience, expertise, energy, and enthusiasm. With his hands-on approach, he was involved in every aspect of the project. He read all manuscript, raising pertinent questions and offering sage advice.

- **Don Williams**, also of Page Designs International, for creating a fresh, new look, which is as user-friendly as it is attractive.

- **Françoise Leffler**, our editor *extraordinaire*, with whom we had the great fortune and pleasure of being able to continue our long collaboration. She provided both continuity and a fresh eye as she delved into another edition of the series, advising us on all things—from the small details to the big picture.

- **Jane Curtis** for her excellent contributions to the first half of this book. Her involvement went beyond her fine writing and choice of engaging topics. She also brought enthusiasm, dedication, and many years of invaluable classroom experience using the series.

- Series co-authors **Irene Schoenberg** and **Jay Maurer** for their suggestions and support, and Irene for sharing her experience in teaching with earlier editions of this book.

- **Julie Schmidt** for her helpful presentation of information and for her input in Part 9.

- **Sharon Goldstein** for her insightful and practical suggestions, delivered with wisdom and wit.

- **Cindy Davis** for her classroom-based recommendations at the very beginning of this edition.

Finally, as always, Marjorie thanks **Rick Smith** for his unswerving support and excellent suggestions. He was a steadfast beacon of light as we navigated our way through our fifth *FOG*.

MF and MB

To the memory of my parents, Edith and Joseph Fuchs—MF
To my parents, Marie and Joseph Maus, and to my son, Luke Frances—MB

Reviewers

We are grateful to the following reviewers for their many helpful comments:

Susanna Aramyan, Glendale Community College, Glendale, CA; **Homeretta Ayala**, Baltimore Co. Schools, Baltimore, MD; **Barbara Barrett**, University of Miami, Miami, FL; **Rebecca Beck**, Irvine Valley College, Irvine, CA; **Crystal Bock Thiessen**, University of Nebraska-PIESL, Lincoln, NE; **Janna Brink**, Mt. San Antonio College, Walnut, CA; **Erin Butler**, University of California, Riverside, CA; **Joice Cain**, Fullerton College, Fullerton, CA; **Shannonine M. Caruana**, Hudson County Community College, Jersey City, NJ; **Tonya Cobb**, Cypress College, Cypress, CA; **David Cooke**, Mt. San Antonio College, Walnut, CA; **Lindsay Donigan**, Fullerton College, Fullerton, CA; **Mila Dragushanskya**, ASA College, New York, NY; **Jill Fox**, University of Nebraska, Lincoln, NE; **Katalin Gyurindak**, Mt. San Antonio College, Walnut, CA; **Karen Hamilton**, Glendale Community College, Glendale, CA; **Electra Jablons**, International English Language Institute, Hunter College, New York, NY; **Eva Kozlenko**, Hudson County Community College, Jersey City, NJ; **Esther Lee**, American Language Program, California State University, Fullerton, CA; **Yenlan Li**, American Language Program, California State University, Fullerton, CA; **Shirley Lundblade**, Mt. San Antonio College, Walnut, CA; **Thi Thi Ma**, Los Angeles City College, Los Angeles, CA; **Marilyn Martin**, Mt. San Antonio College, Walnut, CA; **Eve Mazereeuw**, University of Guelph English Language Programs, Guelph, Ontario, Canada; **Robert Mott**, Glendale Community College, Glendale, CA; **Wanda Murtha**, Glendale Community College, Glendale, CA; **Susan Niemeyer**, Los Angeles City College, Los Angeles, CA; **Wayne Pate**, Tarrant County College, Fort Worth, TX; **Genevieve Patthey-Chavez**, Los Angeles City College, Los Angeles, CA; **Robin Persiani**, Sierra College, Rocklin, CA; **Denise Phillips**, Hudson County Community College, Jersey City, NJ; **Anna Powell**, American Language Program, California State University, Fullerton, CA; **JoAnna Prado**, Sacramento City Community College, Sacramento, CA; **Mark Rau**, American River College, Sacramento, CA; **Madeleine Schamehorn**, University of California, Riverside, CA; **Richard Skinner**, Hudson County Community College, Jersey City, NJ; **Heather Snavely**, American Language Program, California State University, Fullerton, CA; **Gordana Sokic**, Douglas College, Westminster, British Columbia, Canada; **Lee Spencer**, International English Language Institute, Hunter College, New York, NY; **Heather Stern**, Irvine Valley College, Irvine, CA; **Susan Stern**, Irvine Valley College, Irvine, CA; **Andrea Sunnaa**, Mt. San Antonio College, Walnut, CA; **Margaret Teske**, Mt. San Antonio College, Walnut, CA; **Johanna Van Gendt**, Hudson County Community College, Jersey City, NJ; **Daniela C. Wagner-Loera**, University of Maryland, College Park, MD; **Tamara Williams**, University of Guelph, English Language Programs, Guelph, Ontario, Canada; **Saliha Yagoubi**, Hudson County Community College, Jersey City, NJ; **Pat Zayas**, Glendale Community College, Glendale, CA

Credits

Present and Past: Review and Expansion

PART 1

OUTCOMES

- Describe actions, states, and situations that happen regularly, and unchanging facts
- Describe actions that are happening now
- Identify key information in a social science article
- Identify people based on recorded descriptions
- Describe people, what they do and are doing
- Discuss names in different countries
- Write a detailed paragraph about oneself

OUTCOMES

- Describe actions and situations that were completed, or were in progress, in the past
- Describe one past action interrupted by another, or two past actions in progress at the same time
- Identify the order of events in a description
- Describe one's first meeting with someone
- Create a story and present it to the class
- Write about past events in an important relationship

OUTCOMES

- Recognize when to use the simple past, the present perfect, or the present perfect progressive
- Show that something was not completed, using *for* or *since* and time expressions
- Identify key details in a reading or a recording
- Discuss hobbies and interests
- Research an interesting hobby and present findings to the class
- Write about a recent trend

OUTCOMES

- Describe events that happened, or were in progress, before a specific time in the past
- Show the order of two past events, using adverbs and expressions with *by*
- Identify the order of events in a biographical article and in a radio interview
- Discuss talents and past achievements
- Discuss one's schedule for the previous day
- Write about a famous person's life and career

Simple Present and Present Progressive

NAMES

STEP 1   GRAMMAR IN CONTEXT

BEFORE YOU READ

Look at the title of the article. Discuss the questions.

1. What do you think the title means?

2. What are some common first and last names in your native language?

3. Do you have a nickname? If yes, what is it? How did you get it?

READ

▶ 01|01   Read this article about names.

What's in a Name?

Names are different from culture to culture. As a result, students in English language classrooms sometimes need to make adjustments. Yevdokiya Ivanovna Detrova and Jorge Santiago García de Gonzalez provide two interesting examples.

Yevdokiya Ivanovna Detrova is from Russia, but this year she's working and studying in Canada. Yevdokiya is an old-fashioned name, but it's coming back in style. Because her classmates find it difficult to pronounce her name, they use Yevdokiya's nickname—Dusya. In Russia, students always call their teachers by their first name and middle name, for example Viktor Antonovich or Katya Antonovna. A Russian middle name is a *patronymic*—it comes from the father's first name and means "son of . . ." or "daughter of. . . ." So Antonovich means "son of Anton" and Antonovna means "daughter of Anton." Russian students don't use titles like *Mr., Mrs., Miss, Ms.,*[1] or *Professor.* Now, Dusya sometimes hears these titles in class. In addition, several of her English teachers actually prefer to be called by just their first name. Dusya says, "In the beginning, this was very hard for me to do. It still seems a little disrespectful,[2] but I'm getting used to it."

---

1 *Ms.:* (pronounced "miz") used in front of a woman's family name and similar to *Mr.*—
it doesn't show if the woman is married or not
2 *disrespectful:* not polite

Jorge Santiago García de Gonzalez comes from Mexico City. He's currently taking English classes at a language institute in the United States. Jorge is his first, or given, name and Santiago is his middle name. His last name consists of not one but two family names. García is from his father's family and Gonzalez is from his mother's family. Unfortunately, people in the United States often think his name is Mr. Gonzalez, but it's actually Mr. García. To avoid the confusion, Jorge is now planning to use García only. His friends are always trying to convince him to use the English name "George" instead of Jorge. However, he doesn't feel comfortable with an English name. He says, "I like my name, and I don't want to lose my identity."

Names have a clear connection to culture and personal identity. What does your name say about you? It probably says a great deal about where you are from and who you are.

AFTER YOU READ

Ⓐ VOCABULARY Choose the word or phrase that best completes each sentence.

1. When you make an **adjustment**, you make a _____.
   a. promise   b. change   c. mistake

2. Examples **provide** details. They _____ specific information.
   a. ask for   b. understand   c. give

3. If a name is **in style**, many young people _____ it.
   a. have   b. don't like   c. have to spell

4. In some countries, names **consist of** more than one part. They _____ two or more words.
   a. connect   b. take out   c. include

5. If you **convince** a person, that person will _____ with you.
   a. meet   b. agree   c. argue

6. Your name is part of your **identity**. It shows you are _____ others.
   a. different from   b. the same as   c. friendly with

Ⓑ COMPREHENSION Read the statements. Check (✓) *True* or *False*.

	True	False
1. Yevdokiya is now in Russia.	☐	☐
2. Her classmates call her by her nickname.	☐	☐
3. In Russia, she calls her teachers by their first name only.	☐	☐
4. Jorge has a first name, a middle name, and a last name.	☐	☐
5. Jorge's last name is confusing for many people in the United States.	☐	☐
6. Jorge is going to change his first name.	☐	☐

Ⓒ DISCUSSION Work with a partner. Compare your answers in B. Why did you check *True* or *False*?

SIMPLE PRESENT

Affirmative Statements

They **live** in Mexico.
She always **works** here.

Negative Statements

They **don't live** in Mexico.
She **doesn't work** here.

Yes/No Questions

Do they **live** in Mexico?
Does she **work** here?

Short Answers

Yes, they **do**.
Yes, she **does**.

No, they **don't**.
No, she **doesn't**.

Wh- Questions

Where **do** they **live**?
Why **does** she **work** so hard?
Who **teaches** that class?

PRESENT PROGRESSIVE

Affirmative Statements

They**'re living** in Mexico now.
She**'s working** here today.

Negative Statements

They **aren't living** in Mexico now.
She **isn't working** here now.

Yes/No Questions

Are they **living** in Mexico now?
Is she **working** here now?

Short Answers

Yes, they **are**.
Yes, she **is**.

No, they **aren't**.
No, she **isn't**.

Wh- Questions

Where **are** they **living** these days?
Why **is** she **working** so hard?
Who**'s teaching** that class now?

GRAMMAR NOTES

1 Simple Present

Use the **simple present** to show that something **happens regularly** or for **unchanging facts**.

- **happens regularly**
  (*always, usually, often, sometimes, rarely*)

People *always* **call** him Joe.
We *usually* **prefer** first names.
Dusya *sometimes* **uses** nicknames.

- **unchanging facts**

She **comes from** Moscow. It**'s** the capital.

BE CAREFUL! Remember to add *-s* or *-es* to third-person singular (*he, she, it*) of simple present verbs. Use *do/does* in questions and *do not/does not* in negative sentences.

Dusya **lives** in Toronto. She **doesn't live** in Ottawa.
NOT Dusya ~~live~~ in Toronto. She ~~don't live~~ in Ottawa.

USAGE NOTE We often use **adverbs of frequency** (*always, usually,* etc.) with verbs in the simple present. The adverb usually goes **before the verb**. If the verb is *be*, the adverb goes **after** *be*.

Sometimes and *usually* can also go at the **beginning** of the sentence.

Dusya *always* **gets** home at 7:00 p.m.
She *usually* **finishes** her work on time.
She **is** *never* late for class.

We *sometimes* **eat** lunch together.
Sometimes we **eat** lunch together.

2 Present Progressive

Use the present progressive to show that something is **happening now** or **in a longer present time**.

- **happening now**
  (*right now, at the moment*)

A: What's Dusya doing?
B: *Right now*, she**'s studying** in the library.

- **happening in a longer present time, but perhaps not at this exact moment**
  (*this month, this year, these days*)

A: What**'s** Jorge **doing** *these days*?
B: He**'s working** on a new project.

BE CAREFUL! Use *am, is,* and *are* with *-ing* for the present progressive. Do not forget to add *-ing* to the verb.

Dusya **is working** in Canada this year.
NOT Dusya ~~is work~~ in Canada this year.

USAGE NOTE We often use **time expressions** (*right now, this month, these days,* etc.) with verbs in the present progressive. The time expression can go at the **beginning or end** of the sentence. *Now* can also go **after** *be*.

These days, Dusya **is looking** for a new job.
Dusya **is looking** for a new job *these days*.

Now, she **is preparing** for a job interview.
She **is preparing** for a job interview *now*.
She **is** *now* **preparing** for a job interview.

3 Non-Action Verbs

Use non-action verbs to describe **states** or **situations**, but not actions.

Non-action verbs describe:

- **emotions** (*love, hate*)
- **mental states** (*remember, understand*)
- **possession** (*have, own*)
- **wants** (*need, want*)
- **senses** and **perceptions** (*hear, see, look, seem*)

I **hate** my nickname.
Do you **remember** her name?
Diego **has** two family names.
Jan **wants** to change her name.
You **don't look** happy today.

BE CAREFUL! Use the **simple present** with most **non-action verbs**. Do not use the present progressive—even when the verb describes a situation that exists at the moment of speaking.

I **want** to have a special name.
NOT I'm wanting to have a special name.

USAGE NOTE In **informal conversation**, some people use the **present progressive with non-action verbs** such as *be, hear, like, love, miss*, and *see* to show that **a situation is temporary or changing**.

Why **are** you **being** impolite today?
I'm **loving** this class.
I'm really **missing** my friend Jorge.
I'm **hearing** a lot of unusual names now.

USAGE NOTE There is both **an action and a non-action meaning** for some verbs such as *have, come from, think, taste, smell, feel*, and *look*.

NON-ACTION	ACTION
She **has** a nickname.	She **is having** lunch.
(*It's her name.*)	(*She is eating lunch.*)
I **come from** Mexico.	I'm **coming** from school.
(*My country of origin is Mexico.*)	(*I'm on my way from school.*)

4 Other Uses of the Simple Present

Use the simple present for **situations that are not connected to time**—for example, scientific facts and physical laws.

Water **freezes** at 0°C (32°F).
The Earth **orbits** the sun.

Writers often use the simple present in **book or movie reviews**, in **newspaper reports**, and **descriptions of sporting events**.

This book **gives** information about names.
The movie **takes place** in Paris in 1945.

5 Present Progressive with *Always*

You can use the present progressive with *always* to describe a **repeated action**. *Always* usually goes **after** *be*.

She's *always* **smiling**. That's why we call her "Sunshine." It's her nickname.

USAGE NOTE We often use the present progressive to describe a **situation that causes a negative reaction**.

He's *always* **calling** me "Sweetie." I really hate that name.

REFERENCE NOTES

For **spelling rules** for the third-person singular of the **simple present**, see Appendix 22 on page 463.

For **pronunciation rules** for the **simple present**, see Appendix 30 on page 467.

For **spelling rules** on forming the **present progressive**, see Appendix 23 on page 463.

For a list of **non-action verbs**, see Appendix 2 on page 454.

STEP 3   FOCUSED PRACTICE

EXERCISE 1   DISCOVER THE GRAMMAR

GRAMMAR NOTES 1–5   Read this book review. Circle the simple present verbs and underline the present progressive verbs.

● ● ●

THE GAZETTE ONLINE NEWS   FRIDAY, JANUARY 20

Kiss, Bow, or Shake Hands:
How to Do Business in Sixty Countries

Book Review

Are you living or working in a foreign country? Do you worry about making a mistake with someone's name or title? You are right to be concerned. Naming systems vary a lot from culture to culture, and people often have strong feelings about their names. Well, now help is available in the form of an interesting and practical book by Terri Morrison. *Kiss, Bow, or Shake Hands: How to Do Business in Sixty Countries* consists of communication tips, information on cross-cultural naming customs, and much more. It also provides excellent real-world examples. However, it's not just for business people. In today's shrinking world, people are always traveling to and from foreign countries. They're flying to all corners of the world, and they're exchanging emails with people they've never actually met. If you're doing business abroad or making friends across cultures, I recommend this book.

EXERCISE 2 ACTION AND NON-ACTION VERBS

GRAMMAR NOTES 1–3 Complete the sentences. Use the correct form of the verbs in parentheses. Use the present progressive where possible.

1. Many parents in the United States _____ *are choosing* _____ baby names such as Emma and
   (choose)

   Olivia for girls and Noah and Liam for boys these days.

2. At the moment, Jean Twenge _____ research at San Diego State University.
   (do)

   Dr. Twenge _____ that a child's name can have a powerful effect later in life.
   (believe)

3. Some parents _____ to give their children names that are currently in style.
   (want)

   These parents _____ names that their children will like as teens and adults.
   (look for)

4. In her research, Dr. Twenge _____ a change in baby names. More and more
   (notice)

   parents _____ their children names such as Moon, Hershey,[1] and Audi.[2]
   (give)

5. These days, children _____ names with unusual spellings like Mykel (Michael)
   (have)

   or Jayceson (Jason). According to researchers, these names _____ identity
   (cause)

   problems because the children _____ why people can't spell their
   (not know)

   names correctly.

---

1 *Hershey:* a U.S. company that makes chocolate candy
2 *Audi:* a popular car made in Germany

EXERCISE 3 STATEMENTS AND QUESTIONS

GRAMMAR NOTES 1–5 Complete the conversations. Use the correct form of the verbs in parentheses—the simple present or the present progressive.

Conversation 1

MARIO: I _____ *'m trying* _____ to find Greg Costanza. _____ you _____ him?
          1. (try)   **2.** (know)

BELLA: Greg? Oh, you _____ Lucky. That's his nickname. Everyone around here
                       3. (mean)

       _____ him Lucky because he _____ things.
       4. (call)   **5.** (always win)

Conversation 2

LOLA: So you and Anya _____ a baby. That's great! Have you decided on a name yet?
                      1. (expect)

VANYA: We _____ names related to music. Tell me. What _____ you
         2. (look for)

       _____ "Mangena"? It means "melody" in Hebrew.
       3. (think of)

LOLA: It _____ pretty. How _____ you _____ it?
          4. (sound)   **5.** (spell)

Conversation 3

IANTHA: Hi, I'm Iantha.

ALAN: Nice to meet you, Iantha. I'm Alan, but my friends _____*call*_____ me Al. Iantha is an
1. (call)

unusual name. Where _____ it _____? Is it Latin or Greek?
2. (come from)

IANTHA: It's Greek. It _____ "violet-colored flower."
3. (mean)

ALAN: That's pretty. What _____ you _____, Iantha?
4. (do)

IANTHA: Well, I usually _____ computer equipment, but right now
5. (sell)

I _____ at a flower shop. My uncle _____ it.
6. work   7. (own)

ALAN: You _____! I _____ it's true that names _____
8. (joke)   9. (guess)   10. (influence)

our lives!

Conversation 4

ROSA: Dr. Ho, _____ your family name _____ a special meaning in Chinese?
1. (have)

DR. HO: Yes. *Ho* _____ "goodness."
2. (mean)

ROSA: Speaking of goodness, how about a nice cup of tea? The water _____. By the
3. (boil)

way, Dr. Ho, why _____ water _____ so quickly here?
4. (boil)

DR. HO: In the mountains, water _____ at a lower temperature. It's a law of nature.
5. (boil)

EXERCISE 4 EDITING

GRAMMAR NOTES 1–5 Read this post to a class blog. There are eleven mistakes in the use of the simple present and the present progressive. The first mistake is already corrected. Find and correct ten more.

● ● ●

Futura Language School

CLASS BLOG English 047

POSTED SEPTEMBER 16, 2016, AT 15:30:03

Hi, everybody. ~~I write~~ *I'm writing* this note to introduce myself to you, my classmates in English 047. Our teacher is wanting a profile from each of us. At first, I was confused because my English dictionary is defining *profile* as "a side view of someone's head." I thought, "Why does she wants that? She sees my head every day!" Then I saw the next definition: "a short description of a person's life and character." Now I understand what to do, so this is my profile:

My name is Peter Holzer. Some of my friends are calling me Pay-Ha because that is how my initials actually sounding in German. I am study English here in Miami because I want to attend the Aspen Institute of International Leadership in Colorado. Maybe are you asking yourself, "Why he wants to leave Miami for Colorado?" The answer is snow! Of course that means adjustments in my life, but good ones. I am coming from Austria, so I love to ski. It's part of my identity. In fact, my nickname in my family is Blitz (lightning) because always I'm trying to improve my speed.

EXERCISE 5 LISTENING

01|02   **A** You are going to listen to two friends discuss these photos. Their conversation is divided into six parts. Listen to each part. Label each photo with the correct name(s) from the box. Then listen again and check your answers.

| ~~Alex~~ | Bertha | "Bozo" | Karl | Red | "Sunshine" | Vicki |

a. _____   b. _____   c. _Alex_____

d. _____   e. _____   f. _____ and _____

01|02   **B** Listen to each part of the conversation again. Then work with a partner. Discuss your answers in A. Give reasons for your answers.

EXAMPLE: A: OK. How do we know that the little girl in picture C is Alex?
                B: Well, Janine says that Alex is her niece.
                A: Right. She also says parents are now giving names like Alex to girls.
                B: OK. So now, who's Red?

C Work with a partner. Talk about three favorite photos of your family or friends. Use traditional print photos or digital pictures from your phone or a social media page such as Facebook.

EXAMPLE: A: Who's this?
                B: It's Carolina. She's my best friend.
                A: This photo is beautiful. Where is she?
                B: She's walking in the mountains near Rio de Janeiro. Carolina loves the fresh air and trees.

EXERCISE 6 GETTING TO KNOW YOU

Ⓐ GAME Write down your full name on a piece of paper. Your teacher will collect all the papers and redistribute them. Walk around the room. Introduce yourself to other students and try to find the person whose name you have on your piece of paper.

EXAMPLE: A: Hi. I'm Jelena.
B: I'm Eddy.
A: I'm looking for Kadin Saleh. Do you know him?
B: I think that's him over there.

Ⓑ When you find the person you are looking for, find out where he or she comes from and ask about his or her name. You can ask some of the questions below.

EXAMPLE: A: Kadin, where do you come from?
B: I come from Dubai.
A: What does *Kadin* mean?
B: It means "friend" or "companion" in Arabic.

- Where do you come from?
- What does your name mean?
- Which part of your name is your family name?
- Do you use a title? (for example, *Ms., Miss, Mrs., Mr.*)

- What do your friends call you?
- Do you have a nickname?
- What do you prefer to be called?
- How do you feel about your name?
- Other: _____

Ⓒ Finally, introduce your classmate to the rest of the class.

EXAMPLE: This is Kadin Saleh. Kadin comes from Dubai. His name means "friend" or "companion" in Arabic . . .

EXERCISE 7 REAL STUDENTS, REAL LIFE

Ⓐ PROJECT Work with a partner. Choose a busy place at your school where students spend time before and after class. Stay there for five minutes and watch what's happening. Then use the camera on your phone to make two 30-second videos. In the videos, show and explain what students are doing.

EXAMPLE: A: This student is doing homework.
B: The student next to her is using Facebook and posting information for his friends.
A: These students are having a conversation.
B: We don't know what they're talking about, but they look very serious.

B Talk to the students who appear in your videos. Ask for permission to show the videos in class. Then ask the students about their typical activities for that day and time.

EXAMPLE: A: You're in our video. Is it OK to use the video in our English class?
B: Sure.
A: My name is Salvador, and this is May. What's your name?
B: Andy.
A: Hi, Andy. What do you usually do on Tuesday at this time?
B: I always come here. I like to check my Facebook before math class.

C Work in a group. Use your phone to share your videos with your classmates. Then talk about typical activities that students at your school do before and after class.

EXAMPLE: A: What does this person usually do on Tuesday before class?
B: He always goes to the cafeteria and checks his Facebook.
C: And what about this student? What does she do?

EXERCISE 8 A WORLD OF NAMES

A SURVEY Complete this chart with information about your country. Then find out about other countries. Talk to people who are not in your class or do an Internet search. Get information from three additional countries.

Country	How many family names do people use?	What are three typical family names?	Is the order first name + family name, or family name + first name?
Your Country:			
Country #1:			
Country #2:			
Country #3:			

B Work in a group. Compare your answers with those of your classmates. What do you notice about family names around the world?

EXAMPLE: A: Which countries are in your chart?
B: I have Brazil, Spain, Thailand, and Nigeria.
C: Do people in those countries use one or two family names?

A BEFORE YOU WRITE Think about how to introduce yourself. Include information about your name, a typical day in your life, and something special that is going on in your life right now. Give details to show your identity. Complete the outline.

Name: _____ From: _____

Information About My Name: _____

My Typical Day: _____

Something Special in My Life Now: _____

B WRITE Use your outline to write a paragraph that describes who you are. Use the simple present and the present progressive. Try to avoid the common mistakes in the chart.

EXAMPLE: My name is Thuy Nguyen. I come from Vietnam. My Vietnamese name is difficult to pronounce, so my friends always use Tina.... For me, a typical day begins at 6:00 a.m. I usually ... These days, I'm looking for a new apartment. That means I'm ...

Common Mistakes in Using the Simple Present and Present Progressive

Use the **simple present** to describe what **happens regularly** and to give **facts**. Do not use the present progressive.	A typical day **begins** at 6:00 a.m. NOT A typical day ~~is beginning~~ at 6:00 a.m.
Use the **simple present** with most **non-action verbs**. Do not use the present progressive.	I **want** to explain. NOT I ~~am wanting~~ to explain.
Except with non-action verbs, use the **present progressive** to describe what is happening **now**. Do not use the simple present.	Right now, **I'm looking** for a new apartment. NOT Right now, I ~~look~~ for a new apartment.

C CHECK YOUR WORK Read your paragraph. Underline once the verbs in the simple present. Underline twice the verbs in the present progressive. Circle the adverbs of frequency and the time expressions. Use the Editing Checklist to check your work.

Editing Checklist

Did you use ...?

☐ the simple present to describe what happens regularly and to give facts

☐ the present progressive to describe what is happening right now or in a longer present time

☐ the simple present with non-action verbs such as *be*, *like*, *seem*, and *want*

☐ adverbs of frequency and time expressions in the correct position

D REVISE YOUR WORK Read your paragraph again. Can you improve your writing? Make changes if necessary. Give your paragraph a title.

UNIT 1 **REVIEW**

Test yourself on the grammar of the unit.

A Circle the correct words to complete the sentences.

1. Ekaterina study / studies until 10:00 every night.
2. Names like Sarah and Rebekah are coming / come back in style now.
3. How are / do you spell your last name?
4. I don't understanding / understand how to pronounce this name. Can you help me?
5. We often use / are using nicknames with our friends.

B Complete the conversation with the simple present or present progressive form of the verbs in parentheses.

ANA: Hi, Kim! I _____ Jeff Goodale. Is he here?
　　　　　　　　　　1. (look for)

KIM: I _____ he's here somewhere.
　　　　　　2. (think)

ANA: He _____ a cell phone today, so I _____ to give him a
　　　　　　3. (not carry)　　　　　　　　　　　　　　　**4.** (need)
message from Lynn.

KIM: I _____ him! He _____ next to Kevin.
　　　　5. (see)　　　　　　　　　　**6.** (stand)

ANA: Jeff, hi. Call Lynn, OK? She _____ for your call right now.
　　　　　　　　　　　　　　　　　　7. (wait)

JEFF: That _____ serious! Can I use your phone?
　　　　　　8. (sound)

ANA: Sure. I _____ it's an emergency. She just _____ you to buy
　　　　9. (not believe)　　　　　　　　　　　**10.** (want)
a new cell phone.

C Find and correct five mistakes.

Hi Leda,

How do you do these days? We're all fine. I'm writing to tell you that we not living in California anymore. We just moved to Oregon. Also, we expect a baby! We're looking for an interesting name for our new daughter. Do you have any ideas? Right now, we're thinking about *Gabriella* because it's having good nicknames. For example, *Gabby*, *Bree*, and *Ella* all seem good to us. How are those nicknames sound to you? We hope you'll write soon and tell us your news.

Love,
Samantha

Now check your answers on page 475.

Simple Past and Past Progressive

FIRST MEETINGS

OUTCOMES
- Describe actions and situations that were completed, or were in progress, in the past
- Describe one past action interrupted by another, or two past actions in progress at the same time
- Identify the order of events in a description
- Describe one's first meeting with someone
- Create a story and present it to the class
- Write about past events in an important relationship

STEP 1 GRAMMAR IN CONTEXT

BEFORE YOU READ

Look at the title of the article and at the photos. Discuss the questions.

1. Which couples do you recognize?
2. What do you know about them?
3. Do you know how they met?

READ

▶02|01 Read this article about three famous couples.

Super Couples

It's a bird, . . . it's a plane, . . . it's Superman! Disguised as Clark Kent, this world-famous character met Lois Lane while the two were working as newspaper reporters for the *Daily Planet*. At first, Lane wasn't interested in mild-mannered[1] Kent—she wanted to cover stories about "The Man of Steel." In time, she changed her mind. When Kent proposed, Lane accepted. (And she didn't even know he was Superman!)

Superman and Lois Lane are certainly not the only super couple . What were other power couples doing when they met? What did they accomplish together? Let's find out.

---

1 *mild-mannered:* behaving in a quiet, gentle way

Marie and Pierre Curie in their lab

When she was twenty-four, Maria Sklodowska left Poland and moved to Paris. While she was studying at the Sorbonne,[2] she met physicist Pierre Curie. She was planning to return to Poland after her studies, but the two scientists fell in love and got married. While they were raising their daughters, they were also doing research on radioactivity. In 1903, the Curies won the Nobel Prize in physics. Then, in 1906, a horse-drawn carriage hit and killed Pierre while he was out walking. When Marie recovered from the shock, she was able to pursue the couple's work. In 1911, she received her second Nobel Prize. She was the first person to ever receive two Nobel Prizes.

Frida Kahlo first met Diego Rivera in 1922 while she was studying at the National Preparatory School in Mexico City. Rivera was already a well-known artist. He came to the National Preparatory School to paint one of his famous murals.[3] Three years later, at the age of eighteen, Kahlo received serious injuries in a bus accident. While she was recovering, she started painting from bed. One day, she went to see Rivera to ask him for career advice. He was very impressed with her work. Kahlo and Rivera fell in love and got married. Today, they are considered two of Mexico's greatest, most influential artists.

Frida Kahlo and Diego Rivera in their studio

---

2 *Sorbonne:* the University of Paris, in Paris, France
3 *murals:* paintings on a wall

AFTER YOU READ

A VOCABULARY **Complete the sentences with the words from the box.**

accomplish	cover	influential	pursue	recover	research

1. He was doing _____ to learn more about Mexican art.

2. After she graduated from college, she decided to _____ her interest in painting.

3. Successful people _____ a lot during their lifetime.

4. The man was having some psychological problems. It took him many months to _____ from his illness.

5. After that, he became a very _____ writer. He changed people's opinions about mental illness.

6. Newspapers want to _____ important stories.

B COMPREHENSION Circle the word that best completes each sentence.

1. Clark Kent met Lois Lane <u>before / during / after</u> his time at the *Daily Planet*.

2. Lane found out Kent was Superman <u>before / during / after</u> Kent's marriage proposal.

3. Maria Sklodowska met Pierre Curie <u>before / during / after</u> her move to Paris.

4. <u>Before / During / After</u> her marriage, Sklodowska wanted to return to Poland.

5. Frida Kahlo met Diego Rivera <u>before / during / after</u> the time he spent at her school.

6. Rivera began painting murals <u>before / during / after</u> his project at the school.

7. Kahlo began painting <u>before / during / after</u> her recovery from her bus accident.

C DISCUSSION Work with a partner. Compare your answers in B. Why did you choose *before*, *during*, or *after*?

STEP 2   GRAMMAR PRESENTATION

SIMPLE PAST

Affirmative Statements

Maria Sklodowska **studied** in Paris.

Negative Statements

Lois **didn't plan** to marry Clark at first.

Yes/No Questions	Short Answers
Did he **teach**?	**Yes**, he **did**. **No**, he **didn't**.

Wh- Questions

What **did** they **do** in their lab?
Who **worked** in their lab?

Simple Past + Simple Past

She **painted** it when she **recovered**.

Simple Past + Past Progressive

She **met** him while she **was studying**.

PAST PROGRESSIVE

Affirmative Statements

She **was studying** in Paris in 1891.

Negative Statements

She **wasn't planning** to get married.

Yes/No Questions	Short Answers
Was he **teaching**?	**Yes**, he **was**. **No**, he **wasn't**.

Wh- Questions

What **were** they **doing** in their lab?
Who **was working** in their lab?

Past Progressive + Past Progressive

She **was painting** it while she **was recovering**.

Past Progressive + Simple Past

She **was studying** when she **met** him.

GRAMMAR NOTES

Use the simple past to show that something happened and was **completed in the past**.
The focus is on the **completion** of the action or situation.

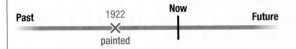

Diego Rivera **painted** his first mural *in 1922*.
(He completed his first mural in 1922.)

Rivera and Kahlo **met** in that same year.

Use the past progressive to show that something was **in progress at a specific time in the past**. The action or situation began before the specific time and may have continued after that time. The focus is on the **duration** of the action or situation, not its completion.

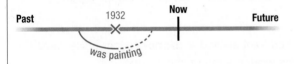

During 1932, Diego Rivera **was painting** murals for the Detroit Institute of Arts.
(During 1932, he continued painting murals for the Detroit Institute of Arts.)

Kahlo and Rivera **were living** in Detroit then.

USAGE NOTE These **action verbs** (*come, do, get, go, look, make, say, try,* and *work*) are the most common verbs in the past progressive. They are common both in speaking and in writing.

What **were** Rivera and Kahlo **doing** in Detroit?
They **were working** on their art.

BE CAREFUL! **Non-action verbs** are not usually used in the progressive.

Kahlo **had** a terrible accident.
NOT Kahlo ~~was having~~ a terrible accident.

Use the past progressive with the simple past to show that **one action interrupted another action in the past**. Use the **simple past** for the **interrupting action**.

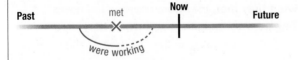

Lois Lane and Clark Kent **met** while they **were working** at the *Daily Planet*.

Use *while* to introduce the action in the **past progressive**.

Use *when* to introduce the action in the **simple past**.

While Kent **was going** to the *Daily Planet*, he **saw** a car accident.

Kent **was going** to the *Daily Planet* **when** he **saw** a car accident.

USAGE NOTE We can also use *when* to introduce the action in the past progressive.

The accident occurred *while* the driver **was making** a left turn.
The accident occurred *when* the driver **was making** a left turn.

4 Past Progressive + *While* or *When*

Use the past progressive with *while* or *when* to show **two actions in progress at the same time in the past**. Use the past progressive in both clauses.

While Superman **was helping** people, Lois Lane **was talking** to the police.

When Superman **was helping** people, Lois Lane **was talking** to the police.

5 Simple Past + Simple Past, or Simple Past + Past Progressive

A sentence with two clauses in the simple past has a very **different meaning** from a sentence with one clause in the simple past and one clause in the past progressive.

• both clauses in the **simple past**

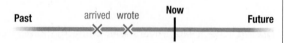

When Kent **arrived** at the newspaper office, Lane **wrote** a report about Superman.

(First he arrived. Then she wrote the report.)

• one clause in the **simple past**, the other clause in the **past progressive**

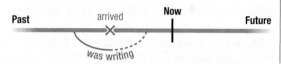

When Kent **arrived** at the newspaper office, Lane **was writing** a report about Superman.

(First she started writing the report. Then he arrived at the office.)

6 Position of the Time Clause

The **time clause** (the part of the sentence with *when* or *while*) can come **at the beginning or the end of the sentence**. The meaning is the same.

• at the **beginning**

While **he was flying**, Superman carried Lois Lane in his arms.

• at the **end**

Superman carried Lois Lane in his arms *while* **he was flying**.

IN WRITING Use a **comma after the time clause** when it comes at the **beginning** of the sentence. Do not use a comma after the main clause when the main clause comes first.

When **they met,** they were covering the news.

They were covering the news *when* **they met**.

NOT They were covering the newsₓ when they met.

REFERENCE NOTES

For **spelling rules of regular past verbs**, see Appendix 24 on page 464.

For a list of **irregular past verbs**, see Appendix 1 on page 453.

For **spelling rules** on forming the **past progressive**, see Appendix 23 on page 463.

For a list of **non-action verbs**, see Appendix 2 on page 454.

EXERCISE 1 DISCOVER THE GRAMMAR

GRAMMAR NOTES 1–6   Read these people's descriptions of how they met important people in their lives. Decide if the statement that follows is *True (T)* or *False (F)*.

1. **LUCKY:** I was riding home on my bike when I saw Elena on a park bench.

    _F_   Lucky saw Elena before he got on his bike.

2. **ROD:** I was climbing a mountain when I met my best friend, Ian.

    _____   Ian was on the mountain.

3. **MARIE:** How did I meet Philippe? I was sitting at home when the phone rang. When I answered, it was the wrong number, but we spoke for an hour!

    _____   Marie knew Philippe before they spoke on the phone.

4. **DON:** When I first met Ana, I was working at the school library. Ana was there doing research.

    _____   Don started his library job after he met Ana.

5. **TONY:** How did I meet my wife? Actually, my cousins invited her to dinner while I was living at their place. After dinner, we started talking and never stopped!

    _____   Tony moved in with his cousins after he met his wife.

6. **MONICA:** I was taking an English class while Dania was taking Spanish. We met in the hall during a break.

    _____   Monica and Dania were students at the same time.

EXERCISE 2 SIMPLE PAST OR PAST PROGRESSIVE

Ⓐ GRAMMAR NOTES 1–6   Complete the conversations. Circle the correct verb forms.

Conversation 1

JASON: Are you OK, Erin? (Were) / Did you (crying) / cry?
                                    1.   2.

ERIN: Yes, but how were / did you knowing / know? I wasn't crying / didn't cry when you
                          3.   4.   5.

         were coming / came in.
              6.

JASON: Your eyes are red.

ERIN: The movie *Frida* was on TV. It's about the Mexican painter Frida Kahlo. It's so sad. When I

         was watching / watched it, I was thinking / thought about her life. She had so many health
              7.   8.

         problems and she never really was recovering / recovered from them.
                                                    9.

Conversation 2

LILY: You won't believe it! I was seeing / saw David and Victoria Beckham in London last week.
                                     1.

TONY: London? What were / did you doing / do in London?
                          2.   3.

LILY: I was there on a business trip, but of course I <u>was finding / found</u> some time for shopping.
                                                     4.

      When I <u>was going / went</u> into Harrods, the Beckhams <u>were walking / walked</u> in the door
                   5.   6.

      right in front of me.

TONY: That's awesome! You <u>were asking / asked</u> them if you could take a selfie with them when
                                             7.

      you <u>were getting / got</u> inside the store, right?
                 8.

LILY: No, I <u>wasn't wanting / didn't want</u> to look like a crazed fan.
                   9.

TONY: OK, so what <u>was happening / happened</u> next?
                   10.

LILY: When I <u>was going / went</u> to the Women's Department, Victoria <u>was looking / looked</u> at
               11.   12.

      jeans. I couldn't control myself anymore, so I <u>was taking / took</u> a photo. Here it is!
                                             13.

Conversation 3

TARO: How <u>were / did</u> you <u>hurting / hurt</u> your foot?
             1.   2.

YOSHI: It was an accident. I <u>was falling / fell</u> on my way to class yesterday. I <u>was slipping / slipped</u>
                          3.   4.

      while I <u>was climbing / climbed</u> the stairs to the third floor.
                   5.

TARO: That's too bad!

YOSHI: Not really. I <u>was feeling / felt</u> sorry for myself when I <u>was sitting / sat</u> in the emergency room,
                         6.   7.

      but suddenly things <u>were changing / changed</u>. I <u>was meeting / met</u> a cool girl who was at the
                              8.   9.

      hospital with her sister. We're going out for pizza tonight.

▶02|02 **B** LISTEN AND CHECK **Listen to the conversations and check your answers in A.**

EXERCISE 3 SIMPLE PAST OR PAST PROGRESSIVE

A GRAMMAR NOTES 1–6 Complete the conversations. Use the simple past or the past progressive form of the verbs in parentheses. See Appendix 1 on page 453 for help with irregular verbs.

Conversation 1

PAZ: What _____were_____ you _____*looking*_____ at just then? You _____.
                           1. (look)   2. (smile)

EVA: I _____ the video of Nicole's wedding. She _____ so happy.
        3. (watch)   4. (look)

PAZ: How _____ she and Matt _____?
                               5. (meet)

EVA: At my graduation party. Matt almost _____ because he was out of town. He
                                    6. (not come)

      _____ a big story for the newspaper. Luckily, his plans _____.
       7. (cover)   8. (change)

      The rest is history.

Conversation 2

DAN: I _____ your Superman website while I _____ for some
          1. (find)   2. (look)

information online. It's great.

DEE: Thanks. When _____ you _____ a Superman fan?
                            3. (become)

DAN: Years ago. I _____ a comic book one day when I _____ to marry
            4. (read)   5. (decide)

Lois Lane! No, just kidding. I _____ to *draw* Lois Lane and Superman.
                             6. (want)

DEE: I _____ a career in graphic arts when I _____ my Superman site.
         7. (pursue)   8. (start)

The website _____ me get my first job.
               9. (help)

DAN: So it looks like Superman was influential in *both* our lives!

Conversation 3

LARA: _____ Jason _____ you when he _____ to see you
              1. (surprise)   2. (come)

last night?

ERIN: Yes! I _____ my apartment when he _____ on the door. When I
         3. (clean)   4. (knock)

_____, we _____ to Fishbone Café. While we
    5. (finish)   6. (go)

_____, Jason _____ me to marry him!
    7. (eat)   8. (ask)

LARA: Congratulations!

ERIN: How much _____ you already _____ about this?
                        9. (know)

LARA: I _____ all the details. But
      10. (not have)

Jason _____ his plans
      11. (mention)

when I _____ him
      12. (see)

yesterday afternoon.

▶ 02|03   **B**   LISTEN AND CHECK
**Listen to the conversations
and check your answers in A.**

EXERCISE 4 CONNECTING CLAUSES WITH *WHEN* OR *WHILE*

GRAMMAR NOTES 3–6 This timeline shows some important events in Monique's life. Use the timeline and the words in parentheses to write sentences about her. Use *when* or *while* and the simple past or past progressive. There is more than one way to write some of the sentences.

born in Canada	moves to Australia	meets Paul	starts medical school	marries	gets medical degree	gets first job	starts practice at Lenox Hospital	has son; starts book	finishes book; does TV interview	book becomes a success; quits job
1983	1998	1999	2005	2006	2009	2010	2012	2013	2014	2015

1. *She met Paul when she moved to Australia.*
   (moves to Australia / meets Paul)

2. *She got married while she was studying medicine.*
   (gets married / studies medicine)

3. _____
   (lives in Australia / gets married)

4. _____
   (completes her medical degree / gets a job)

5. _____
   (practices medicine at Lenox Hospital / has her son)

6. _____
   (writes a book / works at Lenox Hospital)

7. _____
   (does a TV interview / finishes her book)

8. _____
   (leaves her job / her book becomes a success)

EXERCISE 5 EDITING

GRAMMAR NOTES 1–6   Read Monique's email to a friend. There are eleven mistakes in the use of the simple past and the past progressive. The first mistake is already corrected. Find and correct ten more.

Hi Crystal,

I was writing Chapter 2 of my new book when I ~~was thinking~~ *thought* of you. The last time I saw you, you walked down the aisle to marry Dave. That was more than two years ago. How are you? How is married life?

A lot has happened to me since then. While I worked at Lenox Hospital, I decided to pursue a career in writing. In 2014, I was publishing a book on women's health issues. It was quite successful here in Australia. I even had several interviews on TV. When I was receiving a contract to write a second book, I decided to quit my hospital job to write full-time. That's what I'm doing now. Paul, too, has had a career change. While I was writing, he was attending law school. He was getting his degree last summer. Then Paul and his father established their own law firm.

Oh, the reason I thought of you while I wrote was because the chapter was about rashes. Remember the time you were getting that terrible rash? We rode our bikes when you were falling into a patch of poison ivy. And that's how you met Dave! When you were falling off the bike, he offered to give us a ride home. Life's funny, isn't it?

Well, please write soon, and send my love to Dave. I miss you!

Monique

EXERCISE 6 LISTENING

02|04 **Ⓐ** Look at the pictures. Then listen to a woman explain how she met her husband. Listen
again and circle the number of the set of pictures that illustrates the story.

1.

2.

3.

B Listen to the interview again. Then work with a partner. Discuss your answer in A. Why did you choose that set of pictures? Why didn't you choose one of the other two sets of pictures?

EXAMPLE: A: How did you decide which set of pictures to choose?
　　　　　 B: Well, it was because . . .

EXERCISE 7 WHAT ABOUT YOU?

CONVERSATION Work in a group. Think about the first time you met someone who became influential in your life: a best friend, teacher, husband, or wife. Tell your group about the meeting. Answer the questions below.

EXAMPLE: A: I met my best friend in 2013.
　　　　　 B: What were you doing?
　　　　　 A: I was walking to class when this guy came over. . . .
　　　　　 C: What happened then?
　　　　　 A: He started . . .

1. What were you doing?

2. What happened then?

3. How did that person influence your life?

EXERCISE 8 THE TIMES OF MY LIFE

A CONVERSATION Before you talk with a partner, complete this timeline with some important events in your life. Include things that you have accomplished and your first meeting with someone who is significant to you.

Events: _____ _____ _____ _____ _____

_____ _____ _____ _____ _____

Years: ⬜ ⬜ ⬜ ⬜ ⬜

B Work with a partner. Exchange your timelines and ask and answer questions about events on these timelines.

EXAMPLE: A: How did you get your first job?
　　　　　 B: I was studying at the university when I saw an ad for a job in a bookstore.

EXERCISE 9 "IT WAS A DARK AND STORMY NIGHT . . ."[1]

🅐 GAME Work in a group and form a circle. Create your own story. The first person begins with "It was a dark and stormy night." The second person adds one sentence to the story. Continue around the circle until the story is complete. Use your imagination. Choose one student in the group to write each line of the story.

EXAMPLE:

🅑 Share your story. Choose one member of your group to read the group's story to the class.

EXAMPLE: It was a dark and stormy night. The wind was blowing. Samantha was sitting at home alone when suddenly, . . .

---

1 *"It was a dark and stormy night"*: the opening line of a novel by British author Edward Bulwer-Lytton

FROM GRAMMAR TO WRITING

A BEFORE YOU WRITE Think about a relationship that is important to you. Complete the outline.

My First Meeting with _____

Where we met: _____

What we were doing when we met: _____

Important Events in the Relationship

_____ _____ _____

B WRITE Use your outline to write two paragraphs about your important relationship. In the first paragraph, write about your first meeting. In the second paragraph, write about important events in the relationship. Use the simple past and the past progressive. Try to avoid the common mistakes in the chart.

EXAMPLE: I met my friend Andrea while I was living in Germany. . . .

Common Mistakes in Using the Simple Past and Past Progressive

Use the **simple past** for **completed** actions. Do not use the past progressive.	I **met** Andrea in 2014. NOT I ~~was meeting~~ Andrea in 2014.
Use the **past progressive** for **interrupted** actions. Do not use the simple past.	I **was leaving** the airport when I first saw her. NOT I ~~left~~ the airport when I first saw her.
Use a **comma after a time clause when it comes first**. Do not use a comma after the main clause when the main clause comes first.	*While* **I was getting into a taxi,** I fell. NOT I fell╷ while I was getting into a taxi.

C CHECK YOUR WORK Read your paragraphs. Underline once the verbs in the simple past. Underline twice the verbs in the past progressive. Circle *when* or *while*. Use the Editing Checklist to check your work.

Editing Checklist

Did you use . . . ?

☐ the simple past to show the completion of a past action

☐ the past progressive to show the duration of a past action

☐ the simple past with non-action verbs such as *be, like, seem*, and *want*

☐ *when* with a simple past action or a past progressive action

☐ *while* with a past progressive action

☐ commas after time clauses at the beginning of a sentence

D REVISE YOUR WORK Read your paragraphs again. Can you improve your writing? Make changes if necessary. Give your paragraphs a title.

UNIT 2 REVIEW

Test yourself on the grammar of the unit.

(A) Circle the correct words to complete the sentences.

1. I first (met) / was meeting my wife in 2007.

2. She worked / (was working) at the museum the day I went to see a Picasso exhibit.

3. I (saw) / was seeing her as soon as I walked into the room.

4. She (had) / was having long dark hair and a beautiful smile.

5. While / (When) I had a question about a painting, I went over to speak to her.

6. The whole time she was talking, I thought / (was thinking) about asking her on a date.

7. When I left the museum, she (gave) / was giving me her phone number.

(B) Complete the conversation with the simple past or past progressive form of the verbs in parentheses.

A: What ___were___ you ___doing___ when you first ___met___ Ed?
   1. (do)   **2.** (meet)

B: We ___were waiting___ for a bus. We started to talk, and, as they say, "The rest is history."
       3. (wait)

   What about you? How did you meet Karl?

A: Oh, Karl and I ___met___ in school while we ___were studying___ English.
                  4. (meet)   **5.** (study)

   I ___noticed___ him as soon as I ___entered___ the room on the first day
     6. (notice)   **7.** (enter)

   of class.

B: It sounds like it was love at first sight!

(C) Find and correct six mistakes.

It was 2005. I ~~studied~~ *was studying* French in Paris ~~while~~ *when* I met Paul. Like me, Paul was from California. We were both taking the same 9:00 a.m. conversation class. After class, we always ~~were going~~ *went* to a café with some of our classmates. One day, while we ~~was~~ *were* drinking café au lait, Paul was ~~asking~~ *asked* me to go to a movie with him. After that, we started to spend most of our free time together. We really got to know each other well, and we discovered that we had a lot of similar interests. When the course was over, we left Paris and ~~were going~~ *went* back to California together. The next year, we got married!

Now check your answers on page 475.

32   Unit 2

Simple Past, Present Perfect, and Present Perfect Progressive

HOBBIES AND INTERESTS

OUTCOMES
• Recognize when to use the simple past, the present perfect, or the present perfect progressive
• Show that something was not completed, using *for* or *since* and time expressions
• Identify key details in a reading or a recording
• Discuss hobbies and interests
• Research an interesting hobby and present findings to the class
• Write about a recent trend

STEP 1 GRAMMAR IN CONTEXT

BEFORE YOU READ

Look at the photo. Discuss the questions.

1. What is the student doing?
2. Can cooking be a hobby?
3. What do *you* like to do in your free time?

READ

 Read this article from an online student blog about hobbies.

STUDENT VOICES

Adventures in Student Living

BY HANK WASHINGTON

I moved into my first apartment about three months ago. That explains a lot about my new hobby—cooking. My main motivation is eating, but I've also found out that I actually like to cook. And I've been reading food blogs recently. One of the best is *Nutmegs, seven,* by student blogger Elly McCausland.

McCausland is part of a trend among young people in the United Kingdom. They've been learning about delicious, healthy alternatives to fast food. Since April 2010, McCausland has been writing about her passion for cooking on her blog. She often describes new kinds of food that she has discovered. Since she started her blog, she has taken trips to places like Costa Rica and Thailand and has described the connection between her interests in food and

travel. Recently, McCausland's blog has become even more interesting because she has started to grow fruits and vegetables in her garden. I can't wait to read more about how she uses the fresh produce from her garden for breakfast, lunch, and dinner.

Elly McCausland hasn't been experimenting with food all her life. In fact, she survived on cheese sandwiches as a child. McCausland is now 25 years old. She has been studying for a Ph.D. in literature for a couple of years. And of course, she has continued to write about her culinary adventures.

Have you ever wanted to try your hand at[1] cooking? What hobbies have you been enjoying lately? Add a comment to keep the discussion going.

---

1 *try your hand at:* do something for the first time to see if you like it or are good at it

AFTER YOU READ

A VOCABULARY Choose the word or phrase that best completes each sentence.

1. An activity that is part of a **trend** is _____.
   a. necessary   b. expensive   c. popular

2. **Motivation** makes you _____ to do something.
   a. hate   b. want   c. forget

3. An **alternative** gives you _____.
   a. an explanation   b. a choice   c. energy

4. A student with a **passion** for learning probably spends time _____.
   a. at the library   b. in stores   c. at parties

5. A person who **survives** a car accident _____.
   a. dies   b. lives   c. disappears

6. People who **experiment** with food _____ try recipes from different cultures.
   a. never   b. seldom   c. often

B COMPREHENSION Read the list of activities in Elly's life. Which activities are finished? Which are unfinished? Check (✓) *Finished* or *Unfinished*.

	Finished	Unfinished
1. writing the *Nutmegs, seven* blog	☐	☐
2. trying new kinds of food	☐	☐
3. taking a vacation in Costa Rica	☐	☐
4. growing fruits and vegetables	☐	☐
5. eating only cheese sandwiches	☐	☐
6. getting a Ph.D.	☐	☐

C DISCUSSION Work with a partner. Compare your answers in B. Why did you check *Finished* or *Unfinished*?

SIMPLE PAST

Affirmative Statements

I **moved** three months ago.

Negative Statements

She **didn't write** a blog post last night.

Yes/No Questions	Short Answers
Did he **cook** dinner?	**Yes**, he **did**. **No**, he **didn't**.

Wh- Questions

Where **did** he **eat**?

Who **read** the food blog?

PRESENT PERFECT
PRESENT PERFECT PROGRESSIVE

Affirmative Statements

I've **lived** here for three months.
I've **been living** here for three months.

Negative Statements

She **hasn't written** a new blog post.
She **hasn't been writing** lately.

Yes/No Questions	Short Answers
Has he **cooked** dinner? **Has** he **been cooking**?	**Yes**, he **has**. **No**, he **hasn't**.

Wh- Questions

Where **has** he **eaten**?
Where **has** he **been eating**?

Who**'s read** the food blog?
Who**'s been reading** the food blog?

GRAMMAR NOTES

1 Simple Past

Use the simple past to show that something happened and was **completed in the past**.

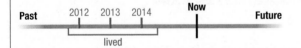

I **lived** in the dorm for two years.
  (I don't live in the dorm now.)

We often use **specific past time expressions** such as *in 2014, last year, last summer, last month,* and *yesterday* with the simple past.

She **traveled** to Thailand *in 2014*.
She **went** to Costa Rica *last summer*.

We often use *ago* with the simple past to show when something started.

They **joined** a cooking club *a year ago*.

Use the present perfect or the present perfect progressive **with *for* or *since*** to show that something **started in the past** but was **not completed**. This action or situation **continues** up to the present and may continue into the future.

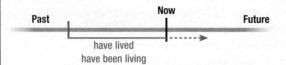

	I've lived in my apartment *for* three months. **I've been living** in my apartment *for* three months. *(I moved to my apartment three months ago, and I'm still living there today.)*
We often use **verbs of duration** such as *live, teach, wear, work,* and *study* in this way.	She**'s worked** hard *for* weeks. She**'s been working** hard *for* weeks.
Use *for* or *since* and a time expression: • *for* + **a length of time** to show *how long* a present condition has been true	She**'s studied** in York *for two years*.
• *since* + **a point of time** to show *when* a present condition *started*	She**'s been studying** there *since she graduated* from high school.

BE CAREFUL! **Time expressions** such as *for the past week, for the last two months,* and *for the past ten years* show that something started in the past but was **not completed**. Use the **present perfect** or the **present perfect progressive**. Do not use the simple past.

I've taken classes here *for the past three years*.
NOT I ~~took~~ classes here for the past three years.
I've been cooking dinner *for the last hour*.
NOT I ~~cooked~~ dinner for the last hour.

BE CAREFUL! The **present perfect** with *for* has a very **different meaning** from the **simple past** with *for*.

He **has taught** a cooking class *for* six months.
(He is still teaching the class.)
He **taught** a cooking class *for* six months.
(He no longer teaches the class.)

BE CAREFUL! Use the **simple past** with expressions that refer to a **specific time in the past**. Do not use the present perfect with a specific time (except after *since*).

He **moved** to London *in 2014*.
NOT He ~~has moved~~ to London in 2014.
He**'s lived** there *since 2014*.

USAGE NOTE It is more common to put the **expression with *for* or *since*** at the **end of the sentence**.

He's been writing *since 2010*. *(more common)*
Since 2010, he's been writing. *(less common)*

IN WRITING Use a **comma** when the expression with *for* or *since* comes at the **beginning** of the sentence. Do not use a comma when the expression with *for* or *since* comes at the end of the sentence.

For several months, I have been reading the blog.
Since I started cooking, my health has improved.
NOT I've been reading the blog_x for several months.
NOT My health has improved_x since I started cooking.

Remember that we usually do not use **non-action verbs** in the progressive.

I've known Elly for a short time.
NOT ~~I've been knowing~~ Elly for a short time.

USAGE NOTE In **informal conversation**, some people use the **progressive** with **verbs of emotion** (*feel, like, love, want*).

She**'s been feeling** a little worried for a while.
I've been wanting to learn how to cook for ages.

3 Present Perfect for an Indefinite Time in the Past

Use the present perfect **without** *for* or *since* to show that something happened at an **indefinite time in the past** and was **completed**.

She**'s written** a new blog post.
> (We don't know when she wrote the blog post, or the time is not important.)

We sometimes use the **present perfect** with **adverbs of time** such as *already, yet, ever, never, just, lately,* and *recently* to show that something happened at an **indefinite time in the past**.

I**'ve** *already* **gone** to the supermarket.
I **haven't had** lunch *yet*.
Have you **seen** Lea *lately*?
He**'s started** to watch food shows *recently*.

USAGE NOTE In American English, we sometimes use the **simple past** with *already, yet, just,* and *recently*.

I**'ve** *already* **eaten**. **or** I *already* **ate**.

BE CAREFUL! Use the **present perfect or the present perfect progressive** with *lately*. Do not use the simple past.

I **have baked** a lot of pies *lately*.
I **have been baking** a lot of pies *lately*.
NOT I ~~baked~~ a lot of pies lately.

We use the **present perfect** (not the simple past) to show that the result of the action or situation is important in the present. The present perfect always has some **connection to the present**.

She**'s completed** her master's degree, and she's studying for a Ph.D.
> (Because she has her master's degree, she can now study for her Ph.D.)

USAGE NOTE We often use the **present perfect** without *for* or *since* to show **how many things** or **how many times** someone has done something.

She**'s read** *three books* about healthy food choices.
She**'s read** that book *three times*.

BE CAREFUL! *She's read that book* and *She's been reading that book* have very different meanings.

She**'s read** that book.
> (She finished the book.)
She**'s been reading** that book.
> (She's still reading the book.)

4 Present Perfect or Simple Past

Use the present perfect or the simple past **with time expressions** for **unfinished time periods** (*today, this week,* etc.) to show **if things might happen again**.

Use the **present perfect** for things that **might happen again** in that time period.

She**'s written** three blog posts *this week*.
> (The week isn't over. She might write another post.)

Use the **simple past** for things that **probably won't happen again** in that period.

She **wrote** three blog posts *this week*.
> (The week isn't over, but she won't write another post.)

BE CAREFUL! *This morning, this afternoon,* and *this evening* can refer to either unfinished or finished time. Use the **simple past** if the time period is **finished**.

I**'ve had** three cups of coffee *this morning*.
> (It's still morning.)
I **had** three cups of coffee *this morning*.
> (It's now afternoon.)

REFERENCE NOTES

For a list of **irregular past verbs**, see Appendix 1 on page 453.

For a list of **irregular past participles** used in forming the **present perfect**, see Appendix 1 on page 453.

STEP 3 **FOCUSED PRACTICE**

EXERCISE 1 DISCOVER THE GRAMMAR

A GRAMMAR NOTES 1–4 Read this article about a famous chef. Circle the simple past verbs. Underline once the verbs in the present perfect. Underline twice the verbs in the present perfect progressive.

One Amazing Chef, One Amazing Hobby

ETHAN STOWELL has been working in the restaurant business for many years. Stowell has received numerous awards as a top chef in the United States. Although he grew up in a family of dancers, Stowell didn't want to join the family business. He quickly realized that his true passion is food. In recent years, Stowell has opened several popular restaurants in Seattle. In addition, he has been collecting cookbooks for years. He has about 2,000 of them!

Ethan Stowell

Since he started his collection in 1995, Chef Stowell has become obsessed with cookbooks. He's been buying new and used books in stores, on websites, at yard sales, and just about anywhere else he can find them. What's more, the books haven't been sitting on shelves all these years. The chef has actually used them to experiment with new kinds of food.

Chef Stowell didn't attend culinary school. Instead, he learned about food by working in restaurants. He got his first cookbooks in order to add to his knowledge. Since then, he has discovered the importance of combining the history of food with his own experiences in life. With this winning combination, he has developed his own style of simply prepared food and has attracted loyal fans.

B Read the statements about Ethan Stowell. Check (✓) *True* or *False*.

		True	False
1.	There have always been many chefs in Ethan Stowell's family.	☐	☑
2.	Stowell has become passionate about food recently.	☐	☐
3.	Stowell bought his first cookbook in 1995.	☐	☐
4.	He has stopped buying cookbooks.	☐	☐
5.	As an alternative to cooking school, he worked in restaurants.	☐	☐
6.	Stowell hasn't read any of his cookbooks yet.	☐	☐
7.	It is possible that Ethan Stowell will win more awards.	☐	☐

EXERCISE 2 SIMPLE PAST, PRESENT PERFECT, OR PRESENT PERFECT PROGRESSIVE

GRAMMAR NOTES 1–3 Complete this article about another hobby—collecting rocks. Circle the correct words.

A Hobby That Helps

High school student Sydney Martin ⟨has always loved⟩ / has always been loving rocks, and
                                                                                    1.
several years ago, she <u>has found / found</u> the perfect way to use her rock collection.
                                    2.

Sydney's rocks come from the Lake Michigan beaches near

her home. She <u>has been using / used</u> them to make necklaces
                        3.

since she <u>has been / was</u> eight years old. In 2005, Sydney
                  4.

<u>has sold / sold</u> her first necklaces to family and friends and
    5.

put the money in the bank. Two years later, when doctors

<u>have told / told</u> Sydney that she had LCH,[1] she immediately
        6.

<u>has known / knew</u> what to do with the profits from her
        7.

Sydney Martin

jewelry. She <u>has decided / decided</u> to give the money to doctors trying to find a cure for
                        8.

LCH, and she <u>hasn't stopped / didn't stop</u> since. Sydney <u>has started / has been starting</u> a
                          9.   **10.**

business, Syd Rocks, to sell her rock jewelry. So far, she <u>has donated / donated</u> more than
                                                                          11.

$420,000. Sydney's motivation is simple. She wants to help in the fight against LCH.

---

1 *LCH:* Langerhans Cell Histiocytosis, a rare blood disease

EXERCISE 3 SIMPLE PAST, PRESENT PERFECT, OR PRESENT PERFECT PROGRESSIVE

GRAMMAR NOTES 1–4 Complete these paragraphs about three people and their hobbies. Use the correct form of the verbs in parentheses—simple past, present perfect, or present perfect progressive. Sometimes more than one answer is correct.

Paragraph 1

May ___*has been taking*___ photos ever since her parents _____
      1. (take)   **2.** (buy)

her a camera when she _____ only ten years old. At first, she only
                                   3. (be)

_____ color snapshots of friends and family, but then she suddenly
      4. (take)

_____ to black and white. Lately, she _____ a lot of
      5. (change)   **6.** (shoot)

nature photographs. This year, she _____ in three amateur photography
                                                    7. (compete)

contests—and it's only April! She hopes to win several awards before the end of this year.

Last month, she _____ second prize for her nighttime photo of a
                          8. (win)

lightning storm.

Paragraph 2

Carlos _____ playing music when he _____ an
            1. (begin)   **2.** (get)

electric guitar for his twelfth birthday. He _____ a day without his guitar
                                                           3. (not spend)

since. In fact, the guitar _____ more than just a way of having some fun
                                     4. (become)

with his friends. Last year, he _____ a local band. Since then, they
                                            5. (join)

_____ all over town, in cafés, at parties, and in concerts. So far this year,
      6. (perform)

the band _____ six concerts, and they have plans for many more.
                7. (give)

Paragraph 3

Kate _____ a beautiful old stamp last month. It is now part of the
          1. (find)

fantastic collection she _____ on for the past two years. At first, she just
                                   2. (work)

_____ stamps from letters that she _____ from friends.
      3. (save)   **4.** (get)

After some time, however, she _____ to look more actively for stamps.
                                            5. (begin)

Lately, she _____ them from special stores and _____
                  6. (buy)   **7.** (trade)

stamps with other collectors on philatelic websites. So far, she _____ over
                                                                                    8. (find)

200 stamps from all over the world.

EXERCISE 4
SIMPLE PAST, PRESENT PERFECT, OR PRESENT PERFECT PROGRESSIVE

GRAMMAR NOTES 1–4 A student is interviewing adventure traveler Rafeh Abad for a research project. Use the words in parentheses to write the student's questions. Use her notes to complete Abad's answers. Choose between the simple past, the present perfect, and the present perfect progressive. Use the present perfect progressive and contractions when possible.

first adventure trip (Lake Louise in Canada) — ten years ago

second adventure (scuba diving trip in Mexico)
   cost — $1,200

from hobby to business — started in 2015
   adventure travel tours along with two employees
   recent trips to Costa Rica, Peru, and Alaska

adventure travel blog — started last year
   1,000 readers in the first two weeks of this month

travel to Africa — not yet

1. (how long / you / do / adventure travel)

   STUDENT: *How long have you been doing adventure travel?*

   ABAD: *I've been doing adventure travel for ten years.*

2. (where / you / go / on your first adventure trip)

   STUDENT: _____

   ABAD: _____

3. (how much / your diving trip in Mexico / cost)

   STUDENT: _____

   ABAD: _____

4. (how long / you and your team / lead / adventure tours)

   STUDENT: _____

   ABAD: _____

5. (what trips / you / take / recently)

   STUDENT: _____

   ABAD: _____

6. (how long / you / write / a travel blog)

   STUDENT: _____

   ABAD: _____

7. (how many people / read / your blog / this month)

STUDENT: _____

ABAD: _____

8. (how many times / you / visit / Africa)

STUDENT: _____

ABAD: _____

EXERCISE 5 EDITING

GRAMMAR NOTES 1–4 Read these comments to the online article about hobbies on page 33.
There are nine mistakes in the use of the simple past, the present perfect, and the present
perfect progressive. The first mistake is already corrected. Find and correct eight more.

● ● ●

COMMENTS

I've been cooking
~~I'm cooking~~ since I was in elementary school. When I was ten years old, my mother has taught
me how to make simple things such as fried eggs and chicken salad. Then we moved on to more
complicated meals. I've always been loving to cook as a way to relax and be creative. Lately, I've
been trying my hand at baking, too. Last month, I made my first strawberry cheesecake. BTW,[1] I've
been reading the *Nutmegs, seven* blog several times. You're right. It's incredible. —**jg20133**

I've been passionate about Do It Yourself since several years. DIY gives me an alternative to
spending lots of money in stores. I have taken a knitting class last year, and since then, I made a
hat, a scarf, and gloves for my boyfriend. My current DIY project is all about upcycling.[2] Last week,
my roommate gave me all of her old magazines, and I've been creating a sculpture from them. I
haven't finished the sculpture yet, but it's going to be beautiful. —**Claudia**

No one has mentioned video games yet. My friends and I have been playing Mortal Kombat vs DC
Universe since this semester has started. We enjoy the challenge. And here's something interesting.
I was a fan of Pokémon all my life. In my opinion, there's nothing better than Pikachu! —**Fanboy**

---

1 *BTW:* a common online and texting abbreviation for "by the way"
2 *upcycling:* using an old product for a new, more valuable purpose

EXERCISE 6 LISTENING

🔊 03|02 **A** Lara and Pablo are discussing hobbies. Listen to their conversation. Read the statements. Then listen again to the conversation and check (✓) *True* or *False*. If there isn't enough information to decide, check (✓) *Don't Know*.

	True	False	Don't Know
1. Pablo's hobby has had a negative effect on his life.	☐	✓	☐
2. One of Pablo's friends explained the importance of hobbies to him.	☐	☐	☐
3. According to Lara, she has had no free time for two weeks.	☐	☐	☐
4. Hobbies can help people do well at school and at work.	☐	☐	☐
5. Pablo has started taking photos of buildings.	☐	☐	☐
6. Pablo is a good photographer because he has become more creative.	☐	☐	☐
7. Lara has still not changed her mind about getting a hobby.	☐	☐	☐

🔊 03|02 **B** Work with a partner. Listen again to the conversation. Discuss your answers in A. Give reasons for your answers.

EXAMPLE: **A:** So, why is the answer for number 1 false?
B: Well, Pablo's hobby hasn't had a negative effect on his life. On the contrary, Lara says he looks happy and relaxed.
A: OK. What about number 2?

🔊 03|02 **C** Work in a group. Listen again to the conversation. Discuss answers to the following questions.

1. What are the advantages of having photography as a hobby? Give examples from your personal knowledge and experience.

   EXAMPLE: **A:** I started taking photos as a way to reduce stress.
   B: How can photography lower your stress level?
   A: Well, for one thing, I've been spending more time outdoors. That means . . .
   C: There are other advantages, too. For example, I've been . . .

2. How can Lara find time for a hobby? Give examples.

3. According to Pablo, everyone needs a hobby to survive. Do you agree with Pablo? Give reasons to support your answer. Include examples.

EXERCISE 7 WHAT ABOUT YOU?

CONVERSATION Work in a group. Talk about your hobbies and interests. What did you do in the past with your hobby? What have you been doing lately? Find out about other people's hobbies.

EXAMPLE: A: Do you have any hobbies, Ben?

B: Yes. Since I was in high school, my hobby has been running.... Recently, I've been training for a marathon. What about you? Do you have a hobby?

C: I collect sneakers. I got my first pair of Nikes when I was ten, and I've been collecting different kinds of sneakers ever since....

EXERCISE 8 DONE, DONE, NOT DONE

Ⓐ INTERVIEW What did you plan to do last month to develop your hobbies and personal interests? Make a list. Include things you did and things that you still haven't done. Do not check (✓) any of the items. Exchange lists with a partner.

Buy a new pair of running shoes.
Research healthy snacks for marathon runners.

Ⓑ Now ask questions about your partner's list. Check (✓) the things that your partner has already done. Answer your partner's questions about your list. When you finish, find out if the information that you recorded on your partner's list is correct.

EXAMPLE: A: Have you bought your new running shoes yet?

B: Yes, I have. I bought them last week.

A: And what about the research on healthy snacks?

B: I haven't done it yet.

A: OK. I think we've talked about everything on our lists. Let's make sure our answers are correct.

EXERCISE 9 NOT YOUR EVERYDAY HOBBY

Ⓐ GROUP PROJECT Work in a group. Choose one of the hobbies from the list to research. Answer some of the questions below.

EXAMPLE: A: Apiculture is beekeeping.
         B: In the past, this was an activity for farmers.
         C: But it has recently become . . .
         D: Right. Since . . .

Hobbies to research:

- apiculture
- cosplay
- couch surfing
- egg carving
- genealogy
- geocaching
- spelunking
- ultimate Frisbee

Possible questions:

- What is the activity?
- When did people start doing the activity?
- Where did the activity start?
- How long has the hobby been popular?
- Why has the hobby become popular?
- What is the most interesting fact that you've learned about the hobby?

Ⓑ Report back to your class. If your group chose the same hobby as another group, do you have the same information about that hobby? Compare answers.

EXAMPLE: A: Beekeeping has been going on for about nine thousand years.
         B: But in the past, it was usually an activity for farmers.
         A: In the twenty-first century, beekeeping has become . . .
         B: Surprisingly, the popularity of beekeeping has been increasing in . . .

FROM GRAMMAR TO WRITING

A BEFORE YOU WRITE Think about trends at your school or among your friends. What is new or different? Think about hobbies, fashion, classroom activities, etc. Complete the outline.

An Interesting Trend: _____

When the Trend Started: _____

Advantages of the Trend: _____

Disadvantages of the Trend: _____

B WRITE Use your outline to write a paragraph about an interesting trend. Use the simple past, the present perfect, and the present perfect progressive. Try to avoid the common mistakes in the chart.

EXAMPLE: Zumba is an exercise program that uses dance styles like salsa and hip hop. People have been doing Zumba for many years. However, it suddenly became . . .

Common Mistakes in Using the Simple Past, Present Perfect, or Present Perfect Progressive

Use the **simple past** with **specific past time expressions**. Do not use the present prefect (except after *since*).	I **started** a Zumba class *two weeks ago*. NOT I've started a Zumba class two weeks ago.
Use the **present perfect** or the **present perfect progressive** to show that something **started in the past** but was **not completed**. Do not use the simple past.	People **have been doing** Zumba *since 1986*. NOT People did Zumba since 1986.
Use the **present perfect** to show that something happened at an **indefinite time in the past** and was **completed**. Do not use the present perfect progressive.	We've **finished** today's Zumba class. NOT We've been finishing today's Zumba class.

C CHECK YOUR WORK Read your paragraph. Circle the verbs in the simple past. Underline once the verbs in the present perfect. Underline twice the verbs in the present perfect progressive. Use the Editing Checklist to check your work.

Editing Checklist

Did you use . . . ?

☐ the simple past for things that happened and were completed in the past

☐ the present perfect and present perfect progressive with *for* or *since* for things that started in the past but were not completed

☐ the present perfect for things that were completed at an indefinite time in the past

D REVISE YOUR WORK Read your paragraph again. Can you improve your writing? Make changes if necessary. Give your paragraph a title.

UNIT 3 REVIEW

Test yourself on the grammar of the unit.

A Circle the correct words to complete the sentences.

1. Isabel was / (has been) interested in yoga since high school.

2. She finally (took) / has taken her first yoga class last week.

3. She has read / (has been reading) a book about yoga. She'll probably finish it tomorrow.

4. She has felt much healthier since she (started) / has started the yoga class.

5. She went / (has gone) to three yoga classes this week, and it's only Tuesday.

6. Isabel's roommate has been doing yoga since / (for) eight months.

7. More and more students became / (have become) fans of yoga in the past several years.

B Complete the sentences with the simple past, present perfect, or present perfect progressive form of the verbs in parentheses.

Lisa _has been working_ on her stamp collection for five years, and she still enjoys
     1. (work)

it. Last year, she _discovered_ a very valuable stamp on an old letter in her attic.
                  2. (discover)

At first, she _didn't know_ it was valuable. She _found out_ after
              3. (not know)   **4.** (find out)

she did some research on the Internet. Of course, she _got_ really
                                                      5. (get)

excited. Since then, she _has been going_ to garage sales and flea markets every
                        6. (go)

weekend. Unfortunately for Lisa, she _hasn't find_ another valuable stamp, but
                                    7. (not find)

she _has been having_ a great time searching.
    8. (have)

C Find and correct five mistakes.

A: How long did¹ you been doing adventure sports?
         have

B: I've gotten interested five years ago, and I haven't stopped since then.
   I got   *→ simple past*

A: You're lucky to live here in Colorado. It's a great place for adventure sports. Did you live
                                                                              Have you lived

   here long?

B: No, not long. I've moved here last year. I used to live in Alaska.
               + moved

A: I haven't go there yet, but I've heard it's great. → *Despoes de haven't va participle*
            gone   *past*

B: It *is* great. When you go, be sure to visit Denali National Park.

Now check your answers on page 475.

Past Perfect and Past Perfect Progressive

MUSICIANS

OUTCOMES
- Describe events that happened, or were in progress, before a specific time in the past
- Show the order of two past events, using adverbs and expressions with *by*
- Identify the order of events in a biographical article and in a radio interview
- Discuss talents and past achievements
- Discuss one's schedule for the previous day
- Write about a famous person's life and career

STEP 1 GRAMMAR IN CONTEXT

BEFORE YOU READ

Look at the photo, the title, and the first paragraph of the article. Discuss the questions.

1. What is the man doing? Describe him.

2. What type of music do you like? Do you enjoy classical music? Which composers?

3. Why do you think the article is called "The People's Conductor"?

READ

04|01 Read this article about Gustavo Dudamel.

Gustavo
Dudamel

The People's Conductor

He's exciting. He's great-looking. He's "The Dude,"[1] and he's changing the way people around the world feel about classical music.

Gustavo Dudamel grew up in Barquisimeto, Venezuela. A child prodigy,[2] he had already started taking music lessons by the early age of four. His father played the trombone in a salsa band, and young Dudamel had been hoping to take up the same instrument. But his arms were too short, and so he studied the violin instead.

It wasn't too long before Dudamel became part of El Sistema—a program created to teach young Venezuelans, mostly from poor families, how to play musical instruments. Many of these kids had been getting into trouble before participating in the program. "The music saved me. I'm sure of this," said Dudamel in a TV interview.

---

1 *dude:* a man (an informal word, used to express positive feelings about the person)

2 *child prodigy:* a very young person who has a great natural ability in a subject or skill

In El Sistema, Dudamel's amazing talent was obvious, and by the time he was fifteen, he had become the conductor of the Simón Bolívar National Youth Orchestra. But that wasn't the first time he had led an orchestra. According to Dudamel, he had been conducting in his imagination since he was six.

On October 3, 2009, Dudamel lifted his baton for the first time as music director of the famed Los Angeles Philharmonic. He was only twenty-eight, and he had just signed a five-year contract as conductor. Tickets for this free concert at the 18,000-seat Hollywood Bowl had become available two months earlier. By the time the Bowl's ticket office opened on August 1, hundreds of people had already arrived. They had been lining up for hours in the hot Californian sun. The tickets were gone in minutes. On October 3, that lucky audience, a mix of all ages and ethnic backgrounds, had come for one thing—to see "Gustavo the Great" conduct. They were not disappointed. By the end of the concert, they had all risen to their feet and had been applauding enthusiastically for ten minutes.

After his successful debut, Dudamel continued to attract new fans to his concerts. To help young people, he worked with the Los Angeles Philharmonic to set up a program modeled on El Sistema, the program that had transformed his life. Today, Dudamel is an award-winning conductor who wants to inspire others and share his love of classical music.

AFTER YOU READ

A VOCABULARY Complete the sentences with the words from the box.

conducted	contract	ethnic	inspired	participated	transformed

1. The experience _____ her life. It really changed everything for her.

2. The pianist's performance _____ me to study piano.

3. How many times has Dudamel _____ the orchestra this season?

4. The audience was a real _____ mix of African Americans, Asians, Hispanics, and whites.

5. Many musicians and singers _____ in the event.

6. One violinist signed a(n) _____ with the orchestra for two years.

B COMPREHENSION Read the statements. Put the events in Dudamel's life in the correct time order (1 = *first*, 6 = *last*).

_____ He became conductor of the Simón Bolívar National Youth Orchestra.

_____ He turned four.

_____ He started a program based on El Sistema.

_____ He became music director of the Los Angeles Philharmonic.

_____ He started taking music lessons.

_____ He became part of El Sistema.

C DISCUSSION Work with a partner. Compare your answers in B. Why did you choose each answer?

PAST PERFECT

Statements

Subject	*Had (not)*	Past Participle		
I You He She It We You They	**had (not)**	**arrived**	in the U.S.	by then.
		become	famous	

Contractions

I had	=	**I'd**
you had	=	**you'd**
he had	=	**he'd**
she had	=	**she'd**
it had	=	**it'd**
we had	=	**we'd**
they had	=	**they'd**
had not	=	**hadn't**

Yes/No Questions

Had	Subject	Past Participle		
Had	you he they	**arrived**	in the U.S.	by then?
		become	famous	

Short Answers

Affirmative			Negative		
Yes,	I he they	**had.**	**No,**	I he they	**hadn't.**

Wh- Questions

Wh- Word		*Had*	Subject	Past Participle	
How many	concerts	**had**	he	**given**	by then?

PAST PERFECT PROGRESSIVE

Statements

Subject	*Had (not) been*	Base Form + *-ing*	
I You He She It We You They	**had (not) been**	**playing**	all over the world by then.

Yes/No Questions

Had	Subject	Been + Base Form + -ing	
Had	you he they	**been playing**	the violin by then?

Short Answers

Affirmative			Negative		
Yes,	I he they	**had.**	**No,**	I he they	**hadn't.**

Wh- Questions

Wh- Word	Had	Subject	Been + Base Form + -ing	
How long	**had**	he	**been playing**	classical music by then?

GRAMMAR NOTES

1 Past Perfect

Use the past perfect to show that something **happened before a specific time in the past**.

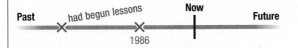

By 1986, Dudamel **had begun** violin lessons.
(Dudamel began taking violin lessons before 1986.)

With the past perfect, the focus is often on the **completion** of the action or situation.

By 2010, Kato **had conducted** Beethoven's Ninth Symphony for the first time.
(The performance took place and ended before 2010.)

2 Past Perfect Progressive

Use the past perfect progressive to show that something was **in progress before a specific time in the past**. The action or situation **may have continued** after that time. The focus is on the **continuation** of the action or situation, not the end result.

By 2010, Kato **had been conducting** an orchestra *for 12 years*.
(She was still conducting in 2010, and possibly continued to conduct.)

USAGE NOTE We also use the past perfect progressive for actions that had **just ended**. You can often still see the results of the action.

She was out of breath. It was clear that she **had been running**.
(She was no longer running when I saw her.)

BE CAREFUL! Do not use the past perfect progressive with most **non-action verbs**.

It was 2008. He **had been** a conductor for two years.
NOT He ~~had been being~~ a conductor for two years.

Use the past perfect or the past perfect progressive with the simple past to show the **time order between two past events**.

Use the **past perfect** or the **past perfect progressive** for the **earlier event**. Use the **simple past** for the **later time or event**.

He **had conducted** once when he **left** for Germany.
(He had conducted once before he left for Germany.)

He **had been conducting** for years when he **left** for Germany.
(He was conducting before he left for Germany.)

USAGE NOTE We often mention **a period of time with the past perfect progressive** to show how long an event was in progress when another event occurred. We often use the **past progressive** when we **do not mention the length of time**.

He **had been studying** in El Sistema *for five years* when he received his first job as a conductor.

He **was studying** in El Sistema when he received his first job as a conductor.

USAGE NOTE When the **time relationship between two past events is clear** (for example, with *before, after, as soon as, until,* and *because*), we often use the **simple past for both events**.

After Dudamel **had joined** El Sistema, he **studied** the violin.
or
After Dudamel **joined** El Sistema, he **studied** the violin.

BE CAREFUL! In sentences with a time clause starting with *when*, notice the difference in meaning between the **simple past** and the **past perfect** in the main clause.

When the concert ended, she **left**.
(First the concert ended. Then she left.)
When the concert ended, she **had left**.
(First she left. Then the concert ended.)

Use **adverbs** such as *already, yet, ever, never,* or *just* with the **past perfect** or **past perfect progressive** to emphasize the **first event**.

A: Jason and I watched Dudamel on YouTube last night. Jason **had *already* seen** him conduct.
B: **Had** you *ever* **seen** him before?
A: No, I hadn't. I **had *never* heard of** him.

BE CAREFUL! Do not put an adverb between the **main verb** and a **direct object**.

I hadn't **seen him *yet*.** **or** I hadn't ***yet* seen him.**
NOT I hadn't ~~seen yet him~~.

CONTINUED ▶

Use **expressions with** *by* to refer to the **second event**.	
• *by* + **time or event**	***By 2006***, Dudamel **had gotten** married. ***By the end of the concert***, they **had been applauding** enthusiastically for ten minutes.
• *by the time* (to introduce a **clause** in the **simple past**)	***By the time he was fifteen***, he **had started** to conduct. ***By the time we got tickets***, we **had been waiting** in line for an hour.
IN WRITING Use a **comma after the time clause or phrase** when it comes at the **beginning** of the sentence. Do not use a comma after the main clause when the main clause comes first.	***By the time I sat down,*** the concert had started. NOT The concert had started ✗ by the time I sat down.

REFERENCE NOTES

For a list of **irregular past participles**, see Appendix 1 on page 453.

For **spelling rules for progressive forms**, see Appendix 23 on page 463.

STEP 3   FOCUSED PRACTICE

EXERCISE 1 DISCOVER THE GRAMMAR

GRAMMAR NOTES 1–4 Read each numbered situation. Decide if the description that follows is *True* (*T*) or *False* (*F*). If there is not enough information to know, write a question mark (*?*).

1. The talk-show host invited the musician on her show because he had won a competition.

    __F__ The musician won the competition after his appearance on the show.

2. When I arrived, the musician had been explaining why he had chosen to play the violin.

    __F__ The musician's explanation was finished.

3. It was 4:00 p.m. They had been selling tickets for an hour.

    __?__ They were still selling tickets at 4:05.

4. When I found my seat, the concert started.

    _____ First the concert started. Then I found my seat.

5. When I found my seat, the concert had started.

    _____ First the concert started. Then I found my seat.

6. When I saw Mei Ling, she was very enthusiastic. She had been rehearsing with Dudamel.

    _____ She wasn't rehearsing when I saw her.

7. By the end of the concert, the audience had fallen in love with Dudamel.

    __F__ The audience fell in love with Dudamel after the concert.

EXERCISE 2 PAST PERFECT STATEMENTS WITH *ALREADY* AND *YET*

GRAMMAR NOTES 1–4 Look at some important events in Gustavo Dudamel's career. Then complete the sentences. Use the past perfect with *already* or *not yet*.

born in Venezuela	began violin lessons	started to study conducting	became conductor of youth orchestra	won prize; met Eloisa Maturen in Germany	got married in Caracas, Venezuela	moved to L.A. as musical director of L.A. Symphony
1981	1985	1992	1999	2004	2006	2009

1. It was 1984. Dudamel <u>hadn't yet begun</u> _____ violin lessons.

2. By age six, he _____ violin lessons.

3. In 1991, he _____ to study conducting.

4. By 2000, he _____ the conductor of an orchestra.

5. Before age twenty-five, he _____ a conducting prize.

6. It was 2003. He and Maturen _____ married.

7. It was 2010. He and Maturen _____ to L.A.

EXERCISE 3 PAST PERFECT QUESTIONS AND SHORT ANSWERS

GRAMMAR NOTE 1 Carly plays cello in an orchestra. Read her diary notes. Then complete the questions about her day and give short answers. Use the past perfect.

DATE: Thursday, December 15, 2016

8:30 took yoga class at the gym

10:00 started rehearsing at the concert hall for Saturday's concert

12:30 ate lunch

2:30 had cello lesson with Sofia Gregor

4:00 gave cello demonstration at Performing Arts High School

6:00 shopped for dress for Saturday night's concert

7:30 did relaxation exercises

8:30 ordered takeout from favorite ethnic restaurant

11:00 fell asleep—forgot to eat!

1. It was 9:30 a.m. Carly was at the gym.

   A: _Had she taken_ _____ her yoga class yet?

   B: _Yes, she had._ _____

2. At 10:15, Carly was at the concert hall.

   A: _____ for Saturday's concert yet?

   B: _____

3. It was 1:30. Carly was in the practice room of the concert hall.

   A: _____ her lunch by that time?

   B: _____

4. At 2:15, Carly was talking to Sofia Gregor.

   A: _____ cello lesson yet?

   B: _____

5. It was 3:30.

   A: _____ her cello demonstration yet?

   B: _____

6. At 4:45, Carly was still at the high school.

   A: _____ for her dress by then?

   B: _____

7. It was 8:00 p.m. Carly was changing her clothes.

   A: _____ her relaxation exercises that day?

   B: _____

8. At 10:00 p.m., Carly was listening to a CD of her last performance.

   A: _____ takeout yet?

   B: _____

9. It was 11:00 p.m. Carly was sleeping.

   A: _____ her dinner yet?

   B: _____

EXERCISE 4 PAST PERFECT PROGRESSIVE STATEMENTS

GRAMMAR NOTE 2 Gustavo Dudamel was a musical child prodigy. Complete the information about two other prodigies. Use the past perfect progressive form of the verbs in parentheses.

Judit Polgár

JUDIT POLGÁR is known as the strongest female chess player who has ever lived. In 1991, she became the youngest Grandmaster ever at age fifteen, which was not really very surprising because Polgar _____had been playing_____ the
1. (play)
game since she was only five years old. For five years, she _____ games
2. (win)
against older chess masters. By age twenty, Polgár was ranked the tenth best player in the world—the first woman to achieve a rating in the top 10. In 2002, she defeated Garry Kasparov, the highest rated player in the world. It was a great personal victory. She had lost to Kasparov in 1994, and she _____ to try again.
3. (wait)
In 2000, Polgár married Gusztav Font. Font, a veterinarian, _____
4. (treat)
Polgár's dog when the two met. Between 2004 and 2007, the couple had two children, and Polgár competed less often. Because she _____ as much, her rank
5. (not compete)
dropped to twentieth, but by 2008, Polgár was playing for Hungary in the Chess Olympiad, her career back on track. Although she is now retired, Polgár is still the best of the best.

AKRIT JASWAL has been called "the world's smartest boy" and "the Mozart of modern medicine." By the age of six, he _____ already _____
6. (read)
Shakespeare in his native village in northern India. Even more amazing, young Jaswal

_____ medical textbooks on his own. He _____ even
7. (study)
_____ surgeries at local hospitals. Then at age seven, he operated on
8. (observe)
a young girl whose hand had been severely injured in a fire. The operation, which he performed for free in his home, was a success, and Jaswal became famous. His family

_____ that their son could start medical school when he was eight,
9. (hope)
but he had to wait three years before he enrolled at Punjab University—the youngest student ever admitted. Jaswal's dream is to someday find a cure for cancer.

EXERCISE 5 PAST PERFECT PROGRESSIVE QUESTIONS

GRAMMAR NOTES 2–4 A talk-show host is making a list of questions for her research
about violinist Midori Goto. Use the words in parentheses to write questions with the past
perfect progressive. Use *when* to introduce the time clause with the simple past.

1. Midori Goto gave her first public performance in Osaka, Japan, at the age of six.

   How long had she been playing violin when she gave her first public performance in Osaka, Japan, at the age of six?
   (how long / she / play violin)

2. Ten-year-old Midori began classes at the Juilliard School in New York City.

   _____
   (where / she / take music lessons)

3. Midori performed with the New York Philharmonic for the first time.

   _____
   (how long / she / study at Juilliard)

4. She made her first recording.

   _____
   (her fans / wait a long time)

5. She started the Midori & Friends program.

   _____
   (what / she / notice about children and music)

6. She became a United Nations Messenger of Peace.

   _____
   (how / she / help children around the world)

7. Young musicians were on stage with her for a concert in Tokyo.

   _____
   (how many hours a day / they / practice)

8. The concert started at 7:00 p.m.

   _____
   (reporters / take photos)

EXERCISE 6 PAST PERFECT OR PAST PERFECT PROGRESSIVE

GRAMMAR NOTES 1–4 Complete this report on El Sistema. Use the past perfect or past perfect progressive form of the verbs in the boxes. Use the past perfect progressive when possible.

come up	help	observe	~~receive~~	show up	teach	win

It was 1975. José Antonio Abreu _____*had received*_____ his degree in economics
                                                    1.
and _____ economics at Simón Bolívar University for years. As an
              2.
economist, he _____ the poverty he saw around him. As a trained
                        3.
musician, he _____ with a creative solution—a music program for
                      4.
children. El Sistema began in a parking garage in 1975. Abreu remembers the first night of the
program. Only eleven children _____, but, Abreu says, he still felt it
                                              5.
was the start of something very big. It was. By 2009, Abreu _____
                                                                          6.
many prizes for his work, and he _____ hundreds of thousands of
                                                7.
Venezuela's kids turn their lives around with music.

arrest	be	go	hope	live	work

Gustavo Dudamel, a world-famous conductor, _____ one of
                                                              8.
those kids. He, in turn, established similar programs, such as Youth Orchestra Los Angeles.
Canadian singer Measha Brueggergosman participated in the program, and in October 2009
the kids attended Dudamel's concert at the Hollywood Bowl. They were wildly enthusiastic.
"A lot of the people . . . _____ never _____ to a classical music
                                                    9.
concert before. They were crying and screaming," she recalls. But Dudamel is only one of El
Sistema's success stories. Here are just two more out of thousands: At age nine, Edicson Ruiz
_____ at a Caracas supermarket to help support his family. El Sistema
          10.
helped him put down the supermarket packages and pick up the bow.[1] He is now a successful
double bass player with the Berlin Philarmonie. And then there's Lennar Acosta. Before he got
his clarinet, Acosta _____ a life of crime. Police _____ already
                              11.
_____ the troubled youth nine times for robbery and drug use. But
          12.
thanks to El Sistema, he traded in his gun for a musical instrument and became a clarinetist at
the Caracas Youth Orchestra. As Abreu said, "Music is a weapon against poverty." It is also a
way to change lives.

---

1 *bow:* a long thin piece of wood used for playing instruments such as the violin, cello, and double bass

EXERCISE 7 TIME ORDER IN SENTENCES

GRAMMAR NOTES 1–4 Combine the pairs of sentences about Edson Natareno, a student in Youth Orchestra Los Angeles. Decide on the correct time order of the sentences. Use the past perfect or the past perfect progressive to express the event that occurred first. Use the past perfect progressive when possible.

1. A teacher heard Edson Natareno singing in her class. She talked to his mother about his musical talent.

   After *a teacher had heard Edson Natareno singing in her class* _____,

   she talked to his mother about his musical talent _____.

2. Edson joined Youth Orchestra Los Angeles in 2007. His mother encouraged him to join.

   _____

   because _____.

3. Edson listened to the sounds of other instruments. He finally decided to play the clarinet.

   _____

   before _____.

4. Edson played music for a year. His story appeared in a newspaper article.

   When _____,

   _____.

5. Edson performed with Youth Orchestra Los Angeles for six years. He traveled to London with the orchestra in 2013.

   By the time _____,

   _____.

6. Edson was able to begin classes at Colburn School. He won a scholarship to the world-famous performing arts school.

   _____

   after _____.

7. Edson graduated from high school. He already played in orchestras with Gustavo Dudamel three times.

   By the time _____,

   _____.

EXERCISE 8 EDITING

GRAMMAR NOTES 1–4 Read this article about Canadian singer Measha Brueggergosman. There are eight mistakes in the use of the past perfect and the past perfect progressive. The first mistake is already corrected. Find and correct seven more.

A Diva¹ with a Difference

MEASHA BRUEGGERGOSMAN'S first-grade teacher urged her parents to give her music lessons. They did, and by age fifteen, she ~~had been deciding~~ *had decided* on a singing career. Not growing up in a large cultural center, she didn't have the chance to attend concerts or the opera. However, by the time she enrolled at the University of Toronto, she listening to classical music on the radio for years, and she participated in her church's music program since childhood.

After she received her degree in Toronto, Brueggergosman had moved to Düsseldorf, Germany, to study. By age twenty-five, she had been performing internationally for several years and had won a number of important prizes. One enthusiastic judge said she had never been meeting a singer with such perfect vocal control. By her thirtieth birthday, Brueggergosman has become both a classical music sensation² and a popular celebrity.

A diva with a Facebook fan club who had develop her own unique fashion style, Brueggergosman's fame continued to grow. However, when she experienced a serious health problem in June 2009, Brueggergosman stopped performing. Amazingly, she recovered in time to sing at the *¡Bienvenido Dudamel!* concert four months later. When she stepped onto the stage at the Hollywood Bowl and began singing, the audience had fallen in love with her again for her beautiful voice, her style, and her bravery. Brava Brueggergosman!

---

1 *diva:* a very successful female opera singer
2 *sensation:* something or someone that causes a lot of excitement or interest

EXERCISE 9 LISTENING

▶04|02 (A) A radio host is interviewing several musicians. Listen to the interview. Read the statements. Then listen again and check (✓) *True* or *False*.

	True	False
1. Before Julio started music lessons, he'd wanted to play the trombone.	☐	☑
2. By the time Marta and Julio got to Berlin, they had become friends.	☐	☐
3. Marta and Julio got married six months after they joined the orchestra.	☐	☐
4. Klaus had seen Dudamel conduct many times before the concert in Caracas.	☐	☐
5. The Dudamel concert inspired Klaus to make a change in his life.	☐	☐
6. Ling decided she wanted a violin before she turned ten.	☐	☐
7. Ling and her sister started taking violin lessons in the same year.	☐	☐
8. After Antonio started making music, he got into a lot of trouble.	☐	☐

▶04|02 (B) Listen to the interview again. Then work with a partner. Discuss your answers in A. Why did you choose *True* or *False*?

EXAMPLE: A: So, the first statement is false.
   B: Right. Julio had been planning to study the flute, but his school gave him a trombone because there was no flute available.
   A: What did you choose for the second statement?

EXERCISE 10 WHAT ABOUT YOU?

CONVERSATION Work in a group. Think about a talent or skill that you have such as playing a musical instrument, drawing, playing basketball, dancing, or taking photos. Tell your group what your talent is and how you developed it. Answer questions from the group.

EXAMPLE: A: I'm good at playing the piano. In fact, I won a piano competition when I was nine years old.
   B: How long had you been playing the piano by then?
   A: Five years.
   C: So you had started piano lessons when you were only four?

EXERCISE 11 THINKING BACK

A CONVERSATION Before you talk with a partner, think about what you did yesterday. Indicate whether it was or wasn't a busy day. Complete the sentences.

Yesterday was / wasn't a busy day for me.

1. By 9:00 a.m., _____ .

2. By the time I got to work/school, _____ .

3. By the time I had lunch, _____ .

4. By the time I left work/school, _____ .

5. By the time I had dinner, _____ .

6. By 9:00 p.m., I _____ .

7. By the time I went to bed, I had done so much/little that I felt _____ .

B Work with a partner. Compare your day with your partner's day.

EXAMPLE: A: By 9:00 a.m., I'd already been practicing the piano for two hours. What about you?
B: By 9:00 a.m., I hadn't even gotten up!

EXERCISE 12 AMAZING CHILD PRODIGIES STORIES

A GROUP PROJECT Work in a group. Choose one of the people listed below, who were child prodigies. Do research about the person and answer some of the questions below.

- Nadia Comaneci, gymnast
- Amadeus Mozart, composer
- Clara Schumann, musician
- Stevie Wonder, musician
- Tiger Woods, golfer
- Sho Yano, physician

Sho Yano

Possible questions:
- When was the person born?
- What special skill(s) did the person have as a child?
- What had the person accomplished by the age of five? Ten? Fifteen?
- What is the most surprising fact that you learned about the person?

EXAMPLE: A: Sho Yano was a child prodigy.
B: He had already started composing music by the age of five.
C: And by the time he was ten, . . .
D: Here's something even more amazing. By his tenth birthday, . . .

B Report back to your class. If your group chose the same person as another group, do you have the same information about that person? Compare answers.

EXAMPLE: A: Sho Yano is a physician and he was a child prodigy.
B: He's also a musician. By the age of five, he had learned how to play the piano.
A: And he had started composing music by the time he was five.
B: By his tenth birthday, . . .

EXERCISE 13 NOW YOU SEE IT, NOW YOU DON'T

PICTURE COMPARISON Work with a partner. Look at the two pictures. There are eleven differences in the pictures. Find and discuss them. Use *by* + past perfect in your discussion.

EXAMPLE: **A:** At 4:00 p.m., the woman wasn't wearing a sweater. By 6:00 p.m., she had put her sweater on.

B: And the boy had fallen asleep.

FROM GRAMMAR TO WRITING

A BEFORE YOU WRITE Find information in the library or on the Internet about the life and career of a musician or singer that you like. Make a timeline using five events in the artist's life and career. Give details.

Events: _____ _____ _____ _____ _____

Years: [ ] [ ] [ ] [ ] [ ]

B WRITE Use your timeline to write two paragraphs about the artist you researched. In the first paragraph, include information about the person's career. In the second paragraph, write about the artist's personal life. Use the past perfect and the past perfect progressive. Try to avoid the common mistakes in the chart.

EXAMPLE: Vanessa-Mae only uses her first name professionally. She was born in Singapore on October 27, 1978. By age five, she had been playing the piano for two years. By the time she was a teenager, she had already made three classical recordings. . . .

Common Mistakes in Using the Past Perfect and Past Perfect Progressive

Use **the past perfect or the past perfect progressive** to show that an event came **first**. Do not use the simple past.	I was late. By the time I arrived, the concert **had started**. NOT By the time I arrived, the concert started.
Use **the past perfect** with most **non-action verbs**. Do not use the past perfect progressive.	Before he left, he **had seemed** tired. NOT Before he left, had been seeming tired.
Use **a comma after the time clause or phrase** when it comes at the **beginning** of the sentence. Do not use a comma after the main clause when the main clause comes first.	*By the end of the evening,* I had decided to attend another concert. NOT I had decided to attend another concert, by the end of the evening.

C CHECK YOUR WORK Read your paragraphs. Underline once the verbs in the past perfect. Underline twice the verbs in the past perfect progressive. Circle the verbs in the simple past. Use the Editing Checklist to check your work.

Editing Checklist

Did you use . . . ?

☐ the past perfect for things that happened before a specific time in the past

☐ the past perfect progressive for things that were in progress before a specific time in the past

☐ time clauses to show the time order between two past events

☐ adverbs or expressions with *by* to show the order of events

☐ commas after time clauses or phrases at the beginning of a sentence

D REVISE YOUR WORK Read your paragraphs again. Can you improve your writing? Make changes if necessary. Give your paragraphs a title.

UNIT 4 REVIEW

Test yourself on the grammar of the unit.

Ⓐ Circle the correct words to complete the sentences.

1. By the time I was ten, I got / ~~had gotten~~ my first violin.

2. It was 2007. I have been studying / ~~had been studying~~ the violin for two years by then.

3. By 2010, I ~~had graduated~~ / had been graduating from Juilliard School of Music.

4. After I finished school, I ~~moved~~ / had been moving to Los Angeles.

5. I had given / ~~hadn't given~~ a concert yet.

Ⓑ Complete the interview with the simple past, past perfect, or past perfect progressive form of the verbs in parentheses. Use the past perfect progressive when possible.

A: You're only twenty-five. How long _____had_____ you _____been playing_____ the
   1. (play)
   violin when you _____joined_____ the Philharmonic Orchestra?
   2. (join)

B: Ten years. By the time I was thirteen, I _____had been decided_____ to become a
   3. (decide)
   professional, and I _____had been practicing_____ for three hours a day. My father was a
   4. (practice)
   musician, and he _____had taught_____ me to play the piano, too.
   5. (teach)

A: _____Had_____ you _____come_____ to this country yet?
   6. (come)

B: Yes. We _____had_____ already _____moved_____ here. We
   7. (move)
   _____had been living_____ here for a year.
   8. (live)

A: Well, congratulations on winning the grand prize. Were you surprised?

B: Very! I _____hadn't been expecting_____ it, so I was very excited.
   9. (not expect)

Ⓒ Find and correct six mistakes.

When five-year-old Sarah Chang enrolled in the Juilliard School, she has [had] already been

playing the violin for more than a year. Her parents, both musicians, had ~~been moving~~ [moved] from

Korea to further their careers. They had ~~gave~~ [given] their daughter a violin as a fourth birthday

present, and Sarah had been ~~practiced~~ [practicing] hard since then. By seven, she [had] already performed

with several local orchestras. A child prodigy, Sarah became the youngest person to receive

the Hollywood Bowl's Hall of Fame Award. She had already been ~~receiving~~ [received] several awards

including the Nan Pa Award—South Korea's highest prize for musical talent.

Now check your answers on page 475.

Future: Review and Expansion

66

PART 2

OUTCOMES

- Discuss future facts, predictions, plans, and scheduled events
- Describe events that will be in progress at a specific time in the future
- Identify key details in a reading or recording
- Discuss schedules and make plans
- Discuss life in the future
- Write about how one's school will be in the future

OUTCOMES

- Describe events that will happen, or will be in progress, before a specific time in the future
- Show the order of two future events, using adverbs and expressions with *by*
- Identify specific information in a business article and a conversation
- Discuss future goals and aspirations
- Write about a classmate's future goals

Future and Future Progressive

LIFE IN THE FUTURE

OUTCOMES
• Discuss future facts, predictions, plans, and scheduled events
• Describe events that will be in progress at a specific time in the future
• Identify key details in a reading or recording
• Discuss schedules and make plans
• Discuss life in the future
• Write about how one's school will be in the future

STEP 1   GRAMMAR IN CONTEXT

BEFORE YOU READ

Look at the picture and at the section titles in the article. Discuss the questions.

1. How will the cities of the future look?

2. What kinds of problems do you think people will face in the future?

3. How do you think they can solve them?

READ

05|01 Read this article about the future.

Cities of the Future

The world's population is exploding. By 2050, futurists[1] predict that 10 billion people will be living on the planet, up to 70 percent of them in cities. At the same time, the oceans are rising as global warming melts the ice at the North and South Poles. This means that while the population is growing, land will be shrinking. In addition, there is not going to be enough fresh water or oil and other types of fuel. Where will people live when room on dry land gets too crowded? How will 10 billion people feed themselves and travel from place to place? We're going to need a lot of innovative solutions. Fortunately, some very creative individuals are already thinking about them. Here's what they are predicting:

Homes: Water World

Some futurists believe that as rising oceans cover the land, the oceans themselves are going to become valuable real estate.[2] Architects and engineers will be building floating cities that will use

---

1 *futurists:* people who predict future events and developments

2 *real estate:* land and houses that people buy and sell

solar, wind, and wave power.[3] Some cities will even be traveling long distances and using their large gardens to supply food. Science fiction? Maybe not. Some of the technology is already being used in underwater hotels and laboratories.

Food: The Sky's the Limit

According to the United Nations Food and Agriculture Organization, the world is going to need 70 percent more food by 2050. This will require additional farmland equal to the size of Brazil. Where will we find it? Dr. Dickson Despommier, of Columbia University, says urban farmers will be growing food on vertical farms, and that "sky farms" in New York will produce enough chicken, vegetables, and fruit to feed the entire city. Instead of fuel-guzzling[4] farm machines, farmers will be using robots for difficult and dangerous work. The farms will also save energy because food won't be traveling into the city by truck from distant farms.

Travel: Back to the Future?

More than eighty years ago, luxurious airships—large "balloons" filled with helium[5]—carried passengers around Europe and across the Atlantic. However, after one terrible accident, travelers stopped using them. Now, with fuel becoming more expensive, airships are coming back. A Spanish company is developing a solar-powered airship that will fly on sunshine during the day and use fuel only at night. Commuters will be taking airships to work, and the company predicts many other uses for the vehicles. For example, disaster relief organizations, such as the Red Cross and Red Crescent Societies, will be using them as flying hospitals to help earthquake and storm victims.

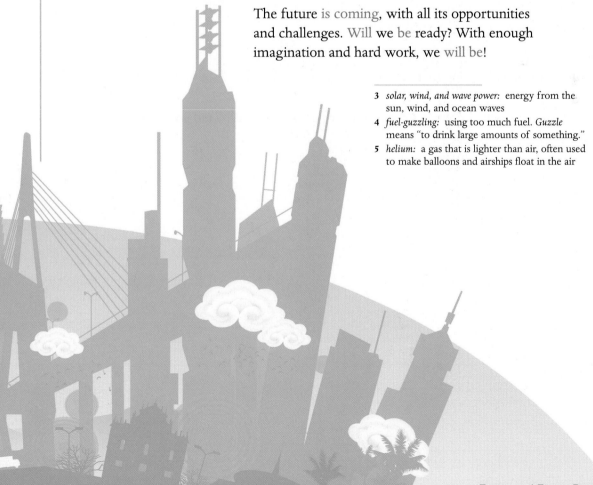

The future is coming, with all its opportunities and challenges. Will we be ready? With enough imagination and hard work, we will be!

3 *solar, wind, and wave power:* energy from the sun, wind, and ocean waves
4 *fuel-guzzling:* using too much fuel. *Guzzle* means "to drink large amounts of something."
5 *helium:* a gas that is lighter than air, often used to make balloons and airships float in the air

AFTER YOU READ

A VOCABULARY **Choose the word or phrase that best completes each sentence.**

1. An **innovative** plan is _____.
   a. new
   b. old
   c. easy

2. Creative **individuals** are _____ that find solutions to problems.
   a. methods
   b. people
   c. machines

3. **Technology** is the _____ we use to do things.
   a. money and skills
   b. machines and knowledge
   c. people and animals

4. A _____ is not usually **vertical**.
   a. tall building
   b. tree
   c. table

5. A(n) _____ is an example of a **vehicle**.
   a. accident
   b. car
   c. hospital

6. A **challenge** is a task that is _____.
   a. new and difficult
   b. easy and safe
   c. in the distant future

B COMPREHENSION **Read the statements. Check (✓) *True* or *False*.**

	True	False
1. The world's population is already growing fast.	☐	☐
2. People are already living on floating cities.	☐	☐
3. Tourists are already staying in underwater hotels.	☐	☐
4. Sky farms are already using robots as workers.	☐	☐
5. A company is already building a solar-powered airship.	☐	☐
6. Commuters are already riding to work in airships.	☐	☐

C DISCUSSION **Work with a partner. Compare your answers in B. Why did you check *True* or *False*?**

FUTURE

Affirmative Statements

We **are going to take**	
We **will take**	the airship at 9:00.
We **are taking**	
We **take**	

Negative Statements

We **are not going to take**	
We **will not take**	the airship at 10:00.
We **are not taking**	
We **don't take**	

Yes/No Questions

Is she **going to take**	
Will she **take**	the airship at 9:00?
Is she **taking**	
Does she **take**	

Short Answers

Affirmative		Negative	
	she **is.**		she **isn't.**
Yes,	she **will.**	No,	she **won't.**
	she **is.**		she **isn't.**
	she **does.**		she **doesn't.**

Wh- Questions

When **is** she **going to take**	
When **will** she **take**	the airship?
When **is** she **taking**	
When **does** she **take**	

FUTURE PROGRESSIVE

Statements

Subject	Be (not) going to/ Will (not)	Be + Base Form + -ing	
People	**are (not) going to** **will (not)**	**be traveling**	to Mars by 2050.

Yes/No Questions

Be/Will	Subject	Going to	Be + Base Form + -ing	
Are	they	**going to**	**be traveling**	to Mars?
Will				

Short Answers

Affirmative		Negative	
Yes,	they **are.**	No,	they**'re not.**
	they **will.**		they **won't.**

Wh- Questions

Wh- Word	Be/Will	Subject	Going to	Be + Base Form + -ing	
When	**are**	they	**going to**	**be traveling**	to Mars?
	will				

GRAMMAR NOTES

1 Referring to Future Events

There are **several ways to refer to future events**. Sometimes only one form of the future is appropriate, but in many cases more than one form is possible.

• *be going to*	I'**m going to take** the airship tomorrow.
• *will*	It'**ll be** a nice trip.
• **present progressive**	It'**s leaving** from Barcelona.
• **simple present**	It **takes off** at 9:00 a.m.

2 Future Facts

For facts or events that you are **certain will happen in the future**, you can use *be going to* or *will*.

• *be going to*	The sun **is going to rise** at 6:43 tomorrow.
• *will*	The sun **will rise** at 6:43 tomorrow.

3 Predictions

For predictions about things you are **quite sure will happen in the future**, you can also use *be going to* or *will*.

• *be going to*	I think people **are going to use** robots for a lot of tasks.
• *will*	I think people **will use** robots for a lot of tasks.

USAGE NOTE We often use *I think* before a prediction.	*I think* almost everyone **is going to have** a robot.
IN WRITING We use *will* more in **formal writing** and *be going to* more in **conversation**.	Prices **will increase** next month. *(formal writing)* Prices **are going to increase** next month. *(conversation)*
BE CAREFUL! Use *be going to* when something that you **notice right now** makes you almost certain an event is going to happen. Do not use *will*.	Look! That robot **is going to serve** our coffee! NOT Look! That robot ~~will serve~~ . . .

4 Future Plans

For plans or things that are **already decided**, use *be going to* or the **present progressive**.

• *be going to*	I**'m going to fly** to Tokyo next week.
• **present progressive**	I**'m flying** to Tokyo next week.

USAGE NOTE We often use the **present progressive** for plans that are **already arranged**.

I**'m flying** to Tokyo next week. I already have a ticket.

USAGE NOTE When the main verb is *go*, it is much more common to use the **present progressive** (*be going*) than *be going to go*.

He**'s going** home at 2:30. *(more common)*
He**'s going to go** home at 2:30. *(less common)*

5 Quick Decisions, Offers, and Promises

For decisions that you make quickly while you are speaking, or to make offers or promises, use *will*.

	A: The Robot Show opens next week.
• **quick decision**	B: Sounds interesting. I think I**'ll go**.
	A: I'd like to go, too, but I don't have a ride.
• **offer**	B: I**'ll drive** you, but I'd like to leave by 7:00.
• **promise**	A: No problem. I**'ll be** ready.

USAGE NOTE *Shall* is not common in American English except for **offers** and **suggestions**.

Shall I pick you up at 8:00? *(offer)*
Shall we take the bus? *(suggestion)*

6 Future Scheduled Events

For scheduled events such as **timetables**, **programs**, and **schedules**, you can use the **simple present**.

• **simple present**	The airship **leaves** at 9:00 a.m.

USAGE NOTE We often use the simple present with verbs such as *begin*, *start*, *leave*, *arrive*, *last*, and *end* to show scheduled events.

The conference **starts** tomorrow morning.
It **lasts** three days.
My final meeting of the day **ends** at 5:00 p.m.

USAGE NOTE We can also use *be going to* and *will* for scheduled future events.

My final meeting **is going to end** at 5:00 p.m.
My final meeting **will end** at 5:00 p.m.

7 Future Progressive

Use the **future progressive** with *be going to* or *will* to show that an action will be **in progress at a specific time in the future.**

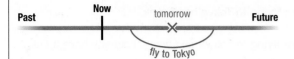

At this time tomorrow, I**'m going to be flying** to Tokyo.
At this time tomorrow, I**'ll be flying** to Tokyo.

USAGE NOTE We often use the **future progressive** instead of the future to make a question about someone's plans **more polite.**	When **are** you **going to hand in** your paper, Ana? When **will** you **be grading** our tests, Professor Lee? *(more polite)*
USAGE NOTE We also use the **future progressive** to ask about future plans in order to request a favor. This makes the request **more polite.**	**Will** you **be going** by the post office tomorrow? I need some stamps.

8 Future Time Clauses

Use **the simple present** or **the present progressive** in **future time clauses.**

In sentences with a **future time clause**, use:

• **future** or **future progressive** in **main clause**

MAIN CLAUSE	TIME CLAUSE
I**'ll call** you when the robot finishes the laundry.	
I**'ll be enjoying** dinner while he is dusting.	

• **present** or **present progressive** in **time clause**

MAIN CLAUSE	TIME CLAUSE
I'll call you when the robot **finishes** the laundry.	
I'll be enjoying dinner while he **is dusting**.	

BE CAREFUL! Do not use the future or the future progressive in the time clause.	**NOT** I'll call you when the robot ~~will finish~~ the laundry. **NOT** I'll be enjoying dinner while he ~~is going to be~~ dusting.
IN WRITING Use a **comma after the time clause or phrase** when it comes at the **beginning** of the sentence. Do not use a comma after the main clause when the main clause comes first.	***When the price drops,*** more people will buy robots. **NOT** More people will buy robots_x when the price drops.

EXERCISE 1   DISCOVER THE GRAMMAR

Ⓐ GRAMMAR NOTES 1–7 Reporter Will Hapin just met his friend Dr. Nouvella Eon at a technology conference. Read their conversation and underline all the verbs that refer to the future.

HAPIN: Nouvella! It's nice to see you. <u>Are you presenting</u> a paper today?

EON: Hi, Will! Yes. In fact, my talk starts at two o'clock.

HAPIN: Oh, I think I'll go. What do you plan to talk about? Will you be discussing robots?

EON: Yes. I'm focusing on personal robots for household work. My talk is called "Creative Uses of Home Robots."

HAPIN: *I* want one of those! But seriously, you promised me an interview on personal robots. Will you be getting some free time in the next few weeks?

EON: I'm not sure. I'll call you after the conference, OK?

HAPIN: Great! Where's your son, by the way? Is he with you?

EON: No. Rocky stays in Denver with his grandparents in the summer. I'm going to visit him right after the conference. He'll be ten years old in a few days. I can't believe it!

HAPIN: It's his birthday, huh? Here, take this little model of the flying car for him.

EON: Oh, he's going to love this! Thanks, Will. So what are you working on these days?

HAPIN: Well, *Futurist Magazine* just published my article on cities of the future. And next month at their convention, I'm interviewing members of the World Future Association about flying cars.

EON That'll be exciting! Good luck!

B Read the conversation again. Complete the chart. List the twelve future verb forms in Part A. Then check (✓) the correct column for each form.

	Facts	Predictions	Plans	Quick Decisions	Promises	Schedules
1. Are you presenting			✓			
2.						
3.						
4.						
5.						
6.						
7.						
8.						
9.						
10.						
11.						
12.						

EXERCISE 2 FORMS OF THE FUTURE

A GRAMMAR NOTES 1–6 Circle the correct words to complete these conversations.

1. **EON:** Which projects do you report / are you going to report on?

   HAPIN: I haven't decided for sure. Probably flying cars.

2. **HAPIN:** Look at those dark clouds!

   EON: Yes. It looks like it's raining / it's going to rain any minute.

3. **EON:** I'd better get back to my hotel room before it starts to rain. Call me, OK?

   HAPIN: OK. I'm talking / I'll talk to you later.

4. **DESK:** Dr. Eon, your son just called.

   EON: Oh, good. I think I'll call / I'm calling him back right away.

5. **EON:** Hi, honey. How's it going?

   ROCKY: Great. And guess what? I go / I'm going fishing with Grandpa tomorrow.

6. **EON:** Have fun, but don't forget you still have to finish that paper.

   ROCKY: I know, Mom. I send / I'm sending it to my teacher tomorrow. I already discussed it with her.

7. **ROCKY:** How's the conference?

   EON: Good. I'm giving / I'll give my talk this afternoon.

8. ROCKY: Good luck. When <u>are you / will you</u> be here?

EON: Tomorrow. The airship <u>lands / will land</u> at 7:00, so I <u>see / I'll see</u> you about 8:00.

9. ROCKY: Great! <u>Are we going / Do we go</u> to the car show on my birthday?

EON: Sure! Oh, I saw Will Hapin, and he gave me something for you. I think <u>you like / you're going to like</u> it.

▶ 05|02 **B** LISTEN AND CHECK   **Listen to the conversations and check your answers in A.**

EXERCISE 3   FUTURE PROGRESSIVE

A GRAMMAR NOTE 7   **Will Hapin is interviewing Nouvella Eon. Complete the interview. Use the future progressive form of the words in parentheses and short answers.**

HAPIN: I noticed that you've been presenting a lot of papers recently. _____*Will*_____ you

_____*be going*_____ to the robotics conference in Tokyo next month?
1. (will / go)

EON: _____*Yes, I will*_____. But I _____. The Japanese are doing very
2.   **3.** (won't present)

innovative things with personal robotics, and I _____ every
4. (be going to / attend)

lecture possible.

HAPIN: What _____ their new robots _____ for us?
5. (be going to / do)

EON: A lot! Oh, personal robots _____ still _____ the elderly
6. (be going to / help)

and individuals with disabilities. But the new 'bots _____ our
7. (will / improve)

lives in a lot of other ways, too. They _____ complicated
8. (will / cook)

recipes. They _____ music and many other creative tasks. So
9. (will / perform)

_____ you _____ one for your family, Will?
10. (be going to / buy)

HAPIN: _____. They look too much like machines to me. _____ their appearance
11.

_____?
12. (be going to / change)

EON: _____—and very soon. Companies are starting to meet that challenge now. In
13.

just a couple of years, they _____ 'bots that look exactly like
14. (will / sell)

humans—and show human emotions.

HAPIN: Amazing! Well, thanks for the interview, Nouvella. Oh! Look at the time. This afternoon, I

_____ a test drive in the new flying car. You should see it. The
15. (be going to / take)

technology is really amazing. Why don't you come with me?

▶ 05|03 **B** LISTEN AND CHECK   **Listen to the interview and check your answers in A.**

EXERCISE 4 FUTURE PROGRESSIVE AFFIRMATIVE AND NEGATIVE STATEMENTS

GRAMMAR NOTE 7 Dr. Eon's family uses a robot for household chores. Look at Botley the Robot's schedule for tomorrow. Write sentences using the words in parentheses and the future progressive.

TOMORROW

8:00	make breakfast
9:00	vacuum
10:00	dust
11:00	shop for food
12:00	do laundry
12:30	make lunch
1:00	recycle the garbage
2:00	pay bills
3:00	give Dr. Eon a massage
5:00	make dinner
6:00	play soccer with Rocky

1. _At 8:05, Botley won't be vacuuming. He'll be making breakfast._
(8:05 / vacuum)

2. _At 9:05, he'll be vacuuming._
(9:05 / vacuum)

3. _____
(10:05 / dust)

4. _____
(11:05 / do laundry)

5. _____
(12:05 / shop for food)

6. _____
(1:05 / recycle the garbage)

7. _____
(2:05 / give Dr. Eon a massage)

8. _____
(3:05 / give Dr. Eon a massage)

9. _____
(5:05 / make dinner)

10. _____
(6:05 / play cards with Rocky)

EXERCISE 5 FUTURE PROGRESSIVE STATEMENTS AND TIME CLAUSES

GRAMMAR NOTES 7–8 Complete the ad for a getaway[1] in space with the verbs in parentheses. In sentences with time clauses, use the future progressive in the main clause. Use the simple present or the present progressive in the time clause.

Need a break? Call today and in just a few days, you _____ *'ll be traveling* _____

1. (travel)

skyward for a week at Starburst Suites Hotel. No rockets necessary—our comfortable

modern elevator _____ you quietly into space while

2. (lift)

everyone else _____ stuck in the crowds and noise back

3. (be)

on Earth. While you _____ a meal on this luxurious

4. (enjoy)

vehicle, a friendly flight robot _____ amazing views of

5. (point out)

our planet from space. And before you _____ it, you

6. (know)

_____ to check into your hotel for a week of "fun

7. (get ready)

near the Sun." After you _____ your spacesuit, you

8. (unpack)

_____ the other guests for a tour. Do you love sunsets?

9. (join)

You're in luck! You _____ sixteen of them every day from

10. (watch)

the hotel's huge windows. Do you prefer adventure? Picture this! While other guests

_____ in the spa, you _____

11. (relax)   **12.** (put on)

your spacesuit for a walk under the stars.

So call for a reservation. Once aboard, we guarantee it—

you _____ about anything

13. (not think)

except returning again and again and again....

STARBURST SUITES HOTEL

---

1 *getaway:* a short vacation trip

EXERCISE 6 EDITING

GRAMMAR NOTES 1–8 Read this article about cars of the future. There are ten mistakes in the use of the future and the future progressive. The first mistake is already corrected. Find and correct nine more.

Flying Cars

YOUR CLASS starts in ten minutes, but you're stuck in traffic. Don't panic. With just a press of

a button, your car will ~~lifts~~ *lift* off the ground, and you'll be on your way to school. No bad roads,

no stop signs, no worries! It seems like science fiction, but it isn't. Experts predict that we'll all

be use these amazing vehicles one day.

According to *Car Trends Magazine*, one model, part car and part plane, is going be on the

market in the not-so-distant future. It will look like a regular car when it's on the road, but its

wings will unfold when the driver will decide to take to the skies. It will runs on the same fuel

for both land and air travel, and you'll be able to keep it in your garage. (But you're still going

need an airport to take off and land.)

A better model will be a vertical takeoff and landing vehicle (VTOL). You won't need to go

to the airport anymore, and all controls will being automatic. Imagine this: You'll be doing your

homework while your car will be getting you to school safely and on time.

And what does this future dream car cost? Well, fasten your seatbelts—the price will going

to be sky-high. At first, it will be about a million dollars, but after a few years, you'll be able to

buy one for "only" $60,000. Don't sell your old vehicle just yet!

EXERCISE 7
LISTENING

▶ 05|04 **A** Four members of the Mars Association are trying to organize a conference on Venus. Listen to their conversation. Then listen again and mark the chart with an *X* for the times each member cannot meet. Then figure out when everyone will be available.

When they're all available:

<u>1st week August</u>

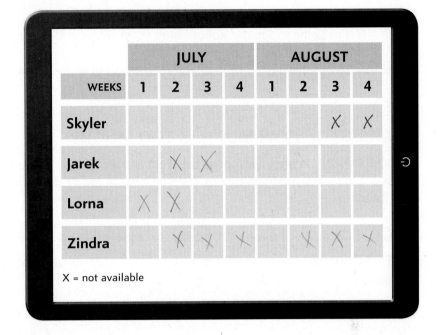

WEEKS	JULY				AUGUST			
	1	2	3	4	1	2	3	4
Skyler							X	X
Jarek		X	X					
Lorna	X	X						
Zindra		X	X	X		X	X	X

X = not available

▶ 05|04 **B** Listen to the conversation again. Then work with a partner. Discuss your answers in A. Explain how you decided when everyone is available.

EXAMPLE: A: When do you think they'll all be available?
            B: Well, Skyler is going to be taking a vacation the last two weeks...
            A: That's right. And Jarek won't...

EXERCISE 8 LET ME CHECK MY CALENDAR

A REACHING AGREEMENT You're going to try to make plans with a partner to do an activity together next week. First, complete your schedule for next week. If you have no plans, write *free*.

	Monday	Tuesday	Wednesday	Thursday	Friday
9:00					
11:00					
1:00					
3:00					
5:00					
7:00					

B Work with a partner. Without showing each other your schedules, find a time to get together. Then make plans.

EXAMPLE: **A:** What are you doing on Tuesday morning?

B: I'm going to see the Robot Show at the Science Museum.

A: I'll go with you. I'll be free at 11:00.

B: Great. The coffee shop opens at 10:00. Shall we meet for coffee first?

EXERCISE 9 HOW MUCH IS TOO MUCH?

A DISCUSSION Before you discuss the work of robots, look at the list of activities. Check (✓) the ones you think robots *Will Be Doing* or *Won't Be Doing* for humans in the near future.

Robots	Will Be Doing	Won't Be Doing
• answer the phone	☐	☐
• drive cars	☐	☐
• find information on the Internet	☐	☐
• go shopping	☐	☐
• guide vacation tours	☐	☐
• have a conversation	☐	☐
• invent new technology	☐	☐
• make dinner	☐	☐
• paint pictures	☐	☐
• plant gardens	☐	☐
• play musical instruments	☐	☐
• report the news	☐	☐
• take a vacation	☐	☐
• take care of children	☐	☐
• teach English	☐	☐
• teach themselves new skills	☐	☐
• write letters	☐	☐
• write laws	☐	☐

B Work in a group. Share and explain your opinions about what robots will be doing for humans. Do you think robots will be doing too much for humans? Why?

EXAMPLE: **A:** I don't think robots will be teaching English, but they'll be taking care of children. Children will think they're fun—like big toys.

B: I think it's a bad idea to have robots take care of children. Children need human contact to help them develop emotional security.

C: Do you think robots will be driving cars?

EXERCISE 10 DR. EON'S CALENDAR

A INFORMATION GAP Work with a partner. Student A will follow the instructions below. Student B will follow the instructions on page 485.

STUDENT A

- Complete Dr. Eon's calendar. Get information from Student B. Ask questions and fill in the calendar. Answer Student B's questions.

  EXAMPLE: A: What will Dr. Eon be doing on Sunday the first?

  B: She'll be flying to Tokyo. What about on the second? Will she be taking the day off?

  A: No, she'll be meeting with Dr. Kato.

FEBRUARY 2077

SUNDAY	MONDAY	TUESDAY	WEDNESDAY	THURSDAY	FRIDAY	SATURDAY
1 fly to Tokyo	2 meet with Dr. Kato	3	4 →→→→	5	6	7 →→
8 take Bullet Train to Osaka	9 sightseeing	10 →→→	11 →	12	13	14 →→
15 fly home	16	17	18 attend energy seminar →→	19	20 →	21 shop with Rocky and Asimo
22	23	24 →→→	25	26	27 →	28 take shuttle to Mars

B Now compare calendars with your partner. Are they the same?

FROM GRAMMAR TO WRITING

A BEFORE YOU WRITE Think about changes that will happen at your school in the future. Make a list of ways that your school will be different twenty-five years from now. Complete the outline.

Changes in the Classrooms, Library, etc.

_____

_____

_____

Changes in the Teachers and Students

_____

_____

_____

B WRITE Use your outline to write two paragraphs about your school twenty-five years from now. Describe what the school will look like and what both teachers and students will be doing. Use different forms of the future. Try to avoid the common mistakes in the chart.

EXAMPLE: Twenty-five years from now, our school will be very different. First, the classrooms are going to be . . .

Common Mistakes in Using the Future and Future Progressive

Use the **present** or the **present progressive** in **future time clauses**. Do not use the future or the future progressive.	You'll be surprised when you **enter** a classroom of the future. **NOT** You'll be surprised when you ~~will enter~~ a classroom of the future.
Use a **comma after the time clause or phrase** when it comes at the **beginning of the sentence**. Do not use a comma after the main clause when the main clause comes first.	***When I return for a visit,*** I'll see many changes. **NOT** I'll see many changes_x when I return for a visit.

C CHECK YOUR WORK Read your paragraphs. Underline once the verbs in the future. Underline twice the verbs in the future progressive. Circle the verbs in the future time clauses. Use the Editing Checklist to check your work.

Editing Checklist

Did you use . . . ?

☐ *be going to* or *will* for facts and predictions

☐ the future progressive for actions that will be in progress at a specific time in the future

☐ the simple present or the present progressive in future time clauses

☐ commas after time clauses at the beginning of a sentence

D REVISE YOUR WORK Read your paragraphs again. Can you improve your writing? Make changes if necessary. Give your paragraphs a title.

UNIT 5 REVIEW

Test yourself on the grammar of the unit.

Ⓐ Circle the correct words to complete the sentences.

1. Our daughter will turns / turn fifteen next week.

2. Are / Do you going to school today?

3. What will you be doing / do at 3:00 this afternoon?

4. The sun will / is going to rise at 6:22 tomorrow morning.

5. Be careful! Your coffee will / is going to spill!

6. While you're / you'll be driving to work tomorrow, we'll be flying to Beijing.

7. Roboid will let us know when he will finish / finishes cooking dinner.

Ⓑ Complete the conversation with the future or future progressive form of the verbs in parentheses or with a short answer. Use the future progressive when possible.

A: What _____are_____ you _____going to be doing_____ at 10:00 tomorrow morning?
1. (do)

B: Ten o'clock? Well, let's see. I _____will be leaving_____ for the airport at 8:30, so at
2. (leave)

10:00, I _____will_____ probably _____be going_____ through airport security.
3. (go)

A: So I guess you _____won't be coming_____ to the office at all tomorrow. → will that cause
4. (not come)

B: Doesn't look like it. Why? _____Is_____ that _____going to cause_____ a problem?
5. (cause)

A: _____No_____, it _____won't_____ won't. It _____will be_____ it is going to be fine. Have a
6. 7. (be)

good trip.

B: Thanks. I _____will see_____ you in a couple of weeks.
8. (see)

Ⓒ Find and correct five mistakes.

stay or be staying

A: How long are you going to staying in Beijing?

I

B: I'm not sure. I'll let you know as soon as I'll find out. OK?

be

A: OK. It's going to be a long flight. What will you doing to pass the time?

working

B: I'll be work a lot of the time. And I'm going to try to sleep.

'll be

A: Good idea. Have fun, and I'm emailing you all the office news. I promise.
I will email

Now check your answers on page 476.

Future Perfect and Future Perfect Progressive

GOALS

OUTCOMES
- Describe events that will happen, or will be in progress, before a specific time in the future
- Show the order of two future events, using adverbs and expressions with *by*
- Identify specific information in a business article and a conversation
- Discuss future goals and aspirations
- Write about a classmate's future goals

STEP 1 GRAMMAR IN CONTEXT

BEFORE YOU READ

Read the definition of *entrepreneur* and look at the photo. Discuss the questions.

1. How are entrepreneurs different from other business people?

2. Who are some famous entrepreneurs?

en•tre•pre•neur /ˌɑntrəprəˈnɜ, -ˈnʊr/ *n.* someone who starts a company, arranges business deals, and takes risks in order to make a profit

READ

▶06|01 Read this article about teen entrepreneur Shubham Banerjee.

Young Entrepreneur Looks Toward the Future

Who is fourteen-year-old entrepreneur Shubham Banerjee, and will he have become a millionaire by his thirtieth birthday? Like other entrepreneurs, Shubham shows great initiative and is willing to take risks in order to succeed. However, money is not his only goal. Shubham wants to use his problem-solving talent to create devices that will help others and make the world a better place.

At the age of twelve, Shubham invented Braigo 1.0, a printer that converts traditional text to braille.[1] He created his printer for a school science project because he wanted to make a better, less expensive braille printer. With money from his father and corporate sponsors,[2] Shubham started his own company,

---

1 *braille:* a system of writing that uses raised dots that blind people can read by touching
2 *sponsors:* people or organizations that pay for the cost of an activity

Braigo Labs, and began developing Braigo 2.0. By the time his printer is available for purchase, he will have been working on the device for several years, and the cost of a braille printer will have dropped from $2,000 to $500 or less. It is important to Shubham that he will have produced an affordable way for the blind and others with limited vision—285 million of them worldwide—to print and read digital documents.

In keeping with his entrepreneurial spirit, Shubham is already finding ways to make his dreams come true. Meanwhile, he is still a teenager who is just beginning high school. By the time he graduates, he will have improved his skills in science and technology. Like most teenagers, he will have played sports and joined clubs. And because education is important to him, Shubham says that he will have applied to several universities to study medical engineering. Clearly, the teen won't have been wasting time, but what about future inventions?

Shubham reports that he already has plans for his next projects. That means by the age of thirty, he will probably have become a well-known engineer working to make the world a better place. As for his millionaire status, there is no doubt that he will have achieved that goal as well.

AFTER YOU READ

A VOCABULARY **Complete the sentences with the words from the box.**

affordable	convert	corporate	initiative	meanwhile	status

1. Entrepreneurs _____ ideas into money-making products.

2. Getting a good education can help you improve your economic _____.

3. You should show _____ instead of waiting to be told what to do.

4. Creative people often have problems following _____ rules.

5. Shoppers are always looking for _____ prices.

6. Price is important, but _____, they want the latest fashion and high quality.

B COMPREHENSION **Read the statements. Check (✓) True or False.**

	True	False
1. Shubham Banerjee's printer will be in stores. Then he will work on Braigo 2.0 for several years.	☐	☐
2. Because of Shubham's invention, braille printers will be more affordable.	☐	☐
3. Shubham will improve his science and technology skills in high school.	☐	☐
4. Shubham will not have time for sports in high school.	☐	☐
5. After he graduates from high school, he will apply to a university.	☐	☐
6. Before his thirtieth birthday, he will probably invent more devices to help people.	☐	☐
7. Shubham will be a millionaire when he is thirty.	☐	☐

C DISCUSSION **Work with a partner. Compare your answers in B. Why did you check** *True* **or** *False***?**

FUTURE PERFECT

Statements

Subject	Will (not)	Have + Past Participle	
I You He She It We They	will (not)	have finished	by next week.

Yes/No Questions

Will	Subject	Have + Past Participle	
Will	you she they	have finished	by next week?

Short Answers

Affirmative				Negative		
Yes,	I she they	will (have).		No,	I she they	won't (have).

Wh- Questions

Wh- Word	Will	Subject	Have + Past Participle	
How much	will	you she they	have finished	by next week?

FUTURE PERFECT PROGRESSIVE

Statements

Subject	Will (not)	Have been + Base Form + -ing	
I You He She It We They	will (not)	have been working	for a month.

Yes/No Questions

Will	Subject	Have been + Base Form + -ing	
Will	you she they	have been working	for a month?

Short Answers

Affirmative		
Yes,	I she they	will (have).

Negative		
No,	I she they	won't (have).

Wh- Questions

Wh- Word	Will	Subject	Have been + Base Form + -ing	
How long	will	you she they	have been working	by then?

GRAMMAR NOTES

1 Future Perfect

Use the future perfect to show that something **will happen before a specific time in the future**. The focus is often on the **completion** of an action or situation.

By next week, he **will have achieved** his goal.
She**'ll have started** to sell her new product *by May*.
I**'ll have been** in college for a year *by then*.
We**'ll have learned** a lot *by the end of this class*.

2 Future Perfect Progressive

Use the future perfect progressive to show that something **will be in progress until a specific time in the future**. The action or situation **may continue** after that time. The focus is on the **continuation** of the action or situation, not the end result.

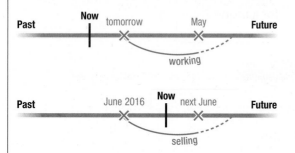

A: I start my job at the computer store tomorrow.
B: But what about our trip in May?
A: *By May*, I**'ll have been working** for six months. I'm sure my boss will give me a week off.

He opened his business in 2016. *By next June*, he**'ll have been selling** computer software for several years.

Notice that the action may start sometime in the future or it may have already started.

BE CAREFUL! Do not use the future perfect progressive with most **non-action verbs**.

By June, we**'ll have owned** our business for five years.
NOT By June, we'll have ~~been owning~~ our business for five years.

3 Future Perfect or Future Perfect Progressive + Simple Present in Time Clause

Use the future perfect or the future perfect progressive with the simple present in the time clause to show the **time order between two future events**.

Use the **future perfect** or the **future perfect progressive** in the main clause for the **earlier event**. Use the **simple present** in the time clause for the **later time or event**.

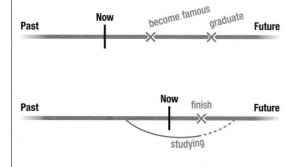

TIME CLAUSE   MAIN CLAUSE
By the time we **graduate**, you **will have become** a famous inventor.
(First you'll become a famous inventor. Then we'll graduate.)

TIME CLAUSE   MAIN CLAUSE
When I **finish** my degree, I**'ll have been studying** here for four years.
(First I'll be studying here for four years. Then I will finish my degree.)

CONTINUED ▶

BE CAREFUL! Use the **simple present** in the **future time clause**. Do not use *will* or *be going to*.	By the time I'm twenty, I'll have started my company. **NOT** By the time ~~I'll be~~ twenty, I'll have started my company. When he **retires**, he'll have been working here for thirty-five years **NOT** When he ~~'s going to retire~~, he'll have been working here for thirty-five years.

4 Adverbs or Expressions with *By* to Show the Order of Events

Use **adverbs** such as *already* and *yet* with the **future perfect** or the **future perfect progressive** to emphasize the **first event**.	A: I can help you clean the apartment tomorrow. B: I'll *already* have finished by then. But I **won't have gone** to the supermarket *yet*. Can you do the shopping?
BE CAREFUL! Do not put an adverb between the **main verb** and a **direct object**.	We **will *already* have completed** our research by Monday. **NOT** We will have ~~completed already our research~~ by Monday. We **will not have taken** the final exam *yet*. **or** We **will not *yet* have taken** the final exam. **NOT** We will not have ~~taken yet the final exam~~.
Use **expressions with** *by* to refer to the **second event**. • *by* + **time or event**	*By the age of thirty*, he **will** probably **have become** a millionaire. *By graduation*, he'**ll have been working** on other creative ideas.
• *by the time* (to introduce a **clause** in the **simple present**)	*By the time he is thirty*, he **will** probably **have become** a millionaire. *By the time he graduates*, he'**ll have been working** on other creative ideas.
IN WRITING Use a **comma after the time clause or phrase** when it comes at the **beginning** of the sentence. Do not use a comma after the main clause when the main clause comes first.	*When he celebrates his thirtieth birthday,* he **will** probably **have become** a millionaire. **NOT** He will probably have become a millionaire_x when he celebrates his thirtieth birthday.

REFERENCE NOTES

For a list of **irregular past participles**, see Appendix 1 on page 453.
For **spelling rules for progressive forms**, see Appendix 23 on page 463.

EXERCISE 1 DISCOVER THE GRAMMAR

GRAMMAR NOTES 1–4 Read each numbered statement from members of a high school club for young entrepreneurs. Choose the sentence (*a* or *b*) that is similar in meaning.

1. By the end of this month, our company will have been doing computer repairs for two years.
   a. The team of students started their business almost two years ago.
   b. The team will continue offering computer services for two more years.

2. Meanwhile, our computer classes for senior citizens will have started.
   a. The students haven't started teaching the classes yet.
   b. The students are already teaching computer skills to senior citizens.

3. Our company is WeRTees. By the next meeting, we'll have finished designing a new t-shirt.
   a. The students will work on the t-shirt design while they are at the next meeting.
   b. The students will work on the design before the next meeting.

4. By the time we graduate, we'll have been selling our t-shirts for the same price for three years.
   a. The t-shirts will be the same price when the students graduate.
   b. The price of the t-shirts will be higher when the students graduate.

5. We have a new company. By 12:00 noon tomorrow, we'll have selected our company's name.
   a. The students know what the name of their company will be.
   b. The students still don't have a name for their company.

6. I won't have completed our team's business plan by noon.
   a. The student will finish at noon.
   b. The student will still be working at noon.

EXERCISE 2 FUTURE PERFECT

GRAMMAR NOTES 1, 4 Debbie Hart has a lot of goals. Look at the timeline. Write sentences describing what Debbie *will have done* or *won't have done* by the year 2022. Use the words in parentheses and the future perfect.

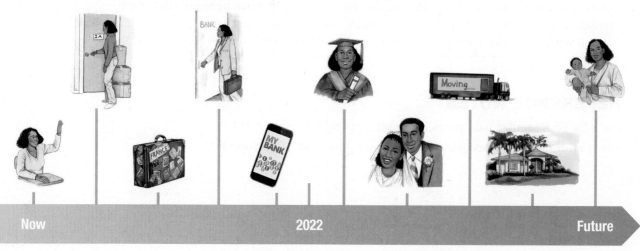

Now   2022   Future

1. By 2022, <u>*Debbie will have started college*</u> .
   (start college)

2. By 2022, _____ .
   (get married)

3. By 2022, _____ .
   (find an affordable apartment)

4. By 2022, _____ .
   (move to Miami)

5. By 2022, _____ .
   (spend a summer in France)

6. By 2022, _____ .
   (start working at a bank)

7. By 2022, _____ .
   (create a new app for online banking)

8. By 2022, _____ .
   (buy a house)

9. By 2022, _____ .
   (graduate from college)

10. By 2022, _____ .
    (become a parent)

EXERCISE 3 SIMPLE PRESENT + FUTURE PERFECT WITH *ALREADY* AND *YET*

GRAMMAR NOTES 1, 3–4 Read Debbie's goals in parentheses. What will or won't she have achieved by the time the second event occurs? Use the information in the timeline from Exercise 2. Write sentences using the words in parentheses and *already* and *yet*.

1. By the time <u>*Debbie finds an affordable apartment, she'll already have started college*</u> .
   (find an affordable apartment / start college)

2. By the time _____ .
   (find an affordable apartment / get married)

3. By the time _____ .
   (start college / spend a summer in France)

4. By the time _____ .
   (graduate from college / find an affordable apartment)

5. By the time _____ .
   (spend a summer in France / find a job at a bank)

6. By the time _____ .
   (graduate from college / create a new banking app)

7. By the time _____ .
   (get married / graduate from college)

8. By the time _____ .
   (move to Miami / buy a house)

9. By the time _____ .
   (become a parent / graduate from college)

10. By the time _____ .
    (buy a house / become a parent)

EXERCISE 4
FUTURE PERFECT OR FUTURE PERFECT PROGRESSIVE

GRAMMAR NOTES 1–4 Ask and answer questions about these people's accomplishments. Use the words in parentheses and choose between the future perfect and the future perfect progressive. Use the calendar to answer the questions.

January						
S	M	T	W	T	F	S
					1	2
3	4	5	6	7	8	9
10	11	12	13	14	15	16
17	18	19	20	21	22	23
24	25	26	27	28	29	30
31						

February						
S	M	T	W	T	F	S
	1	2	3	4	5	6
7	8	9	10	11	12	13
14	15	16	17	18	19	20
21	22	23	24	25	26	27
28						

March						
S	M	T	W	T	F	S
	1	2	3	4	5	6
7	8	9	10	11	12	13
14	15	16	17	18	19	20
21	22	23	24	25	26	27
28	29	30	31			

April						
S	M	T	W	T	F	S
				1	2	3
4	5	6	7	8	9	10
11	12	13	14	15	16	17
18	19	20	21	22	23	24
25	26	27	28	29	30	

May						
S	M	T	W	T	F	S
						1
2	3	4	5	6	7	8
9	10	11	12	13	14	15
16	17	18	19	20	21	22
23	24	25	26	27	28	29
30	31					

June						
S	M	T	W	T	F	S
	1	2	3	4	5	
6	7	8	9	10	11	12
13	14	15	16	17	18	19
20	21	22	23	24	25	26
27	28	29	30			

1. On January 1, Debbie Hart started saving $15 a week.

   QUESTION: _By February 19, how long will Debbie have been saving?_
   (by February 19 / how long / save)

   ANSWER: _By February 19, she'll have been saving for seven weeks._

2. On March 1, Matt Rodriguez began working eight hours a day on his latest invention.

   QUESTION: _____
   (by April 16 / how many days / work)

   ANSWER: _____

3. On March 3, Janet Haddad began reading a book a week.

   QUESTION: _____
   (by June 16 / how many books / read)

   ANSWER: _____

4. On April 24, Don Caputo began running one mile (1.6 km) a day.

   QUESTION: _____
   (how long / run / by May 29)

   ANSWER: _____

5. On April 24, Tania Zakov began running two miles (3.2 km) a day.

   QUESTION: _____
   (how many miles / run / by May 29)

   ANSWER: _____

6. On February 6, Mary Gregory began saving $10 a week.

   QUESTION: _____
   (save $100 / by March 27)

   ANSWER: _____

7. On May 8, Tim Rigg began painting two apartments a week in his building.

   QUESTION: _____
   (how many apartments / paint / by May 29)

   ANSWER: _____

8. Tim's building has twelve apartments.

   QUESTION: _____
   (finish / by June 19)

   ANSWER: _____

EXERCISE 5 EDITING

GRAMMAR NOTES 1–4 Read this blog entry. There are eight mistakes in the use of the future perfect and the future perfect progressive. The first mistake is already corrected. Find and correct seven more.

In Praise of the Business Leaders of Tomorrow

ALEXA IOANNIDIS

will have reached

By 2025, today's young entrepreneurs ~~have reached~~ adulthood. Almost certainly, they'll have converted their creative ideas into cash. And if we're lucky, they'll had shown the corporate world that making money by solving problems and helping others is a good business model to follow.

■ The Inventioneers designed the SMARTwheel to address the problem of drivers, especially teen drivers, who take their hands off the steering wheel when distracted by activities such as texting, talking on the phone, or eating. By the end of next year, more than 3,000 people in the United States will have die, and there will have been more than 400,000 injuries as a result of distracted driving. With the SMARTwheel, drivers will have been receiving a warning to put both hands on the wheel and pay attention before an accident can occur. And it's possible that they'll have changed their driving habits by the time they will be on the road again.

■ Zollipops are Alina Morse's way of helping kids who will eat candy, lots of it, before their next visit to the dentist. "Zollis" are sugar-free, so they won't cause tooth decay. Meanwhile, by the end of this year, Alina will has donated ten percent of the profits from her candy business to health education programs for children.

■ Moziah Bridges has earned status and respect as the teen owner of Mo's Bows. By the time he's twenty-one, Moziah will have been sold his bow ties for nine years. If all goes according to plan, he'll have added already a collection of jackets and pants by then. Moziah's product line currently includes the Go Mo! bow tie, which earns money to send children to summer camp.

How about a round of applause for the business leaders of tomorrow?

EXERCISE 6 LISTENING

▶06|02 **(A)** Listen to the conversation between Iza and her father, Don. They are discussing Iza's daughter Beth, a young entrepreneur. Read the statements. Then listen again and check (✓) *True* or *False*.

	True	False
1. Iza believes that the bicycle business is good for her daughter.	☑	☐
2. When she graduates from high school, Beth will have owned her business for four years.	☐	☐
3. Beth uses math skills to operate her business.	☐	☐
4. Beth will probably stop "thinking outside the box" when she graduates.	☐	☐
5. Don finally changed his mind about Beth's bicycle business.	☐	☐
6. Beth has already started filling out her college applications.	☐	☐
7. Beth is still working on Don's bicycle.	☐	☐

▶06|02 **(B)** Work with a partner. Listen again to the conversation. Discuss your answers in A. Give reasons for your answers.

EXAMPLE: **A:** The answer for number 1 is *True*. Do you know why?
B: According to Iza, her daughter Beth is doing something that she loves. And Beth will have gotten valuable skills from her bicycle business by the time she graduates from high school.
A: OK, I understand. Now, let's talk about number 2.

▶06|02 **(C)** Work in a group. Listen again to the conversation. What will Beth have achieved by the time she graduates from high school? Make a list of her top five achievements.

EXAMPLE: **A:** Beth will have done a lot by the time she graduates. Let's write everything that her mother mentions. Then we can choose her top five achievements.
B: OK. She'll have improved her math skills. What else do you want to put on the list?
C: I think this is important. She will have . . .

EXERCISE 7 BY THE END OF...

CONVERSATION Work with a partner. What will some of the people in your life (including you!) have achieved by the end of this year, this month, or this week? Talk about some of these accomplishments. (Remember, even small accomplishments are important!) Use some of the ideas in the list below and ideas of your own.

EXAMPLE: A: I'm really proud of my roommate. She's always had a problem oversleeping, but by the end of this month, she won't have missed any of her morning classes!

B: That's great. How did she solve her problem?

- making a budget
- managing time
- exercising
- learning new things
- overcoming a bad habit

- starting a good habit
- spending time with friends and family
- _____
- _____
- _____

EXERCISE 8 LONG-TERM GOALS

A CONVERSATION Work in a group. Think of three goals you would like to achieve in the next five to ten years and talk about them. They can be big goals, such as buying a house, or smaller goals, such as learning a new skill.

EXAMPLE: A: I'd like to get fit and then run in a 10 km race. What about you?

B: I want to learn how to use photo editing software like a pro.

C: I'd like to learn to skateboard.

B Arrange your goals on the timeline. Write the goals and the years you want to achieve them.

Goals: _____ _____ _____

_____ _____ _____

Years:

C Discuss your goals in detail. Talk about things you'll need to do before you achieve each goal.

EXAMPLE: A: Before I run my first 10 km race, I'll have been training for three months.

B: By the holidays this year, I'll have taken an online photo-editing class.

C: By then, I'll have bought a skateboard!

A BEFORE YOU WRITE Ask a classmate about his or her goals and what he or she is doing to achieve these goals by the end of the year. Complete the outline.

Classmate's Name	Classmate's Goal(s)	Activities This Year to Achieve Goals	Time Doing Activities by End of Year	Achievements by End of Year

B WRITE Use your outline to write a paragraph about your classmate. Use the future perfect and the future perfect progressive. Try to avoid the common mistakes in the chart.

EXAMPLE: Danny Munca wants to buy a new phone. He got a part-time job in the library to help him save money. By the end of the year, he'll have been working there for two months. He'll have saved about $200 by then, and he'll be able to get his new electronic toy.

Common Mistakes in Using the Future Perfect and Future Perfect Progressive

Use *will have* + **past participle** to form the future perfect. Do not use the base form of the verb.	He **will have saved** $200 by then. NOT He will have ~~save~~ $200 by then.
Use *will have been* + **base form** + *-ing* to form the future perfect progressive. Do not use *will have been* + past participle.	By the end of the year, he**'ll have been working** there for two months. NOT By the end of the year, he'll have been ~~worked~~ there for two months.
Use the **simple present** in a **future time clause**. Do not use *will* or *be going to*.	By the time the year **is** over, he will have learned a lot. NOT By the time the year ~~will be~~ over, he will . . .

C CHECK YOUR WORK Read your paragraph. Underline once the verbs in the future perfect. Underline twice the verbs in the future perfect progressive. Use the Editing Checklist to check your work.

Editing Checklist

Did you use . . . ?

☐ the future perfect for actions that will already be completed by a specific time in the future

☐ the future perfect progressive for actions that will still be in progress at a specific time in the future

☐ time clauses to show the time order between two future events

☐ the simple present in a future time clause

☐ adverbs or expressions with *by* to show the order of events

D REVISE YOUR WORK Read your paragraph again. Can you improve your writing? Make changes if necessary. Give your paragraph a title.

UNIT 6 REVIEW

Test yourself on the grammar of the unit.

A Circle the correct words to complete the sentences.

1. Kareem will <u>has been selling</u> / <u>have been selling</u> his new phone app for six months by January 1.

2. When <u>we get</u> / <u>we'll get</u> to my parents' house, they'll already have eaten dinner.

3. By the end of this week, Mia will <u>exercise</u> / <u>have been exercising</u> for six months.

4. When I finish this story by Sue Grafton, <u>I'll have read</u> / <u>I'll have been reading</u> all of her mysteries.

5. <u>By</u> / <u>Since</u> 2025, he'll have been living here for ten years.

B Complete the conversation with the simple present, future perfect, or future perfect progressive form of the verbs in parentheses. Use the future perfect progressive if possible.

A: Do you realize that in September we _____ here for two years?
   1. (live)

B: Amazing! And you _____ here for four years.
   2. (study)

A: I know. By next year at this time, I _____ .
   3. (graduate)

B: Well, I certainly hope that by the time you _____ ,
   4. (graduate)
   I _____ a good job.
   5. (find)

A: Well, one thing is certain. By that time, we _____ a lot of
   6. (make)
   friends here.

B: Yes. And we _____ almost $2,000 selling our school t-shirts.
   7. (earn)

C Find and correct eight mistakes.

I'm so excited about your news! By the time you read this, you'll already have moving into your new house! And I have some good news, too. By the end of this month, I'll have save $5,000. That's enough for me to buy a used car! And that means that by this time next year, I drive to California to visit you! I have more news, too. By the time I will graduate, I will have been started my new part-time job. I hope that by this time next year, I'll also had finished working on my latest invention—a solar-powered flashlight.

It's hard to believe that in June, we will have been being friends for ten years. Time sure flies! And we'll have been stayed in touch even though we are 3,000 miles apart. Isn't technology a great thing?

Now check your answers on page 476.

Negative and Tag Questions, Additions and Responses

UNIT

7

Negative *Yes/No* Questions and Tag Questions
PLACES TO LIVE

UNIT

8

Additions and Responses: *So, Too, Neither, Not either*, and *But*
SIMILARITIES AND DIFFERENCES

OUTCOMES

- Check information or comment on a situation, using negative *yes/no* questions or tag questions
- Identify key details in interview transcripts and recorded interviews
- Interview a classmate, asking questions and checking information
- Discuss details about cities around the world
- Write an interview transcript about a classmate's home city, including questions and answers

OUTCOMES

- Show similarity, using *so*, *too*, *neither*, or *not either*; and show difference, using *but*
- Identify key details in an article on a scientific topic and in a conversation between two people
- Discuss similarities and differences between two people
- Research a pair of twins and report findings
- Write about the similarities and differences between two people

Negative *Yes/No* Questions and Tag Questions

PLACES TO LIVE

OUTCOMES
- Check information or comment on a situation, using negative *yes/no* questions or tag questions
- Identify key details in interview transcripts and recorded interviews
- Interview a classmate, asking questions and checking information
- Discuss details about cities around the world
- Write an interview transcript about a classmate's home city, including questions and answers

STEP 1   GRAMMAR IN CONTEXT

BEFORE YOU READ

Look at the photos. Discuss the questions.

1. How do these places look to you?
2. Which one of these places would you like to visit or live in? Why?
3. What do you like about the town or city where you live? What don't you like?

READ

07|01   Read these transcripts of on-the-street interviews from cities around the world.

It's a Great Place to Live, Isn't It?

Rio de Janeiro, Brazil

REPORTER: Excuse me. Do you speak English?

LYDIA: Yes, I do. Hey! I've seen you on TV. . . . Aren't you Paul Logan?

REPORTER: That's right. I'm conducting a survey for *Life Abroad Magazine*. You're not from Rio, are you?

LYDIA: No, I'm not. I'm originally from Portugal. You could tell by my accent, couldn't you?

REPORTER: Uh-huh. You don't speak English like a Brazilian. So how do you like living here?

LYDIA: I love it. Just look around you—the beach, the bay, the mountains, the sky. Aren't they gorgeous? I walk along this beach every day on the way to my office.

REPORTER: It's not a bad way to get to work, is it?

LYDIA: It's not a bad place to play, either! There's constant excitement. Besides the beach, there are so many restaurants and clubs. It's a great place to live, isn't it?

Cairo, Egypt

REPORTER: This is one of the oldest markets in Cairo, isn't it?

KINORO: Yes, and it's one of the most interesting. Hey, didn't you buy anything?

REPORTER: Not today. So what brought you from Nairobi to Cairo?

KINORO: My job. I work for a company that supplies Internet services for a lot of businesses here.

REPORTER: It gets extremely hot here in the summer, doesn't it?

KINORO: Yes, but the winters are mild. And it almost never rains. You can't beat that,[1] can you?

Seoul, South Korea

REPORTER: You're a student, aren't you?

ANTON: No, actually, I'm a teacher. I'm teaching a course in architecture at the Kaywon School of Art and Design this semester.

REPORTER: So how do you like living here? Doesn't the cold weather bother you?

ANTON: Not really. I'm from Berlin, so I'm used to it. I love this city. You can see skyscrapers right next to ancient structures.

REPORTER: That's true. That's the old city gate over there, isn't it?

ANTON: Yes. And there are several beautiful palaces nearby.

Vancouver, Canada

REPORTER: You're from England, aren't you?

TESSA: Yes. I moved here ten years ago.

REPORTER: Was it a difficult adjustment?

TESSA: No, not really. First of all, having the same language makes things easy, doesn't it? And people here are very friendly.

REPORTER: Why Canada?

TESSA: England's a very small country. I was attracted by Canada's wide-open spaces. It seems to offer endless possibilities.

---

1 *You can't beat that.*: Nothing is better than that.

AFTER YOU READ

Ⓐ VOCABULARY Choose the word or phrase that best completes each sentence.

1. A _____ is not an example of a **structure**.
   a. bridge   **b.** building   **c.** beach

2. If you're **originally** from South Korea, you _____.
   a. were born there   **b.** still live there   **c.** have relatives there

3. A place with **constant** noise is _____ quiet.
   a. always   **b.** sometimes   **c.** never

4. If you are **attracted** to something, you want to _____ it.
   a. avoid   **b.** get to know   **c.** change

5. A _____ with thirty customers is **extremely** crowded.
   a. small café   **b.** movie theater   **c.** department store

6. If someone **supplies** you with information, he or she _____ the information.
   a. wants   **b.** gives you   **c.** corrects

Ⓑ COMPREHENSION Read the statements. Check (✓) *True* or *False*.

	True	False
1. Lydia doesn't know the reporter.	☐	☐
2. The reporter thinks Lydia is from Rio.	☐	☐
3. The reporter bought a lot of things at the Cairo market.	☐	☐
4. The reporter thinks the cold weather bothers Anton.	☐	☐
5. The reporter thinks Tessa comes from Canada.	☐	☐
6. The move was not a difficult adjustment for Tessa.	☐	☐

Ⓒ DISCUSSION Work with a partner. Compare your answers in B. Why did you check *True* or *False*?

NEGATIVE *YES/NO* QUESTIONS

With *Be* as the Main Verb

Questions		Short Answers		
Be + *Not* + Subject		**Affirmative**		**Negative**
Aren't you from Rio de Janeiro?		**Yes**, I **am**.		**No**, I'm **not**.

With All Auxiliary Verbs Except *Do*

Questions	Short Answers				
Auxiliary + *Not* + Subject + Verb	**Affirmative**		**Negative**		
Aren't you moving?	**Yes**,	I **am**.	**No**,	I'm **not**.
Hasn't he been here before?		he **has**.		he **hasn't**.
Can't they move tomorrow?		they **can**.		they **can't**.

With *Do* as the Auxiliary Verb

Questions	Short Answers				
Do + *Not* + Subject + Verb	**Affirmative**		**Negative**		
Doesn't he live here?	**Yes**,	he **does**.	**No**,	he **doesn't**.
Didn't they move last year?		they **did**.		they **didn't**.

TAG QUESTIONS

With *Be* as the Main Verb

Affirmative Statement	Negative Tag
Subject + *Be*	*Be* + *Not* + Subject
You're from Rio,	aren't you?

Negative Statement	Affirmative Tag
Subject + *Be* + *Not*	*Be* + Subject
You're not from Rio,	are you?

With All Auxiliary Verbs Except *Do*

Affirmative Statement	Negative Tag
Subject + Auxiliary	Auxiliary + *Not* + Subject
You're moving,	aren't you?
He's been here before,	hasn't he?
They can move tomorrow,	can't they?

Negative Statement	Affirmative Tag
Subject + Auxiliary + *Not*	Auxiliary + Subject
You're not moving,	are you?
He hasn't been here before,	has he?
They can't move tomorrow,	can they?

With *Do* as an Auxiliary Verb

Affirmative Statement	Negative Tag
Subject + Verb	*Do* + *Not* + Subject
He lives here,	doesn't he?
They moved last year,	didn't they?

Negative Statement	Affirmative Tag
Subject + *Do* + *Not* + Verb	*Do* + Subject
He doesn't live here,	does he?
They didn't move,	did they?

GRAMMAR NOTES

1 Negative *Yes/No* Questions and Tag Questions

Use negative *yes/no* questions and tag questions to **check information** you believe is true or to **comment on a situation**.

• **checking information** you believe is true	**Doesn't Anton** live in Seoul? Anton lives in Seoul, **doesn't he?** *(The speaker believes that Anton lives in Seoul.)*
• **commenting on a situation**	**Isn't it** a nice day? It's a nice day, **isn't it?** *(The speaker is commenting on the weather.)*

Negative *yes/no* questions and tag questions are **different from affirmative *yes/no* questions**:	
In **affirmative *yes/no* questions**, you have **no idea of the answer**.	**Do you work** here? *(I don't know if you work here.)*
In **negative *yes/no* questions and tag questions**, you have **information** that you want to **check**, or you have an **opinion** and are **looking for agreement**.	**Don't you work** here? *(I think you work here, but I'm not sure.)* This is hard work, **isn't it?** *(I think this is hard work, and I think you agree.)*
USAGE NOTE We use negative *yes/no* questions and tag questions mostly in **conversation** and **informal writing** (notes, emails, text messages, etc.).	**Isn't it** beautiful? *(conversation)* You're moving next week, **aren't you?** *(email)*

2 Forming Negative *Yes/No* Questions

Like affirmative *yes/no* questions, negative *yes/no* questions **begin with a form of *be* or an auxiliary verb**, such as *have, do, will, can,* or *should*.	**Aren't you** Paul Logan? **Haven't I** seen you on TV? **Don't you** like the weather here? **Won't you** be sorry to leave? **Can't you** stay longer?
USAGE NOTE We almost always use **contractions** in negative questions. Full forms are very formal and not very common.	**Shouldn't we** go? *(informal)* **Should we not** go? *(very formal)*
BE CAREFUL! Use *are* in negative questions with *I* and a contraction. Do not use *am*.	**Aren't I** right? NOT ~~Amn't~~ I right?

Form tag questions with **statement + tag**. The statement expresses an **assumption**. The tag means *Isn't that right?* or *Isn't that true?*	STATEMENT TAG
	You're Paul Logan, **aren't you?**
	  (You're Paul Logan. Isn't that right?)
	You're not from Cairo, **are you?**
	  (You're not from Cairo. Isn't that true?)

If the statement verb is **affirmative**, the tag verb is **negative**.	AFFIRMATIVE NEGATIVE You **work** on Thursdays, **don't** you?
If the statement verb is **negative**, the tag verb is **affirmative**.	NEGATIVE AFFIRMATIVE You **don't work** on Thursdays, **do** you?
BE CAREFUL! Adverbs of frequency such as *never*, *rarely*, and *seldom* have a negative meaning. If they are in the statement, the tag verb is affirmative.	You've **never** been to Istanbul, **have** you? NOT You've never been to Istanbul, ~~haven't~~ you?
Begin the **tag** with a **form of *be* or an auxiliary verb**, such as *have, do, will, can,* or *should*. Use the **same auxiliary** that is in the statement.	It's a nice day, **isn't** it? There **are** good schools here, **aren't** there? You've lived here a long time, **haven't** you?
If the statement does not use *be* or an auxiliary verb, use an appropriate **form of *do*** in the tag.	You **come** from London, **don't** you? You **came** from London, **didn't** you?
USAGE NOTE We almost always use **contractions** in the **tag**. Full forms are very formal and not very common.	You can drive, **can't** you? *(informal)* You can drive, **can** you **not**? *(very formal)*
BE CAREFUL! Use *are* in tag questions with *I* and a contraction. Do not use *am*.	I'm right, **aren't I**? NOT I'm right ~~amn't~~ I?
BE CAREFUL! When the subject of the statement is a **noun**, the subject of the tag is the matching **pronoun**. When the subject of the statement is *this* or *that*, the subject of the tag is *it*.	***Tom*** works here, doesn't **he**? NOT Tom works here, doesn't ~~Tom~~? ***That's*** a good idea, isn't **it**? NOT That's a good idea, isn't ~~that~~?

Answer negative *yes/no* questions and tag questions the **same way you answer affirmative *yes/no* questions**.

• *yes* if the information is **correct**	A: **Don't you** work in Vancouver? B: **Yes, I do.** I've worked there for years.
• *no* if the information is **not correct**	A: You work in Vancouver, **don't you**? B: **No, I don't.** I work in Montreal.

PRONUNCIATION NOTE

07|02

Intonation of Tag Questions

In tag questions, our **voice rises** at the end when we expect another person to give us **information**.	A: You're not moving, **are you?** ↗ B: Yes. I'm returning to Berlin.
Our **voice falls** at the end when we are making a comment and expect the other person to **agree**.	A: Seoul is interesting, **isn't it?** ↘ B: Yes, it is.

STEP 3   FOCUSED PRACTICE

EXERCISE 1   DISCOVER THE GRAMMAR

GRAMMAR NOTES 1–4 **Read this conversation between Anton Kada's mother, Petra, and a Canadian neighbor, Ken. Underline all the negative** *yes/no* **questions and circle all the tags.**

PETRA: Hi, Ken. Nice day, (isn't it?)

KEN: Sure is. What are you doing home today? <u>Don't you usually work on Thursdays?</u>

PETRA: I took the day off to help my son. He just got back to Berlin, and he's looking for an

apartment. You don't know of any vacant apartments, do you?

KEN: Isn't he going to stay with you?

PETRA: Well, he just got a new job at an architecture firm downtown. He wants a place of his own in

a quiet area, not one of those neighborhoods with constant noise. Do you know of anything?

KEN: As a matter of fact, I do. The Edwards family lives in a quiet residential neighborhood near the

river. You know them, don't you?

PETRA: Yes, I think Anton went to school with their son. But they're not moving, are they?

KEN: Yes, they're moving back to Vancouver next month.

PETRA: Are they? What kind of apartment do they have?

KEN: A one-bedroom. It's very nice.

PETRA: It's not furnished, is it? Anton really doesn't have

any furniture.

KEN: Can't he rent some? I did that in my first apartment.

PETRA: I don't know. Isn't it less expensive to buy?

A quiet residential neighborhood in Berlin

EXERCISE 2   AFFIRMATIVE AND NEGATIVE TAG QUESTIONS

GRAMMAR NOTE 3   Mr. and Mrs. Edwards are talking about their move to Vancouver.
Match the statements with the tags.

Statements	Tags
_f_ **1.** You've called the movers,	**a.** do we?
___ **2.** They're coming tomorrow,	**b.** is it?
___ **3.** This is going to be expensive,	**c.** don't they?
___ **4.** You haven't finished packing,	**d.** have you?
___ **5.** We don't need any more boxes,	**e.** isn't it?
___ **6.** We need to disconnect the phone,	**f.** haven't you?
___ **7.** The movers supply boxes for us,	**g.** don't we?
___ **8.** Moving is never easy,	**h.** aren't they?

EXERCISE 3   TAG QUESTIONS AND SHORT ANSWERS

Ⓐ GRAMMAR NOTES 3–4   Complete this interview with Tessa Bradley. Use appropriate
tags and short answers.

HOST: You're originally from England, _____ _aren't you_ _____?
        1.

TESSA: _____ _Yes, I am_ _____. I'm from London.
        2.

HOST: You've lived in Vancouver for many years, _____?
        3.

TESSA: _____. Since I came here to teach video arts. Seems like ages ago.
        4.

HOST: You didn't know anyone here, _____?
        5.

TESSA: _____. I was here all alone. And I didn't have a cent to my name. Just
        6.

        some ideas and a lot of hope. It sounds crazy, _____?
        7.

HOST: _____. Not when you look at all the TV shows you've done. Things
        8.

        have sure worked out for you, _____? You've already worked on two
        9.

        big TV series, and you've done some work for the movies as well. You're working on

        another film now, _____?
        10.

TESSA: _____. It's a comedy about some kids who become invisible.
        11.

HOST: Speaking of kids, you and your husband have some of your own, _____?
        12.

TESSA: _____. Two boys and a girl—all very visible!
        13.

HOST: I know what you mean. Do you ever wish they were invisible?

TESSA: Hmm. That's an interesting thought, _____?
        14.

⏺ 07|03   Ⓑ LISTEN AND CHECK   Listen to the conversation and check your answers in A.

EXERCISE 4 NEGATIVE *YES/NO* QUESTIONS AND SHORT ANSWERS

(A) GRAMMAR NOTES 2, 4 Anton Kada is looking at the apartment the Edwards family just left. Complete the negative *yes/no* questions. Write short answers. Use the verbs that are in the sentences following the short answers.

1. OWNER: Hi, you look familiar. *Isn't your name* _____ John Radcliffe?

   ANTON: *No, it isn't* _____ . My name is Anton Kada.

2. OWNER: Oh. _____ this apartment before?

   ANTON: _____ . I've never seen it before. This is the first time.

3. ANTON: The apartment feels hot. _____ air conditioning?

   OWNER: _____ . It has ceiling fans but no air conditioners.

4. ANTON: I notice that there are marks on the walls. _____ them?

   OWNER: _____ . I'm going to paint them next week.

5. OWNER: _____ a nice apartment?

   ANTON: _____ . It's very nice. But I'm not sure I can take it.

6. OWNER: _____ big enough?

   ANTON: _____ . It's big enough, but I can't afford it.

7. OWNER: _____ how much it was before you came here?

   ANTON: _____ . I knew the price, but I was hoping for a bargain.

07|04 (B) LISTEN AND CHECK Listen to the conversations and check your answers in A.

EXERCISE 5 NEGATIVE *YES/NO* QUESTIONS AND TAG QUESTIONS

GRAMMAR NOTES 1–3 Rewrite the sentences. Change the sentence in parentheses into a negative *yes/no* question or a tag question.

ROLAND: Hi, Tessa. *Isn't it a nice day?* or *It's a nice day, isn't it?* _____
          1. (I think it's a nice day.)

TESSA: It sure is. _____
        2. (I think you have a class today.)

ROLAND: I do. But not until 3:00. _____
          3. (I think it's only 2:30 now.)

TESSA: You're right. You have plenty of time. _____
        4. (I'm surprised you don't have a bike.)

ROLAND: I lost it. That's why I'm walking.

TESSA: Well, it's a nice day for a walk. _____
        5. (I think Vancouver is a beautiful city.)

ROLAND: Yes. And a great city for video artists. _____
          6. (I'm pretty sure you're coming to see my film tonight.)

TESSA: I wouldn't miss it. Hey! _____ We took the wrong path.
        7. (I'm pretty sure your class is that way.)

EXERCISE 6 NEGATIVE *YES/NO* QUESTIONS AND TAG QUESTIONS

GRAMMAR NOTES 1–3 Read this information about video artist Nam June Paik. Imagine you are going to interview a guide at the Nam June Paik Art Center in Yongin, South Korea. You are not sure of the information in parentheses. Write negative *yes/no* questions or tag questions to check that information.

Nam June Paik

1. born July 1932 in Korea (in Seoul?)
2. at age 14, studied music (took piano lessons?)
3. family left Korea in 1950 (moved to Tokyo?)
4. moved to Germany in 1956 (originally studied music composition there?)
5. attracted to electronic music (didn't write traditional music, too?)
6. during the 1960s created a new art form with TV screens and video (didn't paint on paper again?)
7. produced a huge art installation for 1988 Seoul Olympics (the structure used 1,003 TV monitors?)
8. after an illness in 1996 started painting on flat surfaces (didn't do any more installations after that?)
9. lived in New York (became a U.S. citizen?)
10. died in January 2006 in Florida (was 75 years old?)

1. <u>Wasn't he born in Seoul? or He was born in Seoul, wasn't he?</u>

2. _____

3. _____

4. _____

5. _____

6. _____

7. _____

8. _____

9. _____

10. _____

EXERCISE 7 RISING AND FALLING TAG QUESTIONS

07|05 PRONUNCIATION NOTE Read the tag questions. Then listen to each question and decide if the voice rises (↗) or falls (↘) at the end of the tag. Draw the correct arrow over the tag.

1. You're originally from Vancouver, aren't you?

2. It's a beautiful city, isn't it?

3. You don't like the weather here, do you?

4. They'll be moving soon, won't they?

5. That building isn't new, is it?

6. There aren't any more vacancies, are there?

7. You've never met Ann, have you?

8. She works around here, doesn't she?

9. This can't be true, can it?

10. I'm really lucky, aren't I?

EXERCISE 8 EDITING

GRAMMAR NOTES 1–4 Tessa Bradley is working on a script for a movie that takes place in Vancouver. There are ten mistakes in the use of negative *yes*/*no* questions, tag questions, and short answers. The first mistake is already corrected. Find and correct nine more.

> **BEN:** It's been a long time, Joe, ~~haven't~~ *hasn't* it?
>
> **JOE:** That depends on what you mean by a long time, doesn't that?
>
> **BEN:** Are not you afraid to show your face here in Vancouver?
>
> **JOE:** I can take care of myself. I'm still alive, amn't I?
>
> **BEN:** Until someone recognizes you. You're still wanted by the police, are you? But that has never bothered you, hasn't it?
>
> **JOE:** I'll be gone by morning. Look, I need a place to stay. Just for one night.
>
> **BEN:** I have to think about my wife and kid. Don't you have any place else to go?
>
> **JOE:** Yes, I do. There's no one to turn to but you. You have to help me.
>
> **BEN:** I've already helped you plenty. I went to jail for you, haven't I? And didn't I kept my mouth shut the whole time?
>
> **JOE:** Yeah, OK, Ben. Don't you remember what happened in Vegas, do you?
>
> **BEN:** You won't let me forget it, will you? OK, OK. I can make a call.

EXERCISE 9 LISTENING

▶ 07|06 **(A)** Listen to the conversations. Read the statements. Then listen again and check (✓) *True* or *False*.

	True	False
1. The man wants to know if Rio is the capital of Brazil.	✓	☐
2. The man thinks Rio has an exciting nightlife.	☐	☐
3. The woman wants to know if Anton was teaching a course in Korea.	☐	☐
4. The woman wants to know if it is hard to find an apartment in Berlin.	☐	☐
5. The woman thinks the man has lived in Tokyo for a long time.	☐	☐
6. The man is sure that the weather is hot in Cairo.	☐	☐
7. The woman thinks Anne is from Vancouver.	☐	☐
8. The woman wants to know if the man is from Vancouver.	☐	☐

▶ 07|06 **(B)** Listen to the conversations again. Then work with a partner. Discuss your answers in A. For each answer, repeat the part of the conversation that explains why you chose *True* or *False*.

EXAMPLE: A: I see that the answer for number 1 is *True*. But isn't the answer actually *False*?
B: No, it isn't. It's *True* because the man is unsure about the capital of Brazil. His voice rises when he says, "Rio isn't the capital of Brazil, is it?" That means he wants to check the information.
A: OK. Now I understand. What's your answer for number 2?

EXERCISE 10 HOW MUCH DO YOU REALLY KNOW?

(A) CONVERSATION You are going to work with a partner. How well do you know him or her? Complete the questions with information about your partner that you think is correct.

EXAMPLE: *You're from Venezuela, aren't you?*

1. _____, aren't you?
2. Don't you _____?
3. _____, haven't you?
4. _____, did you?
5. _____, do you?
6. Aren't you _____?

(B) Now work with your partner. Ask the questions to check your information. Check (✓) each question that has the correct information. Which one of you knows the other one better?

EXAMPLE: A: You're from Venezuela, aren't you?
B: Yes, I am. **or** No, I'm from Colombia.

EXERCISE 11 LONDON AND VANCOUVER

INFORMATION GAP Work with a partner. Student A will follow the instructions below.
Student B will follow the instructions on page 486.

STUDENT A

- What do you know about London? Complete the questions by circling the correct words and writing the tags.

  1. London (is) / isn't the largest city in the United Kingdom, _isn't it_ ?

  2. It is / isn't the capital of the United Kingdom, _____?

  3. London lies on a river / the ocean, _____?

  4. It consists of two / thirty-two "boroughs," or parts, _____?

  5. It has / doesn't have a lot of theaters, _____?

  6. Many / Not many tourists visit London, _____?

  7. It is / isn't a very safe city, _____?

- Ask Student B the questions. Student B will read a paragraph about London and tell you if your information is correct or not.

  EXAMPLE: A: London is the largest city in the United Kingdom, isn't it?
             B: Yes, it is.

- Now read about Vancouver and answer Student B's questions.

  EXAMPLE: B: Vancouver isn't the largest city in Canada, is it?
             A: No, it isn't. It's the third largest city.

VANCOUVER

Vancouver is the third largest city in Canada. Lying on the Pacific coast, it is surrounded on three sides by water and has the largest and busiest seaport in the country. It is also home to Stanley Park, one of the largest city parks in North America. Because of its great natural and architectural beauty and its moderate climate, Vancouver is a very popular place to live. It also attracts millions of tourists each year. It is a very international city, and more than 50 percent of its residents do not speak English as their first language. Today, Vancouver is called the "Hollywood of the North" because of the number of films made in this exciting city.

FROM GRAMMAR TO WRITING

A BEFORE YOU WRITE Interview a classmate about his or her home city. Write eight questions. Use negative *yes/no* questions and tag questions. Ask your questions. Take notes of your classmate's answers.

EXAMPLE: You're originally from Venezuela, aren't you? *Yes—Caracas.*
Isn't that the capital? *Yes.*

B WRITE Use your notes to write up the interview. Include negative *yes/no* questions and tag questions. Try to avoid the common mistakes in the chart.

EXAMPLE: INTERVIEWER: You're originally from Venezuela, aren't you?
MIGUEL: Yes, I am. I'm from Caracas.
INTERVIEWER: Isn't that the capital?
MIGUEL: Yes, it is.

Common Mistakes in Using Negative *Yes/No* Questions and Tag Questions

In **informal conversation**, use **contractions** in negative *yes/no* questions and tags. Do not use full forms.	**Isn't** Caracas the capital of Venezuela? **NOT** ~~Is not~~ Caracas the capital of Venezuela? Caracas is the capital of Venezuela, **isn't it**? **NOT** Caracas is the capital of Venezuela, ~~is it not~~?
Use a **pronoun** in the **tag** that matches the noun in the statement. Do not use a noun in the tag.	**The city** is beautiful, isn't **it**? **NOT** The city is beautiful, isn't ~~the city~~?
If there is an **auxiliary** in the statement, use the **same auxiliary in the tag**. Do not use a different auxiliary in the tag.	You **have** been here since 2016, **haven't** you? **NOT** You have been here since 2016, ~~aren't~~ you?

C CHECK YOUR WORK Read your interview. Underline the negative *yes/no* questions. Circle the tags. Use the Editing Checklist to check your work.

Editing Checklist

Did you use . . . ?

☐ contractions in negative *yes/no* questions

☐ contractions in tags

☐ negative tags with affirmative statements

☐ affirmative tags with negative statements

☐ the same auxiliary in the tag and in the statement

☐ pronouns (not nouns) in tags

D REVISE YOUR WORK Read your interview again. Can you improve your writing? Make changes if necessary. Give your interview a title.

UNIT 7 REVIEW

Test yourself on the grammar of the unit.

A Circle the correct words to complete the sentences.

1. It's a beautiful day, isn't / is it?

2. Didn't / Aren't you order coffee?

3. You've / You haven't heard from Raoul recently, haven't you?

4. That was a great movie, wasn't that / it?

5. Nick hasn't left San Francisco yet, did / has he?

6. Lara can't move out of her apartment yet, can Lara / she?

7. Shouldn't / Should not we leave soon? It's getting late.

B Complete the conversation with negative *yes/no* questions and tag questions. Use the correct verbs and short answers.

A: You haven't lived in Vancouver for very long, _____ you?
                    1.

B: _____. Only for a month. Why are you asking?
        2.

A: You're wearing so many clothes. _____ you hot?
                     3.

B: _____. I think it's freezing today.
        4.

A: Oh, come on. You're not really *that* cold, _____ you?
                   5.

B: I'm originally from Rio de Janeiro. This is my first experience with cold weather. I'll get used

   to it someday, _____ I?
           6.

A: _____. It won't take long, and winter here isn't very bad.
      7.

C Find and correct six mistakes.

A: Ken hasn't come back from Korea yet, has Ken?

B: No, he has. He got back last week. Didn't he call you when he got back?

A: No, he didn't. He's probably busy. There are a lot of things to do when you move, isn't there?

B: Definitely. And I guess his family wanted to spend a lot of time with him, won't they?

A: I'm sure they will. You know, I think I'll just call him. You have his phone number, have you?

B: Yes, I do. Could you wait while I get it from my phone? You're not in a hurry, aren't you?

Now check your answers on page 476.

Additions and Responses: *So, Too, Neither, Not either*, and *But*

SIMILARITIES AND DIFFERENCES

OUTCOMES
- Show similarity, using *so, too, neither,* or *not either*; and show difference, using *but*
- Identify key details in an article on a scientific topic and in a conversation between two people
- Discuss similarities and differences between two people
- Research a pair of twins and report findings
- Write about the similarities and differences between two people

---

STEP 1   GRAMMAR IN CONTEXT

BEFORE YOU READ

Look at the photos of twins. Discuss the questions.

1. What is different about each pair of twins? What is the same?

2. How are *you* similar to family members? How are *you* different?

READ

08|01   Read this article about identical twins.

The Twin Question: Nature or Nurture?

Mark and Gerald are identical twins. Mirror images of each other, they also share many similarities in lifestyle. Mark was a firefighter, and so was Gerald. Mark has never been married, and neither has Gerald. Mark likes hunting, fishing, and old movies. Gerald does too. These similarities might not be unusual in identical twins, except that Mark and Gerald were separated when they were five days old. They

Mark and Gerald

grew up in different states with different families. Neither one knew that he had a twin until they found each other at age thirty-one.

Average people are fascinated by twins, and so are scientists. Because identical twins share the same genes, they offer researchers the chance to study the effect of heredity[1] on health and personality. Identical twins with completely different childhoods allow researchers to investigate the influence of environment.[2]

Scientists have long wondered about the role of heredity and environment in our lives. In other words, which is the more important factor—nature or nurture? The example of Mark and Gerald seems to show the power of genetics. However, the lives of other identical twins separated at birth indicate that the question of nature or nurture is complicated.

Identical twins Anaïs Bordier and Samantha Futerman were adopted soon after their birth in Busan, South Korea. Twenty-five years later, a friend was sure he saw Anaïs in a YouTube video, that is, until he realized the woman on YouTube was American, while Anaïs was French. He told Anaïs immediately. When she saw the video, Anaïs was so shocked to see another person who looked exactly like her that she decided to find out who the American woman was.

Anaïs and Samantha

Anaïs sent a Facebook message to Samantha, and the two began sharing information. During their first face-to-face conversation on Skype, Anaïs felt an instant connection, and so did Samantha. They laughed at the same things, in exactly the same way. They also found they had many other things in common. For example, they both suffered from the same nervous condition as children. In addition, when Anaïs feels stressed, she sleeps, and Samantha does too. Both Anaïs and Samantha want everything they see on a restaurant menu, except for carrots. Anaïs doesn't eat cooked carrots, and neither does Samantha.

However, Samantha and Anaïs are not totally alike. Of course, Samantha speaks American English, while Anaïs speaks British English and her native language, French. But there are other differences as well. Like her adoptive mother, Samantha is an outgoing person, but Anaïs isn't. She is more reserved like *her* adoptive mother. Samantha, an actor, has an excellent memory, but Anaïs doesn't. A fashion designer, she has stronger visual skills.

Clearly, our heredity doesn't completely control our lives. Our environment doesn't either. The lives of twins separated at birth suggest that we have a lot to learn about the complex role these two powerful forces play in shaping human lives.

---

1 *heredity:* the genes we receive from our parents
2 *environment:* everything around us, including family members, religion, education, financial situation, and location

AFTER YOU READ

A VOCABULARY Complete the sentences with the words from the box.

complex	factor	identical	image	investigate	reserved

1. Some parents like to dress their twins in _____ clothes. Others prefer to focus on differences.

2. When Don saw the _____ of his twin in the photo, he thought at first that he was looking at himself.

3. Karyn's sister is friendly and talks a lot, but Karyn is _____.

4. The answer to the question about genetics was too _____ for me to understand.

5. Mia's education was an important _____ in her success.

6. I'm going to _____ twins and their emotional connection for my research project.

B COMPREHENSION Check (✓) the boxes to complete the sentences. Check all the true information from the article.

1. Mark and Gerald have had the same _____.
   ☐ marriage histories   ☐ types of jobs   ☐ hobbies

2. Scientists are fascinated by _____.
   ☐ average people   ☐ twins   ☐ nature and nurture

3. Samantha Futerman sleeps when she is _____.
   ☐ sick   ☐ stressed   ☐ with her sister

4. Anaïs and Samantha do not have the same _____.
   ☐ personality   ☐ appearance   ☐ adoptive mother

5. Anaïs does not _____.
   ☐ like to eat a lot   ☐ have strong visual skills   ☐ remember things perfectly

6. Environment _____ our lives.
   ☐ partly controls   ☐ completely controls   ☐ has a weak effect on

C DISCUSSION Work with a partner. Compare your answers in B. Why did you check the boxes you checked?

SIMILARITY: *SO* AND *NEITHER*

Affirmative

Statement	Addition	
Subject + Verb	*And so*	Verb* + Subject
Amy *is* a twin,	and so	*am* I.
She *has* traveled,		*have* we.
She *can* **ski**,		*can* they.
She *likes* dogs,		*does* Bill.

* The verb in the addition is a form of *be*, an auxiliary, or a modal.

Negative

Statement	Addition	
Subject + Verb + *Not*	*And neither*	Verb + Subject
Amy *isn't* a twin,	and neither	*am* I.
She *hasn't* **traveled**,		*have* we.
She *can't* **ski**,		*can* they.
She *doesn't* **like** dogs,		*does* Bill.

SIMILARITY: *TOO* AND *NOT EITHER*

Affirmative

Statement	Addition	
Subject + Verb	*And*	Subject + Verb + *Too*
Amy *is* a twin,	and	I *am* **too**.
She *has* **traveled**,		we *have* **too**.
She *can* **ski**,		they *can* **too**.
She *likes* dogs,		Bill *does* **too**.

Negative

Statement	Addition	
Subject + Verb + *Not*	*And*	Subject + Verb + *Not either*
Amy *isn't* a twin,	and	I'*m not* **either**.
She *hasn't* **traveled**,		we *haven't* **either**.
She *can't* **ski**,		they *can't* **either**.
She *doesn't* **like** dogs,		Bill *doesn't* **either**.

DIFFERENCE: *BUT*

Affirmative + Negative

Statement	Addition	
Subject + Verb	*But*	**Subject + Verb + *Not***
Amy *is* a twin,		I'*m not*.
She *has* traveled,	but	we *haven't*.
She *can* ski,		they *can't*.
She *likes* dogs,		Bill *doesn't*.

Negative + Affirmative

Statement	Addition	
Subject + Verb + *Not*	*But*	**Subject + Verb**
Amy *isn't* a twin,		I *am*.
She *can't* ski,	but	we *can*.
She *hasn't* traveled,		they *have*.
She *doesn't* like dogs,		Bill *does*.

GRAMMAR NOTES

1 Additions to Show Similarity or Difference

Additions are clauses or short sentences that **follow a statement**. Use additions to **avoid repeating** the information in the statement.

Additions express **similarity** or **difference** with the information in the statement.

- **similarity**

  STATEMENT   ADDITION
  Anaïs sleeps a lot, **and so does Samantha**.
  (Anaïs sleeps a lot. Samantha sleeps a lot.)

- **difference**

  STATEMENT   ADDITION
  Anaïs grew up in France, **but Samantha didn't**.
  (Anaïs grew up in France. Samantha didn't grow up in France.)

2 Additions Showing Similarity with *So*, *Too*, *Neither*, or *Not Either*

Additions showing similarity can be **clauses or short sentences**. They use *so*, *too*, *neither*, or *not either* to express **similarity**.

Most additions of similarity are **clauses** starting with *and*.

CLAUSE
Mark is a firefighter, **and so is Gerald**.
Mark is a firefighter, **and Gerald is *too***.
Mark isn't married, **and *neither* is Gerald**.
Mark isn't married, **and Gerald *isn't either***.

CONTINUED ▶

	SENTENCE
Additions of similarity can also be **short sentences**.	Mark is a firefighter. **So is Gerald.**
	Mark is a firefighter. **Gerald is *too*.**
	Mark isn't married. ***Neither* is Gerald.**
	Mark isn't married. **Gerald *isn't either*.**

	AFFIRMATIVE STATEMENT
Use *so* or *too* if the addition follows an **affirmative statement**. *So* and *too* have the same meaning.	Mark **is** a firefighter, and **so is** Gerald.
	Mark **is** a firefighter, and Gerald **is** *too*.
	(Mark is a firefighter. Gerald is a firefighter.)

	NEGATIVE STATEMENT
Use *neither* or *not either* if the addition follows a **negative statement**. *Neither* and *not either* have the same meaning.	Mark **didn't** marry. ***Neither* did** Gerald.
	Mark **didn't** marry. Gerald **did*n't either*.**
	(Mark isn't married. Gerald isn't married.)

BE CAREFUL! Notice the **word order** after *so* and *neither*. The verb comes before the subject.	**So is Gerald.** NOT So ~~Gerald is~~.
	Neither did Gerald. NOT Neither ~~Gerald did~~.

USAGE NOTE People sometimes use *as well* in additions that follow an affirmative statement.	Mark enjoys fishing, **and Gerald does *as well*.**
	Mark is a fan of old movies, **and Gerald is *as well*.**

3 Additions Showing Difference with *But*

Additions showing difference are **clauses** starting with *but*. They use *but* to express **difference**.

	AFFIRMATIVE NEGATIVE
If the statement is **affirmative**, the addition is **negative**.	Ana **has** short hair, ***but* Eva doesn't**.
	Ana **lived** in Mexico, ***but* Eva didn't**.

	NEGATIVE AFFIRMATIVE
If the statement is **negative**, the addition is **affirmative**.	Ana **doesn't like** to read, ***but* Eva does**.
	Ana **didn't speak** English, ***but* Eva did**.

4 Verbs in Additions

Additions always use a form of *be*, an **auxiliary verb**, or a **modal**.

If the statement uses *be*, use *be* in the addition.	I**'m** a twin, and so **is** my cousin.

If the statement uses an auxiliary verb (*be*, *have*, *do*, or *will*) or a modal (*can*, *could*, *should*, *would*, or *must*), use the **same auxiliary verb or modal** in the addition.	My twin sister and I **have** always lived together, and so **have** my cousins.
	I **can't** drive, and neither **can** my twin.

If the statement doesn't use *be* or an auxiliary verb, use an appropriate form of *do* in the addition.	Bill **owns** a dog, and so **does** Ed.
	Bill **bought** a Chevrolet, and so **did** Ed.

BE CAREFUL! The verb in the addition **agrees with the subject of the addition**, not with the subject of the statement.	**They've** learned Spanish, and so **has she**.
	NOT They've learned Spanish, and so ~~have she~~.

In **conversation**, you can use **short responses** with *so, too, neither, not either,* or *but.*

Use *so, too, neither,* or *not either* to express **agreement** with another speaker.	**A: I like** sports. **B: *So do I.* or I do *too.***
	A: I don't like sports. **B: *Neither* do I. or I *don't either.***
Use *but* to express **disagreement** with another speaker. You can often leave out *but.*	**A: I wouldn't like** to have a twin. **B:** Oh, *(but)* **I would.**
USAGE NOTE In **informal speech**, we often say *Me too* to express agreement with an affirmative statement and *Me neither* to express agreement with a negative statement.	**A: I think** twin studies are fascinating. **B: *Me too.***
	A: I don't know any mirror-image twins. **B: *Me neither.***

STEP 3   FOCUSED PRACTICE

EXERCISE 1 DISCOVER THE GRAMMAR

GRAMMAR NOTES 1–5 Read these short conversations between Erica and several of her friends. Decide if the statement that follows each conversation is *True* (*T*) or *False* (*F*).

1. CAROL: I went to Neil's party last night.
   ERICA: But I didn't.

   __T__ Erica wasn't at Neil's party.

2. LISA: Ed told me he saw you at Neil's party last night. I thought you weren't going.
   ERICA: I was in the library last night. So was my roommate. You can ask her.

   _____ Erica's roommate was at Neil's party.

3. DAVE: Most people weren't taking pictures at Neil's party, but Pete was. Here they are.
   ERICA: And here's a photo of that girl who looks . . . just like me!

   _____ Pete was taking pictures.

4. JIM: I met someone who looks just like you last night. Her name is María.
   ERICA: I know . . . I have long black hair and big blue eyes, and she does too.

   _____ María has long black hair and big blue eyes.

5. JIM: One more thing. María doesn't like to dance. Neither do you.
   ERICA: Now this is getting interesting.

   _____ Erica likes to dance.

6. JIM: I'd like to find out more about María.

ERICA: Me too.

_____ Both Jim and Erica want to find out more about María.

7. ERICA: Everyone is talking about someone named María, but I haven't met her.

AMY: I haven't either.

_____ Amy hasn't met María.

8. ERICA: Dave is having a party tonight. I can't go, but you can.

AMY: Right, and if I'm lucky, I'll meet María, your long lost twin!

_____ Amy can't to go to Dave's party tonight.

EXERCISE 2 ADDITIONS

GRAMMAR NOTES 1–4 **Circle the correct words to complete this paragraph about being a twin.**

Sometimes being a twin can cause trouble. In high school, I was in Mr. Jacobs's history class. Neither /(So) was Joe. One day we took a test. The results were identical.
1.

I got questions 18 and 20 wrong. Joe did so / too.
2.

I didn't spell *Constantinople* correctly, and either / neither did Joe. The teacher
3.

was sure we had cheated. As a result, I got an F on the test, and so did / got Joe. We
4.

tried to convince Mr. Jacobs that it was just a coincidence. After all, I had sat on the

left side of the room, but Joe didn't / hadn't. As always, he sat on the right. But Mr.
5.

Jacobs just thought we had developed some complex way of sharing answers across

the room. Our parents believed we were honest, but Mr. Jacobs didn't / weren't. The
6.

principal didn't either / too. They finally agreed to give us another test.
7.

Even though we were in separate rooms and cheating *couldn't* be a factor, I

got questions 3 and 10 wrong. Guess what? Neither / So did Joe. Our teacher was
8.

astounded, and / but we weren't.
9.

EXERCISE 3 SHORT RESPONSES

Ⓐ GRAMMAR NOTE 5 Two twins are talking. They agree on everything. Complete their conversation with short responses.

MARTA: I love having someone who's my mirror image. I'm so happy we finally found each other.

CARLA: So _____am I_____. I always felt like something was missing from my life.
         1.

MARTA: So _____. I always knew I had a double somewhere out there.
         2.

CARLA: I can't believe how alike we look!

MARTA: Neither _____.
               3.

CARLA: And we like and dislike all the same things.

MARTA: Right. I hate lettuce.

CARLA: I _____. And I detest liver.
          4.

MARTA: So _____. I love pizza, though.
          5.

CARLA: So _____. Especially with mushrooms. But I can't stand pepperoni.
          6.

MARTA: Neither _____.
               7.

CARLA: This is amazing! I'd like to find out if our husbands have a lot in common, too.

MARTA: So _____! That might be fun to investigate!
          8.

▶08|02 Ⓑ LISTEN AND CHECK Listen to the conversation and check your answers in A.

EXERCISE 4 ADDITIONS FOR SIMILARITY OR DIFFERENCE

GRAMMAR NOTES 1–4 Look at this chart about the twins' husbands. Then complete the sentences about them. Add statements with *so, too, neither, not either,* and *but*.

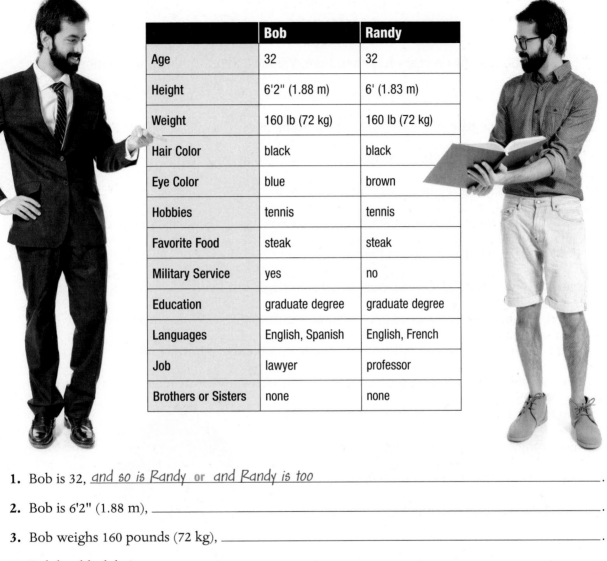

	Bob	Randy
Age	32	32
Height	6'2" (1.88 m)	6' (1.83 m)
Weight	160 lb (72 kg)	160 lb (72 kg)
Hair Color	black	black
Eye Color	blue	brown
Hobbies	tennis	tennis
Favorite Food	steak	steak
Military Service	yes	no
Education	graduate degree	graduate degree
Languages	English, Spanish	English, French
Job	lawyer	professor
Brothers or Sisters	none	none

1. Bob is 32, *and so is Randy* or *and Randy is too* _____.

2. Bob is 6'2" (1.88 m), _____.

3. Bob weighs 160 pounds (72 kg), _____.

4. Bob has black hair, _____.

5. Bob doesn't have green eyes, _____.

6. Bob plays tennis, _____.

7. Bob likes steak, _____.

8. Bob served in the military, _____.

9. Bob has attended graduate school, _____.

10. Bob doesn't speak French, _____.

11. Bob became a lawyer, _____.

12. Bob doesn't have any brothers or sisters, _____.

EXERCISE 5 EDITING

GRAMMAR NOTES 1–5 Read this composition about two brothers. There are six mistakes in the use of sentence additions. The first mistake is already corrected. Find and correct five more.

My Brother and I

My brother is just a year older than I am. We have a lot of things in common. We look alike. In fact, sometimes people ask us if we're twins. I am 5'10", and so ~~he is~~ *is he*. I have thick black hair and dark brown eyes. So he does. He wears glasses, and I do too. We also share some of the same interests. I love to play soccer, and he too. Both of us swim every day, but I can't dive, and either can he.

Although there are a lot of similarities between us, there are also many differences. For example, he likes eating all kinds of food, but I don't. Give me hamburgers and fries every day! My brother doesn't want to go to college, but I don't. I believe it's important to get as much education as possible, but he wants to get real-life experience. I like to read a lot and think carefully about complex problems, but my brother is a man of action. I think our personalities are an important factor in these choices. I am reserved and easygoing, but he doesn't. He talks a lot and has strong opinions. When I think about it, despite the many things we have in common, we really are more different than similar.

EXERCISE 6   LISTENING

08|03   **A**   A couple is on their first date. Listen to their conversation. Look at the information. Listen again to the couple's conversation. Check (✓) the correct box(es).

	Man	Woman			Man	Woman
1. loves Italian food	✓	✓	6. enjoys fiction		☐	☐
2. cooks	☐	☐	7. plays sports		☐	☐
3. eats out a lot	☐	☐	8. watches sports on TV		☐	☐
4. enjoys old movies	☐	☐	9. loves documentaries		☐	☐
5. reads biographies	☐	☐	10. wants to see the documentary		☐	☐

08|03   **B**   Listen to the conversation again. Then work with a partner. Discuss your answers in A. Explain your choices.

EXAMPLE: A: So, the answer to number 1 is the man *and* the woman.
          B: Right. That's because the man says, "I really love Italian food." And then the woman says, "So do I."
          A: OK. Now, what about number 2? Who cooks?

EXERCISE 7   FIND SOMEONE WHO...

A   GAME   Complete the statements. Then read your statements to a classmate. He or she will give you a short response. Check (✓) the items the two of you have in common. Then do the same with another classmate.

EXAMPLE: A: I like to walk in the rain.
          B: So do I. **or** Oh, I don't. I like to stay home and watch TV.

I have these things in common with:

	(Classmate 1)	(Classmate 2)
1. I like to _____.	☐	☐
2. I never _____.	☐	☐
3. I love _____. (name of food)	☐	☐
4. I can't _____.	☐	☐
5. I would like to _____.	☐	☐
6. I've never _____.	☐	☐
7. When I was younger, I didn't _____.	☐	☐
8. I'll never _____.	☐	☐

B   Count the number of checkmarks for each of the two classmates. Which classmate do you have more in common with?

EXERCISE 8 CAN YOU TELL THEM APART?

PICTURE COMPARISON Work with a partner. Look at the pictures of twins Michael and Matthew. How many things do they have in common? How many differences can you find? Discuss their similarities and differences.

EXAMPLE: A: Michael has a mustache, and so does Matthew.
 B: Michael doesn't . . .

EXERCISE 9 TOGETHER AGAIN

Ⓐ GROUP PROJECT Work in a group. Choose one of the sets of twins listed below, all of whom were separated at birth and then later reunited. Do research about the twins and answer some of the questions.

- Paula Bernstein and Elyse Schein
- Adriana Scott and Tamara Rabi
- Jim Springer and Jim Lewis
- Debbie Mehlman and Sharon Poset

Possible Questions:
- When and where were the twins born?
- Where did each twin grow up?
- What kind of environment (family, school, education, etc.) did each twin grow up in?
- What similarities do the twins have?
- What differences do the twins have?
- What interesting facts did you learn about the twins?

Paula Bernstein and Elyse Schein

EXAMPLE: A: Paula Bernstein and Elyse Schein were born in New York City in 1968.
B: Paula grew up there, and so did Elyse.
C: They have a lot in common. When they met for the first time, Paula was a writer, and so was Elyse.
A: But there were differences, too. Paula was married, but Elyse . . .

B Report back to your class. If your group chose the same pair of twins as another group, do you have the same information about those twins? Compare answers.

EXAMPLE: A: Paula Bernstein and Elyse Schein were born in New York City.
B: That's right. Paula grew up in New York, and Elyse did too.
A: Then Paula stayed in New York, but Elyse didn't. She moved to Paris.
B: Here's something interesting. When they first met, they had the same job. Paula was a writer, and . . .

EXERCISE 10 WHAT DO *YOU* THINK ABOUT NATURE VS. NURTURE?

DISCUSSION Work in a group. Which do you think is more important, nature or nurture? Give examples from your research in Exercise 9 and your own experience to support your views.

EXAMPLE: A: I think that nature is more important. Look at Paula and Elyse. They . . .
B: Right. Paula . . . , and Elyse does too.
C: I disagree. I think . . .
D: So do I. For example, . . .

FROM GRAMMAR TO WRITING

A BEFORE YOU WRITE Think about two people you know who are close (twins, siblings, spouses, friends, etc.). List their similarities and differences (in appearance, personalities, daily activities, hobbies, etc.). Complete the outline.

Names: _____ and _____

Similarities	Differences
_____	_____
_____	_____
_____	_____

B WRITE Use your outline to write two paragraphs about the people you are describing. In the first paragraph, focus on their similarities. In the second paragraph, focus on their differences. Use *so, too, neither, not either*, and *but*. Try to avoid the common mistakes in the chart.

EXAMPLE: My friends Kim and Ann are identical twins, but they work very hard to be separate individuals. Kim is 5'3", and so is Ann. Kim . . .

Common Mistakes in Using Additions and Responses

Use the **correct word order** with *so* and *neither*: **verb + subject**. Do not use subject + verb.	Kim is 5'3", and **so is Ann**. NOT Kim is 5'3", and so ~~Ann is~~.
Use the **same auxiliary verb or modal** in the addition as in the statement.	Kim **has** won several awards, but Ann **hasn't**. NOT Kim has won several awards, but Ann ~~didn't~~.
Use **correct agreement**. The verb in the addition **agrees with the subject of the addition**, not with the subject of the statement.	**I wear** a lot of jewelry, but **my twin doesn't**. NOT I wear a lot of jewelry, but my twin ~~do not~~.

C CHECK YOUR WORK Read your paragraphs. Underline once the additions of similarity. Underline twice the additions of difference. Circle *so, too, neither, not either*, and *but*. Use the Editing Checklist to check your work.

Editing Checklist

Did you use . . . ?

- [ ] *so, too, neither*, or *not either* to express similarity
- [ ] *so* or *too* after an affirmative statement
- [ ] *neither* or *not either* after a negative statement
- [ ] *but* to express difference
- [ ] the correct form of *be, have, do, will*, or a modal in the additions

D REVISE YOUR WORK Read your paragraphs again. Can you improve your writing? Make changes if necessary. Give your paragraphs a title.

UNIT 8 REVIEW

Test yourself on the grammar of the unit.

Ⓐ Circle the correct words to complete the sentences.

1. Mary lives in Houston, and so lives / does Jan.

2. Doug moved to Florida. So / Neither did his brother.

3. Mia hasn't gotten married. Her sister has too / hasn't either.

4. My friends play tennis, but / so I don't.

5. I often stay up late, but she does / doesn't.

6. Dan enjoys traveling, and I do so / too.

7. I don't like peanuts. My husband doesn't neither / either.

Ⓑ Combine each pair of sentences. Use an addition with *so*, *too*, *neither*, *not either*, or *but*.

1. I speak Spanish. My brother speaks Spanish.

   _____

2. I can't speak Russian. My brother can't speak Russian.

   _____

3. Jaime lives in Chicago. His brother lives in New York.

   _____

4. Chen doesn't play tennis. His sister plays tennis.

   _____

5. Diego doesn't eat meat. Lila doesn't eat meat.

   _____

Ⓒ Find and correct eight mistakes.

My friend Alicia and I have a lot in common. She comes from Los Angeles, and so I

do. She speaks Spanish. I speak too. Her parents are both teachers, and mine do too. She

doesn't have any brothers or sisters. Either do I. There are some differences, too. Alicia is very

reserved, but I am. I like to talk about my feelings and say what's on my mind. Alicia doesn't

like sports, but I don't. I'm on several school teams, and she isn't. I think our differences make

things more interesting, and so do Alicia!

Now check your answers on page 477.

Gerunds, Infinitives, and Phrasal Verbs

PART 4

OUTCOMES

- Discuss activities or make general statements, using gerunds or infinitives
- Explain the purpose of an action, using an infinitive
- Identify key details in a social science article and in a conversation
- Discuss food and fast-food restaurants
- Write about the food at one's school, expressing one's opinion

OUTCOMES

- Describe how someone forces, causes, persuades, or allows someone else to do things
- Describe how someone makes things easier for someone else
- Identify key information and ideas in an opinion article and in a conversation
- Describe how someone has influenced one's life
- Research and discuss animals in captivity
- Write about keeping animals in captivity

OUTCOMES

- Use phrasal verbs in everyday speech
- Recognize the difference between transitive/intransitive and separable/inseparable phrasal verbs
- Identify specific information in a magazine article and in a telemarketing phone call
- Discuss telemarketing and advertising
- Write about an experience you had on the phone

Gerunds and Infinitives: Review and Expansion

FAST FOOD

OUTCOMES
- Discuss activities or make general statements, using gerunds or infinitives
- Explain the purpose of an action, using an infinitive
- Identify key details in a social science article and in a conversation
- Discuss food and fast-food restaurants
- Write about the food at one's school, expressing one's opinion

STEP 1   GRAMMAR IN CONTEXT

BEFORE YOU READ

Look at the title of the article and at the photos. Discuss the questions.

1. What do you think of fast-food restaurants?
2. Do you eat in fast-food restaurants? Why or why not?

READ

▶09|01   Read this article about fast-food restaurants.

Fast Food
in a
Fast World

"I'll have a hamburger, fries, and a Coke." The language may change, but you can expect to hear this order in hundreds of countries all around the world. In fact, dining in fast-food restaurants has become a way of life for millions and millions of people from Buenos Aires, Argentina, to Ho Chi Minh City, Vietnam.

The Plusses

What is it about eating on the run that so many of us find appealing? Of course, the most obvious answer is that, true to its name, fast food is fast. In today's hectic society, people don't want to waste time. But apart from the speed of ordering and getting served, satisfied customers mention other factors such as convenience, reliability, price, and, yes, good taste!

Many people choose to eat fast food because it's convenient. There are so many fast-food locations that they can stop to have a quick meal almost anywhere. People who don't like to cook are especially happy to find one of these restaurants on their way home from work or school. In addition, because fast-food restaurants usually belong to chains,[1] customers like their reliability. They say they can count on finding the same things every time, every place.

Price is also very important. In fast-food restaurants, people can eat large amounts of food without it costing an arm and a leg.[2] Finally, there are also people who simply enjoy eating fast food. They love the taste of foods like burgers, tacos, and pizza. For these people, a fast-food restaurant is the perfect place to go.

The Minuses

Not everyone is in favor of fast-food restaurants spreading over the globe. In fact, a lot of people would prefer not to have the same fast-food chains in every country they visit. "Walking down the Champs-Elysées just isn't as romantic as it once was. When I see the same restaurants everywhere I go, I feel that the world is shrinking too much," complained one traveler. But there are more serious objections, too.

Nutritionists[3] point to the health consequences of eating fast foods since they are generally high in calories, fat, and salt, but low in fiber and nutrients. They blame the world-wide problem of obesity, in part, on eating fast food. Social critics condemn fast-food chains for introducing these unhealthy foods to other countries and for not paying their workers enough. Then there's the question of pollution. Those hamburgers come wrapped in a lot of paper and plastic, which creates waste that pollutes the air and water. It's a high price to pay for convenience.

It's obvious that people have strong opinions about fast food. Like it or not, it's easy to see that fast-food restaurants are a big part of our world. And one thing is certain—they are here to stay.[4]

Fast Facts

- French fries are the most popular fast food, followed by burgers, fried chicken, pizza, and tacos.

- Men tend to eat fast food more often than women.

- It's not unusual to get a drive-thru order in less than 3 minutes.

- The average American spends $100 a month on fast food.

- More than 13 million people around the world have jobs in fast-food restaurants.

---

1 *chains:* restaurants, hotels, or stores with the same name, appearance, products, and owner

2 *costing an arm and a leg:* being extremely expensive

3 *nutritionists:* experts on what people should eat

4 *here to stay:* permanent, continuing to exist for a long time

AFTER YOU READ

A VOCABULARY Complete the sentences with the words from the box.

appealing	consequence	convenience	globe	objection	reliability

1. As a food writer, Ozawa travels all over the _____ . Last year, he visited restaurants in forty countries.

2. I have no _____ to the report about fast food. I agree with everything it says.

3. I love the _____ of eating at Burg's. It's open 24 hours a day!

4. People like the _____ of the restaurant information on Zagat.com. They know the site's research is carefully done.

5. A(n) _____ of the nutrition report was that some people stopped eating fast food.

6. The idea of low-cost, healthy food choices is very _____ .

B COMPREHENSION Choose the word or phrase that best completes each sentence.

1. Fast-food restaurants are _____ .
   a. unpopular   **b.** expensive   **c.** everywhere

2. The article mentions _____ as a main reason for fast food's popularity.
   a. cleanliness   **b.** attractiveness   **c.** quick service

3. Many fast-food restaurants serve _____ .
   a. fries   **b.** vegetable burgers   **c.** low-fat food

4. _____ happy to see fast-food chains all around the globe.
   a. Some people are   **b.** Everyone is   **c.** Nobody is

5. One big objection to fast food is that it is _____ .
   a. cheap   **b.** unhealthy   **c.** bad-tasting

6. According to the article, workers at fast-food chains don't _____ .
   a. eat well   **b.** make enough money   **c.** have enough family time

C DISCUSSION Work with a partner. Compare your answers in B. Why did you choose these words and phrases?

GERUNDS AND INFINITIVES

<table>
<tr><td colspan="2">Gerunds</td><td colspan="2">Infinitives</td></tr>
<tr><td colspan="2">Gerund as Subject</td><td colspan="2">It + Infinitive</td></tr>
<tr><td colspan="2">Eating fast foods is convenient.</td><td colspan="2">It's convenient to eat fast foods.</td></tr>
<tr><td colspan="2">Verb + Gerund</td><td colspan="2">Verb + Infinitive</td></tr>
<tr><td colspan="2">They recommend reducing fats in the food.</td><td colspan="2">They plan to reduce fats in the food.</td></tr>
<tr><td colspan="2">Verb + Gerund or Infinitive</td><td colspan="2">Verb + Gerund or Infinitive</td></tr>
<tr><td colspan="2">She started eating fries every day.</td><td colspan="2">She started to eat fries every day.</td></tr>
<tr><td colspan="2">Preposition + Gerund</td><td colspan="2">Adjective + Infinitive</td></tr>
<tr><td colspan="2">We're tired of reading calorie counts.</td><td colspan="2">We were surprised to read the number of calories.</td></tr>
<tr><td colspan="2">Possessive + Gerund</td><td colspan="2">Object Pronoun + Infinitive</td></tr>
<tr><td colspan="2">I didn't like his ordering fries.</td><td colspan="2">I urged him to order fries.</td></tr>
</table>

GRAMMAR NOTES

1 Gerunds as Subjects

A **gerund** (base form + **-ing**) is a verb used as a noun. We often use a **gerund** as the **subject** of a sentence.	**Cooking** is a lot of fun.
A gerund can have a **negative** form (**not** + base form + **-ing**).	**Not exercising** leads to health problems.
BE CAREFUL! A gerund is often part of a phrase. When a **gerund phrase** is the **subject** of a sentence, make sure the following verb is in the **third-person singular**.	**Eating too many fries *is*** unhealthy. NOT Eating too many fries ~~are~~ unhealthy.
IN WRITING There are often spelling changes when you add **-ing** to the base form of the verb.	**BASE FORM** **GERUND** waste wast**ing** permit permit**ting** die d**ying**

2 Verb + Gerund

	VERB + GERUND
A gerund often **follows certain verbs** as the **object** of the verb (*avoid, consider, discuss, dislike, enjoy, recommend*, etc.).	My brother *avoids* **eating** fried food. Many people *enjoy* **eating** fast food.
USAGE NOTE We often use *go + gerund* to describe activities such as *shopping, dancing, fishing, skiing,* and *swimming*.	People often eat fast food when they *go* **shopping**. I'm always hungry after I *go* **swimming**.
USAGE NOTE In **formal** English, you can use a **possessive** (*Anne's, the boy's, my, your, his, her, its, our, their*) before a gerund. In **informal** English, many people use **nouns** or **object pronouns** instead of possessives before a gerund.	I dislike *Julio's* **eating** fast foods. *(formal)* I dislike *his* **eating** fast foods. *(formal)* I dislike *Julio* **eating** fast foods. *(informal)* I dislike *him* **eating** fast foods. *(informal)*

3 Verb + Infinitive

An **infinitive** is *to* + base form of the verb. We can use an infinitive **after the verb** in a clause.	They *hope* **to open** a new restaurant.
An infinitive can have a **negative** form (*not + to* + base form).	She *chose* **not to give up** meat.

An infinitive often follows certain verbs. There are three combinations:
 	
• **verb + infinitive**
  (*agree, can't wait, decide, deserve*, etc.)
 	
• **verb + object (noun/pronoun) + infinitive**
  (*cause, challenge, convince, encourage*, etc.)
 	
• **verb + infinitive** or **verb + object + infinitive**
  (*ask, expect, request, want*, etc.)
	VERB + INFINITIVE
	They *agreed* **to cook** with less fat.
	My sister *can't wait* **to try** the low-fat burger.
	
	VERB + OBJECT + INFINITIVE
	She *convinced Max* **not to order** fries.
	I *encouraged them* **to buy** the 2-for-1 special.
	
	VERB + INFINITIVE
	I *wanted* **to try** that new restaurant.
	VERB + OBJECT + INFINITIVE
	I *wanted my sister* **to try** it, too.

BE CAREFUL! We usually **do not repeat** *to* when there is **more than one infinitive**.	We plan **to stay** home, **watch** a movie, and **eat** pizza. NOT We plan to stay home, ~~to~~ watch a movie, and ~~to~~ eat pizza.

4 Verb + Gerund or Infinitive

Some verbs are **followed by a gerund or an infinitive** (*begin, continue, hate, love,* etc.). The **meaning is the same.**	I *love* **cooking** with my friends. I *love* **to cook** with my friends.
BE CAREFUL! When **two or more verbs** follow another verb, we use the **same form** of the verb. (In writing, this is called *parallel structure*.)	I *love* **walking** and **doing** yoga. NOT I love walking and ~~to do~~ yoga. I *love* **to walk** and **do** yoga. NOT I love to walk and ~~doing~~ yoga.

BE CAREFUL! A few verbs (for example, *stop, remember,* and *forget*) can be followed by either a gerund or an infinitive, but the **meanings are very different.**	She *stopped* **eating** pizza.
	  (She doesn't eat pizza anymore.)
	She *stopped* **to eat** pizza.
	  (She stopped another activity in order to eat pizza.)
	
	He *remembered* **meeting** her.
	  (He remembered that he had already met her in the past.)
	He *remembered* **to meet** her.
	  (First he arranged a meeting with her. Then he remembered to go to the meeting.)
	
	I never *forgot* **eating** lunch at the Burg.
	  (I ate lunch at the Burg, and I didn't forget the experience.)
	I never *forgot* **to eat** lunch.
	  (I always ate lunch.)

5 Preposition or Phrasal Verb + Gerund

A **gerund** is the only verb form that can **follow a preposition** (*about, against, at, between, by, for, from, in, of, on,* etc.).	PREP. + GERUND I read an article *about* **counting** calories. People save time *by* **eating** fast food.

A **gerund** follows these common combinations:
  • **verb + preposition**
    (*advise against, approve of, worry about,* etc.)
  • **adjective + preposition**
    (*excited about, famous for, interested in,* etc.)
	VERB + PREP. + GERUND
	I don't *approve of* **eating** fast food every day.
	
	ADJECTIVE + PREP. + GERUND
	We're very *interested in* **trying** different types of food.

BE CAREFUL! Use a **gerund**, not the base form of the verb, **after expressions with the preposition** *to* (*look forward to, be opposed to, object to,* etc.).	We *look forward to* **having** dinner with you. NOT We look forward ~~to have~~ dinner with you.
A **gerund** is the only verb form that can follow a **phrasal verb** (*count on, end up, give up, keep on, put off,* etc.).	PHRASAL VERB + GERUND My brother *gave up* **drinking** Coke. My parents *kept on* **eating** fast food.

6 Infinitives After Adjectives or Nouns

You can use an infinitive after **certain adjectives or nouns**:

- **adjective + infinitive**
  (*afraid, angry, curious, eager, easy, glad, possible,* etc.)

- **noun + infinitive**
  (*chance, decision, offer, price, reason, right, time,* etc.)

ADJECTIVE + INFINITIVE
They're *eager* **to try** the new taco.
She was *glad* **to hear** about the healthy menu.

NOUN + INFINITIVE
She has the *right* **to eat** what she wants.
I don't have *time* **to take** a break.

Sometimes *for* + **noun/pronoun** goes before the infinitive.

ADJ.   INFINITIVE
It's very **easy *for students* to eat** fast food.

NOUN   INFINITIVE
It's a high **price *for them* to pay**.

7 Infinitives of Purpose

You can use an infinitive to explain the **purpose of an action**.

An infinitive of purpose can explain the purpose of an action. It often **answers the question *Why?***

A: *Why* does he always order fast food?
B: He does it **to save** time.

USAGE NOTE In **conversation**, we often answer the question *Why?* with an incomplete sentence beginning with *to*.

A: *Why* did you stop eating fast food?
B: **To lose** weight.

USAGE NOTE We can use *in order (not) to* in **formal speech** and **formal writing** when we explain the purpose of an action.

Older people should exercise regularly *in order to* **remain** healthy. *(medical report)*

USAGE NOTE In everyday **conversation** and **informal writing**, we usually express a **negative purpose** with *because* + a **reason** or *so that* + a **reason**.

I sleep a lot *because* **I don't want to get sick**. *(conversation)*
I sleep a lot *so that* **I don't get sick**. *(email)*

8 Gerunds and Infinitives for General Statements

To make **general statements** you can use:

- **gerund as subject**

- *it* + **infinitive**

They have the **same meaning**.

Cooking is fun.

***It*'s fun to cook**.

REFERENCE NOTES

For **spelling rules for base form of verb + *-ing***, see Appendix 23 on page 463.

For a more complete list of **verbs that can be followed by gerunds**, see Appendix 10 on page 459.

For more complete lists of **verbs that can be followed by infinitives**, see Appendices 11 and 13 on pages 459 and 460.

For a more complete list of **verbs that can be followed by either gerunds or infinitives**, see Appendix 12 on page 459.

For a list of **verb + preposition combinations**, see Appendix 17 on page 460.

For a list of **adjective + preposition expressions**, see Appendix 16 on page 460.

For a list of **adjectives that can be followed by infinitives**, see Appendix 14 on page 460.

For a list of **nouns that can be followed by infinitives**, see Appendix 15 on page 460.

For a list of **phrasal verbs**, see Appendix 4 on page 455.

STEP 3 FOCUSED PRACTICE

EXERCISE 1 DISCOVER THE GRAMMAR

GRAMMAR NOTES 1–8 Read this questionnaire about fast-food restaurants. Underline the gerunds and circle the infinitives. (In Exercise 7 on page 149, you will complete the questionnaire with your own information.)

FAST-FOOD QUESTIONNAIRE

It is increasingly common (to see) fast food in countries around the globe. Please complete this questionnaire about eating at fast-food restaurants. Check (✔) all the answers that apply to you.

1. In my opinion, eating fast food is _____.
   ☐ healthy ☐ unhealthy ☐ convenient ☐ inexpensive ☐ fun

2. Which meals are you used to eating at a fast-food restaurant?
   ☐ breakfast ☒ lunch ☒ dinner ☐ snacks ☐ None

3. Which types of fast food do you like to eat?
   ☒ hamburgers ☐ pizza ☐ fried chicken ☐ tacos ☐ sushi
   ☐ Other: _____ ☐ None

4. To select a fast-food restaurant, what kind of information do you use?
   ☐ advice of friends ☐ online menus ☐ advertisements ☐ prices ☐ Other: _____

5. How often are you likely to eat at a fast-food restaurant?
   ☒ 1–3 times a week ☐ 4–6 times a week ☐ more than 6 times a week ☐ Never

6. How much do you enjoy going to fast-food restaurants?
   ☐ I like it very much. ☒ It's just OK. ☐ I don't enjoy it. ☐ I never go.

7. How do you feel about seeing the same fast-food restaurants all over the world?
   ☐ I like it. ☒ I have no objections. ☐ I don't like it.

8. Do you think the government should require fast-food restaurants to include healthy choices?
   ☒ Yes ☐ No

EXERCISE 2 GERUND OR INFINITIVE

GRAMMAR NOTES 1–8 Complete the information about fast-food favorites. Use the correct form—gerund or infinitive—of the verbs in parentheses. See Appendices 10–17 on pages 459–460 for help.

Calorie Content of Fast-Food Favorites

People are starting ____to think____ about the consequences of ____going____ to
1. (think)   2. (go)

fast-food restaurants, especially when they want ____to maintain____ a healthy lifestyle. If
3. (maintain)

you are one of these people, here are some facts ____to consider____ before you order.
4. (consider)

• ____Ordering____ a Big Mac will "cost" you about 540 calories.
5. (order)

• ____Having____ a Taco Bell taco is much less fattening. One taco has only about
6. (have)

190 calories.

• If you want ____to lose____ weight, you should also consider ____getting____ a
7. (lose)   8. (get)

Subway turkey sandwich. It contains around 280 calories.

• You'll probably end up ____gaining____ weight if you eat a lot of pepperoni pan pizza.
9. (gain)

A single slice at Pizza Hut has about 370 calories.

• You should give up ____eating____ french fries! An order at Wendy's contains about
10. (eat)

410 calories.

• Think about ____choosing____ an egg roll instead of fries. A Panda Express egg roll has
11. (choose)

just a little over 200 calories.

• Nutritionists advise people ____to avoid____ fried chicken. A drumstick at KFC contains
12. (avoid)

about 120 calories—but people usually eat much more!

EXERCISE 3 VERB + GERUND OR INFINITIVE

GRAMMAR NOTES 2–4 Read each conversation and complete the summary statement. Use the correct form of a verb from the box followed by the gerund or infinitive form of the verb in parentheses. See Appendices 10–12 on page 459 for help.

| admit | deserve | ~~forget~~ | recommend | remember | stop | try | volunteer |

1. CUSTOMER: Uh, didn't I order fries, too?
   SERVER: That's right, you did. I'll bring them right away.

   SUMMARY: The server ___forgot to bring___ the fries.
   (bring)

2. FATHER: That Little Burg Meal isn't enough for you anymore. Have a Big Burg, OK?
   CHILD: OK, but I really wanted the toy in the Little Burg Meal.

   SUMMARY: The father ___recommended ordering___ a Big Burg.
   (order)

3. MOM: This car is a mess! Somebody, throw out all those fast-food containers!
   STAN: I'll do it, Mom.

   SUMMARY: Stan ___volunteer to throw out___ the fast-food containers.
   (throw out)

4. PAT: Hi, Renee. Want to go to Pizza Hut with us?
   RENEE: Thanks, but I can't eat fast food now. I'm training for the swim team.

   SUMMARY: Renee ___stopped eating___ fast food.
   (eat)

5. EMPLOYEE: Thanks for the raise. I can really use it.
   MANAGER: You've earned it. You're our best drive-through server.

   SUMMARY: The employee ___deserves to receive___ a raise.
   (receive)

6. MOTHER: I think you should quit that fast-food job. Your grades are suffering.
   CAROL: It's hard to decide. I need to save for college, but if my grades are bad . . .

   SUMMARY: Carol ___tried to decide___ whether to keep her job.
   (decide)

7. MOM: You're not eating dinner. You had some fast food on the way home, didn't you?
   CHRIS: Well, . . . actually, I stopped at Arby's, but I only had fries.

   SUMMARY: Chris ___admits going___ to Arby's after school.
   (go)

8. TIM: I used to stay in the Burg's playground for hours when I was little.
   WANG: Yeah, me too. My mother couldn't get me to leave.

   SUMMARY: The boys ___remembered playing___ in the Burg's playground.
   (play)

EXERCISE 4 GERUND OR INFINITIVE WITH AND WITHOUT OBJECT

GRAMMAR NOTES 1–7 Complete these letters to the editor of a school newspaper. Use the correct forms of the words in parentheses. See Appendices 10–17 on pages 459–460 for help.

STUDENT NEWS

TO THE EDITOR

Yesterday, my roommate Andre _____ *wanted me to have* _____ lunch with him in the
1. (want / I / have)

dining hall. I was surprised about _____ there because last year
2. (Andre / choose / go)

he and I had _____ the dining hall. It just wasn't appealing to
3. (decide / not use)

us. But when we went in yesterday, instead of _____ the usual
4. (find)

greasy fries and mystery meat, I was happy _____ the colorful
5. (see)

Taco Bell sign. In my opinion, _____ to fast foods is really
6. (change)

the thing _____. The administration made a great choice.
7. (do)

I _____ fast food and I _____
8. (support / they / sell)   9. (appreciate / my friend / encourage)

me to give campus food another try.

M. Rodriguez

TO THE EDITOR

I'm writing this letter _____ my anger and terrible
10. (express)

disappointment at _____ fast-food chains in the dining halls.
11. (have)

When a classmate and I went to eat yesterday, I _____ the
12. (expect / find)

usual healthy choices of vegetables and salads. I _____ a
13. (not expect / see)

fast-food court. In my opinion, it's simply wrong _____ fast food
14. (bring)

into the college dining hall. The consequence of _____ the right
15. (not eat)

food is bad health. As a commuter, I _____ the convenience of a
16. (need / have)

healthy meal option every evening before class. But I usually _____
17. (try / stay away)

from fast foods. I _____ a salad bar so that
18. (urge / the administration / set up)

students like me can _____ meals on campus. I'm sure other
19. (keep on / buy)

commuters will agree with my objections.

B. Chen

EXERCISE 5 EDITING

GRAMMAR NOTES 1–8 Read these posts to an international online discussion group. There are eleven mistakes in the use of gerunds and infinitives. The first mistake is already corrected. Find and correct ten more. See Appendices 10–17 on pages 459–460 for help.

READ RESPONSES | POST A NEW RESPONSE | RETURN TO INDEX | PREVIOUS | NEXT

Re: love those tacos

eating **or** *to eat*

I love ~~eat~~ tacos for my lunch. I think they're delicious, convenient, nutritious, and inexpensive. I don't mind to have the same thing every day! And I'm not worried about any health consequences. What do you think?

Re: vegetarian travel

I'm a vegetarian. I stopped to eat meat two years ago to lose weight and improve my overall health. I feel a little nervous about traveling to other countries. I'm interested in go to Ghana and other countries in the region in September. Is it easy to find meatless dishes there?

Re: takoyaki

Hi! I am Paulo, and I come from Brazil. I travel a lot, and I enjoy to try different foods from all over the globe. I hope I have a chance trying takoyaki (fish balls made with octopus) when I go to Japan. Is there a takoyaki shop you can recommend my going to? I look forward to hear from you.

Re: Cheap and delicious in Seoul

Eat in Seoul is one of life's great pleasures. It's easy find delicious food at reasonable prices. I suggest to try *kimbap*. It's made with steamed rice and fresh ingredients such as carrots and spinach, rolled in seaweed—a little like Japanese sushi. I'd be happy to post the recipe if you want having it.

EXERCISE 6   LISTENING

▶ 09|02   **A**   Two college students, Lily and Victor, are discussing their responses to a food-service survey. Listen to their conversation. Look at the list of possible changes. Listen again to the conversation. Check (✓) the possible changes that each student agrees with.

School Food-Service Survey ~~Survey~~ ~~urvey~~

We're changing and you can help! Please complete the survey by checking (✔) the changes you want to see.

	name	Lily name	Victor name
1. Introducing Burger Queen fast foods	☐	☐	☑
2. Showing fat and calorie contents of each serving	☐	☐	☐
3. Providing more healthy choices	☐	☐	☐
4. Lowering prices	☐	☐	☐
5. Improving food quality	☐	☐	☐
6. Offering international foods	☐	☐	☐
7. Starting breakfast at 6:30 a.m.	☐	☐	☐

▶ 09|02   **B**   Listen again to the conversation. Then work with a partner and discuss the questions.

1. Did Lily follow Victor's advice about the meatloaf in the school cafeteria?

     EXAMPLE: A: I don't remember hearing anything about meatloaf. Do you?
               B: Victor told Lily not to eat it. But she decided to get it anyway, and it was terrible.

2. What is the purpose of the school-cafeteria survey?

3. What kinds of changes in the cafeteria is Lily most interested in?

4. What kinds of changes is Victor most interested in?

5. Is the food at Lily and Victor's school the same as or different from the food at your school?

C   Work with a partner. Take the survey. Then discuss your answers.

EXAMPLE: A: Do you agree with Lily or Victor about having Burger Queen in the cafeteria?
           B: I agree with Victor.
           A: Me too. Lily's meat loaf sounds terrible. I'd prefer to have a burger!

EXERCISE 7 IF YOU ASK ME . . .

A QUESTIONNAIRE Give your opinions about fast food. Complete the fast-food questionnaire in Exercise 1 on page 143.

B Work with a partner. Compare your answers on the questionnaire.

EXAMPLE: A: What's your answer to number 1?

B: In my opinion, fast food is convenient and cheap. How do you feel about eating fast food?

A: I agree. And it's not healthy, but it is fun!

C Have a class discussion about your answers. Tally the results.

EXAMPLE: Fifteen students agree that eating fast food is convenient and fast.

EXERCISE 8 A WORLD OF FAST FOOD

CROSS-CULTURAL COMPARISON Work in a group. Describe popular fast food in your country. The food can be from an international fast-food restaurant or local fast food.

EXAMPLE: A: In Germany, we like to order the Big Rösti at McDonald's. It's a burger with bacon, cheese, and a potato pancake on it. *Rösti* is the German word for potato pancake.

B: The potato pancake is on the burger? I'm all for trying that! It sounds delicious.

C: In addition to eating at fast-food restaurants, people in Mexico like to buy food from street vendors. My favorite is *elote*. It's . . .

EXERCISE 9 HEALTHY CHOICES

A GROUP PROJECT Work in a group. Use the websites of some popular fast-food restaurants to answer this question: Is it possible to have healthy food choices at a fast-food restaurant? Answer some of the questions below as you do your research.

EXAMPLE: A: Let's go online now to get nutrition information.

B: OK. We can start by looking at the salads.

C: What do you think about the crispy chicken salad?

D: I don't know. Some of the burgers seem to have fewer calories.

Possible questions:

- What is the total calorie count for a specific meal?
- How much salt does the meal have?
- What is the vitamin content of the food?
- Which menu items could replace a hamburger?
- What food sizes are available?
- How fresh is the food?

B Report back to your class. Compare your answers.

EXAMPLE: A: We were surprised to see that some of the salads on this menu have more fat and calories than burgers.

B: Right. But it depends on the size of the burger and what you eat with the burger.

A: We decided to make our own combination meal of a hamburger with a side salad.

B: Good choice!

A BEFORE YOU WRITE Think about the types of food that students can buy at your school (for example, pizza, burgers, salads, tacos, and sushi). Complete the outline.

Types of Food	Plusses	Minuses
_____	_____	_____
_____	_____	_____

B WRITE Use your outline to write two paragraphs. In the first paragraph, describe the food at your school. In the second paragraph, give your opinion about the food. Use gerunds and infinitives. Try to avoid the common mistakes in the chart.

EXAMPLE: I eat at school every day because I live on campus. I would like to describe my dining experience. The food here is . . .

Common Mistakes in Using Infinitives and Gerunds

Use a **gerund after certain verbs**, such as *dislike*, *enjoy*, and *suggest*. Do not use an infinitive.	I *suggest* **making** changes in the cafeteria food. NOT I suggest to make changes in the cafeteria food.
Use a **gerund after a preposition** or **a phrasal verb**. Do not use an infinitive.	I object **to eating** so much fried food. NOT I object to eat so much fried food. Last semester, I *ended up* **gaining** weight. NOT Last semester, I ended up to gain weight.
Use **parallel structure** when **two or more verbs** follow another verb. Use either infinitives or gerunds. Do not use infinitives and gerunds together.	The cafeteria should *continue* **providing** a salad bar and **serving** hot vegetarian meals. NOT The cafeteria should continue providing a salad bar and to serve hot vegetarian meals.

C CHECK YOUR WORK Read your paragraphs. Underline the gerunds. Circle the infinitives. Use the Editing Checklist to check your work.

Editing Checklist

Did you use . . . ?
- [ ] gerunds as subjects
- [ ] correct verbs + gerunds
- [ ] correct verbs + infinitives
- [ ] prepositions (or phrasal verbs) + gerunds
- [ ] infinitives after certain adjectives or nouns
- [ ] *it* + infinitive for general statements
- [ ] parallel structure

D REVISE YOUR WORK Read your paragraphs again. Can you improve your writing? Make changes if necessary. Give your paragraphs a title.

UNIT 9 REVIEW

Test yourself on the grammar of the unit.

A Complete the paragraph with the gerund or infinitive form of the verbs in parentheses.

Cost and convenience often persuade people _____ fast-food restaurants. If
                                              1. (use)

you are eating a fast-food lunch _____ money, think about _____
                                   2. (save)   **3.** (order)

from the special value menu. A fast-food dinner can leave you free _____ or
                                                                       4. (relax)

_____ instead of _____ food. _____ for fast food is
   5. (study)   **6.** (prepare)   **7.** (stop)

a cheap and convenient way _____ . But try _____ fast food too
                              8. (eat)   **9.** (not have)

often. _____ at home provides better quality food for less money.
         10. (cook)

B Read each conversation and complete the summary statement (S). Use the correct
form of the words in parentheses.

1. **DAD:** You used to love Taco Bell as a kid.
   TIM: I *did*? Did you take me there a lot?

   S: Tim _____
                        (remember / go)
   to Taco Bell.

2. **AL:** I'm sick of eating fast food.
   NAN: You should take a cooking class.

   S: Nan _____
                        (want / Al / take)
   a cooking class.

3. **CHU:** I ate in the cafeteria today.
   KAY: That's strange. You hate that food.

   S: Kay _____
                        (wonder about / Chu / eat)
   in the cafeteria.

4. **DEB:** Would you like to have dinner now?
   TAO: Sure! I haven't eaten since breakfast.

   S: Tao _____
                        (stop / have)
   lunch.

5. **IAN:** Did you mail that letter I gave you?
   LIZ: Oops. Sorry. I'll mail it tomorrow.

   S: Liz _____
                        (forget / mail)
   Ian's letter.

C Find and correct five mistakes.

A: I was happy to hear that the cafeteria is serving salads now. I'm eager trying them.

B: Me too. Someone recommended to eat more salads to lose weight.

A: It was that TV doctor, right? He's always urging we to exercise more, too.

B: That's the one. He's actually convinced me to stop to eat meat.

A: Interesting! That would be a hard decision for us making, though. We love to barbecue.

Now check your answers on page 477.

Make, Have, Let, Help, and *Get*

ZOOS AND MARINE THEME PARKS

OUTCOMES
- Describe how someone forces, causes, persuades, or allows someone else to do things
- Describe how someone makes things easier for someone else
- Identify key information and ideas in an opinion article and in a conversation
- Describe how someone has influenced one's life
- Research and discuss animals in captivity
- Write about keeping animals in captivity

STEP 1 GRAMMAR IN CONTEXT

BEFORE YOU READ

Look at the photos. Discuss the questions.

1. How do you think the animals feel? Why do they feel that way?
2. Do you think people should use animals for entertainment?

READ

▶10|01 Read this article about performance animals.

That's Entertainment?

"Ooooh!" cries the audience as the orcas leap from the water in perfect formation. "Aaaah!" they shout as the trainer rides across the pool on the nose of one of the graceful giants. For years, dolphins, orcas, and other sea

mammals have been making audiences cheer at marine theme parks around the world. But how do trainers get nine-ton whales to do acrobatic tricks[1] or make them "dance"?

It's not easy. Traditional animal trainers controlled animals with collars and leashes and made them perform by using cruel punishments. Then, in the 1940s, marine theme parks wanted to have dolphins do tricks. The first trainers faced big problems. You can't get a dolphin to wear a collar. And you can't punish a dolphin—it will just swim away from you! This challenge made the trainers develop a kinder, more humane method to teach animals.

This method, positive reinforcement, uses rewards rather than punishments for training. To begin teaching, a trainer lets an animal act freely. When the trainer sees the "correct" behavior, he or she rewards the animal immediately, usually with food. The animal quickly learns that a reward follows the behavior. For complicated acts, the trainer breaks the act into many smaller parts and has the animal learn each part separately.

Positive reinforcement has completely changed our treatment of animals in zoos. Elephants, for example, need a lot of physical care. However, traditional trainers used force to make elephants "behave." Elephants sometimes rebelled and hurt or even killed their keepers. Through positive reinforcement, elephants at modern zoos have learned to stand at the bars of their cage and let keepers draw blood for tests and take care of their feet. Gary Priest, a former orca trainer, helped the keepers train the elephants at the San Diego Zoo. Do the elephants like the new system? "They love it! They'll do anything we ask," Priest said.

Unfortunately, not all trainers use positive reinforcement. Animal rights organizations have found abuses[2] of animal actors by circuses and other entertainment companies. And the question remains: Even with kind treatment, should we keep these animals captive[3] and have them perform just for our entertainment?

---

1 *acrobatic tricks:* the kind of acts that animals and people do at the circus (example: walking on a wire)
2 *abuses:* examples of cruel or violent treatment
3 *keep...captive:* keep animals or people in a place that they are not allowed to leave

AFTER YOU READ

A VOCABULARY Match the words with their definitions.

_____ 1. cruel
a. related to the body, not the mind

_____ 2. humane
b. causing pain

_____ 3. reinforcement
c. having a position in the past, but not now

_____ 4. physical
d. kind to people or animals

_____ 5. rebel
e. to fight against someone in power

_____ 6. former
f. a way of strengthening or encouraging an action

B COMPREHENSION Read the statements. Check (✓) *True* or *False*.

	True	False
1. It's easy to train orcas and dolphins.	☐	☐
2. Many dolphins wear collars.	☐	☐
3. Methods of animal training have changed a lot since the 1940s.	☐	☐
4. Trainers give rewards so that animals will act freely.	☐	☐
5. Zoo elephants and their keepers have a better relationship now.	☐	☐
6. The author of the article is in favor of using animals for entertainment.	☐	☐

C DISCUSSION Work with a partner. Compare your answers in B. Why did you check *True* or *False*?

STEP 2 GRAMMAR PRESENTATION

MAKE, HAVE, LET, HELP, AND *GET*

Make, Have, Let, Help				
Subject	Make/Have/Let/Help	Object	Base Form	
They	(don't) **make have let help***	animals them	**learn**	tricks.

* Help can also be followed by an infinitive.

Get, Help				
Subject	Get/Help	Object	Infinitive	
They	(don't) **get help**	animals them	**to learn**	tricks.

GRAMMAR NOTES

1 Make, Have, and Get

Use *make*, *have*, and *get* to talk about things that someone **causes another person (or an animal) to do**.

Make, *have*, and *get* show **how much choice** a person or animal has about doing an action.

Make + **object** + **base form** of the verb means **to force** a person or animal to do something (there is **no choice**).

The trainer **made *the elephant* perform** tricks for the audience.
(The trainer forced the elephant to perform tricks.)

Have + **object** + **base form** of the verb means **to cause** a person or animal to do something (there is **some choice**).

Some people **have *their pets* do** tricks.
(Some people cause their pets to do tricks.)

Get + **object** + **infinitive** means **to persuade** a person or animal to do something by giving reasons or rewards (there is **a choice**).

Jan **got *her parents* to take** her to the zoo for a school assignment.
(Jan persuaded her parents to take her.)

NO CHOICE

↑

↓

CHOICE

BE CAREFUL! *Get* is always followed by **object** + **infinitive**, not the base form of the verb.

INFINITIVE
You can't **get *a dolphin* to wear** a collar.
NOT You can't get a dolphin ~~wear~~ a collar.

Make can also mean **to have an effect** on someone or something.

The monkeys always **make *me* laugh**.
(They have this effect on me.)

When the effect is a **feeling**, we often use *make* + **object** + **adjective**.

ADJECTIVE
Cruel treatment of animals **makes *me* angry**.
(Cruel treatment of animals causes me to feel angry.)

2 Let

Let + **object** + **base form** of the verb means **to allow** a person or animal to do something.

Our teacher **let *us* leave** early after the test.
(Our teacher allowed us to leave early.)
Some zoos **let *animals* interact** with humans.
(Some zoos allow animals to interact with humans.)

BE CAREFUL! *Let* is always followed by **object** + **base form** of the verb, not an infinitive.

Zoos usually **let *people* take** photos.
NOT Zoos usually let people ~~to take~~ photos.

3 Help

Help means **to make something easier** for a person or an animal.

Help can be followed by:
- **object** + **base form** of the verb
- **object** + **infinitive**

They have the **same meaning**.

She **helped *me* do** the homework.

She **helped *me* to do** the homework.
(She made it easier for me to do the homework.)

EXERCISE 1 DISCOVER THE GRAMMAR

GRAMMAR NOTES 1–3 Read each numbered statement. Choose the sentence (*a* or *b*) that is similar in meaning.

1. Ms. Bates got the principal to arrange a class trip to the zoo.

   a. Ms. Bates arranged the class trip.

   b. The principal arranged the class trip.

2. Mr. Goldberg had us do research about animals.

   a. Mr. Goldberg did the research for us.

   b. We did the research.

3. My teacher made me rewrite the report.

   a. I wrote the report again.

   b. I didn't write the report again.

4. She got me to do research on tropical birds.

   a. I agreed to do the research.

   b. I didn't agree to do the research.

5. The zoo lets small birds and animals wander freely inside the habitat.[1]

   a. They can go where they want.

   b. They have to stay in cages.

6. Chi was sick, so her teacher didn't let her go on the trip to the zoo.

   a. Chi stayed home.

   b. Chi went on the trip.

7. The homework was complicated, but Paulo helped Maria finish it.

   a. Paulo did Maria's homework for her.

   b. Both Paulo and Maria worked on her homework.

8. Their trip to the zoo made the students really appreciate animals.

   a. The trip forced the students to appreciate animals.

   b. The trip changed the students' opinions of animals.

---

1 *habitat*: in a zoo, a place outdoors or in a building that is like the natural environment of the animals

EXERCISE 2 MEANING OF *MAKE, HAVE, LET, HELP,* AND *GET*

GRAMMAR NOTES 1–3 Students in a conversation class are talking about their experiences with authority figures.[1] Complete the sentences by circling the correct verb. Then match each situation with the person in authority.

Situation

___c___ **1.** I was tired, so he didn't help / (have) me play in the second half of the game.

_____ **2.** I didn't really want to work overtime this week, but she had / let me work late because some of my co-workers were sick.

_____ **3.** I forgot to turn on my headlights before I left the parking lot a few nights ago. She made / got me pull over to the side of the road and asked to see my license.

_____ **4.** At first, we rebelled when he told us to write in our journals, but then he explained how important it was. Finally, he had / got us to try it.

_____ **5.** My check was delayed in the mail. I told him what had happened, and he made / let me pay the rent two weeks late.

_____ **6.** I needed to get a blood test for my physical exam. She got / had me roll up my sleeve and make a fist.

_____ **7.** We're a big family, and we all have our own chores. While she washed the dishes, she helped / had me dry. My brother, a former high school wrestling star, swept the floor!

_____ **8.** I'm an only child, and when I was young, I felt lonely. He let / got me sleep over at my friend's house.

_____ **9.** I wasn't paying attention, and I hit a parked car. He let / helped me to get the money for all of the repairs.

Person in Authority

a. my teacher

b. the doctor

~~**c.**~~ my soccer coach

d. my father

e. a police officer

f. my insurance agent

g. my landlord

h. my boss

i. my mother

---

1 *authority figures:* people who are or seem powerful

EXERCISE 5 EDITING

GRAMMAR NOTES 1–3 Read this email petition about orcas. There are eight mistakes in the use of *make*, *have*, *let*, *help*, and *get*. The first mistake is already corrected. Find and correct seven more.

LET THEM GO!

Blackfish, a documentary film about orcas in captivity, made people ~~to think~~ *think* about the use of these magnificent mammals in marine theme parks. Public pressure even got SeaWorld to change the orca shows at its theme parks. But the orcas are still in captivity. So it's time for action.

In captivity, an orca can't have normal physical or emotional health. In the wild, an orca swims freely and has a complex social life in a large family group. However, marine theme parks and aquariums make this animal lives in a small, chemically treated pool where it may get sick and die. There are arguments that captive orcas have helped humans learned about them. However, orcas cannot behave naturally in captivity when trainers have them to perform embarrassing tricks for a "reward." How can watching tricks or seeing orcas in a small pool help we understand them?

Don't let these beautiful animals suffering this cruel treatment for human entertainment! First, help us end orca shows. Stop going to these shows, and get your friends and family stop also. Next, we must make marine theme parks and aquariums stop buying orcas. And they must let experts to retrain the orcas now in captivity and release them to a normal life. Write to your government officials and tell them how you feel.

Help us help the orcas! It's the humane thing to do. Sign this petition and send it to everyone you know.

EXERCISE 6 LISTENING

▶10|02 **A** Listen to the conversation between a student and his writing teacher. Read the statements. Then listen again and check (✓) *True* or *False*.

	True	False
1. Ms. Jacobson originally made Simon write about animals in zoos.	☐	☑
2. She let him change the topic of his essay.	☐	☐
3. She had him remove some details from his second paragraph.	☐	☐
4. She got him to talk about his uncle.	☐	☐
5. She helped him correct a grammar mistake.	☐	☐
6. Simon got Ms. Jacobson to correct the gerunds in his essay.	☐	☐
7. Ms. Jacobson made Simon look for the gerunds in his essay.	☐	☐
8. She let Simon make an appointment for another conference.	☐	☐

▶10|02 **B** Listen to the conversation again. Then work with a partner. Do you think Ms. Jacobson is a good writing teacher? Why or why not? Discuss your answers.

EXAMPLE: **A:** Ms. Jacobson let Simon explain why he was worried about his essay. That's good.
  B: I agree. And she used positive reinforcement. However, she made him . . .

EXERCISE 7 A HELPING HAND

CONVERSATION Work with a partner. Talk about a person who helped you learn something new (for example, a parent, other relative, teacher, or friend). Answer the questions below.

EXAMPLE: A: My older brother was a big help to me when I was a teenager.
            B: Oh? What did he do?
            A: Well, he got me to try a lot of new things. He even taught me . . .

1. What did the person get you to do that you had never done before?
2. How did this person help you?
3. How did it make you feel?
4. Did he or she let you make mistakes in order to learn?

EXERCISE 8 FOR OR AGAINST?

Ⓐ DISCUSSION You are going to have a discussion about keeping animals in captivity for human entertainment. Use the Internet to research reasons for and against keeping animals in zoos and marine theme parks. Take notes.

Ⓑ Work in a group. Discuss whether you are for or against using animals for entertainment. Use *make*, *have*, *let*, *help*, and *get*.

EXAMPLE: A: I think it's cruel to make wild animals live in small habitats.
            B: I'm not sure. Having them perform . . .
            C: I think zoos can help us . . .
            D: Zoos make me feel . . .

FROM GRAMMAR TO WRITING

A BEFORE YOU WRITE Think about the arguments for and against keeping animals in zoos and marine theme parks. Then think about your own opinion. Complete the outline.

Arguments For	Arguments Against	My Opinion
_____	_____	_____
_____	_____	_____
_____	_____	_____

B WRITE Use your outline to write three paragraphs. In your first paragraph, give the arguments for keeping animals in zoos and marine theme parks. In your second paragraph, give the arguments against. Give your own opinion in the third paragraph. Use *make*, *have*, *let*, *help*, and *get*. Try to avoid the common mistakes in the chart.

EXAMPLE: Many people believe that it is good to have animals live in captivity. They believe animals help . . .
    On the other hand, other people want to let animals live freely in the wild. According to these people . . .
    In my opinion . . .

Common Mistakes in Using *Make, Have, Let, Help*, and *Get*

Use the **base form** of the verb **after** *make*, *have*, and *let*. Do not use an infinitive.	Should we **make** animals **live** in captivity? NOT Should we make animals ~~to live~~ in captivity?
Use an **infinitive after** *get*. Do not use the base form of the verb.	My friend **got** me **to agree** with his opinion. NOT My friend got me ~~agree~~ with his opinion.
Use an **object pronoun after** *make*, *have*, *let*, *help*, and *get*. Do not use a subject pronoun.	Most marine animal parks **have them** do tricks. NOT Most marine animal parks have ~~they~~ do tricks.

C CHECK YOUR WORK Read your paragraphs. Underline *make*, *have*, *let*, *help*, and *get* + object + verb. Use the Editing Checklist to check your work.

Editing Checklist

Did you use . . . ?

- ☐ object + base form of the verb after *make*, *have*, and *let*
- ☐ object + base form or infinitive after *help*
- ☐ object + infinitive after *get*
- ☐ the correct verb to express your meaning

D REVISE YOUR WORK Read your paragraphs again. Can you improve your writing? Make changes if necessary. Give your paragraphs a title.

UNIT 10 REVIEW

Test yourself on the grammar of the unit.

A Circle the correct words to complete the sentences.

1. I didn't know what to write about, so my teacher <u>helped / made</u> me choose a topic by suggesting ideas.

2. Before we began to write, she <u>had / got</u> us research the topic online.

3. At first, I was annoyed when my teacher <u>let / made</u> me rewrite the report.

4. She was fantastic. She always <u>let / helped</u> me ask her questions.

5. It was a good assignment. It really <u>made / got</u> me to think a lot.

B Complete the sentences with the correct form of the verbs in parentheses. Choose between affirmative and negative and use pronoun objects.

1. When I was little, my parents _____ a pet. They said I was too young.
   (let / have)

2. When I was ten, I finally _____ me a dog. His name was Buttons.
   (get / buy)

3. It was a lot of responsibility. My parents _____ him every day.
   (make / walk)

4. They _____ him, too. He ate a lot!
   (have / feed)

5. I was annoyed at my older brother. He _____ care of Buttons.
   (help / take)

6. Sometimes, I _____ Buttons a bath. Both enjoyed it.
   (get / give)

7. When I have children, I plan to _____ a pet. It's a great experience.
   (let / have)

C Find and correct eight mistakes.

Lately, I've been thinking a lot about all the people who helped me adjusting to moving here when I was a kid. My parents got me join some school clubs, so I met other kids. Then my dad helped me improved my soccer game so that I could join the team. And my mom never let me to stay home. She made me to get out and do things. My parents also spoke to my new teacher and had she call on me a lot, so the other kids got to know me quickly. Our next-door neighbors helped, too. They got I to walk their dog Red, and Red introduced me to all her human friends! The fact that so many people wanted to help me made me to realize that I was not alone. Before long, I felt part of my new school, my new neighborhood, and my new life.

Now check your answers on page 477.

Phrasal Verbs: Review and Expansion

TELEMARKETING

OUTCOMES
- Use phrasal verbs in everyday speech
- Recognize the difference between transitive/intransitive and separable/inseparable phrasal verbs
- Identify specific information in a magazine article and in a telemarketing phone call
- Discuss telemarketing and advertising
- Write about an experience you had on the phone

STEP 1   GRAMMAR IN CONTEXT

BEFORE YOU READ

Look at the cartoon. Discuss the questions.

1. Who do you think is calling the man? How does the man feel about the call?

2. Do you receive unwanted calls? How do you feel about them?

READ

11|01   Read this magazine article about telemarketers.

Welcome Home!

You just got back from a long, hard day at the office. You're exhausted. All you want to do is take off your jacket, put down your briefcase, and relax over a great dinner. Then, just as you're about to sit down at the table, the phone rings. You hesitate to pick it up. It's probably just another telemarketer trying to talk you into buying something you really don't need. But, what if it's not? It could be important family news that you don't want to miss out on. You have to find out!

"Hello?" you answer nervously.

"Good evening. Is this Mr. Groaner?" a strange voice asks. You know right away that it's a telemarketer. Your last name is Groden. "We have great news for you! You've been chosen to receive an all-expenses-paid trip to the Bahamas! It's an offer you can't afford to turn down!"

"I just got home. Can you call back tomorrow when I'm still at work?"

Telemarketing—the practice of selling products and services by phone—is spreading throughout the world as the number of phones goes up and phone rates come down. To most people, annoying calls from telemarketers are about as welcome as a bad case of the flu.

What can be done about this invasion of privacy?[1] Experts have come up with several tactics that you can try out.

- Sign up to have your phone number placed on a Do Not Call list. If you're on the list and telemarketers keep on calling, write down the date and time of the call, and find out the name of the organization calling you. You can then report the call to the proper authorities.

- Use Caller ID to help identify telemarketers. If an unfamiliar number shows up, don't pick up the phone. Even better, use the Block This Caller feature on your phone to prevent future calls from getting through.

- If you *have* answered the phone, say (firmly but politely!): "I'm hanging up now," and get off the phone.

- Ask the telemarketing company to take you off their list. But don't count on this happening immediately. You may have to ask several times before it takes effect.

None of these measures will eliminate all unwanted telephone solicitations,[2] but they should help cut down the number of calls that you receive.

Telemarketing, however, is part of a larger problem. We are constantly being flooded with unwanted offers and requests. Junk mail fills up our mailboxes (and later our trash and recycling cans when we throw it out). And the invasion is, of course, not limited to paper. When you turn on your computer and check your email, you have to deal with spam, the electronic equivalent of junk mail.

What's the solution? Leave home? Move to a desert island? Maybe not. They'll probably get to you there anyway!

---

1 *invasion of privacy:* interrupting or getting involved in another's personal life in an unwelcome way
2 *solicitations:* asking someone for something such as money or help

AFTER YOU READ

Ⓐ VOCABULARY Circle the word or phrase that best completes each sentence.

1. If you **eliminate** a problem, the problem disappears / gets better / gets worse.

2. The **authorities** are people that buy / control / write about things.

3. A useful **feature** of phones is text messaging / telemarketing / junk mail.

4. If two things are **equivalent**, they are the same / different / valuable.

5. Telemarketers' **tactics** are their products / sales methods / prices.

6. When you speak **firmly**, you show that you are worried / curious / certain.

COMPREHENSION **Read the statements. Check (✓) True or False.**

	True	False
1. Mr. Groden got a call from a telemarketer in the morning.	☐	☐
2. Mr. Groden quickly figured out that it was a telemarketing call.	☐	☐
3. More people now have phones, so telemarketing is becoming a global problem.	☐	☐
4. If your name is on a Do Not Call list, you will not get telemarketing calls.	☐	☐
5. You can do something to stop *all* of these unwanted calls.	☐	☐
6. Telemarketing is just one example of an invasion of privacy.	☐	☐

C **DISCUSSION** **Work with a partner. Compare your answers in B. Why did you choose *True* or *False*?**

STEP 2   GRAMMAR PRESENTATION

PHRASAL VERBS: REVIEW AND EXPANSION

Separable Transitive

Subject	Verb	Particle	Object (Noun)
She	**picked**	**up**	the phone.

Separable Transitive

Subject	Verb	Object (Noun/ Pronoun)	Particle
She	**picked**	the phone it	**up**.

Inseparable Transitive

Subject	Verb	Particle	Object (Noun/ Pronoun/Gerund)
He	**counts**	**on**	your calls. them.
They	**keep**	**on**	calling. doing it.

Intransitive

Subject	Verb	Particle
They	**sat**	**down**.

Phrasal Verb + Preposition

Subject	Verb	Particle	Preposition	Object (Noun/ Pronoun)
I	**hung**	**up**	**on**	the caller. him.
They	**came**	**up**	**with**	this idea. it.

GRAMMAR NOTES

1 Form of Phrasal Verbs

A **phrasal verb** (also called a *two-word verb*) has **two parts**: a verb and a particle.

	VERB + PARTICLE
• phrasal verb = verb + particle	I **got off** the phone quickly.

These are some **common particles** that combine with verbs to form a phrasal verb:

		VERB + PARTICLE
• *in*	(*call in, fill in, turn in*)	I **turned in** the form.
• *out*	(*find out, throw out, try out*)	I **throw out** my junk mail.
• *up*	(*fill up, hang up, pick up*)	I don't **pick up** the phone.
• *down*	(*sit down, turn down, write down*)	I **write down** the date and time of each call.
• *on*	(*count on, put on, turn on*)	I **turn on** my computer to check my email.
• *off*	(*get off, take off, turn off*)	I **get off** the phone as soon as I can.

Particles look like prepositions, but they act differently. Particles often **change the meaning** of the verb, but prepositions do not.

VERB + PREPOSITION
I **looked up** and saw a large bird.
   (I looked toward the sky.)

VERB + PARTICLE
I **looked up** his number online.
   (I tried to find his number.)

2 Meaning of Phrasal Verbs

A **phrasal verb** has a **special meaning**. It is often very different from the meaning of its parts.

PHRASAL VERB	MEANING	
call in	hire	Let's **call in** an expert to help.
find out	discover	Did you **find out** who was calling you?
turn down	reject	I **turned down** their offer.

USAGE NOTE Phrasal verbs are **less formal** than one-word verbs with similar meaning. They are very **common in everyday speech.**

They **set up** Do Not Call lists. *(less formal)*
They **established** Do Not Call lists. *(more formal)*

BE CAREFUL! Like other verbs, phrasal verbs often have **more than one meaning.**

Please **turn down** the radio. It's too loud.
   (Please lower the volume.)
I **turn down** all telemarketing offers.
   (I reject all telemarketing offers.)

BE CAREFUL! Use the **correct particle**. The particle often changes the meaning of the phrasal verb.

We **handed** *in* our homework.
   (We submitted our homework.)
Then the teacher **handed** *out* our next assignment.
   (Then the teacher distributed our next assignment.)

3 Separable Transitive Phrasal Verbs

Many phrasal verbs are **transitive**—they **take an object**. Most transitive phrasal verbs are **separable**.

PHRASAL VERB	MEANING
call off something	cancel
pick out something	choose
take off something	remove

PHRASAL VERB + OBJECT
Let's **call off** *the meeting*.
I **picked out** *the chair* I like best.
Take off *your coat*.

With a separable transitive phrasal verb, the **noun object** can go:

- **after** the particle

VERB + PARTICLE + OBJECT
I just **took off** *my coat*.

- **between** the verb and the particle

VERB + OBJECT + PARTICLE
I just **took** *my coat* **off**.

BE CAREFUL! When the **object** is a **pronoun**, it must go **between** the verb and the particle. Do not put the pronoun after the particle.

I **took** *it* **off**.
NOT I ~~took off it~~.

USAGE NOTE When the **noun object** is part of a **long phrase**, we usually **do not separate** the verb and particle of a phrasal verb.

I **filled out** *the form from the Do Not Call registry*.
NOT ~~I filled the form from the Do Not Call registry out.~~

With a small group of transitive phrasal verbs, the verb and particle **must be separated**.

PHRASAL VERB	MEANING
ask someone *over*	invite to one's home
see something *through*	complete

Ask *Ian* **over**.   NOT Ask ~~over Ian~~.
I **saw** *the job* **through**.   NOT I saw ~~through the job~~.

4 Inseparable Transitive Phrasal Verbs

Some transitive phrasal verbs are **inseparable**.

With inseparable transitive phrasal verbs, both **noun and pronoun objects** always go **after** the particle. Do not separate the verb from its particle.

I **ran into** *Ed* at work.   NOT I ~~ran Ed into~~ at work.
I **ran into** *him* at work.   NOT I ~~ran him into~~.

A few phrasal verbs can have a **gerund** (verb + -*ing*) as an **object**. The gerund always comes **after** the particle.

They **kept on** *calling*.
Mike **put off** *reporting* the calls to the authorities.

5 Intransitive Phrasal Verbs

Some phrasal verbs are **intransitive**—they do **not take an object**.

PHRASAL VERB	MEANING	VERB + PARTICLE
catch on	become popular	The Do Not Call list has **caught on** everywhere.
sign up	register	Margaret **signed up** last month.
show up	appear	If an unfamiliar number **shows up**, don't answer.

With intransitive phrasal verbs, the verb and particle are **never separated**.

He's been away and just **got back** yesterday.
NOT He's been away and just ~~got yesterday back~~.

USAGE NOTE Intransitive phrasal verbs are often action verbs and they occur frequently in the **imperative**.

Please **come in**.
Don't **call back**!

IN WRITING Intransitive phrasal verbs are very **common in conversation**, but they are **rare in formal writing**.

Her efforts **paid off**. *(conversation)*
Her efforts **were worthwhile**. *(formal writing)*

6 Transitive or Intransitive Phrasal Verbs

Like other verbs, some phrasal verbs can be **both transitive and intransitive**. The meaning is often the same.

He **called** *me* **back**.
He **called back**.
  (He returned my phone call.)

BE CAREFUL! Some phrasal verbs have a completely **different meaning** when they are transitive or intransitive.

We **made up** *a story*. *(We invented a story.)*
We **made up**. *(We ended a disagreement.)*

7 Phrasal Verb + Preposition Combinations

Some **phrasal verbs** are used **in combination with a preposition** (such as *at, from, for, of, on, to,* or *with*).

A **phrasal verb + preposition combination** (also called a *three-word verb*) is usually **inseparable**. The **object** comes **after the preposition**.

PHRASAL VERB + PREPOSITION	MEANING	
come up with something	invent	She **came up *with*** a way to stop junk mail.
drop out of something	quit	He **dropped out *of*** school and got a job.
hang up on someone	end a phone call suddenly	Why did you **hang up *on*** me? I was still talking.

REFERENCE NOTES

For a list of **separable phrasal verbs**, see Appendix 4 on page 455.

For a list of **inseparable transitive phrasal verbs**, see Appendix 4 on page 455.

For a list of **phrasal verbs that must be separated**, see Appendix 4 on page 455.

For a list of **phrasal verb + preposition combinations**, see Appendix 4 on page 455.

For a list of **intransitive phrasal verbs**, see Appendix 5 on page 457.

EXERCISE 1 DISCOVER THE GRAMMAR

A GRAMMAR NOTES 1–7 Read this article about ways of dealing with telemarketers. Underline the phrasal verbs. Circle the objects. See Appendices 4 and 5 on pages 455 and 457 for help.

Getting the Last Laugh

Although your phone number is on the Do Not Call list, every night you still end up with calls from telemarketers. Lots of them. Why not have some fun then? We came up with these amusing tactics:

- When the telemarketer asks, "How are you today?"—tell her! Go over every detail. Don't leave anything out. Say, "I have a headache you wouldn't believe, and my back is acting up again. I ran into an old friend, and I couldn't remember her name! Now I can't figure out the instructions for downloading..."

- When a telemarketer calls during dinner, request his home telephone number so you can call him back. When he refuses, ask him to hold on. Put the phone down and keep on eating until you hear the dial tone.

- Ask the telemarketer to spell her first and last name and the name of the company. Tell her to speak slowly—because you're taking notes. Ask questions until she gives up answering and hangs up.

- To credit card offers, say, "Thanks a lot! My company just laid me off, and I really need the money!"

B Write down a phrasal verb from the article next to its meaning.

1. _____ causing problems

2. _____ review

3. _____ ends a phone call

4. _____ ended employment

5. _____ invented

6. _____ return a call

7. _____ wait

8. _____ omit

9. *end up with* _____ have an unexpected result

10. _____ stop holding

11. _____ understand

12. _____ met accidentally

EXERCISE 2 MEANING OF PHRASAL VERBS

GRAMMAR NOTE 2 A *scam* is a dishonest plan, usually to get money from people. Read about how to avoid some common scams. Complete the information with the correct forms of the phrasal verbs from the boxes. See Appendices 4 and 5 on pages 455 and 457 for help.

end up with	hang up	let down	~~throw out~~

I just _____ *threw out* _____ my first issue of *Motorcycle Mama*. I'm nobody's mama, and I
         1.
don't own a motorcycle, so how did I _____ this subscription? Well, my
                                   2.
neighbor's son was raising money for his soccer team, and I didn't want to _____ him
_____. It's easy to _____ on telemarketers, but it's hard to
     3.   **4.**
say *no* to your friends and neighbors.

fall for	get to	help out	watch out for

The magazine company _____ me through a friendship. It's one of the
                                5.
ways "persuasion professionals" get us to say *yes*. Of course it's OK to _____
                                                  6.
the local soccer team. But a lot of people _____ scams because of similar
                                7.
techniques. Learn to identify and _____ these common scams.
                                8.

find out	give back	go along with	turn down

When someone gives you something, naturally you want to _____ something
_____. This desire to return a favor can cost you money when a telemarketer
     9.
announces you've won a vacation or a new car. Beware! These offers aren't free. When people
_____ them, they always _____ that there's a tax or a fee
     10.   **11.**
to collect the "free" prize. Since they've accepted the offer, they feel obligated to pay. You should
_____ these offers _____. These are scams and they are illegal.
                                12.

count on	fill out	pick out	put on	turn up

A TV actor will _____ a doctor's white jacket and talk about cough
                      13.
medicine. In a magazine ad, a woman in a business suit will help you _____
                                              14.
the best investment firm. Ads with fake "authority figures" are quite easy to identify, but there's an
Internet scam called *phishing* that's harder to recognize. For example, the phisher sends emails that
seem to be from well-known banks. They tell you that a problem with your account has
_____. Then they send you to an Internet site to _____
     15.   **16.**
forms with your account information. The *spoofed* site looks like the real thing, but a real bank will
never ask for your information over the Internet. You can _____ that!
                                              17.

EXERCISE 3 SEPARABLE PHRASAL VERBS AND PRONOUN OBJECTS

A GRAMMAR NOTE 3 Complete the conversations. Use the correct form of the phrasal verb from the first line of the conversation. Include a pronoun object.

1. **A:** Tell Ana not to pick up the phone. It's probably a telemarketer. They call constantly.

    B: Too late. She's already _picked it up_____.

2. **A:** You can't turn down this great offer for cat food!

    B: I'm afraid I have to _____. I don't *have* a cat.

3. **A:** Did you fill out the online Do Not Call form?

    B: I _____ yesterday. I hope this will take care of the problem. I'm tired of these calls.

4. **A:** I left out my office phone and cell phone numbers on that form.

    B: Why did you _____?

5. **A:** Remember to call your mother back.

    B: I _____ last night.

6. **A:** Did you write down the dates of the calls?

    B: I _____, but then I lost the piece of paper.

7. **A:** Can you take my mother's name off your calling list?

    B: Sure. We'll _____ right away.

8. **A:** Let's turn the phone off and have dinner.

    B: I can't _____. I'm expecting an important call.

▶11|02 **B** LISTEN AND CHECK Listen to the conversations and check your answers in A.

EXERCISE 4 SEPARABLE AND INSEPARABLE PHRASAL VERBS

GRAMMAR NOTES 3–4, 7 Complete the ads from spam emails. Use the correct forms of the phrasal verbs and objects in parentheses. Place the object between the verb and the particle when possible. See Appendices 4 and 5 on pages 455 and 457 for help.

LOSE Weight

_____Take those extra pounds off_____ fast! Love bread and cake?
1. (take off / those extra pounds)

Don't _____.
2. (give up / them)

No diet! No pills! No exercise! No worries! Just choose your target weight.

You'll _____ in no time. Our delicious
3. (get to / it)

drinks will _____ while you drop the
4. (fill up / you)

pounds. _____ at no cost. It's FREE
5. (try out / our plan)

for one month. _____ today!
6. (sign up for / it)

Want to know more? Click here for our information request form.

_____ to get our brochure.
7. (fill out / it)

Just _____ and watch those pounds come off! If you do not want to
8. (stick to / our plan)

receive emails from us, we will be more than happy to _____ our list.
9. (take off / you)

MAKE $$$$! WORKING FROM HOME!

_____ cash and increase your savings
1. (turn into / your hobby)

without leaving your home!

My home-based business _____ a day.
2. (take in / $2,000)

That's right—and I _____ every week.
3. (turn down / work)

Sure, I could _____, but I'd rather
4. (take on / employees)

teach you how to _____. This is an
5. (go after / those jobs)

easy business, and you can _____ in a few days. Click on the $, and I'll
6. (set up / it)

_____ right away. _____. If you
7. (send out / the materials)   **8.** (check out / them)

don't like them, _____.
9. (send back / them)

It's as simple as that! Don't _____! Act now! This offer is a money machine,
10. (put off / your decision)

so don't _____. Start to _____ by
11. (pass up / it)   **12.** (cash in on / this great opportunity)

next week!

EXERCISE 5 EDITING

GRAMMAR NOTES 1–7 **Read this transcript of a phone call between a telemarketer (TM) and Janis Linder (JL). There are thirteen mistakes in the use of phrasal verbs. The first mistake is already corrected. Find and correct twelve more. See Appendices 4 and 5 on pages 455 and 457 for help.**

JL: Hello?

TM: This is Bob Watson from *Motorcycle Mama*. I'm calling to offer you a 12-month subscription for the low price of just $15 a year. Can I ~~sign up you~~ *sign you up*?

JL: No thanks. I'm trying to eliminate clutter, so I'm not interested in any more magazine subscriptions. Besides, I just sat up for dinner.

TM: Why don't you at least try out it for six months? This is a great opportunity. Don't miss it out on!

JL: Sorry, I'm really not interested. I don't even have a motorcycle.

TM: Really? When I got on my first motorcycle, I didn't want to get off. Owning a motorcycle is great! You should look into it. And you can count *Motorcycle Mama* on. We'll tell you everything you need to know. Let me send you a free copy of our magazine, and you can look over it.

JL: I'll say this as firmly as I can. I'm not interested. And no matter what you say, I'm not going to fall it for. Please take my name out your list. If you keep on call, I'll notify the authorities. Goodbye.

TM: No, hold out! Don't hang up! Don't turn this great offer off! Chances like this don't come around every day!

JL: OK. I have an idea. Why don't you give me your phone number, and I'll call back you during *your* dinner?

(The telemarketer hangs the phone.)

JL: And good-bye to you, too!

EXERCISE 6 LISTENING

▶11|03 **A** Listen to the conversation between Mr. Chen and a telemarketer. Read the statements. Then listen again and check (✓) *True* or *False*.

	True	False
1. Mr. Chen hangs up immediately.	☐	☑
2. The telemarketer says she wants to help Mr. Chen out with his phone rates.	☐	☐
3. With the Get Together Program, Mr. Chen might run out of minutes.	☐	☐
4. There's a charge for setting up the new phone plan.	☐	☐
5. Mr. Chen figured out the cost of the Get Together Program cell phone.	☐	☐
6. The telemarketer is going to give Mr. Chen some time to think over the plan.	☐	☐
7. Mr. Chen is going to sign up for the service.	☐	☐

▶11|03 **B** Listen to the conversation again. Then work with a partner. Make a list of the advantages and disadvantages of the Get Together Program.

EXAMPLE: **A:** Well, one advantage is that you can call up as many people as you want and talk for as long as you want because of the unlimited minutes.
B: But I think the plan probably leaves out international calls. The telemarketer didn't say anything about international calls. That's a disadvantage.

EXERCISE 7 TO PICK UP OR NOT TO PICK UP

A DISCUSSION Work with a partner. Discuss these questions about telemarketing.

1. What do you think of telemarketing? Does it offer consumers anything positive? Or is it equivalent to junk mail?

EXAMPLE: **A:** I think telemarketing is a terrible idea.
B: It doesn't bother me. I just politely say I have to hang up, and then I get off the phone.

2. Should telemarketing be illegal? Do you go along with the idea of Do Not Call lists? Should some organizations be allowed to keep on calling you? If yes, what kind?

3. Do you think people should just hang up when telemarketers call? Or should they put them off with a polite excuse, such as, "Thanks. I'll think it over."?

B Work in a group. Compare your answers in A with those of your classmates.

EXAMPLE: **A:** My partner and I don't agree about telemarketing, but we came up with . . .
B: We both feel that telemarketing is a huge problem. We hang up, but the telemarketers call back the next day.
C: Have you tried . . . ?
D: We think . . .

EXERCISE 8 SELLING TACTICS

DISCUSSION Work with a group. Bring in an ad from a magazine, a piece of junk mail, spam, or an ad from the Internet. Discuss the ads and the questions below. Use some of the phrasal verbs in the box in your discussion.

EXAMPLE: **A:** I think this ad is trying to get to anyone who wants to make money fast.
B: I agree. It's not really aimed at a specific group of people.
C: It's probably a scam. When you click on OK, I bet they try to get money *from* you! Do you think people would fall for this?

- What group of people might want this product or service (children, teenagers, older people, men, women)?
- What tactics does the ad use to get people to want this product or service?
- Is this an honest offer or a scam? What makes you think so?

cash in on s.t.	fall for s.t.	get to s.o.	miss out
catch on	fill s.t. out	go after s.o.	miss out on s.t.
count on s.t.	find s.t. out	help s.o. out	pay off
end up	get ahead	leave s.t. out	send s.t. back
end up with s.t.	get s.t. out of s.t.	make s.t. up	turn s.t. down

FROM GRAMMAR TO WRITING

A BEFORE YOU WRITE Think about an experience you have had on the phone. It could be a conversation with a friend, a wrong number, or a telemarketing call. Complete the outline.

What Happened During the Phone Call	What I Learned from the Experience
_____	_____
_____	_____
_____	_____

B WRITE Use your outline to write two paragraphs about the experience you had on the phone. In the first paragraph, describe what happened during the call. In the second paragraph, write about what you learned from the experience. Use phrasal verbs. Try to avoid the common mistakes in the chart.

EXAMPLE: When I first got to this country, I had difficulty understanding English on the phone. Because I couldn't figure out what people were saying to me, I often ended up getting into trouble. One day, there was a message on my cell phone. It sounded important, so I called back. That's when I found out . . .

Common Mistakes in Using Phrasal Verbs

Use the **correct particle**. The wrong particle changes the meaning of the verb.	I **picked *up*** the phone when it rang. *(I answered the phone.)* I **picked *out*** the phone because of its features. *(I selected the phone.)*
Put **pronoun** objects **between** the verb and the particle in transitive **separable** phrasal verbs. Do not put pronoun objects after the particle.	When the phone rang, I **picked *it* up**. NOT I ~~picked up it~~.
Put **pronoun** objects **after** the particle in transitive **inseparable** verbs. Do not put pronoun objects after the verb.	Think about this plan before you **settle on *it***. NOT before you ~~settle it on~~.

C CHECK YOUR WORK Read your paragraphs. Underline the phrasal verbs. Circle the objects. Use the Editing Checklist to check your work.

Editing Checklist

Did you use . . . ?

☐ phrasal verbs

☐ the correct particles

☐ pronoun objects between the verb and the particle of separable phrasal verbs

☐ pronoun objects and noun objects after the particle of inseparable phrasal verbs

D REVISE YOUR WORK Read your paragraphs again. Can you improve your writing? Make changes if necessary. Give your paragraphs a title.

UNIT 11 REVIEW

Test yourself on the grammar of the unit.

A Match each phrasal verb with its meaning.

_____ **1.** pick up   **a.** remove

_____ **2.** look into   **b.** meet by accident

_____ **3.** take off   **c.** complete (a form)

_____ **4.** fill out   **d.** return

_____ **5.** run into   **e.** research

_____ **6.** get back   **f.** lift

_____ **7.** give up   **g.** quit

B Complete each sentence with the correct form of the phrasal verb and object in parentheses. Place the object between the verb and particle when possible.

1. I had to _____ .
       (get through with / my work)

2. The phone rang. I didn't want to _____ , but I did.
       (pick up / it)

3. It was Ada. I can always _____ to call late!
       (count on / her)

4. I asked her to _____ in the morning.
       (call back / me)

5. Then I _____ .
       (get off / the phone)

6. I _____ and went to bed.
       (put on / my pajamas)

7. Finally, I _____ and fell asleep.
       (turn off / the lights)

C Find and correct six mistakes.

I'm so tired of telemarketers calling up me as soon as I get back from work or just when I sit up for a relaxing dinner! It's gotten to the point that I've stopped picking the phone when it rings between 6:00 and 8:00 p.m. up. I know I can count on it being a telemarketer who will try to talk me into spending money on something I don't want. But it's still annoying to hear the phone ring, so sometimes I turn off it. Then, of course, I worry that it may be someone important. So I end up checking caller ID to find out. I think the Do Not Call list is a great idea. Who thought up it? I'm going to sign for it up tomorrow!

Now check your answers on page 477.

Adjective Clauses

PART 5

OUTCOMES
- Identify or give additional information about people, places, or things, using adjective clauses with correct subject relative pronouns
- Identify personality traits in a psychology article
- Identify the people described in a conversation
- Take a personality quiz and discuss the results
- Discuss personality traits
- Write about the qualities of a good friend

OUTCOMES
- Identify or give additional information about people, places, or things, using adjective clauses with correct object relative pronouns
- Identify key details in an online book review
- Identify the image described in a recording
- Describe your hometown or city
- Research a successful immigrant and report findings
- Write about a place from one's childhood

Adjective Clauses with Subject Relative Pronouns

PERSONALITY TYPES AND FRIENDS

STEP 1   GRAMMAR IN CONTEXT

BEFORE YOU READ

Look at the cartoon and at the definitions. Discuss the questions.

1. What is the personality of an extrovert? An introvert?

2. Can people with very different personalities get along?

READ

▶12|01   Read this article about extroverts and introverts.

Extroverts and Introverts

Extrovert: someone who loves being in a group of people

Introvert: someone who avoids extroverts

Nadia, who needs to spend several hours alone each day, avoids large social gatherings whenever possible. She hates small talk, and at office holiday parties, which are "must-attend" events, she's always the first one to leave.

You probably know someone like Nadia. Maybe you're even one of those people that nag[1] a friend like her to get out more. If so, stop! Nadia is an introvert, and there's really nothing wrong with that. Introverts are people that get their energy by spending time alone. Their opposites are extroverts, people whose energy comes from being around others. Neither type is better than the other. However, because there are so many more extroverts than introverts, there is a lot of misunderstanding about the introverts among us.

---

1 *nag:* keep telling someone, in way that is very annoying, to do something

First, people have a tendency to think that all introverts are shy. Not so. Shy people fear social situations, but many introverts just try to avoid the ones that drain[2] their energy. Nadia, who is great at leading big, noisy business meetings, isn't afraid of those meetings. But she needs a lot recovery time afterwards. Unlike extroverts, who love the small talk at those meetings, she prefers private conversations that focus on feelings and ideas.

Secondly, people also assume that you have to be an extrovert (or act like one) in order to succeed. However, every day the news is full of examples that contradict that belief. Microsoft's Bill Gates is one famous introvert who comes to mind. Another is successful businesswoman Andrea Jung. Jung, who grew up in a traditional Chinese family, considers herself "reserved," but not shy. A writer who has studied the personality traits of business leaders points out that the one trait which absolutely defines successful leaders is creativity. Introverts are known for being creative, so it shouldn't be a surprise to find many of them at the top of their professions.

What happens when an extrovert and an introvert become friends or fall in love? Opposites attract, but can first attraction survive really big personality differences? Yes, but only if both can accept the other person's needs—and it's not always easy. Extroverts, who have to talk through everything before they even know what they think, can drive an introvert crazy. Nadia, who always thinks before she speaks, doesn't always understand their need to talk. On the other hand, many extroverts, who reach for their cell phones after two minutes alone, can't see why an introvert like Nadia requires so much time by herself. (Is that really *normal*? they wonder.) However, if both people take the time to understand the other's personality type, the results can pay off. The introvert, who has a rich inner life, can help the extrovert become more sensitive to feelings. And the risk-loving extrovert can help the introvert develop a sense of adventure. As a result, each friend's personality becomes more complete.

It's important to remember that no one is a pure introvert or extrovert. In fact, we are probably all "ambiverts," people who act like introverts in some situations and extroverts in others. Like everyone else, you have a unique personality—your own special combination of traits that makes you *you*!

---

2 *drain:* use too much of something so that there is not enough left

AFTER YOU READ

A VOCABULARY   **Complete the sentences with the words from the box.**

contradict	require	sensitive	tendency	trait	unique

1. Extroverts have a _____ to reach for their cell phones.

2. Rahul is so _____. He knows when I'm upset even when I hide my feelings.

3. Nadia hates to _____ people, even when they're obviously wrong.

4. Introverts _____ time alone. They get very unhappy without it.

5. No two people are exactly alike. Everyone is _____.

6. Creativity is a personality _____ of many introverts. It's part of who they are.

COMPREHENSION Read each description. Check (✓) *Introvert* or *Extrovert*.

Who . . . ?	Introvert	Extrovert
1. gets energy from being alone	☐	☐
2. gets energy from other people	☐	☐
3. enjoys small talk	☐	☐
4. likes to talk about ideas and feelings	☐	☐
5. talks while thinking	☐	☐
6. thinks before talking	☐	☐
7. is sensitive to feelings	☐	☐
8. likes to take risks	☐	☐

C DISCUSSION Work with a partner. Compare your answers in B. Why did you choose *Introvert* or *Extrovert*?

STEP 2   GRAMMAR PRESENTATION

ADJECTIVE CLAUSES WITH SUBJECT RELATIVE PRONOUNS

Adjective Clauses After the Main Clause

Main Clause			Adjective Clause		
Subject	Verb	Noun/Pronoun	Subject Relative Pronoun	Verb	
I	read	a book	*that* *which*	discusses	personality.
An introvert	is	someone	*that* *who*	needs	time alone.
			Whose + Noun		
I	have	a friend	*whose* personality	is	like mine.

Adjective Clauses Inside the Main Clause

Main Clause	Adjective Clause			Main Clause (cont.)	
Subject	Subject Relative Pronoun	Verb		Verb	
The book	*that* *which*	**discusses**	**personality**	is	by Ruben.
Someone	*that* *who*	**needs**	**time alone**	may be	an introvert.

	Whose + Noun				
Ana,	*whose* **personality**	**is**	**like mine,**	loves	parties.

GRAMMAR NOTES

1 Purpose of Adjective Clauses

Use **adjective clauses** to **identify** or give **additional information** about **nouns**. The nouns can refer to:

- **people**

I have a ***friend* who avoids parties**.
(The clause who avoids parties *identifies the friend.)*

- **places**

She lives in ***Miami*, which is my hometown**.
(The clause which is my hometown *gives additional information about Miami.)*

- **things**

She has a ***job* that is very interesting**.
(The clause that is very interesting *gives additional information about the job.)*

Adjective clauses can also identify or describe **indefinite pronouns** such as *one, someone, somebody, something, another,* and *other(s)*.

Nadia would like to meet ***someone* who is funny**.
(The clause who is funny *describes the person that Nadia would like to meet.)*

You can think of **sentences with adjective clauses** as a **combination of two sentences**.	*I have a classmate.* + *He is an extrovert.* = I have a classmate **who is an extrovert**.
The **adjective clause follows the noun or pronoun** it is identifying or describing. The adjective clause can come:	
• **inside** the main clause	*My friend calls often.* + *She lives in Rome.* = My friend **who lives in Rome** calls often.
• **after** the main clause	*She has a son.* + *He is a successful doctor.* = She has a son **who is a successful doctor**.
BE CAREFUL! **Do not separate an adjective clause** from the noun or pronoun that it identifies or gives information about.	My friend **who lives in Berlin** seldom calls me. **NOT** My friend ~~seldom calls me who lives in Berlin~~.

Adjective clauses begin with **relative pronouns**. Relative pronouns can be **subjects**.	
Relative pronouns that can be the **subject** of the clause are *who*, *that*, and *which*. Use:	
• *who* or *that* for **people**	SUBJECT I have a **friend *who*** loves spending time alone. SUBJECT I have a **friend *that*** loves spending time alone.
• *which* or *that* for **places** or **things**	SUBJECT There's a **meeting *which*** starts at 10:00 a.m. SUBJECT There's a **meeting *that*** starts at 10:00 a.m.
Relative pronouns always have the **same form**. They do not change for singular and plural nouns or pronouns, or for males and females.	That's the **person *that*** gives great parties. Those are the **people *that*** give great parties. That's the **man *who*** gives great parties. That's the **woman *who*** gives great parties.
USAGE NOTE In **conversation**, we use *that* more often than *who* and *which*. It's less formal.	Nadia is a person ***that*** avoids parties. *(less formal)* Nadia is a person ***who*** avoids parties. *(more formal)*
BE CAREFUL! **Do not use a subject pronoun** (*I*, *you*, *he*, *she*, *it*, *we*, *they*) and a subject relative pronoun in the same adjective clause.	Scott is someone ***who* enjoys** parties. **NOT** Scott is someone who ~~he~~ enjoys parties.
BE CAREFUL! **Do not leave out the subject relative pronoun** in an adjective clause.	Sarah is another person ***who* has** fun at parties. **NOT** Sarah is another person ~~has fun at parties~~.

4 Whose

Some adjective clauses begin with the possessive form *whose*.

Use *whose* + **noun** to show **possession** or **relationship**.	*My friend has a son. + His name is Max.* = My friend has a son *whose* name is Max.
Use *whose* to refer to:	
• people	**Friends** *whose* interests are different can help each other.
• things	I work at a **company** *whose* offices are in London.
BE CAREFUL! **Do not use** *who* + possessive adjective (*my, your, his, her, its, our, their*) instead of *whose*.	Deb is a woman *whose* **personality** is reserved. NOT Deb is a woman ~~who her~~ personality is reserved.

5 Verbs in Adjective Clauses

The **verb in the adjective clause** is **singular** if the subject relative pronoun refers to a singular noun or pronoun. The verb is **plural** if it refers to a plural noun or pronoun.	Ben is my **friend** *who* **lives** in Boston. Al and Ed are my **friends** *who* **live** in Boston.
BE CAREFUL! When *whose* + **noun** is the subject of the adjective clause, **the verb agrees with the noun subject** of the adjective clause.	Ed is a man *whose* **friends are** like family. NOT Ed is a man whose friends ~~is~~ like family.

6 Identifying and Nonidentifying Adjective Clauses

There are two kinds of adjective clauses, **identifying** and **nonidentifying**.

An **identifying** adjective clause is **necessary to identify** the noun it refers to.	I have a lot of good friends. My friend **who lives in Chicago** visits me often. *(The adjective clause is necessary to identify which friend.)*
A **nonidentifying** adjective clause gives **additional information** about the noun it refers to. It is **not necessary to identify** the noun. The noun is often **already identified** with an adjective such as *first, last, best,* or *most,* or the noun is the name of a person or place.	I have a lot of good friends. My *best* friend, **who lives in Chicago**, visits me often. *(The friend has already been identified as the person's best friend. The adjective clause gives additional information, but it isn't needed to identify the friend.)*
BE CAREFUL! **Do not use** *that* to introduce nonidentifying adjective clauses. Use *who* for people and *which* for places and things.	**Ed,** *who* introduced us at the party, called me last night. NOT Ed, ~~that~~ introduced us at the party, called me last night. My favorite city is **Miami,** *which* reminds me of home. NOT My favorite city is Miami, ~~that~~ reminds me of home.

CONTINUED ▶

CONTINUED ▶

IN WRITING Use **commas** to separate a nonidentifying adjective clause from the rest of the sentence.	NONIDENTIFYING ADJECTIVE CLAUSE Bill Gates, **who is a well-known introvert,** founded Microsoft in 1975. NONIDENTIFYING ADJECTIVE CLAUSE I work at Microsoft, **which is located in Seattle.**
BE CAREFUL! **Without commas**, an adjective clause has **a very different meaning** from an adjective clause with commas.	IDENTIFYING ADJECTIVE CLAUSE My friends **who are extroverts** love parties. *(My friends have different personalities. The adjective clause is necessary to identify which ones love parties.)* NONIDENTIFYING ADJECTIVE CLAUSE My friends, **who are extroverts,** love parties. *(All of my friends are extroverts. They all love parties.)*

PRONUNCIATION NOTE

▶ 12|02 **Pronunciation of Identifying and Nonidentifying Adjective Clauses**

In **writing**, we use **commas** around **nonidentifying adjective clauses**.	My sister Marie, **who lives in Seattle,** is an introvert.
In **speaking**, we **pause** briefly **before and after** **nonidentifying** adjective clauses.	My sister Marie [PAUSE] **who lives in Seattle** [PAUSE] is an introvert.
We **do not pause** before and after **identifying** adjective clauses.	My sister **who lives in Seattle** is an introvert.

EXERCISE 1   DISCOVER THE GRAMMAR

GRAMMAR NOTES 1–6   Read this article about two other personality types. Circle the relative pronouns and underline the adjective clauses. Then draw an arrow from the relative pronoun to the noun or pronoun that it refers to.

It's All How You Look at It

It's half empty!

It's half full!

Look at the photo. Do you see a glass (which) is half full or a glass which is half empty? For optimists, people who have a positive view of life, the glass is half full. For pessimists, people who have a negative view of life, the glass is half empty.

Most of us know people who have a strong tendency to be either optimistic or pessimistic. I have a friend whose life motto is "Things have a way of working out." Even when something bad happens, Cindi remains optimistic. Last year, she lost a job that was extremely important to her. She didn't get depressed; she just thought "Well, maybe I'll find a new job that's even better than this one!" But then there is the example of Monica, who always sees the dark side of every situation, even when something good happens. She recently won a lot of money in

a contest. Is she happy about this windfall? Not really. She worries that she won't know how to spend the money wisely. And now she's also worried that her friend Dan, who is struggling to start his own business, will be jealous of her. Cindi and Monica are women whose outlooks on life are as different as day and night.

Former U.S. president Harry Truman defined the two personalities very well: "A pessimist is one who makes difficulties of his opportunities, and an optimist is one who makes opportunities of his difficulties." However, people can learn to make these tendencies less extreme—even Cindi and Monica. Experts who study personality types agree: Half full or half empty, you may not be able to change how much water is in your glass, but you can often change how you view the situation and how you respond to it.

EXERCISE 2 RELATIVE PRONOUNS AND VERBS

GRAMMAR NOTES 3–6 Complete the statements in the personality quiz. Circle the correct words. (In Exercise 9, you will take the quiz.)

Personality Quiz

Do you agree with the following statements? Check (✔) *True* or *False*.

	TRUE	FALSE
1. People (who)/ which talk a lot tire me.	☐	☐
2. On a plane, I always talk to the stranger who take / takes the seat next to me.	☐	☐
3. I'm the kind of person that / which needs time to recover after a social event.	☐	☐
4. My best friend, that / who talks a lot, is just like me.	☐	☐
5. I prefer to have conversations which focus / focuses on feelings and ideas.	☐	☐
6. I am someone whose favorite activities include / includes reading and doing yoga.	☐	☐
7. People whose / their personalities are completely different can be close friends.	☐	☐
8. I'm someone that always see / sees the glass as half full, not half empty.	☐	☐
9. Difficult situations are often the ones that provide / provides the best opportunities.	☐	☐
10. Introverts, that / who are quiet, sensitive, and creative, are perfect friends.	☐	☐

EXERCISE 3 IDENTIFYING ADJECTIVE CLAUSES

Ⓐ GRAMMAR NOTES 1–4, 6 We often use identifying adjective clauses to define words. First, match the words on the left with the descriptions on the right.

_h_	**1.** difficulty	**a.**	This situation gives you a chance to experience something good.
____	**2.** extrovert	**b.**	This attitude shows your ideas about your future.
____	**3.** introvert	**c.**	This ability makes you able to produce new ideas.
____	**4.** opportunity	**d.**	This person usually sees the bright side of situations.
____	**5.** opposites	**e.**	This person requires a lot of time alone.
____	**6.** optimist	**f.**	This money was unexpected.
____	**7.** outlook	**g.**	This person usually sees the dark side of situations.
____	**8.** pessimist	~~h.~~	This problem is hard to solve.
____	**9.** creativity	**i.**	These people have completely different personalities.
____	**10.** windfall	**j.**	This person requires a lot of time with others.

B Now write definitions with adjective clauses for the words on the left. Use the correct description on the right and an appropriate relative pronoun.

1. <u>A difficulty is a problem which is hard to solve.</u> **or** <u>A difficulty is a problem that is hard to solve.</u>

2. _____

3. _____

4. _____

5. _____

6. _____

7. _____

8. _____

9. _____

10. _____

EXERCISE 4 NONIDENTIFYING ADJECTIVE CLAUSES

GRAMMAR NOTES 1–6 Combine the pairs of sentences. Make the second sentence in each pair an adjective clause. Use the correct punctuation. Make any other necessary changes.

1. I'm attending English 101. It meets three days a week.

   <u>I'm attending English 101, which meets three days a week.</u>

2. Sami is an optimist. He's in my English class.

   <u>Sami, who is in my English class, is an optimist.</u>

3. He drives to school with his sister Jena. She wants to go to law school.

   _____

4. Jena is always contradicting him. She loves to argue.

   _____

5. This personality trait never annoys cheerful Sami. He just laughs.

   _____

6. Jena is going to have a great career. Her personality is perfect for a lawyer.

   _____

7. I always look forward to the class. The class meets three days a week.

   _____

8. San Antonio has a lot of community colleges. San Antonio is in Texas.

   _____

9. My school has students from all over the world. It's one of the largest colleges in the country.

   _____

EXERCISE 5 IDENTIFYING OR NONIDENTIFYING ADJECTIVE CLAUSES

GRAMMAR NOTES 1–6 **Read each conversation. Then use the first and last sentences in the conversation to help you write a summary statement. Use adjective clauses. Remember to use commas where necessary.**

1. A: This article is really interesting.
   B: What's it about?
   A: It discusses the different types of personalities.

   SUMMARY: *This article, which discusses the different types of personalities, is really interesting.*

2. A: The office party is going to be at the restaurant.
   B: Which restaurant?
   A: You know the one. It's across the street from the library.

   SUMMARY: _____

3. A: I liked that speaker.
   B: Which one? We heard several!
   A: I forget his name. He talked about optimists.

   SUMMARY: _____

4. A: Bill and Sue aren't close friends with the Swabodas.
   B: No. The Swabodas' interests are very different from theirs.

   SUMMARY: _____

5. A: I lent some chairs to the new neighbors.
   B: Why did they need chairs?
   A: They're having a party tonight.

   SUMMARY: _____

6. A: I'm watching an old video of Jason.
   B: Look at that! He was telling jokes when he was five!
   A: I know. This totally defines his personality.

   SUMMARY: _____

7. A: My boyfriend left me a lot of plants to water.
   B: How come?
   A: He's visiting Venezuela with some friends.

   SUMMARY: _____

EXERCISE 6 IDENTIFYING OR NONIDENTIFYING ADJECTIVE CLAUSES

▶12|03 PRONUNCIATION NOTE **Listen to the sentences. Add commas if you hear pauses around the adjective clauses.**

1. My neighbor, who is an introvert, called me today.

2. My neighbor who is an introvert called me today.

3. My brother who is one year older than me is an extrovert.

4. My sister who lives in Toronto visits us every summer.

5. My friend who is in the same class as me lent me a book.

6. The book which is about personality types is really interesting.

7. The article that won a prize is in today's newspaper.

8. My boyfriend who hates parties actually agreed to go to one with me.

EXERCISE 7 EDITING

GRAMMAR NOTES 1–6 **Read this student's essay about a friend. There are ten mistakes in the use of adjective clauses and their punctuation. The first mistake is already corrected. Find and correct nine more.**

Good Friends

A writer once said friends are born, not made. In other words, we immediately

become friends with people who ~~they~~ are compatible with us. I have to contradict this

writer. Last summer, I made friends with someone which is very different from me.

In July, I went to Mexico City to study Spanish for a month. In our group, there were

twenty students and five adults, who was all language teachers. Two of the teachers

stayed with friends in Mexico City, and we saw those teachers only during the day. But

we spent a lot of time with the teachers, who stayed with us in the dormitory. They

were the ones who helped us when we had problems. After my first two weeks, I had

a problem it was getting me down. Mexico City, that is a very exciting place, was too

distracting. I'm a real extrovert—someone who he wants to go out all the time—and I

stopped going to my classes. As a result, my grades suffered. When they got really bad,

I wanted to leave. Bob Taylor, who was the most serious teacher in the dorm, was very

sensitive to those feelings. But he was also optimistic about my situation. He helped

me get back into my courses which were actually pretty interesting. I managed to do

well after all! After the trip, I kept writing to Mr. Taylor, who's letters are always friendly

and encouraging. Next summer, he's leading another trip what sounds great. It's a

three-week trip to Spain. I hope I can go.

EXERCISE 8 LISTENING

▶12|04 **A** Some friends are at a high school reunion. They haven't seen one another for twenty-five years. Listen to their conversation. Look at the picture. Then listen again to the conversation and write the correct name next to each person.

| Ann | Asha | ~~Bob~~ | Kado | Pat | Pete |

▶12|04 **B** Listen to the conversation again. Then work with a partner. Discuss your answers in A. Explain your choices.

EXAMPLE: **A:** So, the man who is standing is Bob.
    B: Right. And what about Ann? Which person is Ann?
    A: She's the woman who . . .

EXERCISE 9 GETTING PERSONAL

A CONVERSATION Think about your own personality traits. Then take the quiz in Exercise 2 on page 190.

B Work with a partner. Talk about your answers to the quiz. What do you think your answers show about your personality?

EXAMPLE: A: Question 1. People who talk a lot tire me. That's true.
B: I think that means you're probably an introvert. It isn't true for me. I talk a lot, and I enjoy people who talk a lot, too.

EXERCISE 10 QUOTABLE QUOTES

DISCUSSION Work in a group. Read these quotes about friends and personality types. Choose three quotes and discuss them. What do they mean? Do you agree with them? Why or why not? Give examples from your own experience to support your ideas.

1. Show me a friend who will weep[1] with me; those who will laugh with me I can find myself.
   —*Slavic proverb*

   EXAMPLE: A: I think this means it's easier to find friends for good times than for bad times.
   B: I agree. A true friend is someone who is there for you during good *and* bad times.
   C: My best friend in high school was like that. She was someone who . . .

2. An optimist is a guy that has never had much experience.
   —*Don Marquis (U.S. writer, 1878–1937)*

3. He is wise who can make a friend of a foe.[2]
   —*Scottish proverb*

4. A pessimist is one who makes difficulties of his opportunities, and an optimist is one who makes opportunities of his difficulties.
   —*Harry Truman (U.S. president, 1884–1972)*

5. Wherever you are, it is your own friends who make your world.
   —*Ralph Barton Perry (U.S. philosopher, 1876–1957)*

6. A true friend is somebody who can make us do what we can.
   —*Ralph Waldo Emerson (U.S. writer, 1803–1882)*

---

1 *weep:* cry
2 *foe:* enemy

EXERCISE 11 WHAT ARE FRIENDS FOR?

A QUESTIONNAIRE Complete the questionnaire. Check (✓) all the items that you believe are true. Then add your own ideas.

A friend is someone who...

- ☐ **1.** always tells you the truth
- ☐ **2.** has known you for a very long time
- ☐ **3.** cries with you
- ☐ **4.** lends you money
- ☐ **5.** talks to you every day
- ☐ **6.** helps you when you are in trouble
- ☐ **7.** listens to your problems
- ☐ **8.** does things with you
- ☐ **9.** respects you
- ☐ **10.** accepts you the way you are
- ☐ **11.** is sensitive to your feelings
- ☐ **12.** gives you advice
- ☐ **13.** keeps your secrets
- ☐ **14.** never contradicts you

Other: _____

_____

_____

B Work with a partner. Compare your answers to the questionnaire. Discuss the reasons for your choices.

EXAMPLE: **A:** I think a friend is someone who always tells you the truth.
B: I don't agree. Sometimes the truth can hurt you.

C After your discussion, tally the results of the whole class. Discuss the results.

EXAMPLE: **A:** I'm surprised. Only three people said a friend is someone who always tells you the truth.
B: I'm not surprised. You want friends that are honest, but maybe not always.
C: I agree. The truth could be something that's painful. A friend might want to protect you.

FROM GRAMMAR TO WRITING

A BEFORE YOU WRITE Think about your friends. Complete the outline.

A Good Friend Is Someone Who...   **Description of My Best Friend**

_____   _____

_____   _____

B WRITE Use your outline to write two paragraphs about your best friend. In the first paragraph, describe what a good friend should do. In the second paragraph, describe your best friend. Use adjective clauses with subject relative pronouns. Try to avoid the common mistakes in the chart.

EXAMPLE: Ralph Waldo Emerson said, "A true friend is somebody who can make us do what we can." I completely agree. A friend is someone who...

My best friend, whose name is Fran, is the perfect example of a true friend. She...

Common Mistakes in Using Adjective Clauses with Subject Relative Pronouns

Use an adjective clause **after a noun or pronoun** to **identify** or **give additional information** about a person, place, or thing. Do not separate the adjective clause and the noun or pronoun.	A *person* who is a true friend will always help you. NOT A person ~~will always help you who is a true friend~~.
Use *who*, *which*, or *that* as the **subject relative pronoun** in an adjective clause. Do not use subject pronouns (*I*, *you*, *he*, *she*, *it*, *we*, *they*).	I have a friend *who* is always there for me. NOT I have a friend ~~he~~ is always there for me. NOT I have a friend who ~~he~~ is always there for me.
Use a **singular verb** in the adjective clause if the subject relative pronoun refers to a singular noun or pronoun. Use a **plural verb** if the relative pronoun refers to a plural noun or pronoun.	I have **a friend *who* understands** me. NOT I have a friend who ~~understand~~ me. Joe has **friends *who* understand** him. NOT Joe has friends who ~~understands~~ him.

C CHECK YOUR WORK Read your paragraphs. Underline the adjective clauses. Circle the relative pronouns. Use the Editing Checklist to check your work.

Editing Checklist

Did you use...?

☐ *who*/*that* for people, *which*/*that* for places and things, *whose* for possession or relationship

☐ the correct verb form in adjective clauses

☐ identifying adjective clauses to identify a noun

☐ nonidentifying adjective clauses to give more information about a noun

☐ commas to separate nonidentifying adjective clauses

D REVISE YOUR WORK Read your paragraphs again. Can you improve your writing? Make changes if necessary. Give your paragraphs a title.

UNIT 12 REVIEW

Test yourself on the grammar of the unit.

A Circle the correct words to complete the sentences.

1. I have a lot of friends who is / are introverts.

2. Maria is someone whose / who idea of a good time is staying home.

3. Ben, who always think / thinks carefully before he speaks, is very sensitive to people's feelings.

4. He lives in Los Angeles, which / that is a city I'd love to visit.

5. He wrote a book about personality types that / it is very interesting.

6. My friend who / which read it liked it a lot.

B Complete each sentence with a relative pronoun (*who*, *which*, *that*, or *whose*) and the correct form of the verb in parentheses.

1. Thinkers and Feelers are types of people _____ very differently.
   (behave)

2. A Thinker, _____ facts to make decisions, is a very logical person.
   (use)

3. Emotions, _____ usually _____ a Feeler, are more important
   (convince)
   than facts to this personality type.

4. A Thinker is someone _____ always _____ fairly and honestly.
   (speak)

5. A Feeler avoids saying things _____ another person's feelings.
   (hurt)

6. I dislike arguments, _____ usually _____ me. I guess I'm a Feeler.
   (upset)

7. Ed, _____ personality _____ different from mine, loves to argue.
   (be)

C Find and correct seven mistakes. Remember to check punctuation.

It's true that we are often attracted to people which are very different from ourselves. An extrovert, which personality is very outgoing, will often connect with a romantic partner who are an introvert. They are both attracted to someone that have different strengths. My cousin Valerie who is an extreme extrovert, recently married Bill, whose idea of a party is a Scrabble game on the Internet. Can this marriage succeed? Will Bill learn the salsa, that is Valerie's favorite dance? Will Valerie start collecting unusual words? Their friends, that care about both of them, are hoping for the best.

Now check your answers on page 478.

Adjective Clauses with Object Relative Pronouns
THE IMMIGRANT EXPERIENCE

OUTCOMES
• Identify or give additional information about people, places, or things, using adjective clauses with correct object relative pronouns
• Identify key details in an online book review
• Identify the image described in a recording
• Describe your hometown or city
• Research a successful immigrant and report findings
• Write about a place from one's childhood

STEP 1   GRAMMAR IN CONTEXT

BEFORE YOU READ

Look at the photo on page 200 and at the title of the reading. Discuss the questions.

1. Who is the man in the photo? Where is he?

2. How do you think he feels?

READ

  Read this post from a class blog.

Sociology 139
The Immigrant Experience

HOME   ABOUT THIS BLOG   POSTS

Stories of a New Generation of Immigrants

Posted on March 21, 2016 by Alicia Arash — Leave a Comment

Immigrant Voices: 21st-Century Stories is one of the best books that I've ever read. The stories which editors Achy Obejas and Megan Bayles selected for the anthology[1] are powerful. They offer a compelling view into the lives of the current generation of immigrants to the United States. Of the eighteen stories in the book, my personal favorite is "Absence."

"Absence" is about Wari, a painter from Lima, Peru. His experiences illustrate many of the issues immigrants encounter. As he walks on the streets of New York, Wari is excited about the newness around him. But he is alone. The people who he loves are in Lima,

---

1 *anthology:* a book of stories or poems by different authors

Adjective Clauses with Object Relative Pronouns   **199**

and he is unable to communicate with almost everyone he meets because he doesn't speak English. Most importantly, he wonders if he is still an artist. After all, his paint, brushes, and pencils are among the things that he left in Peru.

Wari's problems began at the U.S. Embassy in Lima, where he went for a visa. Wari had an invitation from an American university to exhibit his paintings. His plan was to get a three-month visa, which he could use for a double purpose. He hoped to show his artwork and also to have enough time to make a decision about whether to remain in the United States. Instead of three months, he received a visa for only one month, but he continued preparing for the day when he would fly from Lima to Miami and on to New York. When he got to Miami, an immigration officer said Wari didn't have enough money to stay in the United States for one month and reduced his visa to just two weeks.

When "Absence" ends on the evening of Wari's art exhibit, the big questions remain unanswered. Is Wari ready for life outside of Peru? Will he lose his connection to the place where he grew up? Will he experience poverty and loneliness as he struggles with life in a new country?

My grandfather, with whom I have a close relationship, came to the United States as a young man. Maybe because of him, I feel connected to the people whose stories I read in *Immigrant Voices*. However, I'm certain this is a book that you'll be interested in, too. Once you start reading, you won't put it down!

AFTER YOU READ

VOCABULARY Complete the sentences with the words from the box.

compelling	encounter	generation	issue	poverty	struggle

1. Every day, I _____ new words in English, but I try to meet the challenge.

2. It's always interesting to hear the older _____ talk about how life used to be.

3. My grandfather was very poor. He left his country to escape from a life of _____.

4. The stories in the book are _____. I couldn't stop reading them.

5. The food in this country is a(n) _____ for me. I don't want to eat anything here.

6. Life can be difficult for immigrants, who often _____ to learn a lot in a very short time.

Ⓑ COMPREHENSION Check (✓) the boxes to complete the statements. Check all the true information from the blog post.

1. Alicia Arash _____ the book *Immigrant Voices*.
   ☐ recommends   ☐ has read   ☐ selected stories for

2. Wari's experiences are _____ the experiences of many immigrants.
   ☐ similar to   ☐ better than   ☐ harder than

3. Wari _____ in the United States.
   ☐ speaks English with everyone   ☐ has family and friends   ☐ has nothing to paint with

4. Wari got his visa at the embassy in _____.
   ☐ Lima   ☐ Miami   ☐ New York

5. Wari wanted a three-month visa in order to _____, but he got a two-week visa instead.
   ☐ attend his art exhibit   ☐ decide if he would immigrate   ☐ learn English

6. Alicia Arash feels a connection to _____.
   ☐ Wari   ☐ the immigrants in the book   ☐ her grandfather

Ⓒ DISCUSSION Work with a partner. Compare your answers in B. Why did you check the boxes your checked?

ADJECTIVE CLAUSES WITH OBJECT RELATIVE PRONOUNS OR *WHERE* AND *WHEN*

Adjective Clauses After the Main Clause

Main Clause			Adjective Clause		
Subject	Verb	Noun/Pronoun	(Object Relative Pronoun)	Subject	Verb
He	read	the book	(*that*) (*which*)	she	**wrote**.
She	is	someone	(*who[m]*)	I	**respect**.
			Whose + Noun		
That	is	the author	*whose* book	I	**read**.
			Where/(*When*)		
She	loves	the city	*where*	she	**grew up**.
They	cried	the day	(*when*)	they	**left**.

Adjective Clauses Inside the Main Clause

Main Clause	Adjective Clause			Main Clause (cont.)	
Subject	(Object Relative Pronoun)	Subject	Verb	Verb	
The book	(*that*) (*which*)	I	**read**	is	great.
Someone	(*who[m]*)	you	**know**	was	there.
	Whose + Noun				
The man	*whose* sister	you	**know**	writes	books.

Main Clause	Adjective Clause			Main Clause (cont.)	
Subject	*Where*/(*When*)	Subject	Verb	Verb	
The library	*where*	I	**work**	has	videos.
The summer	(*when*)	she	**left**	passed	slowly.

GRAMMAR NOTES

1 Object Relative Pronouns

In Unit 12, you learned about adjective clauses in which the **relative pronoun** was the **subject** of the clause.	SUBJECT *Achy Obejas is a writer.* + ***She** was born in Cuba.* = SUBJECT Achy Obejas, ***who was born in Cuba***, is a writer.
A **relative pronoun** can also be the **object** of an adjective clause.	OBJECT *Obejas is also a journalist.* + *I saw **her** on TV.* OBJECT Obejas, ***who I saw on TV***, is also a journalist.
Like subject relative pronouns, **object relative pronouns** come at the **beginning** of the adjective clause.	SUBJECT Ben, ***who lives in California***, is a journalist. OBJECT Ben, ***who we just met***, reports on music.
Relative pronouns (subject or object) always have the **same form**. They do not change for singular and plural nouns or pronouns, or for males and females.	That's the **student *who*** I met. Those are the **students *who*** I met. That's the **man *who*** I met. That's the **woman *who*** I met.
The subject and the verb of the adjective clause follow the **object relative pronoun**. The **verb in the adjective clause** is singular if the subject of the clause is singular. It is plural if the subject of the clause is plural.	OBJ. + SUBJ. + VERB I like the blog posts ***which she writes***. I like the blog posts ***which they write***.
BE CAREFUL! **Do not use an object pronoun** (*me, you, him, her, it, us, them*) and an object relative pronoun in the same adjective clause.	She is the writer ***who* I saw** on TV. NOT She is the writer who I saw ~~her~~ on TV.

2 Identifying and Nonidentifying Adjective Clauses

As you have seen in Unit 12, there are two kinds of adjective clauses:	
• **identifying**	IDENTIFYING ADJECTIVE CLAUSE I read a lot of books. The book **which I just finished** was very powerful. *(The adjective clause is necessary to identify which book I mean.)*
• **nonidentifying**	NONIDENTIFYING ADJECTIVE CLAUSE I read a lot of books. ***This*** book, **which I just finished**, was very powerful. *(I'm pointing to the book, so the adjective clause isn't necessary to identify it. The clause gives additional information.)*
IN WRITING Use **commas** to separate a **nonidentifying** adjective clause from the rest of the sentence. In **speaking**, use short **pauses** to separate the **nonidentifying** adjective clause.	*The Rice Room*, **which I read last year,** is a great book. *The Rice Room* [PAUSE] **which I read last year** [PAUSE] is a great book.

Relative pronouns that can be the **object of the verb** in an adjective clause are *who(m)*, *which*, and *that*.

Use *whom*, *who*, or *that* for **people**:	VERB + OBJ. *She's a woman.* + *I admire **her**.* =
• *whom*	She's a woman ***whom** I admire.* MORE FORMAL
• *who*	She's a woman ***who** I admire.*
• *that*	She's a woman ***that** I admire.*
You can also **leave out the object relative pronoun** in an **identifying** adjective clause.	She's a woman **I admire.** LESS FORMAL

Use *which* or *that* for **things**:	VERB + OBJ. *I read a book.* + *She wrote **it**.* =
• *which*	I read a book ***which** she wrote.* MORE FORMAL
• *that*	I read a book ***that** she wrote.*
You can also **leave out the relative pronoun** in **identifying** adjective clauses.	I read a book **she wrote.** LESS FORMAL

USAGE NOTE In **conversation**, most people use *that* or **no relative pronoun** for the object of the verb in an **identifying** adjective clause.	IDENTIFYING ADJECTIVE CLAUSE A: Did you read the article ***that** Alicia posted?* B: Yes. I like all the articles **she puts on our blog.**

BE CAREFUL! **Do not use** *that* in a **nonidentifying** adjective clause.	NONIDENTIFYING ADJECTIVE CLAUSE Alicia's post, ***which** we all read*, was interesting. NOT Alicia's post, ~~that~~ we all read, was interesting.

BE CAREFUL! **Do not leave out the relative pronoun** in a **nonidentifying** adjective clause.	NONIDENTIFYING ADJECTIVE CLAUSE I remember Wari, ***who** she described very clearly.* NOT I remember Wari, ~~she described very clearly~~.

Relative pronouns that can be the **object of a preposition** in an adjective clause are *who(m)*, *which*, and *that*.

Use *whom*, *who*, or *that* for **people**:	PREP. + OBJ. *He's the writer. + I work **for him**. =*
• preposition + *whom*	He's the writer **for whom** I work. MORE FORMAL
• *whom* . . . + preposition	He's the writer **whom** I work **for**.
• *who* . . . + preposition	He's the writer **who** I work **for**.
• *that* . . . + preposition	He's the writer **that** I work **for**.
You can also **leave out the object relative pronoun** in an **identifying** adjective clause.	He's the writer I work **for**. LESS FORMAL

Use *which* or *that* for **things**:	PREP. + OBJ. *This is a book. + I am interested **in it**. =*
• preposition + *which*	This is a book **in which** I am interested. MORE FORMAL
• *which* . . . + preposition	This is a book **which** I am interested **in**.
• *that* . . . + preposition	This is a book **that** I am interested **in**.
You can also **leave out the relative pronoun** in **identifying** adjective clauses.	This is a book I am interested **in**. LESS FORMAL

USAGE NOTE In **conversation**, most people use *that* or **no relative pronoun** for the object of a preposition in an **identifying** adjective clause. The **preposition** comes at the **end of the clause**.	IDENTIFYING ADJECTIVE CLAUSE A: Here's the story **that** she was talking **about**. B: But it isn't the story **I've been looking for**!

BE CAREFUL! Do not use *that* in a **nonidentifying** adjective clause.	NONIDENTIFYING ADJECTIVE CLAUSE Wari's story, **which** I was impressed **by**, was powerful. NOT Wari's story, ~~that~~ I was impressed by, was powerful.

BE CAREFUL! Do not leave out the relative pronoun in a **nonidentifying** adjective clause.	NONIDENTIFYING ADJECTIVE CLAUSE My grandmother, **who** I often write **to**, lives in Peru. NOT My grandmother, ~~I often write to~~, lives in Peru.

5 Whose

Some adjective clauses begin with *whose* + noun object to show possession or relationship.	
Whose + noun object comes at the beginning of the adjective clause. You cannot leave out *whose*.	POSS. + NOUN OBJ. *They're the immigrants.* + *We read **their stories**.* = They're the immigrants ***whose stories** we read.*
The noun following *whose* can be the object of: • the verb in the adjective clause • a preposition in the adjective clause	OBJECT VERB The professor ***whose** class we like* studies immigration. OBJECT PREP. She's an author ***whose** book we're excited **about**.*
Use *whose* to refer to: • people • things	I like **authors** ***whose*** books I can feel connected to. It's a **book** ***whose*** main character I love.
BE CAREFUL! Do not use *who* + possessive adjectives (*my, your, his, her, its, our, their*) instead of *whose*.	He's a writer ***whose*** stories I will never forget. **NOT** He's a writer ~~who his~~ stories I will never forget.

6 Where and When

Where and *when* can also begin adjective clauses.	
Use: • *where* for a place • *when* (or *that*) for a time	That's the library ***where*** she works. I remember the day ***when*** I met him. I remember the day ***that*** I met him.
You can leave out *when* or *that* in identifying adjective clauses.	I remember the day I met him.
USAGE NOTE Instead of *where*, we sometimes use preposition + *which/that* to begin an adjective clause.	The building ***where*** I live is old. The building ***in which*** I live is old. The building ***which*** I live ***in*** is old. The building ***that*** I live ***in*** is old.
We can also leave out *which* or *that*. Preposition + *which/that* is more formal than *where*.	The building I live ***in*** is old.
BE CAREFUL! Do not use a preposition with *where*.	The street ***where*** they live is quiet. **NOT** The street where they live ~~on~~ is quiet.
BE CAREFUL! *Where* cannot be the subject of an adjective clause.	New York is a city ***that has many immigrants***. **NOT** New York is a city ~~where~~ has many immigrants.

REFERENCE NOTE

For more information on **identifying and nonidentifying adjective clauses**, see Unit 12 on page 187.

EXERCISE 1 DISCOVER THE GRAMMAR

Ⓐ GRAMMAR NOTES 1–6 Read a second blog post by Alicia Arash. Underline the adjective clauses and circle the relative pronouns, *where*, and *when*. Then draw an arrow from each relative pronoun to the noun or pronoun that it refers to.

● ● ●

Sociology 139
The Immigrant Experience

HOME   ABOUT THIS BLOG   POSTS

When Reality Hits Home

Posted on March 22, 2016 by Alicia Arash — Leave a Comment

In the compelling story "Absence," author Daniel Alarcón explains what happens to most immigrants. Eventually, there is a day (when) the newness of a new country ends. Suddenly, the things that immigrants used to be interested in become annoying. Even worse, these things become problems for the immigrant. For example, the stores where they shop suddenly seem small, crowded, and expensive. Or they continue to struggle with English, which they have been studying for many months.

At this point, the list of things that immigrants miss from their home country begins to grow. They think about the boss whose name they once wanted to forget. Amazingly, they remember him as someone who they respected and admired. They have memories of quiet streets and beautiful parks where their children played without a care in the world. And the food back home was fresh and mouth-wateringly delicious. Most of all, they remember the warmth of the people, with whom they could always connect. They miss the feeling of fitting in and belonging.

Fortunately, 21st-century immigrants can call or Skype with friends and family who they've left behind. They can also use money that they've earned in their new country to travel back to their old country for a visit. Immigrants of previous generations didn't have these advantages.

B Read this conversation between Alicia and her classmate Ade. There are six adjective clauses without relative pronouns. The first one is already underlined. Find and underline five more. Then add appropriate relative pronouns.

ADE: The two articles ^*that* or *which* you posted on our class blog are great!

ALICIA: Thanks. I wrote the first one the day I finished reading *Immigrant Voices*. You can tell I was really excited about the book, can't you?

ADE: You're not alone. My sister loves immigrant literature. It's something she talks about all the time. In fact, the "birthday box" she sent me last week had a copy of *Immigrant Voices* in it.

ALICIA: Have you read it yet?

ADE: Not yet. But I will. It's on the list of things I'm going to do after midterm exams.

ALICIA: Well, as I said in my blog post, you'll love the book. By the way, you're from Nigeria, aren't you?

ADE: I was born in Nigeria. But this is the country I grew up in. I think of myself as Nigerian-American.

EXERCISE 2 RELATIVE PRONOUNS AND VERBS

GRAMMAR NOTES 1–4, 6 Complete this interview from a high-school newspaper. Use *who(m)*, *that*, *which*, *where*, or *when* and the correct forms of the verbs in parentheses.

The
Grover   September 19, 2016
              page 3   **MEET YOUR
                                                            CLASSMATES**

Maniya, _____ *who* _____ a lot of our readers already

_____ *know* _____, has been at Grover High for three years
    1. (know)

now. We interviewed Maniya, who is from the Philippines, about

her experiences as a new immigrant in the United States.

INTERVIEWER: How did your family choose Atlanta, Maniya?

MANIYA: My cousin, _____ we _____ with at first, lives here.
                                              2. (stay)

INTERVIEWER: What were your first impressions?

MANIYA: At first, it was a lot of fun. We arrived here at the beginning of the summer,

_____ there _____ no school, so I didn't feel much
                              3. (be)

pressure to speak English.

INTERVIEWER: What problems did you encounter when you finally went to school?

MANIYA: Of course, the class in _____ I _____ the biggest
                                                        4. (have)
problems at first was English. I struggled to write compositions and to say the

things _____ I _____ to say. It was really a big issue
                                    5. (want)
for me. Now it's much easier. I have a much stronger connection to English now.

INTERVIEWER: What was the biggest change for you when you got here?

MANIYA: We used to live in a big house, _____ there _____
                                                                              6. (be)
always a lot of people. We were several generations under one roof. Here I live

with just my parents and sister, _____ I _____
                                                                  7. (take care of)
after school.

INTERVIEWER: How did you learn English so quickly?

MANIYA: At night, I write words and idioms on a small piece of paper _____

I _____ in my pocket. Then I study them at school whenever I have
        8. (put)
a chance between classes.

INTERVIEWER: Is there anything _____ you still _____ trouble with?
                                                                  9. (have)
MANIYA: One thing _____ I still _____ hard to do is to make
                                              10. (find)
jokes in English. Some things are funny in Tagalog but not in English.

EXERCISE 3 IDENTIFYING ADJECTIVE CLAUSES

GRAMMAR NOTES 1–6 Complete the story. Use the sentences from the box. Change them
to identifying adjective clauses and use relatives pronouns, *where*, or *when*.

I drank coffee there every day.	I knew her sister from school.	Many students attended it.
I had to leave Cracow then.	I loved it very much.	We both felt very good about it.

Cracow is a city in Poland ___*that I loved very much* **or** *which I loved very much*___.
                                                                              1.

I lived there until I came to the United States. My parents owned a café in the town center

_____. One day, I met a woman
                                    2.

there _____. Her sister and I were in
                            3.

a class together _____. The woman
                                    4.

and I felt a strong connection _____.
                                                  5.

For me, the day _____ was very sad.
                            6.

EXERCISE 4 NONIDENTIFYING ADJECTIVE CLAUSES

GRAMMAR NOTES 1–6 **Complete this article about Ben Fong-Torres. Use the sentences in parentheses to write nonidentifying adjective clauses with relative pronouns, *where*, or *when*. Don't forget to add commas.**

Ben Fong-Torres was born in Alameda, California, in 1945. He was the son of first-generation Chinese parents. To escape a life of poverty, his father immigrated to the Philippines and then to the United States _, where he settled down_____. His mother came to the
1. (He settled down there.)
United States ten years later _____.
2. (Their marriage was arranged by relatives then.)

Fong-Torres, along with his brother and sister, grew up in the city of Oakland, California

_____. His family owned a Chinese
3. (There was a large Chinese community there.)
restaurant _____ when they were not in school.
4. (All the children worked there.)
Young Ben was always an enthusiastic reader of cartoons and a huge fan of popular music

_____. At the age of twelve, Ben went with his
5. (He heard it on the radio.)
father to Texas _____. Ben encountered problems
6. (They opened another Chinese restaurant there.)
there because he was among people who had had no previous contact with Asians.

Back in Oakland, after the failure of the Texas restaurant, Ben got jobs writing for various

magazines and newspapers. His interviews with hundreds of rock stars included the Beatles and

the Rolling Stones _____. He also did an
7. (He loved their music.)
interview with Ray Charles _____. Fong-Torres
8. (He won an award for it.)
was a DJ for San Francisco radio station KSAN, which

plays rock music, and in 1976 he won an award for

broadcasting excellence.

Fong-Torres and his wife Dianne Sweet

_____
9. (He married her in 1976.)
still live in San Francisco. He hosts many events

for the Chinese-American community in that

city and continues to write about music for

publications such as the e-zine (Internet

magazine) www.AsianConnections.com.

Dianne and Ben Fong-Torres

EXERCISE 5 IDENTIFYING AND NONIDENTIFYING ADJECTIVE CLAUSES

GRAMMAR NOTES 1–6 Combine the pairs of sentences. Make the second sentence in each pair an adjective clause. Make any other necessary changes. Use relative pronouns, *where*, or *when* only when necessary.

1. That's the house. I grew up in the house.

   That's the house I grew up in. or *That's the house where I grew up.*

2. I lived with my parents and my siblings. You've met them.

   _____

3. I had two sisters and an older brother. I felt a close connection to my sisters.

   _____

4. My sisters and I shared a room. We spent nights talking there.

   _____

5. My brother slept on the living room couch. I hardly ever saw him.

   _____

6. It was a large old couch. My father had made the couch himself.

   _____

7. My best friend lived across the hall. I loved her family.

   _____

8. We went to the same school. We both studied English there.

   _____

9. Mr. Robinson was our English teacher. Everyone was a little afraid of Mr. Robinson.

   _____

10. After school, I worked in a bakery. My aunt and uncle owned it.

   _____

11. They sold delicious bread and cake. People stood in line for hours to buy the bread and cake.

   _____

12. My brother and sisters live far away now. I miss them.

   _____

13. When we get together, we like to talk about the old days. We all lived at home then.

   _____

EXERCISE 6 EDITING

GRAMMAR NOTES 1–6 Read this student's book report. There are eleven mistakes in the use of adjective clauses with object relative pronouns and their punctuation. The first one is already corrected. Find and correct ten more.

Eva Hoffman spent her early childhood in Cracow, Poland, the city ~~that~~ *where* or *in which* she was born.

When she was thirteen, she moved with her family to Vancouver, Canada. Her autobiography,

Lost in Translation: A Life in a New Language, that she wrote in 1989, describes her

experiences as she leaves Cracow, the city which she called it home.

In spite of her family's poverty and small, crowded apartment, Ewa Wyda (Hoffman's

Polish name) loved her native city. It was a place when life was lived intensely. She used

to visit the city's many cafés with her father, that she watched in lively conversations with

his friends. Hoffman remembers her neighbors as people, who she spent many happy hours

with. Among them was Marek, who apartment she visited almost daily and who she always

believed she would one day marry.

Madame Witeszczak who Ewa took piano lessons from, was the last person which Ewa

said goodbye to before she left Poland. "What do you think you'll miss most?" her teacher

asked. "Everything. Cracow. The school . . . you. Everything . . ."

At her new school in Vancouver, Hoffman is given her English name, Eva, that her

teachers find easier to pronounce. Ewa, however, feels no connection to the name. In fact,

she feels no connection to the English name of anything what she feels is important. All her

memories are still in her first language, Polish.

The story of Eva as she grows up and comes to terms with her new identity and language

is fascinating and moving. It's a familiar story that all immigrants can relate to.

EXERCISE 7   LISTENING

▶13|02   **A**   Look at the pictures. Then listen to an author's description of her childhood room. Listen again and circle the number of the picture that the woman describes.

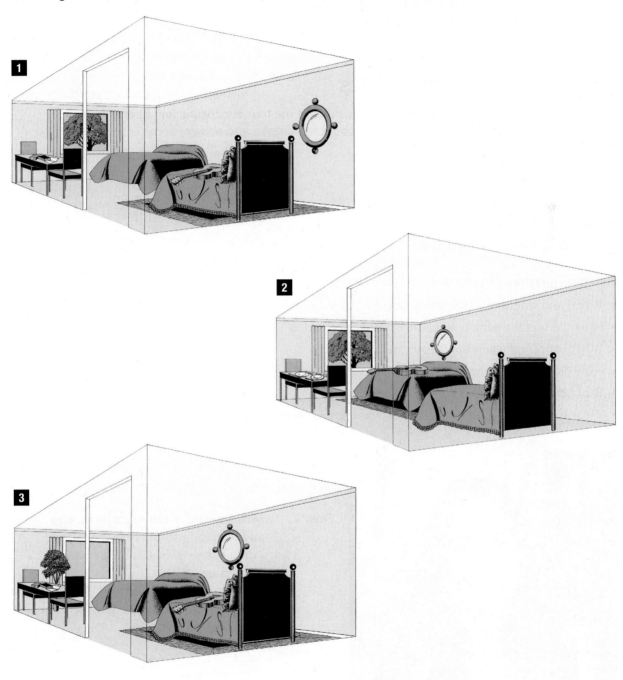

▶13|02   **B**   Listen to the interview again. Then work with a partner. Discuss your answer in A. Why did you choose that picture? Why didn't you choose one of the other two pictures?

EXAMPLE: A: How did you decide which room to choose?

           B: First of all, the bed that Maria's sister slept in . . .

EXERCISE 8 HOME SWEET HOME

CONVERSATION Work with a partner. Talk about the people and places in your hometown that are important to you. Use three of your own photos or pictures that you found on the Internet.

EXAMPLE: A: I love my hometown. This is the street where we lived before we moved here.
B: Is that the house you grew up in?
A: Yes, it is. I lived there until I was fifteen.

EXERCISE 9 SUCCESS STORIES

(A) GROUP PROJECT Work in a group. Choose one of the four successful immigrants to the United States listed below. Do research about the person and answer some of the questions.

- José Hernández, astronaut
- Mila Kunis, actress
- Jhumpa Lahiri, author
- Jerry Yang, Internet entrepreneur

Possible questions:
- When and where was the person born?
- How old was the person when he or she immigrated?
- What happened when the person immigrated?
- How did the person become successful?
- What connection does the person have to his or her country of birth?
- What is the most interesting fact that you learned about the person?

EXAMPLE: A: Mila Kunis is famous for the movies and television shows that she's made.
B: I didn't know this. Look. She was born in Ukraine.
C: Her family immigrated . . .
D: During the first months that she lived in the United States . . .

B Report back to your class. If your group chose the same person as another group, do you have the same information about that person? Compare answers.

EXAMPLE: A: Mila Kunis is famous for all the Hollywood movies that she's made.
   B: Don't forget about television. Here's a list of the shows that she's appeared in.
   A: She was born in Ukraine.
   B: Right. But her family immigrated . . .
   A: . . .

EXERCISE 10 QUOTABLE QUOTES

DISCUSSION Work in a group. Read these quotes about home. Choose three quotes and discuss them. What do they mean? Do you agree with them? Why or why not? Give examples from your own experience to support your ideas.

1. Home is where the heart is.
   —*Pliny the Elder (Roman soldier and encyclopedist, 23–79)*

   EXAMPLE: A: I think this means that home is not always a place.
      B: I agree. It's a feeling that you have.
      C: I think it can be a place or person that you love.

2. Home is where one starts from.
   —*T. S. Eliot (British poet, 1888–1965)*

3. Home is the place where you feel happy.
   —*Salman Rushdie (Indian author, 1947–)*

4. Home is a place you grow up wanting to leave, and grow old wanting to get back to.
   —*John Ed Pearce (U.S. journalist, 1917–2006)*

5. Home is not where you live but where they understand you.
   —*Christian Morgenstern (German poet, 1871–1914)*

6. Home is the place where, when you have to go there, they have to take you in.
   —*Robert Frost (U.S. poet, 1874–1963)*

Ⓐ BEFORE YOU WRITE Think about a place from your childhood. Complete the outline.

Place: _____

Description of the Place	Why the Place Was Important to Me
_____	_____
_____	_____

Ⓑ WRITE Use your outline to write two paragraphs about an important place from your childhood. In the first paragraph, describe the place. In the second paragraph, explain why the place was important to you. Use adjective clauses with object relative pronouns, *where*, or *when*. Try to avoid the common mistakes in the chart.

EXAMPLE: The town where I grew up was the perfect place for a child. Living there was like living in an earlier century. We didn't lock our doors, and my best friend, who I saw every day, could visit anytime she wanted to. The house that my family owned was . . .

Common Mistakes in Using Adjective Clauses with Object Relative Pronouns

Use *who(m)*, *which*, or *that* as **the object relative pronoun** in an adjective clause. Do not use an object pronoun (*me*, *you*, etc.) and an object relative pronoun in the same adjective clause.	I remember the big dinners *that* we had on holidays. NOT I remember the big dinners that we had ~~them~~ on holidays.
Use *who(m)*, *which*, *whose*, *where*, or *when* to start **nonidentifying** adjective clauses. Do not use *that*.	My best friend, *who* I saw daily, lived nearby. NOT My best friend, ~~that~~ I saw daily, lived nearby.
Use *where* or **preposition** + *which / that* to describe a place. Do not use *where* + preposition.	The town *where* I lived was quiet. NOT The town where I lived ~~in~~ was quiet.

Ⓒ CHECK YOUR WORK Read your paragraphs. Underline the adjective clauses. Circle the relative pronouns, *where*, and *when*. Use the Editing Checklist to check your work.

Editing Checklist

Did you use . . . ?

☐ adjective clauses with object relative pronouns *who(m)*, *which*, or *that*

☐ *whose* to show possession or relationship

☐ *where* to show place and *when* to show time

☐ the correct verb form in adjective clauses

☐ commas to separate nonidentifying adjective clauses from the rest of the sentence

Ⓓ REVISE YOUR WORK Read your paragraphs again. Can you improve your writing? Make changes if necessary. Give your paragraphs a title.

UNIT 13 REVIEW

Test yourself on the grammar of the unit.

(A) Circle the correct words to complete the sentences.

1. Mrs. Johnson, <u>whom / whose</u> dog I walk, lives next door.

2. She lives in an old house <u>that / who</u> her father built.

3. It's right next to the park <u>where / when</u> I run every morning.

4. She has a daughter <u>which / who</u> I went to school with.

5. We became best friends in 2005, <u>where / when</u> we were in the same class.

6. Ann, <u>that / who</u> I still call every week, moved to Canada last year.

(B) Complete each sentence with a relative pronoun, *where*, or *when*.

1. Today, I took a trip back to Brooklyn, _____ I grew up.

2. The emotions _____ I felt were very powerful.

3. I saw the house _____ my family lived in for more than ten years.

4. I saw some old neighbors _____ I remembered well.

5. Mrs. Gutkin, _____ son I used to do homework with, still lives next door.

6. It was wonderful to see Mrs. Gutkin, _____ I've always liked.

7. I'll never forget the day _____ I moved away from this neighborhood.

(C) Find and correct seven mistakes.

I grew up in an apartment building who my grandparents owned. There was a small

dining room when we had family meals and a kitchen in that I ate my breakfast. My aunt,

uncle, and cousin, in who home I spent a lot of my time, lived in an identical apartment on

the fourth floor. I remember the time that my parents gave me a toy phone set that we used it

so I could talk to my cousin. There weren't many children in the building, but I often visited

the building manager, who's son I liked. I enjoyed living in the apartment, but for me the day

where we moved into our own house was the best day of my childhood.

Now check your answers on page 478.

Modals: Review and Expansion

PART 6

OUTCOMES

- Express ability, possibility, advice, necessity, prohibition, conclusions, or future possibility with a range of modals and similar expressions
- Identify key information in a social science article
- Identify key details in a conversation
- Discuss social networking, giving opinions
- Write a blog entry about one's plans for the near future

OUTCOMES

- Express past advisability, regret, or criticism with past modals
- Identify people's opinions in a psychology article
- Identify key details in a recorded personal narrative
- Discuss past situations and decide what people should or should not have done
- Complete a survey and discuss the results
- Write about a past problem and what one should or should not have done

OUTCOMES

- Speculate about past events, expressing possible or probable conclusions
- Draw conclusions based on the information in an article about archaeology
- Identify key details in a conversation and draw conclusions
- Discuss ancient objects and historical facts, and speculate about them
- Write about an unsolved mystery

Modals and Similar Expressions: Review

SOCIAL NETWORKING

OUTCOMES
- Express ability, possibility, advice, necessity, prohibition, conclusions, or future possibility with a range of modals and similar expressions
- Identify key information in a social science article
- Identify key details in a conversation
- Discuss social networking, giving opinions
- Write a blog entry about one's plans for the near future

STEP 1   GRAMMAR IN CONTEXT

BEFORE YOU READ

Look at the picture. Discuss the questions.

1. Do you use social networking sites? Which ones?
2. Do you use social media for connecting with friends, or for school or business?

READ

▶ 14|01   Read this article about social networking.

A bigail Thompson's school friends can find out what she is doing almost every minute by checking Facebook. Vince Stevenson stays in touch with his family the same way. Vince says, "I had to join. My grandkids all use it, and I want to be involved in their lives." Magda Tilia, an English teacher in Romania, has created an international online community for her class, using another social media site. Her students are able to discuss lessons and chat with other students in France, Turkey, and Greece. She says, "Students don't have to use the site. Class is just more fun for the ones who do."

Besides staying connected, social networking can also be a great tool for making new friends. But, just like making friends at work or school, you have to make the effort to "meet" people with similar interests. Is *Survivor* a reality TV show you could never miss? If so, you might consider joining a *Survivor* interest group and beginning conversations with people there. Once you've made some friends, you should keep posting comments, photos, and videos that people can respond to.

However, while you're having fun getting to know people, you must never forget that what you put on the Internet isn't really private. Even if your posts are only available to friends, embarrassing content can still become public. So maybe you'd better think twice before posting those party photos. Once they're out there, you can't take them back!

Social networking is a great resource for students. When you're applying to school, you can network by chatting with current students. They could give you an inside view of the school you're interested in. Once in school, you can form study groups, organize your schedule, and much more. But be careful: You might also find yourself wasting valuable study time.

Recently, Abigail has decided she's got to limit her social media use. "I must waste hours a day online! I'm always chatting, and not doing homework," she said. But she's still a big fan. "I believe everyone ought to use social networking," she is quick to point out. "It's a big world out there, and you can meet a lot of interesting new people and stay connected with those you already know. You just have to know when to say 'enough is enough' and sign off."

AFTER YOU READ

A VOCABULARY Complete the sentences with the words from the box.

content	involved	limit	network	resource	respond

1. How did she _____ to your invitation to join your online community?

2. That website has a lot of interesting _____. I really like the photos.

3. He's very _____ with his family. He's always texting them.

4. Five hours a day is too much. Try to _____ your time online.

5. The Internet is a great _____. You can learn a lot online.

6. I used the Internet to _____ with other people when I was looking for a job.

B COMPREHENSION Read the statements. Check (✓) *True* or *False*.

	True	False
1. Magda Tilia's students are required to use social media.	☐	☐
2. It's not always easy to meet people with similar interests.	☐	☐
3. It's good to regularly post photos, comments, and videos on your interest group's site.	☐	☐
4. Embarrassing photos remain private on the Internet.	☐	☐
5. Students should avoid using social networking.	☐	☐
6. Abigail thinks everyone should use social networking.	☐	☐

C DISCUSSION Work with a partner. Compare your answers to the questions in B. Why did you check *True* or *False*?

MODALS AND SIMILAR EXPRESSIONS: REVIEW

Ability or Possibility: *Can and Could*

Subject	Modal	Base Form of Verb	
She	can (not)	join	now.
	could (not)		last year.

Ability or Possibility: *Be able to*

Subject	*Be able to*		Base Form of Verb	
She	is (not)	able to	join	now.
	was (not)			last year.

Advice: *Should, Ought to, Had better*

Subject	Modal	Base Form of Verb	
You	should (not) ought to had better (not)	post	photos.

Necessity or Prohibition: *Must and Can't*

Subject	Modal	Base Form of Verb	
You	must (not) can't	post	photos.

Necessity: *Have (got) to*

Subject	*Have to* *Have (got) to*	Base Form of Verb	
They	(don't) have to have got to	post	photos.
He	has to has got to		

Conclusions: *May, Might, Could, Must, Can't*

Subject	Modal	Base Form of Verb	
They	may (not) might (not) could (not) must (not) can't	know	him.

Conclusions: *Have (got) to*

Subject	*Have to* *Have got to*	Base Form of Verb	
They	have to have got to	know	him.
He	has to has got to		

Future Possibility: *May, Might, Could*

Subject	Modal	Base Form of Verb	
It	may (not) might (not) could	happen	soon.

GRAMMAR NOTES

1 Modals and Similar Expressions: Functions and Forms

Modals are auxiliary verbs. We use modals (such as *can*, *should*, and *might*) and similar expressions (such as *be able to*, *have to*, and *had better*) to express **social functions** and **logical possibilities**.

Social functions include:

- **ability** or **possibility**
  (*can, could, be able to*)

  He **can learn** to use it.
  He**'s able to learn** quickly.

- **advice**
  (*should, ought to, had better*)

  She **should join** Facebook.
  You**'d better not give** your home address.

- **necessity**
  (*have to, have got to, must*)

  You **have to register** to use this site.
  You **must create** a strong password.

- **prohibition**
  (*must not, can't*)

  You **must not give** anyone your password.
  Children under thirteen **can't join**.

Logical possibilities include:

- **conclusions**
  (*may, might, could, must, have to, can't*)

  It **could be** the best site.
  There **must be** other good sites.

- **future possibility**
  (*may, might, could*)

  I **may join**.
  Sean **might join**, too.

BE CAREFUL! Modals have **only one form**. They do not have *-s* in the third person singular. Always use **modal + base form** of the verb.

She **might post** photos.
NOT She ~~mights~~ post photos.
NOT She might ~~to post~~ photos.

However, with the expressions ***have to*** and ***be able to***, the form of the verb changes.

She ***has* to register** in order to use the site.
He ***had* to change** his password yesterday.
They ***weren't* able to sign on**.

---

2 Ability or Possibility

Use ***can***, ***could***, or ***be able to*** to express **ability** or **possibility**.

- **present** ability or possibility

  She **can speak** French.
  We **aren't able to view** his site.

- **past** ability or possibility

  Before she took lessons, she **could speak** French, but she **wasn't able to speak** English.

- **future** ability or possibility

  She **can register** for class soon.
  She**'ll be able to register** tomorrow.
  She**'s going to be able to attend** next semester.

USAGE NOTE ***Can*** is much more common than *be able to* for ability or possibility.

She **can speak** French. *(more common)*
She **is able to speak** French. *(less common)*

3 Advice

Use *should*, *ought to*, and *had better* to express **advice**.

• *should*	You **should watch** *Survivor* tonight.
• *ought to*	Terri **ought to watch** it, too.
• *had better* for **urgent advice** (when you believe something bad will happen if the person does not follow the advice)	You**'d better spend** less time online or your grades will go down.

USAGE NOTE *Should* is much more common than *ought to*.

They **should join**. *(more common)*
They **ought to join**. *(less common)*

Use *should* to **ask for advice**.

Should I **join** Facebook?

Use *shouldn't* and *had better not* for **negative advice**.

You **shouldn't spend** so much time online.
You**'d better not stay up** too late.

4 Necessity

Use *have to*, *have got to*, and *must* to express **necessity**.

• *have to*	I **have to get** a new email address.
• *have got to*	You**'ve got to see** this cartoon! It's really funny!
• *must*	People **must register** to use this site.

USAGE NOTE We use *have got to* in **conversation** and in **informal writing**. It often expresses strong feeling.

You**'ve got to keep** your password private. It's very important for Internet safety.

USAGE NOTE When we use *must* in **conversation**, the speaker is usually in a position of power or expressing urgent necessity.

You **must go** to bed right now, Tommy!
(mother talking to her young son)

You **must see** a doctor about that terrible cough!
(friend talking to a friend)

IN WRITING *Must* is common in **writing**, such as forms, signs, and manuals.

You **must be** at least 13 years old to join.
(instructions for joining a networking site)

Students **must post** their homework today.
(teacher to students on an online course site)

5 Prohibition

Use **must not** or **can't** to express **prohibition** (things that are against the rules or law).

• *must not*	Students **must not leave** before the test ends. *(written instructions on a test form)*
• *can't*	You **can't leave** yet. The test isn't over. *(teacher speaking to a student)*

USAGE NOTE *Can't* is much more common than *must not* in conversation.	We **can't do** that. *(more common)* We **must not do** that. *(less common)*
BE CAREFUL! *Must* and *have to* have very similar meanings. However, *must not* and *don't have to* have very different meanings. Use *must not* for **prohibition**. Use *don't have to* when something is **not necessary**.	They **must not stay up** past 10:00. *(They are not allowed to stay up past 10:00.)* They **don't have to stay up** past 10:00. *(It isn't necessary for them to stay up past 10:00.)*

6 Conclusions

Use **must**, **have to**, **have got to**, **may**, **might**, and **could** to express **conclusions** ("best guesses") about situations using the facts you have.

We use modals and similar expressions to show how **certain or uncertain** we are about our conclusions.

Affirmative		Negative
must	**VERY CERTAIN**	*can't, couldn't*
have (got) to		*must not*
may		*may not*
might, *could*	**LESS CERTAIN**	*might not*

FACT	**AFFIRMATIVE CONCLUSION**
That photo looks just like Abigail.	It **must be** Abigail. *(very certain)*
Abigail knows Al.	They **may be** friends. *(less certain)*

FACT	**NEGATIVE CONCLUSION**
Al doesn't watch TV.	He **can't be** a member of the *Survivor* fan group. *(very certain)*
I couldn't find Al's name on Facebook.	He **may not** use his real name. *(less certain)*

For **questions** about conclusions, use *can*, *could*, or expressions such as *Do you think . . . ?* or *Is it possible that . . . ?* However, in **answers**, you can use *must (not)*, *have (got) to*, *may (not)*, *might (not)*, *could(n't)*, and *can't*.

A: **Could** Magda's students **be** online now?
B: No, they **can't be**. The lab is closed.
A: **Do you think she knows** how to set up an online study group?
B: She **must**. She set up a group for her class.

Use *may*, *might*, and *could* to express the **possibility** that something **will happen** in the future.

May, *might*, and *could* have very similar meanings. You can use any one to express **future possibility**.	Ted **may get** online later.
• *may*	Ted **might get** online later.
• *might*	Ted **could get** online later.
• *could*	*(It's possible Ted will get online later, but I'm not sure.)*
To express the possibility that something will not happen in the future, you can use *may not* or *might not*. You cannot use *could not*.	I **may not join** Facebook.
• *may not*	I **might not join** Facebook.
• *might not*	*(It's possible I won't join Facebook, but I'm not sure.)*

USAGE NOTE We usually do not begin questions about possibility with *may* or *might*. Instead we use *will* or *be going to* and phrases such as *Do you think . . . ?* or *Is it possible that . . . ?* However, we often use *may*, *might*, or *could* in short answers to these questions.	A: **Will** Josh **join** our Facebook study group? B: He **might not**. He's very involved with his job right now, so he doesn't have much free time. A: **Do you think it'll help** us pass chemistry? B: It **could**. People say study groups help.

STEP 3   FOCUSED PRACTICE

EXERCISE 1   DISCOVER THE GRAMMAR

Ⓐ GRAMMAR NOTES 1–7   Read the FAQ about joining Facebook. Underline the modals and similar expressions. Also underline the verbs that follow.

FAQ About Facebook

How do I join Facebook?

It's easy. You just have to complete an online form with some basic information—your name, birthday, and gender. Oh, and you must have an email address.

Are there any age restrictions?

Yes. You must be 13 or older to join.

I'm worried about privacy. Do I really have to provide personal information such as my date of birth?

Yes, you do. But you will be able to hide personal information if you'd like.

Do I have to post a photo of myself?

It's not required, but most people do. To get the full benefit of making connections, you ought to give as much information as you feel comfortable with. Remember: Facebook is a great resource, so get involved!

Can someone post a photo of me without my permission?

Yes. As long as it doesn't break any of Facebook's rules, people don't have to ask. However, if the photo is embarrassing, a lot of users feel the poster really ought to get permission.

What if I don't like a photo that someone has posted of me?

Unfortunately, Facebook cannot remove a photo if it hasn't broken any rules. If you're unhappy with the photo, however, you can remove your name from it.

There must be some dangers in social networking. What should I do to protect myself?

The number 1 rule is this: You must not give your password to anyone. Ever. Also, you should never give out information that strangers could use to contact you in the real world.

B Write each underlined modal/expression + verb from A under the correct category.

Ability or Possibility	Advice	Necessity	Prohibition
1.	1.	1. *have to complete*	1.
2.	2.	2.	
3.	3.	3.	**Conclusions**
			1.
4.	4.	4.	
		5.	**Future Possibility**
			1.
		6.	

EXERCISE 2 AFFIRMATIVE AND NEGATIVE

GRAMMAR NOTES 1–7   Circle the correct words to complete these posts on a social networking site.

CONVERSATIONS ONLINE

Abigail Thompson wrote at 6:30 a.m.

I can't / shouldn't believe I slept this late again! This might / has got to stop—
$\underline{1.}$ $\underline{2.}$
or I'm going to fail my early class.

Aneesh Hussain wrote at 6:35 a.m.

LOL! You'd better / may stop posting and get going, girl! We have tests today.
$\underline{3.}$

Adam Hall wrote at 6:55 a.m.

Hey, maybe you should / must get off Facebook a little earlier every night.
$\underline{4.}$

Vince Stevenson wrote at 7:00 a.m.

I just saw the weather forecast. Looks like we couldn't / 'll be able to do that
$\underline{5.}$
fishing trip this weekend. Tell the kids to get their stuff ready Friday night—they

must / can't sleep late on Saturday!
$\underline{6.}$

Ellie Stevenson wrote at 7:30 a.m.

Good Morning, Dad. Macy says we ought to / must not bring the video
$\underline{7.}$
camera—she's sure she'll catch the biggest fish. Ben's bringing some friends,

so we 'll have to / won't have to find the big cooler. Do you have it?
$\underline{8.}$

Ben Stevenson wrote at 4:00 p.m.

Grandpa, I think our boat may not / can't be big enough. Dylan wants to
$\underline{9.}$
come with us, too. What do you think? Should / May we rent a bigger one?
$\underline{10.}$

228   Unit 14

Magda Tilia wrote at 9:00 p.m.

Hi, class. Great work today! I <u>can / ought to</u> see your English improving every
11.$$

week. Next week <u>couldn't / could</u> be the last time you <u>can / should</u> chat
12.$$ 13.$$

with your Eukliedis High School friends in Greece—they're going on summer

break. So please show up online for them. See you Friday—and remember, I

<u>must / 'd better not</u> get your journals by then. I'll make comments and send
14.$$

them back right away.

> **Lucian Banika** wrote at 9:30 p.m.
>
> Ms. Tilia, I won't <u>have to / be able to</u> come to class on Friday because
> 15.$$
>
> of a family problem. I <u>could / must</u> leave my journal in your mailbox on
> 16.$$
>
> Thursday. Is that OK?

Abigail Thompson wrote at 8:01 p.m.

It's 8:00—time for *Survivor*! I guess all you fans <u>must / must not</u> be in front of
17.$$

your TVs right now. Who's your favorite contestant so far? Who <u>should / may</u>
18.$$

they kick off the island tonight? Any comments?

> **Ben Sutter** wrote at 8:15 p.m.
>
> My favorite is Christine. She <u>may not / must</u> be the best contestant, but
> 19.$$
>
> she's pretty good, and she works hard. Mel <u>has to / could</u> be the one they
> 20.$$
>
> kick off. I'm sure of it—there's no excuse for keeping him.

> **Sara Fry** wrote at 9:00 p.m.
>
> Hi, everybody. I'm posting from my phone. I'm on a camping trip so I
>
> <u>can / couldn't</u> watch *Survivor* tonight. Let me know what happened, please.
> 21.$$
>
> And Abigail—you <u>must / shouldn't</u> go to sleep now!
> 22.$$

EXERCISE 3 AFFIRMATIVE AND NEGATIVE

GRAMMAR NOTES 1–4, 6–7 Complete these posts to a reality TV message board. Rewrite the phrases in parentheses. Use modals and similar expressions.

[Follow-Ups] [Post a Reply] [Message Board Index]

bigfan: Any comments about *Pop Idols* last night? I _____*couldn't believe*_____
1. (didn't have the ability to believe)

Jennifer Tasco didn't win!

    aisha: I watched it, and you _____ more wrong. Jason
                                         2. (it's impossible for you to be)

    deserved the prize. He's a star. Jennifer isn't.

Kitsdad: Tonight on *Get a Job*, Ronald Turner interviewed Mary-Elizabeth and Shashank. Too

bad that Turner _____ only one of them. I actually think that
                   3. (has the ability to keep)

he _____ Mary-Elizabeth, but I really think Shashank
          4. (will possibly get rid of)

_____ the one to go.
5. (it's a good idea for Shashank to be)

    winz1: Everybody knows that Shashank was really very sick last week. He even

    _____ to the doctor! If you don't know that, then you
          6. (it was necessary for him to go)

    _____ very much about the show.
    7. (it's very certain that you don't know)

Elly: *Survivor* is starting again soon! I love that show, and now that I'm not in school anymore,

I _____ missing classes to watch the next episodes. They
   8. (it won't be necessary to worry about)

_____ to Palau this year, but it's not certain yet. I wish *I* were
9. (will possibly go)

going to Palau!

    bigfan: Elly, you _____ the show. And who knows?
                   10. (it would be a good idea to get on)

    You _____ a million dollars!
        11. (it's possible for you to win)

EXERCISE 4 EDITING

GRAMMAR NOTES 1–7 Read the article about Wikipedia. There are nine mistakes in the use of modals and similar expressions. The first mistake is already corrected. Find and correct eight more.

Wikipedia (pronounced WIK-i-PEE-dee-a)

It's fast (*wiki* means *quick* in Hawaiian); it's convenient (you ~~must not~~ *don't have to* go to the library); and, best of all, it's free. It's the world's most popular online encyclopedia, and you don't even have to register to use it. It's called "the free encyclopedia that anyone can edits." Volunteers around the world contribute to the millions of articles on its website, which are usually more up-to-date than what you may find in a book. You can't also click on hyperlinks to get more information. But, critics say, users ought be aware that the content may not always be 100 percent accurate. A "paper" encyclopedia has professional editors who fact check every article. Not so with Wikipedia. As a result, many teachers say their students should rely on it when they write reports. It's wrong to think that just because an article is on a famous website, it must be reliable. It mights be a good starting point when researching a topic, but writers should then check the facts with other sources. Then there is always the issue of plagiarism.[1] Remember: Wikipedia information is free to use and edit, but you don't have to copy other people's writing without giving them credit. It's against the law!

Along with the freedom of Wikipedia come some dangers. People can "vandalize" articles. This means that they maliciously[2] insert wrong information into a text or remove important facts. Wikipedia says it deals quickly with these attacks, but, again, users has to be aware that information could be wrong.

Online encyclopedias have changed the way we get information. Will they one day replace paper encyclopedias? It's very possible. But for now, it might be a good idea to hold on to that library card. In the meantime, it's safe to say that despite some disadvantages, an online encyclopedia can't be a very useful resource if you are careful and use common sense.

---

1 *plagiarism:* using someone else's words in your own work without giving that person credit
2 *maliciously:* doing something to deliberately hurt someone

EXERCISE 5 LISTENING

▶14|02 **A** Listen to this conversation about Facebook. Complete the conversation with the modal verbs that you hear.

A: Lea, you really _____*must*_____ join Facebook. You're my only friend who isn't on it.
                                        1.

B: I just don't have time for it. There are too many other things that I _____ do.
                                                                                        2.

A: You _____ have some free time.
              3.

B: Sure I do. But I _____ afford to spend it online. Besides, isn't it dangerous?
                        4.

A: Not really. Of course, you _____ be careful and use common sense. Just like
                                   5.
with other things.

B: Well, I guess you _____ be right.
                          6.

A: Trust me. It's a lot of fun. And you _____ meet a lot of interesting people.
                                             7.

B: I _____ join Facebook to meet interesting people. But on second thought, I
        8.
suppose it _____ be fun to reconnect with old friends.
             9.

A: Exactly. You really _____ give it some thought. Will you think about it?
                            10.

B: _____ we _____ chat online if I join?
                          11.

A: Sure.

B: In that case, I _____!
                        12.

▶14|02 **B** Read the statements. Then listen to the conversation again and check (✓) *True* or *False*.

	True	False
1. The woman uses Facebook.	☐	☑
2. The woman is very busy.	☐	☐
3. The man thinks Facebook is dangerous.	☐	☐
4. The man thinks it's possible to meet interesting people online.	☐	☐
5. The woman would like to make new friends online.	☐	☐
6. The man thinks the woman should join Facebook.	☐	☐
7. The woman agrees that joining Facebook is a good way to make new friends.	☐	☐
8. The man and woman can chat online on Facebook.	☐	☐
9. The woman promises to consider joining Facebook.	☐	☐

C Work with a partner. Discuss the answers in B.

EXAMPLE: **A:** So, the answer to number 1 is *False*.
          B: Yes. The man says that the woman must join Facebook.
          A: Right. That means she isn't on Facebook now. What did you put for number 2?

EXERCISE 6 ALL ABOUT ABIGAIL

DISCUSSION   Look at Abigail Thompson's profile on a social networking site. Work with a partner and discuss the site. Use modals and similar expressions. Answer the questions below.

1. What information shouldn't Abigail have on her profile? What should she keep?

   EXAMPLE: A: She should protect her privacy better. For example, she shouldn't give so much personal information.
   B: That's true. It could be dangerous to give your real address and . . .
   A: I think Abigail might . . .

2. Does she have too many social networking friends? Why or why not?

3. What skills and talents do you think Abigail has?

4. What can you guess about her interests?

Abigail shares other profile information with her friends.
Click here to make friends.

Abigail Thompson

Female; Age 17
63 Winter Drive
Orlando, Florida, USA

Networks: Waterfront High School
Disney Resorts

Interests: My guitar class, part-time job at Disney Resorts, working out with friends Danny and Mica

Music: Anything on the guitar, Rihanna, Taylor Swift, Justin Bieber

Movies: *Titanic, Avatar, Finding Dory, Mean Girls, Amélie*

TV: *Survivor*! I must be this show's biggest fan!

Books: Books? What are they?

Abigail's bumper stickers:

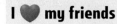 I ♥ my friends HANG UP AND DRIVE! My friends are **awesome** I ♥ music It's never too late to have a happy childhood

Abigail's friends:
Abigail has 840 Friends (top 3)

Ben   Sara   Jesse

Abigail's quizzes and games:
Desert Island
Know–It–All

EXERCISE 7 CLASS WEBSITE

Ⓐ REACHING AGREEMENT Work in a group. Imagine you are designing a class website. Answer the questions below.

1. What information should you include about students and your class?

    EXAMPLE: A: I think we should post photos of class members.
               B: OK. But we'd better not give too much personal information.
               C: I agree. We shouldn't post addresses, for example.

2. What information shouldn't you include about students and your class?

3. Who can and can't post on the site (for example, classmates, teacher, friends, and family)?

4. What content and features might or might not students want (for example, photos, videos, chat, discussion forums, fun quizzes, and games)?

5. Which links to other Internet sites could be helpful resources (for example, online dictionaries and information about other countries)?

6. What are ways you can get your classmates involved in the website?

Ⓑ Make a list of the things that will appear on your website. Compare your list with the lists of other groups.

EXERCISE 8 DESERT ISLAND

Ⓐ PROBLEM SOLVING Many websites have fun quizzes that people link to their pages. Before you work in a group, take this quiz about surviving on a desert island.

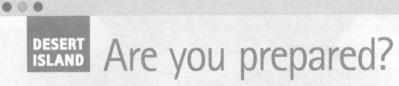

DESERT ISLAND Are you prepared?

Imagine you are in a group on a reality TV show called **Desert Island.** What should you do? Take the quiz.

1. You only have time to grab one thing. What *must* you have to survive?
    - ○ We've got to bring a knife.
    - ○ We should take a mirror.
    - ○ We'll need a fishing rod.
    - ○ Other

2. You've just arrived on the island. What should you do first?
    - ○ We'd better take a nap.
    - ○ We should build a campfire.
    - ○ We ought to find fresh water.
    - ○ Other

3. There are no fast-food places on the island. What's for dinner?

○ Maybe we can catch some fish.
○ We could eat insects.
○ There must be a village nearby where we could get food.
○ Other

4. The island is getting boring. How can you pass the time?

○ We could explore the island.
○ We've got to build a shelter.
○ We should practice swimming.
○ Other

5. There are other people on the island! You hear their voices. What should you do?

○ We should say hello.
○ Avoid them. They may not be friendly.
○ Watch first. They may be friendly.
○ Other

6. Planes and ships sometimes pass by. How can you attract their attention?

○ We've got to build a big fire on the beach.
○ We could use a mirror to signal them.
○ We should scream loudly.
○ Other

Ⓑ **Work in a group. Compare your choices and decide what your group should do.**

EXAMPLE A: We've got to bring a mirror. With a mirror, we can start a fire. . . .
 B: I think we should bring a fishing rod. We have to be able to get food. . . .
 C: I agree. If we can only bring one item, I think we'd better choose the fishing rod. . . .

EXERCISE 9 FOR OR AGAINST

DISCUSSION As a class, discuss the advantages and the disadvantages of online social networking. You can use the ideas below and your own knowledge and experience.

EXAMPLE: A: With social networking, you can find out other students' opinions about schools.
 B: You could also learn about jobs.
 C: You might even . . .

• How can social networking help people?
• What should you do to get the most benefit from networking?
• What are some of the problems?
• What are some of the things you must do to be safe and protect your privacy?
• Do the advantages outweigh the disadvantages?

FROM GRAMMAR TO WRITING

A BEFORE YOU WRITE Think about your plans for next week. Complete the chart.

Things I'm going to do	
Things I might do	
Things I should do	
Things I have to do	
Things I don't have to do	

B WRITE Use your ideas in A to write a blog entry about things that you are *going to do*, *might do*, *should do*, and things you *have to* or *don't have to do*. Try to avoid the common mistakes in the chart.

EXAMPLE: Next week is going to be a busy week. I have exams on Monday and Wednesday, so I really should study this weekend. I've got to bring that math grade up. I've finally chosen some colors, so on Saturday I'm going to paint the living room. I can't do it myself in one weekend, so I posted my plan on Facebook. I might ask some friends to help me. . . .

Common Mistakes in Using Modals and Similar Expressions

Use the **base form** of the verb after modals. Do not add *-s* for the third-person singular (*he, she, it*).	She **should study** this weekend. **NOT** She should ~~studies~~ this weekend.
Use ***don't have to*** for things that are not necessary. Do not use ***must not***.	I **don't have to work** on Monday. It's a holiday. **NOT** I ~~must not work~~ on Monday.

C CHECK YOUR WORK Read your blog entry. Underline the modals and similar expressions plus the verbs following them. Use the Editing Checklist to check your work.

Editing Checklist

Did you use . . . ?

- [ ] the base form of the verb after the modals
- [ ] *may, might, could, may not,* or *might not* for future possibility
- [ ] *should, ought to, had better, shouldn't,* or *had better not* for advice
- [ ] *have (got) to, must,* or *don't have to* for necessity or no necessity

D REVISE YOUR WORK Read your blog entry again. Can you improve your writing? Make changes if necessary.

UNIT 14 REVIEW

Test yourself on the grammar of the unit.

Ⓐ Circle the correct words to complete the sentences.

1. Were you able to <u>get</u> / <u>got</u> in touch with Carla?

2. I'll leave Ian a message on Facebook. He <u>couldn't</u> / <u>may</u> see it there.

3. You <u>'ve got</u> / <u>must</u> to see my photos of our class trip. They're really funny.

4. I <u>can't</u> / <u>not able to</u> log on right now. I'll try again later.

5. Could this online course <u>helps</u> / <u>help</u> me get a job?

6. You ought to <u>post</u> / <u>posted</u> information about your school activities.

7. The rules say that to join this site you <u>must not</u> / <u>don't have to</u> be under 13.

8. Tania is still too young. But she'll <u>can</u> / <u>be able to</u> join next month.

9. Is he right? He <u>might</u> / <u>might be</u>.

Ⓑ Rewrite the phrases in parentheses using modals and similar expressions.

1. You _____ personal information on the Internet.

(it's a very bad idea to give)

2. We _____ today or we won't be able to attend classes.

(it's urgent that we register)

3. Sasha _____ online. I'm sure she's studying for her test.

(it's almost certain that Sasha isn't)

4. Takumi _____ more sleep. He fell asleep in class again today.

(it's absolutely necessary that Takumi get)

5. Sorry, you _____ here. See the sign?

(it's against the rules to eat)

6. Paulo _____ to the party tonight, but he hasn't decided yet.

(it's possible Paulo will come)

Ⓒ Find and correct five mistakes.

1. Could that being Amelie in this photograph?

2. With this site, I must not call to keep in touch with friends. It's just not necessary.

3. I don't know this person. I guess I'd not better accept him as a friend on my Facebook page.

4. That doesn't look anything like Anton. It doesn't have to be him.

5. Were you able remove that embarrassing photo?

Now check your answers on page 478.

Advisability in the Past

REGRETS

STEP 1   **GRAMMAR IN CONTEXT**

BEFORE YOU READ

Look at the photo. Discuss the questions.

1. How do you think the man feels?

2. What is he thinking about?

3. What are some typical things that people have regrets about?

READ

▶15|01   Read this article from a popular psychology magazine.

Useless Regrets

> *For all sad words of tongue or pen, The saddest are these:*
> *"It might have been."* —John Greenleaf Whittier

Regrets. Everyone has them. Psychiatrist Nathan S. Kline, M.D., says it's normal to feel deep regret about things in the past that you think you should have done and did not do—or the opposite, about things you did and feel you should not have done. However, if we think about our past mistakes, we can often learn from them. For example, a student who fails a test learns that he or she should have studied more and can improve on the next test.

    Thinking too much about past mistakes and missed opportunities, on the other hand, can create such bad feelings that people can become paralyzed. As a result, they find that they can't move on with their lives. In their book, *Woulda, Coulda, Shoulda: Overcoming Regrets, Mistakes, and Missed Opportunities*, Arthur Freeman and Rose DeWolf have analyzed how people respond to regrets. They argue that people should not say, "I should've done better." Instead, they tell people to ask themselves: "What could I have done differently? Did I really have the skills, money, and experience at the time to get the

My parents shouldn't have discouraged me.

I ought to have applied to college.

I should've been rich and famous by now.

I could've become a doctor.

results I hoped for?" When people examine their feelings of regret about the past, they often find that they are based on a misunderstanding of the situation. For example, perhaps the student who thinks she ought to have spent more time studying really couldn't have done so because she was too exhausted from job and family responsibilities.

According to recent ideas in psychology, our feelings are mainly the result of the way we perceive reality, not reality itself. Once people realize how unrealistic their feelings of regret often are, they are more ready to let go of them. Psychiatrist David Burns, M.D., suggests specific strategies for dealing with useless feelings of regret and getting on with the present. One amusing technique is to spend ten minutes a day writing all the things you think you should or shouldn't have done that day. Then say them all aloud (better yet, record them), and listen to yourself. When you recognize how foolish most feelings of regret sound, the next step is to let go of them and to start dealing with the problems you face right now. After all, you can't change the past.

AFTER YOU READ

A VOCABULARY **Choose the word or phrase that best completes each sentence.**

1. If you **perceive** a situation negatively, you _____ about it in a negative way.
   a. worry　　　　　　**b.** think　　　　　　**c.** ask

2. A **strategy** is a(n) _____.
   a. plan of action　　**b.** state　　　　　**c.** Internet site

3. If a person is physically **paralyzed**, he or she can't _____.
   a. think　　　　　　**b.** hear　　　　　　**c.** move

4. An **unrealistic** goal is often _____.
   a. impossible　　　　**b.** not popular　　　**c.** really smart

5. If you **examine** something, you look at it carefully in order to _____ something about it.
   a. change　　　　　**b.** learn　　　　　**c.** teach

6. An **exhausted** person is very _____.
   a. tired　　　　　　**b.** excited　　　　　**c.** unhappy

B COMPREHENSION **Read the statements. Which ones would the following people probably agree with?**

a. Kline　　　**b.** Freeman and DeWolf　　　**c.** Burns　　　**d.** Whittier

_____ **1.** It's very sad that people have regrets.

_____ **2.** You are probably regretting doing something that you could not control.

_____ **3.** There can be a positive side to regretting.

_____ **4.** It is quite natural to feel bad about mistakes that you have made.

_____ **5.** You can spend so much time feeling regret that you can't get on with your life.

_____ **6.** If you make a list of your regrets every day, they may start to sound a little silly.

C DISCUSSION **Work with a partner. Discuss your answers in B. Why did you choose each answer? Do you agree with the people's opinions?**

ADVISABILITY IN THE PAST: *SHOULD HAVE, OUGHT TO HAVE, COULD HAVE, MIGHT HAVE*

Statements

Subject	Modal	*Have*	Past Participle	
I You He They	should (not) ought (not) to could might	have	told	her.

Contractions

should have	=	**should've**
could have	=	**could've**
might have	=	**might've**
should not have	=	**shouldn't have**

Yes/No Questions

Should	Subject	*Have*	Past Participle	
Should	he	**have**	told	her?

Short Answers

Affirmative			
Yes,	he	**should**	**have.**

Negative			
No,	he	**shouldn't**	**have.**

Wh- Questions

Wh- Word	*Should*	Subject	*Have*	Past Participle	
When	should	he	have	told	her?

GRAMMAR NOTES

1 **Modals of Advisability in the Past: Meanings**

Use the modals *should have*, *ought to have*, *could have*, and *might have* to express **past advisability**.

When we use modals of past advisability with *I* and *we*, they often express **regret** about something that happened.	*I* **should have applied** to college. *(I didn't apply, and now I'm sorry.)* *We* **could have gone** to a much better school. *(We didn't go to a better school. Now we regret our choice.)*
When we use modals of past advisability with *you*, *she*, *he*, or *they*, they often express **criticism** about something that happened.	*You* **could have called** us. We waited for hours. *(It was wrong of you not to call us.)* *She* **should not have made** that comment. *(It was wrong of her to make that comment.)*

In **affirmative statements**, use *should have, ought to have, could have,* and *might have*. USAGE NOTE *Should have* is the most common form.	He **should have taken** the exam. *(most common)* He **ought to have studied** more. He **could have left** home earlier. He **might have asked** the teacher for help.
USAGE NOTE It is very common to use the **contractions** *should've, could've,* and *might've* in speech, emails, and informal notes.	You **should've** tried harder, Lisa. *(more common)* You **should have tried** harder, Lisa. *(less common)*
In **negative statements**, use *should not have* or *shouldn't have,* and *ought not to have* to express something that was not advisable in the past.	He **should not have missed** the exam. He **shouldn't have gone** to the party. He **ought not to have left** so late.
USAGE NOTE *Shouldn't have* is much more common than *ought not to have*.	They **shouldn't have closed** the library. *(common)* They **ought not to have closed** the library. *(rare)*
BE CAREFUL! Do not use *couldn't have* or *might not have* for **past advisability**. *Couldn't have* means something was impossible. *Might not have* means something was possible, but not probable.	He **shouldn't have arrived** late. NOT He couldn't have arrived late. *(impossible)* NOT He might not have arrived late. *(probably not)*
In **questions**, use *should have*. It is very rare to use *ought to have*.	**Should** he **have called** the teacher? Who **should** he **have called**? Who **ought** he **to have called**? *(rare)*
BE CAREFUL! In **short answers**, include the modal + *have*.	A: **Should** we **have sent** a thank-you note? B: Yes, we **should have**. NOT Yes, ~~we should~~.

PRONUNCIATION NOTE

▶ 15|02   **Pronunciation of *Should have, Could have, Might have,* and *Ought to have***

In **informal conversation**, we often pronounce *have* or its contraction *'ve* in a past modal like the word "a."	I **should have** called you.
	   (shoulda)
	They **could have** helped more.
	   (coulda)
	They **might have** told me sooner.
	   (mighta)

We sometimes pronounce *ought to have* like "oughta of."	They **ought to have** come on time. *(oughta of)*

REFERENCE NOTE

Could have and *might have* are also used for **speculations about the past**, see Unit 16 on page 255.

EXERCISE 1 DISCOVER THE GRAMMAR

GRAMMAR NOTES 1–2 Read each numbered statement. Then choose the sentence (a or b) that is true.

1. I shouldn't have called him.
   (a.) I called him, and now I regret it.
   b. I didn't call him, and now I regret it.

2. My parents ought to have moved away from that neighborhood.
   a. They're going to move, but they're not sure when.
   b. Moving was a good idea, but they didn't do it.

3. I should've studied psychology.
   a. I didn't study psychology, and now I'm sorry.
   b. I studied psychology, and now I think it was a big mistake.

4. He might have warned us about the traffic.
   a. He didn't know, so you can't blame him for not telling us.
   b. He knew, and he was wrong not to tell us.

5. Felicia could have been a vice president by now.
   a. It's too bad that Felicia didn't become a vice president.
   b. It's great that Felicia is a vice president.

6. They shouldn't have lent him their car.
   a. It was wrong of them not to lend him their car.
   b. It was a mistake to lend him their car.

7. I ought not to have bought that sweater.
   a. I bought the sweater, and now I'm sorry I did.
   b. I didn't buy the sweater, and now I regret my decision.

EXERCISE 2 STATEMENTS, QUESTIONS, AND SHORT ANSWERS

Ⓐ GRAMMAR NOTE 2 A class is discussing an ethical[1] problem. Read the problem.
Complete the discussion with the correct form of the verbs in parentheses or with short
answers. Choose between affirmative and negative. Use contractions when possible.

> **PROBLEM:** Greg, a college student, worked successfully for a clothing store for a year. He spent
> most of his salary on books and tuition. One week, he wanted some extra money to buy a sweater
> to wear to a party. He asked for a raise, but his boss, Mr. Thompson, refused. The same week, Greg
> discovered an extra sweater in a shipment he was unpacking. It was very stylish and just his size.
> Greg "borrowed" it for the weekend and then brought it back. Mr. Thompson found out and fired him.

TEACHER: _____Should_____ Mr. Thompson _____have given_____ Greg a raise?
                                                          1. (should / give)

STUDENT A: Yes, he _____should've_____ . After all, Greg had worked there for a
                                  2.

whole year, and it's normal to get a raise after a year. In my opinion, Mr. Thompson

_____shouldn't have refused_____ at that point.
            3. (should / refuse)

STUDENT B: But maybe Mr. Thompson couldn't afford to give Greg a raise. Anyway, Greg still

_____ the sweater. It wasn't his.
            4. (should / take)

TEACHER: What strategy _____ Greg _____ instead?
                                                            5. (should / use)

STUDENT C: He _____ Mr. Thompson to sell him the sweater. Then
                    6. (might / ask)

he _____ for it slowly, out of his salary.
        7. (could / pay)

STUDENT A: He _____ his old clothes to the party. His behavior was
                    8. (ought to / wear)

destructive. He just hurt himself by taking the sweater.

TEACHER: Well, _____ Mr. Thompson _____ Greg?
                                                            9. (should / fire)

STUDENT B: No, he _____ the situation more carefully before taking
                        10. (could / examine)

action. Greg had been a good employee for a year, and he brought the sweater back. Now

Greg's reputation might be ruined.

TEACHER: Well, how _____ Mr. Thompson _____
                                                            11. (should / handle)

the situation?

STUDENT C: I think that he _____ Greg. He really
                                  12. (ought to / warn)

_____ Greg without any warning.
            13. (should / fire)

▶ 15|03 Ⓑ LISTEN AND CHECK **Listen to the discussion and check your answers in A.**

---

1 *ethical:* about what is right and wrong

EXERCISE 3 AFFIRMATIVE AND NEGATIVE STATEMENTS

GRAMMAR NOTE 2 Complete Greta's regrets or complaints about the past using the modals in parentheses. Choose between affirmative and negative.

1. I didn't go to college. Now I'm depressed about my job.

   I *should've gone to college* _____.
                                              (should)

2. My brother quit his job. He thought he could find another job right away. *I knew right away that he was being unrealistic, but I didn't warn him. That was inconsiderate of me.*

   I _____.
                                              (might)

3. I feel sick. I ate all the chocolate.

   I _____.
                                              (should)

4. Christina didn't come over. She didn't even call. My entire evening was ruined.

   She _____.
                                              (might)

5. I tried to tell Christina how I felt, but it was useless. She just didn't listen to me.

   She _____.
                                              (could)

6. I jogged 5 miles yesterday, and now I'm exhausted.

   I _____.
                                              (should)

7. I didn't apply for a good job because the application process was so long. I gave up.

   I _____.
                                              (should)

8. I didn't invite Cynthia to the party. Now she's angry at me.

   I _____.
                                              (should)

9. Yesterday was my birthday, and my brother didn't call. My feelings are hurt.

   He _____.
                                              (might)

10. I didn't do the laundry yesterday, so I don't have any clean socks. Everyone else gets their laundry done on time. Why can't I?

    I _____.
                                             (ought to)

EXERCISE 4 *SHOULDA, COULDA, MIGHTA,* AND *OUGHTA HAVE*

▶15|04 PRONUNCIATION NOTE Listen to the conversations and write the full forms of the words you hear.

1. **A:** Doug _____*ought to have*_____ sent that email.

   B: I know. But you _____ told him that yesterday.

2. **A:** We _____ taken the train.

   B: You're right. We _____ been home by now.

3. **A:** I guess I _____ accepted that job.

   B: Well, maybe you _____ waited a few days before deciding.

4. **A:** You _____ washed that T-shirt in cold water.

   B: I guess I _____ read the label before I washed it.

5. **A:** I _____ asked my sister to lend me some money.

   B: She's your sister! She _____ offered to help.

EXERCISE 5 EDITING

GRAMMAR NOTES 1–2 Read this journal entry. There are six mistakes in the use of modals. The first mistake is already corrected. Find and correct five more.

December 15

About a week ago, Jennifer was late for work again, and Doug, our boss, told me he wanted to fire her. I was really upset. Of course, Jennifer shouldn't ~~had~~ *have* been late so often, but he might has talked to her about the problem before he decided to let her go. Then he laughed and told me to make her job difficult for her so that she would quit. He thought it was amusing! I just pretended I didn't hear him. What a mistake! It was unrealistic to think the problem would just go away. I ought confronted him right away. Or I could at least have warned Jennifer. Anyway, Jennifer is still here, but now I'm worried about my own job. Should I have telling Doug's boss? I wonder. Maybe I should handle things differently last week. The company should never has hired this guy. His behavior isn't normal! I'd better figure out some techniques for handling these situations.

EXERCISE 6 LISTENING

▶ 15|05 Ⓐ Jennifer is taking Dr. David Burns's advice by recording all the things she regrets at the end of the day. Look at Jennifer's list. Then listen to her recording. Listen again and check (✓) the things she did.

TO DO

- ☐ Do homework
- ☑ Walk to work
- ☐ Make $100 bank deposit
- ☐ Buy coat
- ☐ Call Aunt Rose
- ☐ Call Ron
- ☐ Go to supermarket
- ☐ Finish David Burns's book

▶ 15|05 Ⓑ Work with a partner. Listen again. Discuss Jennifer's regrets about the items on her list. Answer the questions.

1. What *didn't* she do that she should've done? Why?

   EXAMPLE: A: She didn't do her homework.
   B: Right. She should've done it.
   A: Now she has to get up early to do it.
   B: She should've done it right away. She shouldn't have waited.

2. What did she do that she shouldn't have done?

3. What could she have done differently to avoid the problem?

EXERCISE 7 YOU BE THE JUDGE!

A SURVEY A *sense of obligation* is a feeling that you (or someone else) should have done or shouldn't have done something. How strong is your sense of obligation? Complete this survey.

Sense of Obligation Survey (S.O.S.)

INSTRUCTIONS: Read each situation. Circle the letter of your most likely response.

1. You want to lose 10 pounds, but you just ate a large dish of ice cream.
   a. I shouldn't have eaten the ice cream. I have no willpower.
   b. I deserve to enjoy things once in a while. I'll do better tomorrow.

2. Your friend quit her job. Now she's unemployed.
   a. Maybe she was really depressed at work. It's better that she left.
   b. She shouldn't have quit until she found another job.

3. You had an appointment with your doctor. You arrived on time but had to wait more than an hour.
   a. My doctor should have scheduled better. My time is valuable, too.
   b. Maybe there was an emergency. I'm sure it's not my doctor's fault.

4. You bought a coat for $140. A day later, you saw it at another store for $100.
   a. That was really bad luck.
   b. I should have looked around before I bought the coat.

5. Your brother didn't send you a birthday card.
   a. He could have at least called. He's so inconsiderate.
   b. Maybe he forgot. He's been really busy lately.

6. You just got back an English test. Your grade was 60 percent.
   a. That was a really difficult test.
   b. I should have studied harder.

7. You just found out that an electrician overcharged you.
   a. I should have known that was too much money.
   b. How could I have known? I'm not an expert.

8. You forgot to do some household chores that you had promised to do. Now the person you live with is angry.
   a. I shouldn't have forgotten. I'm irresponsible.
   b. I'm only human. I make mistakes.

9. You got a ticket for driving 5 miles per hour above the speed limit.
   a. I ought to have obeyed the speed limit.
   b. The police officer could've overlooked it and not given me the ticket. It was only 5 miles over the speed limit.

10. You went to the movies but couldn't get a ticket because it was sold out.
    a. I should've gone earlier.
    b. Wow! This movie is really popular!

B Put a check (✓) next to each of the answers below that you have. Give yourself one point for each answer that is checked. The higher your score, the stronger your sense of obligation.

☐ 1. a   ☐ 2. b   ☐ 3. a   ☐ 4. b   ☐ 5. a   ☐ 6. b   ☐ 7. a   ☐ 8. a   ☐ 9. a   ☐ 10. a

My Score _____

C Work with a partner and compare your survey results.

EXAMPLE: A: What was your answer to Question 1?
           B: I said I shouldn't have eaten the ice cream. What about you?

EXERCISE 8 WHAT A DISASTER!

GAME Work with a partner. Look at the picture of Alicia's apartment. What should she have done? What shouldn't she have done? Write as many sentences as you can in five minutes. When you are done, compare your answers with those of your classmates. Who had the most answers?

EXAMPLE: A: She should have paid the electric bill.
           B: She shouldn't have left the window open.

EXERCISE 9 DID THEY DO THE RIGHT THING?

PROBLEM SOLVING Work in a group. Read and discuss each situation. Examine the people's actions. Did they do the right thing or should they have done things differently?

Situation 1: Andrew was in his last year of college when he decided to run for student council president. During his campaign, a school newspaper reporter asked him about something she had discovered about his past. In high school, Andrew had once been caught cheating on a test. He had admitted his mistake and repeated the course. He never cheated again. Andrew felt that the incident was over, and he refused to answer the reporter's questions. The reporter wrote the story without telling Andrew's side, and Andrew lost the election.

EXAMPLE: A: Should Andrew have refused to answer questions about his past?
B: I don't think so. It's useless to refuse to answer reporters' questions. They always report about it anyway.
C: I agree. He should've . . .

Situation 2: Sheila is a social worker who cares deeply about her clients. Recently, there was a fire in her office building. After the fire, the fire department declared the building unsafe and wouldn't allow anyone to go back in. Sheila became worried and depressed because all her clients' records were in the building. She needed their names, telephone numbers, and other information in order to help them. She decided to take the risk, and she entered the building to get the records. She thought she was doing the right thing, but her supervisor perceived the situation differently and fired her.

Situation 3: Pierre's wife has been sick for a long time. One day, the doctor told Pierre about a new medicine that might save her life. He warned Pierre that the medicine was still experimental, so Pierre's insurance would not pay for it. At the pharmacy, Pierre discovered that the medicine was so expensive that he didn't have enough money to pay for it. The pharmacist refused to let Pierre pay for it later. At first, Pierre was paralyzed by fear and hopelessness. Then he took extra work on nights and weekends to pay for the medicine. Now he's too exhausted to take care of his wife as well as he had before.

FROM GRAMMAR TO WRITING

Ⓐ BEFORE YOU WRITE Think about a problem you have had. Discuss it with a classmate. Answer these questions:

1. What was the problem? _____

2. What did you do about it? _____

3. What should you have done differently? _____

4. What did you learn from the situation? _____

Ⓑ WRITE Use your answers to write three paragraphs about the problem you had. In the first paragraph, describe the problem and what you did. In the second, evaluate what you should or should not have done. In the third, write about what you learned. Try to avoid the common mistakes in the chart.

EXAMPLE: A few years ago, I needed a job. I saw an ad for an assistant in a store that was twenty miles from my home. I took the job and immediately regretted my decision. The commute was long, the pay wasn't good, the boss was terrible, and the hours were long. But, I really needed the money so I stayed on for five months.

It was a terrible decision, and I was miserable. I shouldn't have taken a job so far away. Before I took the job, I should have spoken to other people who already worked there. I also should have . . .

I learned from this mistake. In the future, I will . . .

Common Mistakes in Using Modals of Advisability in the Past

Use *should have*, *ought to have*, *could have*, *might have* + **past participle** for **affirmative** past advisability. Do not use *have* + simple past.	I **should have gone** sooner. NOT I should have went sooner.
Use *shouldn't have* or *ought not to have* for **negative** past advisability. Do not use *couldn't have* or *might not have*.	I **shouldn't have taken** that job. It was a mistake. NOT I couldn't have taken that job. NOT I might not have taken that job.

Ⓒ CHECK YOUR WORK Read your paragraphs. Underline the modals of past advisability. Use the Editing Checklist to check your work.

Editing Checklist

Did you use . . . ?

☐ *should have, ought to have, could have, might have* + past participle in affirmative statements

☐ *should not have* and *ought not to have* + past participle in negative statements

☐ *to* after *ought*

Ⓓ REVISE YOUR WORK Read your paragraphs again. Can you improve your writing? Make changes if necessary. Give your writing a title.

UNIT 15 REVIEW

Test yourself on the grammar of the unit.

Ⓐ Circle the correct words to complete the sentences.

1. I got a C on my test. I should <u>had / have</u> studied more.

2. I <u>ought / should</u> to have asked for help.

3. Dara <u>could / couldn't</u> have offered to help me. She's very good at math.

4. The teacher might have <u>gave / given</u> me a little more time.

5. I was exhausted. I <u>couldn't / shouldn't</u> have stayed up so late the night before.

6. What <u>should I / I should</u> have done differently?

Ⓑ Rewrite the sentences with the correct form of the modals in parentheses. Choose between affirmative and negative.

1. I regret that I didn't study for the math test.

   _____
   (should)

2. It was wrong of you not to show me your class notes.

   _____
   (could)

3. I regret that I stayed up so late the night before the test.

   _____
   (should)

4. It was wrong of John not to call you.

   _____
   (ought to)

5. I blame you for not inviting me to join the study group.

   _____
   (might)

Ⓒ Find and correct nine mistakes.

   I shouldn't have stay up so late. I overslept and missed my bus. I ought have asked Erik

for a ride. I got to the office late, and my boss said, "You might had called." She was right.

I shouldn't have called. At lunch, my co-workers went out together. They really could of

invited me to join them. Should have I said something to them? Then, after lunch, my mother

called. She said, "Yesterday was Aunt Em's birthday. You could've sending her a card!" I really

think my mother might has reminded me. Not a good day! I shouldn't have just stayed in bed.

Now check your answers on page 479.

OUTCOMES
- Speculate about past events, expressing possible or probable conclusions
- Draw conclusions based on the information in an article about archaeology
- Identify key details in a conversation and draw conclusions
- Discuss ancient objects and historical facts, and speculate about them
- Write about an unsolved mystery

STEP 1   GRAMMAR IN CONTEXT

BEFORE YOU READ

Look at the photo. Discuss the questions.

1. When and where do you think the man lived?

2. Why is he called the Iceman?

3. What was his occupation?

READ

16|01   Read this article about an ancient mystery.

The Iceman

On September 19, 1991, two German tourists were hiking in the Alps between Austria and Italy when they discovered a corpse[1] half buried in the ice. They assumed the body must have belonged to a mountain climber who had recently died as the result of an accident. They couldn't have imagined the truth. The body belonged to a man who had lived more than 5,000 years ago. Not only that, he might have been the victim of a brutal murder!

Who was he? What was he doing in that remote[2] location? How did he die? In the decades since this discovery, scientists have been trying to answer these questions. The ice preserved the body amazingly well. In fact, it is the oldest intact[3] human body ever found. As a result, scientists from all over the world have X-rayed[4] and examined him. The Iceman, as he is called, has become the subject of much speculation.

Found in the ice, alongside the Iceman, were many objects. He had weapons—a copper axe,[5] a knife, a bow and arrows. Some of his clothing also survived—snowshoes, a coat, a belt, leggings, a cap. He also had a backpack and a bag, which contained some tools and dried mushrooms. These objects provide clues to the man himself and to what might have happened to him. The axe, for example, was very valuable, and it indicates that the Iceman may have been a very important and wealthy person in his community.

---

1 *corpse:* a dead body
2 *remote:* far away
3 *intact:* not damaged
4 *have X-rayed:* have taken photographs that use radiation to go through solid objects in order to see the inside of the body
5 *axe:* a tool with a heavy metal blade on a long handle, used for cutting wood

At first, scientists believed that the Iceman must have died accidently during a winter storm. However, in 2001, X-rays told another story. There was an arrowhead[6] buried in the Iceman's left shoulder. The new theory was that he was the victim of a violent attack and must have bled to death as a result of this wound. Later examination discovered wounds to other parts of his body, including his head. This led to the speculation that he may have died from a head injury. Someone could have followed him up the mountain and attacked him while he was trying to run away.

Then, in 2009, scientists discovered another clue to the mystery of the Iceman's death. A more powerful X-ray (a CT scan) showed a very full stomach. The Iceman had eaten a big meal just before his death—not the behavior of someone trying to run for his life. This led investigators to believe that the killer couldn't have been a stranger to the Iceman. He had to have known him.

Could the Iceman have fallen and hit his head after the shot from the arrow, or did an attacker hit him over the head with a rock? Why were many of his arrows unfinished and not ready to use? Why didn't his attacker take the valuable axe? Theories about the Iceman's life and death have changed a lot over time as a result of advances in medical technology. And although much has been learned about him, there are still more secrets to learn from this amazing man, frozen in time for more than 5,000 years.

---

6 *arrowhead:* the pointed piece at the end of an arrow, which is used as a weapon along with a bow

Age at Time of Death:
about forty-five years old
Age at Time of Discovery:
more than 5,000 years old
Height: 5'5" (1.65 meters)
Weight: 110 lbs (50 kg)
Hair Color: brown
Eye Color: brown
Cause of Death: head wound? arrow shot?

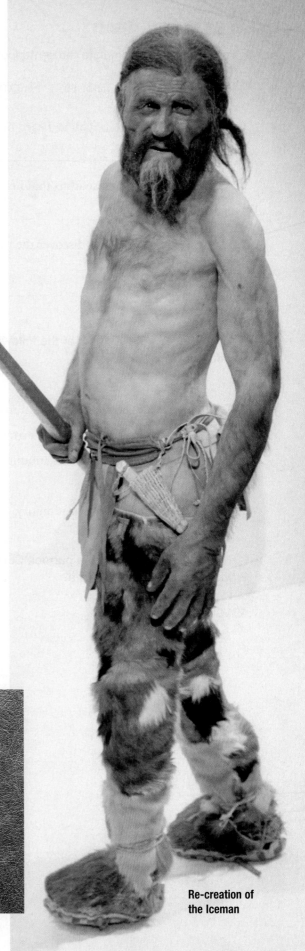

Re-creation of the Iceman

AFTER YOU READ

Ⓐ VOCABULARY **Complete the sentences with the words from the box.**

assume	decade	indicate	preserve	speculation	victim

1. I _____ you've heard of him. He's very famous.

2. There is a lot of _____ about the cause of his death.

3. One theory about his death is that he was a murder _____.

4. What did the X-ray _____? Did he have any broken bones?

5. At first, detectives didn't discover the murder weapon. It took more than a(n) _____ before it was located.

6. How did scientists _____ the body after they discovered it?

Ⓑ COMPREHENSION **Which of the following statements are *Probably True* or *Possibly True*?**

	Probably True	Possibly True
1. The Iceman had been an important man in his community.	☐	☐
2. He bled to death because of the arrow wound.	☐	☐
3. Someone followed him up the mountain.	☐	☐
4. The Iceman knew his killer.	☐	☐
5. The Iceman died from a head injury.	☐	☐

Ⓒ DISCUSSION **Work with a partner. Compare your answers in B. Why did you check *Probably True* or *Possibly True*?**

SPECULATIONS ABOUT THE PAST: *MAY HAVE, MIGHT HAVE, COULD HAVE, MUST HAVE, HAD TO HAVE*

Statements

Subject	Modal/*Had to*	*Have*	Past Participle	
He	**may (not)** **might (not)** **could (not)** **must (not)** **had to**	**have**	**been**	a very important man.

Contractions

may have	=	**may've**
might have	=	**might've**
could have	=	**could've**
must have	=	**must've**
could not	=	**couldn't**

Note: We usually do not contract *may not have, might not have,* or *must not have.*

Questions

Do/Be	Subject	Verb	
Did	he	**know**	his killer?
Was			alone?

Short Answers

Subject	Modal/*Had to*	*Have*	*Been*
He	**may (not)** **might (not)** **could (not)**	**have.**	
	must (not) **had to**	**have**	**been.**

Yes/No Questions: *Could*

Could	Subject	*Have*	Past Participle	
Could	he	**have**	**known**	his killer?
			been	alone?

Short Answers

Subject	Modal/*Had to*	*Have*	*Been*
He	**may (not)** **might (not)** **could (not)**	**have.**	
	must (not) **had to**	**have**	**been.**

Wh- Questions: *Could*

Wh- Word	*Could*	*Have*	Past Participle	
Who	**could**	**have**	**killed**	him?
What			**happened**	to him?

GRAMMAR NOTES

1 Speculations About the Past with Possible Conclusions

Use *may have*, *might have*, and *could have* + past participle to speculate about a fact in the past when you are **unsure** about your conclusions. Your conclusions are **possible**, not certain.

	The Iceman had a knife with him. *(fact)*
• *may (not) have*	He **may have been** a hunter.
• *might (not) have*	He **might not have felt** safe in the mountains.
• *could have*	He **could have expected** trouble.

2 Speculations About the Past with Probable Conclusions

Use *must have*, *had to have*, and *couldn't have* + past participle to speculate about a fact in the past when you are **almost certain** about your conclusions. Your conclusions are **probable**.

	The arrow wasn't in the Iceman's back. *(fact)*
• *must have*	Someone **must have removed** it.
• *must not have*	He **must not have wanted** to leave evidence.
• *had to have*	Someone **had to have taken** it out.
Use *couldn't have* to express **impossibility**.	He **couldn't have survived** the injury.
USAGE NOTE We often use *couldn't have* to express a feeling of disbelief.	He **couldn't have been** a farmer. His hands were much too soft.

3 Questions

Questions about past possibility almost always use *could have* + past participle.	**Could** the killer **have followed** him up the mountain?
USAGE NOTE *May have* and *might have* + past participle are not very common in questions, and they sound very formal and academic.	**Could** he **have known** his killer? *(common)* **Might** he **have known** his killer? *(not common)*

4 Short Answers

There are two ways to give short answers to questions about past possibility.

In **short answers** to questions about past possibility, use:	
• **modal** + *have been* when the questions include a form of *be*	A: *Were* the hikers surprised to discover the Iceman? B: They **must have *been***. They certainly didn't expect to find a corpse on the mountain.
• **modal** + *have* when the questions do not include a form of *be*	A: **Did** they **notify** the police? B: They **must have**. The police came the next day.

PRONUNCIATION NOTE

Pronunciation of *Could(n't) have*, *May have*, and *Might have*

In **informal conversation**, we often pronounce *could have*, *may have*, and *might have* as "could of," "may of," and "might of." We often pronounce *couldn't have* as "couldn't of."	**A:** This **could have** been a tool. *(could of)* **B:** Or, it **may have** been a weapon. *(may of)* **A:** That's true. It **might have** been a knife. *(might of)* **B:** It **couldn't have** been a weapon. It's not sharp. *(couldn't of)*
Remember that you can also pronounce *could have* "coulda" and *might have* "mighta."	**A:** It **could have** been a tool. *(coulda)* **B:** It **might have** been a knife. *(mighta)*

REFERENCE NOTE

Could have and *might have* are also used for **past advisability**, see Unit 15 on page 240.

STEP 3 FOCUSED PRACTICE

EXERCISE 1 DISCOVER THE GRAMMAR

GRAMMAR NOTES 1–2 Match the facts with the speculations.

Facts about the Iceman

_*h*_ **1.** The Iceman had a knife with him.

_____ **2.** His hands were very soft.

_____ **3.** He had warm clothes with him.

_____ **4.** His legs were strong and powerful.

_____ **5.** His axe was very valuable.

_____ **6.** His stomach was full.

_____ **7.** Some of his bones were broken.

_____ **8.** There was blood on his coat.

Speculations

a. He must have expected cold weather.

b. He might have fallen.

c. He may have been rich.

d. He had to have walked a lot.

e. He couldn't have been a farmer.

f. It could have come from an animal.

g. He must have eaten right before he died.

~~**h.**~~ He could have been a hunter.

EXERCISE 2 AFFIRMATIVE AND NEGATIVE STATEMENTS

GRAMMAR NOTES 1–2 Read more about the Iceman. Complete the sentences with the correct form of the words in parentheses. Choose between affirmative and negative.

The Iceman and His Possessions

Just like the Iceman's body tells us a lot about his life and death, his clothing and other possessions reveal a lot about him.

The Axe: This copper axe is very valuable. From it, we learn that the Iceman

_____ _must have been_ _____ a very important member of his
       1. (must / be)

community. It is even possible that he _____
           2. (might / be)

a community leader. If so, his death _____
          3. (could / happen)

for political reasons. Someone _____ to take
          4. (might / want)

his place as a leader. One of the most interesting facts about the axe, of

course, is that the killer didn't remove it from the scene of the murder. There

has been much speculation about the reason for this. The most believable

answer is that the killer _____ people to see
          5. (must / want)

him with it. People _____ the axe as
          6. (could / identify)

belonging to the Iceman and that _____ in
          7. (might / result)

some kind of punishment.

Re-creation of the Iceman's axe

The Bow and Arrows: The bow and some of the arrows were unfinished. The reason for this is still

not clear, and we may never know the answer. But, like the axe, they tell us a lot. The killer didn't

take them with him. He _____ that these items could identify him.
          8. (must / worry)

The Shoes: The construction of the shoes is very complicated. They use three kinds of material—

grass, animal skins, and some kind of cord. They were also waterproof. Because of their complicated

and detailed design, some people think the Iceman _____ them
          9. (could / make)

himself. They believe that there _____ professional shoemakers in
          10. (must / be)

his community that made shoes for the community members.

The Mushrooms: These were in the bag that the Iceman _____
               11. (may / wear)

around his waist. People probably used them as medicine. The fact that the Iceman had dried

mushrooms with him indicates that he _____ sick.
          12. (might / be)

EXERCISE 3 QUESTIONS AND SHORT ANSWERS

GRAMMAR NOTES 3–4 A reporter is interviewing an archaeologist for a magazine article.
Complete the interview questions and short answers.

Q: The food in his stomach, from different locations, shows that before his death high in the Alps,

the Iceman went up the mountain, then walked down to the valley below, and then climbed up

the mountain again. This had to have been a very long and difficult walk. What

_____<u>could have been</u>_____ the reason for this strange behavior? _____<u>Could</u>_____ he
        1. (could be)

_____<u>have thought</u>_____ that someone was following him?
        2. (could / think)

A: He _____<u>might have</u>_____. Some people think that he probably felt that his life was in
        3. (might)

danger, and he was trying to escape.

Q: What did the Iceman do? At that time in history, people were just beginning to farm.

_____ he _____ a farmer?
                4. (could / be)

A: No, he _____. His hands were much too soft. They were definitely not
            5. (could)

the hands of a farmer working the land.

Q: Well, then. _____ he _____ a hunter?
                  6. (could / be)

A: He _____. That's a real possibility. Or he might've been a shepherd.
            7. (could)

Climbing up and down the mountains with his sheep could explain why his legs were so strong.

Q: The Iceman's body is covered with markings that look like tattoos. What _____ they

_____?
        8. (could / mean)

A: No one knows for sure, but they might have been part of a medical procedure—something like

the ancient Chinese art of acupuncture, which uses needles to relieve pain.

Q: There has been a lot of speculation about why the killer left the valuable axe at the scene of the

crime. But what about the arrow shaft? Why didn't he take that, too? _____ it

_____ the killer?
        9. (could / identify)

A: Yes, it _____. Unlike the axe, the arrow belonged to the killer, so that
          10. (could)

might have identified him.

Q: On his last day, _____ the Iceman _____ that someone had
                    11. (could / know)

followed him up the mountain?

A: No, he _____. A person running for his life doesn't stop and eat a big
         12. (must)

meal. However, some people disagree with this interpretation.

EXERCISE 4 SPECULATIONS ABOUT THE PAST

GRAMMAR NOTES 1–2 Read about these other puzzling events. Then rewrite the answers to the questions about their causes. Substitute a modal phrase for the underlined words. Use the modals and similar expressions in parentheses.

Dinosaurs existed on the Earth for about 135 million years. Then, about 65 million years ago, these giant reptiles all died in a short period of time. What could have caused the dinosaurs to become extinct?

1. It's likely that the Earth became colder. (must)

   The Earth must have become colder.

2. Probably, dinosaurs didn't survive the cold. (must not)

   _____

3. It's been suggested that the dinosaurs became extinct because a huge meteor hit the Earth. (might)

   _____

In 1924, Albert Ostman went camping alone in Canada. Later, he reported that he had an encounter with a Bigfoot (a large, hairy creature that looks human). He said the Bigfoot had kidnapped him and taken him home, where the Bigfoot family treated him like a pet. Ostman escaped after several days. What do you think happened? Could a Bigfoot really have kidnapped Ostman?

4. A Bigfoot didn't kidnap Albert Ostman—that's impossible. (couldn't)

   _____

5. Ostman probably saw a bear. (must)

   _____

6. It's possible that Ostman dreamed about a Bigfoot. (could)

   _____

7. Some people think that he made up the story. (might)

   _____

In 1932, a man was taking a walk around Scotland's beautiful Loch Ness. Suddenly, a couple hundred feet from shore, the water bubbled up and a huge monster appeared. The man took a photo. When it was developed, the picture showed something with a long neck and a small head. Since then, many people have reported similar sightings. What do you think? Did the man really see the Loch Ness monster?

8. <u>Most likely</u> the man changed the photo. (have to)

_____

9. <u>Perhaps</u> the man saw a large fish. (might)

_____

10. <u>It's possible that</u> the man saw a dead tree trunk. (may)

_____

11. <u>It's impossible that</u> a dinosaur was in the lake. (couldn't)

_____

EXERCISE 5 COULD'VE, COULDN'T HAVE, MAY'VE, AND MIGHT'VE

▶ 16|03 PRONUNCIATION NOTE Listen to the short conversations. Write the contracted forms of the past modals you hear.

1. A: What was that used for?

   B: I'm not sure. It _____ *could've* _____ been a spoon.

2. A: I called Rahul yesterday afternoon, but there was no answer.

   B: Oh. He _____ gone to the museum.

3. A: Is Sara still on Easter Island?

   B: I'm not sure. She _____ left already.

4. A: I think I saw John yesterday.

   B: You _____ seen him. He's in Peru.

5. A: Do you agree with the author's conclusion?

   B: I don't know. He _____ been wrong.

6. A: Alice got an A on her archaeology test.

   B: She _____ been happy.

7. A: Could they have sailed that far in small boats?

   B: Sure they _____. They were expert sailors.

EXERCISE 6 EDITING

GRAMMAR NOTES 1–3 Read this student's essay about Easter Island. There are ten mistakes in the use of modals and similar expressions. The first mistake is already corrected. Find and correct nine more.

Rapa Nui

Rapa Nui (Easter Island) is a tiny island in the middle of the Pacific. To get there, the first settlers had to ~~had~~ *have* traveled more than 1,000 miles (1,609 kilometers) in open boats. Some scientists believed only the Polynesians of the Pacific Islands could have make the journey. Others thought that Polynesians couldn't have carved the huge stone statues on Rapa Nui. They speculated that Mayans or Egyptians maybe have traveled there. (Some people even said that space aliens might helped!) Finally, a University of Oslo scientist was able to study the DNA from ancient skeletons. Professor Erika Halberg announced, "These people has to have been the descendants[1] of Polynesians."

We now know that the islanders built the statues, but we have also learned that they must had solved even more difficult problems. The first settlers came sometime between the years 400 and 700. At first, Rapa Nui must be a paradise with its fishing, forests, and good soil. Their society may have grown too fast for the small island, however. Botanical studies show that by the 1600s, they had cut down the last tree. The soil must not have washed away, so they couldn't farm. And with no wood to build boats, they couldn't have able to fish. For a period of time, people starved and fought violently, but when the Dutch discovered Rapa Nui in 1722, they found a peaceful, healthy population growing fields of vegetables. How the islanders could have learned in this short period of time to live peacefully with so few resources? For our troubled world today, this might be the most important "mystery of Easter Island."

---

1 *descendants:* people related to people who lived a long time ago

STEP 4 — COMMUNICATION PRACTICE

EXERCISE 7 LISTENING

16|04 **A** Some archaeology students are speculating about objects they have found at various sites. Read the statements. Then listen to the conversations. Listen again and check (✓) *True* or *False* for each statement. Correct the false statements.

	True	False
1. The woman thinks that people might have used the tool for ~~building~~ *cutting* things.	☐	☑
2. The man thinks people could have worn this object around their necks.	☐	☐
3. The woman thinks this object might have been a hole for shoelaces.	☐	☐
4. The man thinks this piece came from the bottom of an object.	☐	☐
5. The woman thinks that the people who made this object were very smart.	☐	☐
6. The man thinks this object is a rock.	☐	☐

B Work with a partner. Discuss your answers in A.

EXAMPLE: A: The answer to number 1 is *False*.
B: Right. The woman thinks people might have used the tool for cutting high grass.
A: So, what did you put for number 2?

16|04 **C** Look at the pictures. Listen again to the conversations. Then work with your partner. Together, decide which objects the people are talking about and match the pictures with the correct conversation.

EXAMPLE: A: In the first conversation, I think they are discussing the object in picture *f* because the woman says it might have been a tool.
B: Hmm. But the item in *c* might have been a tool, too.
A: That's true, but the woman says it looks like a knife. The object in picture *f* is the only one that looks like a knife. The item in *c* couldn't have been a knife.
B: Good point, and then she says . . .

a. _____   b. _____   c. _____   d. _____   e. _____   f. _/_

EXERCISE 8 WHAT COULD THEY HAVE USED THEM FOR?

PICTURE DISCUSSION   Work in a group. Look at the objects that archaeologists have found in different places. Speculate on what they are and how people might have used them. Share your ideas with the rest of the class. The answers are on page 265.

1. Archaeologists found this object in the sleeping area of an ancient Chinese house. It's about the size of a basketball.

   EXAMPLE: A: I think people might have used this as a footstool. It's the right size.
   B: You're right. The floor must have gotten very cold at night.
   C: People could have rested their feet on this.

2. Archaeologists found this in Turkey. People in many places have used objects like this on their clothing for thousands of years. This one is about 3,000 years old. It's the size of a small cell phone.

3. These objects were used by ancient Egyptians. The handles are each about the length of a toothbrush.

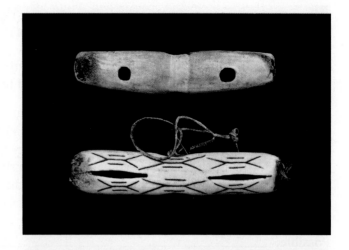

4. People in the Arctic started using these around 2,000 years ago. They used them when they were hunting or traveling. They are small enough to put in your pocket.

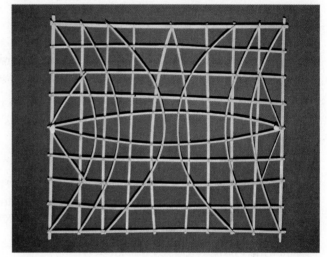

5. Polynesian people used these when they traveled. They made them with sticks, coconut fiber, and seashells. This one is about 1 foot (30 centimeters) wide and 1 foot long.

EXERCISE 9 THE ICEMAN REVISITED

DISCUSSION **Work in a group. Speculate on the reasons for these facts about the Iceman.**

1. Before he died, the Iceman climbed up the mountain, then went down, and then climbed up again. Why?

    EXAMPLE: A: He may have left something important below and needed to get it.
    B: That's possible. It might have been too heavy to carry everything up the mountain at one time.
    C: Or, he might have thought someone was following him and he was trying to escape him.

2. He was in a very remote area of the mountains. What was he doing there?

3. He had a bow and arrows, but they were unusable. Why didn't he finish them?

4. He had several broken bones. Why?

5. No one discovered his body for more than 5,000 years. Why not?

(A) BEFORE YOU WRITE Read the paragraph about an unsolved mystery. What do you think happened? Work with a partner. Speculate and take notes.

In 2004, archaeologists discovered a jar with seven very well-made leather shoes. Someone had hidden them in a small space between two walls in the ancient Egyptian temple in Luxor. The shoes were more than 2,000 years old and in very good condition. Two pairs belonged to children. One pair belonged to an adult. The seventh shoe belonged to an adult. Who hid the shoes and why? Why were there only seven? Why didn't anyone return for them?

Very Certain: _____

Possible: _____

Impossible: _____

(B) WRITE Use your notes in A to write a second paragraph about the shoes. Use modals and your speculations. Try to avoid the mistakes in the chart.

EXAMPLE: The shoes present a mystery. Who were the owners and what could have happened to them? From the quality of the shoes, we can speculate that . . .

Common Mistakes in Using Modals of Speculations About the Past

Use **must have** when you are almost certain about your conclusion. Do not use *may have*, *might have*, or *could have*.	They **must have been** shocked when they learned the age of the Iceman. It's hard to believe! NOT They ~~might have been~~ shocked . . .
Use **may not have**, **might not have**, and **must not have** when you think that something is not possible. Do not use *didn't have to have*.	The police **may not have realized** the importance of the Iceman. How could they have known? NOT The police ~~didn't have to have realized~~ . . .
Use **couldn't have** when you think something is impossible. Do not use *may not have* or *might not have*.	You **couldn't have seen** her. She's away. NOT You ~~might not have seen~~ her. . . .

(C) CHECK YOUR WORK Read your paragraph. Underline the modals or similar expressions that speculate about the past. Use the Editing Checklist to check your work.

Editing Checklist

Did you use . . . ?

☐ *may have*, *might have*, and *could have* for things in the past you are unsure about

☐ *must have* and *had to have* for things in the past you are almost certain about

☐ *couldn't have* to show disbelief or impossibility

☐ *could have* for questions about past possibility

(D) REVISE YOUR WORK Read your paragraph again. Can you improve your writing? Make changes if necessary.

UNIT 16 REVIEW

Test yourself on the grammar of the unit.

(A) Circle the correct words to complete the sentences.

1. Mayans built large cities. They <u>must / must not</u> have had an advanced civilization.

2. Their civilization disappeared. It <u>might not / might not have</u> rained enough to grow crops.

3. Look at this bowl. They could <u>of / have</u> used this to serve food.

4. You must have <u>taken / took</u> a hundred photos today.

5. Trish didn't come on the tour. She <u>may / couldn't</u> have been sick. She wasn't feeling well.

6. I can't find my wallet. I could <u>had / have</u> dropped it in the hotel gift shop.

7. Carla <u>must / couldn't</u> have gotten our postcard. We just mailed it yesterday.

(B) Rewrite the sentences in parentheses using past modals.

1. Dan didn't call me back yesterday. He _____ .
   (Maybe he didn't get my message.)

2. Selina got a C on the test. She _____ .
   (It's almost certain that she didn't study.)

3. Why didn't Fahad come to dinner? He _____ .
   (It's not possible that he forgot our date.)

4. Myra _____ . I saw a woman there who looked like her.
   (It's possible that Myra was at the movies.)

5. The server didn't bring our dessert. She _____ .
   (She probably forgot.)

6. Jan didn't say hello to me today. He _____ .
   (It's almost certain that he didn't see me.)

(C) Find and correct seven mistakes.

Why did the Aztecs build their capital city in the middle of a lake? Could they had wanted

the protection of the water? They might have been. Or the location may has helped them

to control nearby societies. At first, it must have being an awful place, full of mosquitoes

and fog. But it must no have been a bad idea—the island city became the center of a very

powerful empire. To succeed, the Aztecs had to have became fantastic engineers quite

quickly. When the Spanish arrived, they couldn't have expect the amazing palaces, floating

gardens, and well-built canals. They must have been astounded.

Now check your answers on page 479.

The Passive

PART 7

OUTCOMES

- Recognize when to use the passive and when to mention the agent
- Use the passive with different tenses
- Identify specific information in a magazine article about geography
- Identify key details in an academic lecture
- Discuss and interpret international proverbs
- Discuss products found in geographical locations
- Write an essay about a familiar country

OUTCOMES

- Express certainty, ability, possibility, impossibility, advice, or necessity with passive modals and similar expressions
- Identify key information in a social science article
- Identify details in a science-fiction movie dialog
- Discuss rules for group living in close quarters
- Discuss pros and cons of investing money in space projects
- Write about the ideal school for diplomacy

OUTCOMES

- Describe services that people have done for them by others, using the passive causative
- Identify key information in an article about beauty
- Identify details in a conversation about tasks needing to be done
- Discuss preparations for a trip to another country
- Discuss steps people from different cultures take to improve their appearance
- Write about preparations for an upcoming event

17

The Passive: Overview
GEOGRAPHY

OUTCOMES
- Recognize when to use the passive and when to mention the agent
- Use the passive with different tenses
- Identify specific information in a magazine article about geography
- Identify key details in an academic lecture
- Discuss and interpret international proverbs
- Discuss products found in geographical locations
- Write an essay about a familiar country

STEP 1   GRAMMAR IN CONTEXT

BEFORE YOU READ

Look at the title of the article and at the photo. Discuss the questions.

1. What is geography?

2. Have you ever studied geography in school? If yes, did you enjoy it?

3. Is geography an important subject? Why or why not?

READ

▶17|01 Read this article about *National Geographic*, a famous magazine.

Geography: The Best Subject on Earth

Geography is the study of the Earth and its people. It sounds exciting, doesn't it? Yet for decades, students yawned just hearing the word. They were forced to memorize the names of capital cities, important rivers and mountains, and natural resources. They were taught where places were and what was produced there. But they weren't shown how our world looks and feels.

And then came *National Geographic*. From the Amazon rain forest to the Sahara Desert, and from Baalbek to Great Zimbabwe, the natural

and human-made wonders[1] of our world have now been brought to life by its fascinating reporting and beautiful photographs, such as the one on page 270, which was taken by photojournalist[2] Reza Deghati, of a man planting a palm tree in Saudi Arabia.

The National Geographic Society was formed in Washington, D.C., in 1888 by a group of professionals including geographers, explorers, teachers, and mapmakers. Nine months later, the first *National Geographic* magazine was published so that the Society could fulfill its mission: to spread knowledge of and respect for the world, its resources, and its inhabitants.

In 1995, the first foreign-language edition of *National Geographic* was published in Japan. Today, the magazine is printed in English and more than forty local languages and sold all over the world. *National Geographic* also puts out a number of special publications. *National Geographic Explorer*, for example, has been created for classrooms. Other publications feature travel and adventure. *National Geographic* TV programs are watched in over 440 million homes in more than 170 countries, and digital editions are read by hundreds of thousands of people a month.

The study of geography has come a very long way since 1888. The Society's mission has been fulfilled. In fact, it has even been extended to include worlds beyond Earth. From the deep seas to deep space, geography has never been more exciting.

---

1 *wonders:* things that make you feel surprise and admiration
2 *photojournalist:* someone who takes photos and writes reports for newspapers and magazines

AFTER YOU READ

A VOCABULARY **Match the words with their definitions.**

_____ **1. mission**

_____ **2. respect**

_____ **3. publication**

_____ **4. inhabitant**

_____ **5. explorer**

_____ **6. edition**

a. a book or magazine sold to the public

b. someone who travels for the purpose of discovery

c. an important purpose

d. the total number of copies of a magazine or book printed at the same time

e. one of the people living in a particular place

f. an attitude that shows you think someone or something is valuable or important

B COMPREHENSION **Answer the questions.**

1. Who memorized names of capital cities? _____

2. What brought the wonders of our world to life? _____

3. Who took the photo of the Saudi man planting a palm tree? _____

4. Who formed the National Geographic Society? _____

5. Who reads digital editions of *National Geographic*? _____

6. How has the Society's mission changed? _____

C DISCUSSION **Work with a partner. Compare your answers in B. Do you agree?**

THE PASSIVE

Active	Passive
Millions of people **buy** it.	It **is bought** by millions of people.
Someone **published** it in 1888.	It **was published** in 1888.
They **have reached** their goal.	Their goal **has been reached**.

Passive Statements

Subject	Be (not)	Past Participle	(By + Object)	
It	**is** (not)	**bought**	**by** millions of people.	
It	**was** (not)	**published**		in 1888.
Their goal	**has** (not) **been**	**reached**.		

Yes/No Questions

Be/ Have	Subject	(Been +) Past Participle	
Is **Was**	it	**sold**	in Japan?
Has		**been sold**	

Short Answers

Affirmative				Negative		
Yes,	it	**is.** **was.** **has (been).**		No,	it	**isn't.** **wasn't.** **hasn't (been).**

Wh- Questions

Wh- Word	Be/ Have	Subject	(Been +) Past Participle
Where	**is** **was**	it	**sold?**
	has		**been sold?**

GRAMMAR NOTES

1 Active and Passive Sentences

Active and passive sentences often have similar meanings, but a different focus.

Active sentences focus on the agent (the person or thing doing the action).	Millions of people *read* the magazine. *(The focus is on the people.)*
Passive sentences focus on the object (the person or thing receiving the action).	The magazine *is read* by millions of people. *(The focus is on the magazine.)*

2 Forms of the Passive

Form the passive with *be* + past participle.

• simple present • simple past • present perfect	It *is printed* in more than forty languages. It *was published* for the first time in 1888. They *have been* sold all over the world.
Only transitive verbs (verbs that have objects) have passive forms.	TRANSITIVE VERB + OBJECT Ed Bly **wrote** that article. That article **was written** by Ed Bly. *(passive form)*
BE CAREFUL! Intransitive verbs do not have passive forms.	INTRANSITIVE VERB It **arrived** on Monday. NOT It ~~was arrived~~ on Monday. *(no passive form)*

3 Uses of the Passive

Use the passive when the agent (the person or thing doing the action) is unknown or not important.	The magazine **was started** in 1888. *(I don't know who started it.)* The magazine **is sold** online. *(It is not important who sells it.)*
Use the passive when you want to avoid mentioning the agent.	Some mistakes **were made** in that article. *(I know who made the mistakes, but I don't want to blame the person.)*

4 The Passive with *By* + Agent

Use the passive with *by* if you mention the agent.

Only mention the agent when it is important information.	The photographs in this article are wonderful. They **were taken *by a professional***. One of the first cameras **was invented *by Alexander Wolcott***.
BE CAREFUL! In most cases, you do not need to mention an agent in passive sentences. Do not include an agent if the information is not necessary.	Ed Bly took a really great photo. It **was taken** last February. NOT Ed Bly took a really great photo. It was taken last February ~~by him~~.

EXERCISE 1 DISCOVER THE GRAMMAR

GRAMMAR NOTES 1–4 **Read the statements. Check (✓) *Active* or *Passive*.**

	Active	Passive
1. The first *National Geographic* magazine was published in October 1888.	☐	☑
2. Today, millions of people read the magazine.	☐	☐
3. The magazine is translated from English into forty other languages.	☐	☐
4. My cousin reads the Russian edition.	☐	☐
5. Some of the articles are written by famous writers.	☐	☐
6. *Young Explorer*, another publication, is written for kids.	☐	☐
7. The publication is known for its wonderful photography.	☐	☐
8. A *National Geographic* photographer took the first underwater color photos.	☐	☐
9. Photographers are sent all over the world.	☐	☐
10. The articles show a lot of respect for nature.	☐	☐
11. That picture was taken by Reza Deghati.	☐	☐
12. *National Geographic* is sold at newsstands.	☐	☐

EXERCISE 2 ACTIVE OR PASSIVE

GRAMMAR NOTES 1–4 **The chart shows some of the forty language editions that *National Geographic* publishes. Use the chart to complete the sentences. Some sentences will be active; some will be passive.**

Language	Number of Speakers*
Arabic	240
Chinese (all varieties)	1,200
English	340
Japanese	130
Korean	77
Russian	110
Spanish	410
Turkish	71

*first-language speakers in millions

1. Spanish *is spoken by 410 million people* _____.

2. Around 110 million people *speak Russian* _____.

3. Arabic _____.

4. _____ Chinese.

5. _____ by 77 million people.

6. _____ 130 million people.

7. Approximately 340 million people _____.

8. _____ 71 million people.

EXERCISE 3 *WH-* QUESTIONS AND STATEMENTS

Ⓐ GRAMMAR NOTE 2 Jill Jones, a magazine journalist, is preparing for a trip to Bolivia. Look at the online travel quiz she is going to take. Complete the questions with the correct form of the verbs in parentheses. Then take the quiz. Guess the answers!

T R A V E L   Q U I Z

Destination: La Paz, Bolivia

1. In which part of the country ____is____ the capital _____located_____?
(locate)
　○ the north　　　　○ the center　　　　◉ the west

2. When _____ La Paz _____?
(establish)
　○ 1448　　　　○ 1548　　　　○ 1648

3. Which of these items _____ in La Paz?
(produce)
　○ agricultural tools　　○ cars　　　　○ electric appliances

4. What _____ the main street in La Paz _____?
(call)
　○ La Rambla　　　　○ El Prado　　　　○ El Alto

5. Which sport _____ the most in La Paz?
(play)
　○ baseball　　　　○ soccer　　　　○ basketball

The Passive: Overview　**275**

B Complete the sentences with the correct form of the verbs in parentheses. The sentences contain the answers to the questions in A. Did you guess the answers correctly?

1. The highest capital in the world, La Paz _____<u>was built</u>_____ in a canyon in the west of the
   (build)
   country. It _____ by mountains, such as the beautiful Illimani mountain,
   (surround)
   which _____ by snow all year.
   (cover)

2. The city _____ in 1548 by Spanish settlers.
   (establish)

3. Agricultural tools along with food and tobacco products, clothing, and building materials

   _____ in the capital.
   (make)

4. The main street's name changes in different parts of the city, but the tree-lined section in

   downtown La Paz _____ as El Prado.
   (know)

5. Soccer is the most popular sport. The city has several soccer teams. The Strongest, which

   _____ in 1908, has won many tournaments.
   (form)

EXERCISE 4 QUESTIONS, STATEMENTS, AND SHORT ANSWERS

A GRAMMAR NOTE 2 Jill Jones is interviewing a Bolivian cultural attaché for an article she's writing. Complete her interview with the passive form of the correct verbs from the boxes and with short answers.

grow	~~inhabit~~	spell

JONES: Thanks for giving me some time today. Here's my first question: _____<u>Was</u>_____ the area

   first _____<u>inhabited</u>_____ by the Inca?
   1.

ATTACHÉ: _____<u>No, it wasn't</u>_____. Long before the Inca, the Aymara
   2.

   created a great civilization around Lake Titicaca. In fact, the

   Aymara still live in Bolivia.

JONES: Interesting. Now, let's talk about farming. I know potatoes are

   an important food crop[1] in the mountains of the Andes.

   _____ corn _____ there as well?
   3.

ATTACHÉ: _____. The climate is too cold for corn. But
   4.

   quinoa grows well there.

JONES: Quinoa? _____ that _____ with a *k*?
   5.

---

1 *crop:* a plant such as corn or wheat which is grown by a farmer

eat	mine[2]	use

ATTACHÉ: _____ . You spell it with a *q—q-u-i-n-o-a*. Quinoa is a traditional
                    6.

grain, like corn and wheat in other places. It _____ by the
                                                              7.

inhabitants of the Andes since ancient times. In fact, it's been a major source of food

for more than 5,000 years.

JONES: Now, everyone thinks of llamas when they think of Bolivia. What _____ these

animals _____ for?
                    8.

ATTACHÉ: Oh, for many things—clothing, meat, transportation. But they only do well high in

the Andes.

JONES: I see. And what about other resources? I know that tin is extremely important in

Bolivia. Where _____ it _____?
                                        9.

find	make	speak

ATTACHÉ: Well, the richest sources of tin _____ in the Andes.
                                                          10.

JONES: And how about the eastern part of the country? What resources are in that region?

ATTACHÉ: In the Oriente? Oil and natural gas.

JONES: OK. Let's talk about languages now. I know Spanish is the official language of Bolivia.

But, what other languages _____ in the country?
                                          11.

ATTACHÉ: Actually, more people speak Native American languages than Spanish.

JONES: That's interesting. Now, I know scientists love Bolivia for its

wildlife. Are there still many jaguars there?

ATTACHÉ: Yes. In the last decades, conservation _____ a
                                                                12.

top priority by our government. It's become their mission to

protect jaguars and other rare and beautiful animals. We must

show these animals respect, or we risk losing them.

JONES: Well, thank you very much for your time. I'll send you a copy of

our publication as soon as the article comes out.

▶17|02 **B** LISTEN AND CHECK **Listen to the interview and check your**
answers in A.

---

2 *mine:* to dig into the ground to get gold, coal, tin, and other natural resources

EXERCISE 5 AFFIRMATIVE AND NEGATIVE STATEMENTS

GRAMMAR NOTES 2–4 Read Jill Jones's article. Her editor has circled in red six mistakes in spelling or fact. Rewrite the correct sentences with information from Exercise 4. You will write two sentences for each item. The first sentence will show why the sentence is incorrect. The second sentence will give the correct information.

A Land of Contrasts
by Jill Jones

Visitors to Bolivia are amazed by the contrasts and charmed by the beauty of this South American country's landscapes—from the breathtaking Andes in the west to the tropical lowlands in the east.

Two-thirds of Bolivia's 10 million people are concentrated in the cool western highlands, or *altiplano*. Today, as in centuries past, corn and kuinoa are grown in the mountains. Llamas are raised only for transportation And tin, Bolivia's richest natural resource, is mined in the high Andes.

The Oriente, another name for the eastern lowlands, is mostly tropical. Rice is the major food crop there. Rubber, oil, and natural gas are also found in this region.

Bolivia is home to many fascinating forms of wildlife. The condor, for example, is still seen flying above the highest mountains. Boa constrictors, jaguars, and many other animals are found in the rain forests.

Hundreds of years before the Inca flourished, a great civilization was created on the shores of the Pacific, probably by ancestors of Bolivia's Aymara people. Their descendants still speak the Aymara language. Today, Native American languages are still widely spoken in Bolivia. Although Portuguese is spoken in the government, Quechua and Aymara are used more widely by the people. Traditional textiles are woven by hand. Music is played on reed pipes whose tone resembles the sound of the wind blowing over the high plains in the Andes.

Lake Titicaca

1. <u>Corn isn't grown in the mountains. Potatoes are grown there.</u>

2. _____

3. _____

4. _____

5. _____

6. _____

EXERCISE 6 INCLUDING OR DELETING THE AGENT

GRAMMAR NOTES 3–4 **Read Ed Bly's soccer trivia column. Complete the information with the correct form of the verbs in the first set of parentheses. If the agent (in the second set of parentheses) is necessary, include it in your answer. If not, cross it out.**

Soccer Trivia

• Soccer is the most popular sport in the world. It <u>is played by more than 20 million people</u>.
  1. (play) (more than 20 million people)

• It _____<u>is called</u>_____ football _____ in 144 countries.
  2. (call) ~~(people)~~

• Except for the goalie, players _____ to use their hands.
  3. (not allow) (the rules)

  Instead, the ball _____.
  4. (control) (the feet, the head, and the body)

• Soccer _____ very much in the United States until thirty years
  5. (not play) (people)

  ago. Since then, the game _____.
  6. (make popular) (Pelé, Beckham, and other international stars)

• Forms of soccer _____ for thousands of years.
  7. (play) (different cultures)

• A form of soccer _____ in China 2,000 years ago.
  8. (enjoy) (Chinese people)

• It _____ in 1365—his archers spent
  9. (ban) (King Edward III of England)

  too much time playing and too little time practicing archery.

• Medieval games _____ for entire days, over miles of territory.
  10. (play) (players)

• Every four years, the best soccer teams in the world compete in the World Cup tournament.

  This event _____.
  11. (organize) (FIFA)

GRAMMAR NOTES 1–4 Read this short biography of photojournalist Reza Deghati. (He took the photo on page 270.) There are eight mistakes in the use of the passive. The first mistake is already corrected. Find and correct seven more.

Seeing the World

REZA DEGHATI ~~is~~ *was* born in Tabriz, Iran, in 1952. When he was only fourteen years old, he began teaching himself photography. At first, he took pictures of his own country—its people and its architecture. When he was twenty-five, he was decided to become a professional. During a demonstration, he was asked by a French news agency to take photos. He only shot one and a half rolls of film (instead of the usual twenty to forty), but his photos was published in *Paris Match* (France), *Stern* (Germany), and *Newsweek* (U.S.A.).

Reza, as he is knew professionally, has covered several wars, and he has be wounded on assignment.[1] Among all his assignments, the project dearest to his heart is photographing children, who he calls "the real victims of war." He has donated these photos to humanitarian organizations. Always concerned with the welfare of children, Reza has made it his life's mission to help them receive an education. His organization AINA created, in part, to achieve this goal.

When he was interviewed by an interviewer, Reza was asked to give advice to wannabe[2] photojournalists. He replied, "There is a curtain between the photographer and the subject unless the photographer is able to break through it.... Open your heart to people, so they know you care."

Today, Reza Deghati lives in Paris. His photos is widely distributed in more than fifty countries around the world, and his work is published in *National Geographic* as well as many other internationally famous publications.

---

1 *wounded on assignment:* injured on the job
2 *wannabe:* (informal for want-to-be) a person who wants to become a member of a specific profession

EXERCISE 8 LISTENING

▶17|03 **A** Listen to a teacher talk about the country of Haiti. Then listen again and complete the student's notes.

Haiti

1. Officially, Haiti _____is called_____ the Republic of Haiti.

2. It _____ on the island of Hispaniola, which it shares with the Dominican Republic.

3. Haiti _____ by more than 10.6 million people.

4. Both French and Haitian Creole _____ in Haiti.

5. Haiti _____ really _____ by Christopher Columbus.

6. In 1492, Haiti _____ by the Taino people.

7. Haiti _____ by Spain for more than 100 years, and then by France.

8. Vetiver, a plant, _____ to make perfume, body creams, and soap.

9. Coffee, mangoes, nuts, corn, rice, and other crops _____ in Haiti.

10. Many of these crops _____ to other countries.

11. Haiti _____ by more than a million tourists each year.

12. Since 2012, several new hotels _____ in Haiti.

Hispaniola

DOMINICAN REPUBLIC

HAITI

PORT-AU-PRINCE

SANTO DOMINGO

▶17|03 **B** Work with a partner. Listen again. What did you learn about Haiti? What, if anything, surprised you?

EXAMPLE: **A:** I didn't know that two languages are spoken in Haiti.
  B: Me neither. I knew that French is spoken there, but I didn't know about Haitian Creole.
  A: I was also surprised to find out that . . .

EXERCISE 9 QUOTABLE QUOTES

DISCUSSION Work in a group. Read the proverbs from around the world. Choose three proverbs and discuss them. What do you think they mean? Are there proverbs from other cultures that mean the same thing?

1. Rome wasn't built in a day. (*English*)

    EXAMPLE: A: I think this means that big projects aren't finished quickly.
    B: Yes. They take a lot of time and you have to be patient.
    C: There's a proverb in French that means the same thing: "Paris wasn't built in a day."

2. He who was bitten by a snake avoids tall grass. (*Chinese*)

3. He ran away from the rain and was caught in a hailstorm. (*Turkish*)

4. Never promise a fish until it's caught. (*Irish*)

5. Write the bad things that are done to you in sand, but write the good things that happen to you on a piece of marble. (*Arab*)

6. Skillful sailors weren't made by smooth seas. (*Ethiopian*)

7. From one thing, ten things are known. (*Korean*)

8. What is brought by the wind will be carried away by the wind. (*Iranian*)

Rome, Italy

EXERCISE 10 THE PHILIPPINES

A INFORMATION GAP · Work with a partner. Student A will follow the instructions below. Student B will follow the instructions on page 487.

STUDENT A

- The Philippines consists of many islands and has many natural resources. Look at the map of Luzon and complete the chart. Write *Y* for *Yes* if Luzon has a particular resource and *N* for *No* if it does not.

- Student B has the map of Mindanao. Ask Student B questions about Mindanao and complete the chart for Mindanao.

  EXAMPLE: A: Is tobacco grown in Mindanao?
  B: No, it isn't.

- Student B doesn't have the map of Luzon. Answer Student B's questions about Luzon.

  EXAMPLE: B: Is tobacco grown in Luzon?
  A: Yes, it is. It's grown in the northern and central part of the island.

			MINDANAO	LUZON
G R O W		tobacco	N	Y
		corn		
		bananas		
		coffee		
		pineapples		
		sugar		
R A I S E		cattle		
		pigs		
M I N E		gold		
		manganese		
P R O D U C E		cotton		
		rubber		
		lumber		

B When you are finished, compare the charts. Are they the same?

EXERCISE 11 TRIVIA QUIZ

A GAME *National Geographic Explorer* often has games and puzzles. Work with a partner. Complete this quiz. Then compare answers with your classmates. The answers are at the bottom of this page.

Do you know…?

1. Urdu is spoken in _____.
  a. Ethiopia   **b.** Pakistan   **c.** Uruguay

2. Air conditioning was invented in _____.
  a. 1902   **b.** 1950   **c.** 1980

3. The X-ray was invented by _____.
  a. Thomas Edison   **b.** Wilhelm Röntgen   **c.** Marie Curie

4. The Petronas Towers in Kuala Lumpur were designed by _____.
  a. Minoru Yamasaki   **b.** César Pelli   **c.** I. M. Pei

5. The 2016 Summer Olympics were held in _____.
  a. Brazil   **b.** Canada   **c.** Japan

6. An ocean route from Portugal to the East was discovered by Portuguese explorer _____.
  a. Hernán Cortés   **b.** Louis Jolliet   **c.** Vasco da Gama

7. A baby _____ is called a *cub*.
  a. cat   **b.** dog   **c.** jaguar

B Work with your partner. Make up your own quiz questions with the words in parentheses. Ask another pair to answer your questions.

1. _____ "Guernica" was painted _____ by _b_.
      (paint)
  a. ___Monet___   **b.** ___Picasso___   **c.** ___El Greco___

2. _____ by ____.
      (invent)
  a. _____   **b.** _____   **c.** _____

3. _____ by ____.
      (compose)
  a. _____   **b.** _____   **c.** _____

4. _____ by ____.
      (write)
  a. _____   **b.** _____   **c.** _____

Answers to Trivia Quiz: 1. b; 2. a; 3. b; 4. b; 5. a; 6. c; 7. c

FROM GRAMMAR TO WRITING

A BEFORE YOU WRITE   Complete the chart with information about a country you know well.

Name of country	
Geographical areas	
Crops grown in each area	
Animals raised in each area	
Natural resources found in each area	
Birds or animals found in each area	
Languages spoken	
Art, handicrafts, or music created	

B WRITE   Use the information to write an essay about the country. Use the passive. Try to avoid the common mistakes in the chart.

EXAMPLE: Turkey is both a European and an Asian country. European Turkey is separated from Asian Turkey by the Sea of Marmara, the Bosphorus, and the Dardanelles. Citrus fruits, such as lemon and oranges, and tobacco are grown in . . .

Common Mistakes in Using the Passive

Use the correct form of *be* + **past participle** to form the passive. Do not use the base form of the main verb.	Oranges **are grown** in Turkey. NOT Oranges are ~~grow~~ in Turkey.
Only mention the **agent** when it is important information. Do not mention the agent when it is unnecessary information.	Tobacco **is grown**. NOT Tobacco is grown ~~by tobacco farmers~~.

C CHECK YOUR WORK   Read your essay. Underline all the passive forms. Circle *by* + agent. Use the Editing Checklist to check your work.

Editing Checklist

Did you use . . . ?

- [ ] passive sentences to focus on the object
- [ ] the correct form of the passive (*be* + past participle)
- [ ] *by* if you mentioned the agent
- [ ] the agent only when it was important information

D REVISE YOUR WORK   Read your essay again. Can you improve your writing? Make changes if necessary. Give your essay a title.

UNIT 17 REVIEW

Test yourself on the grammar of the unit.

Ⓐ Complete with active and passive sentences.

Active	Passive
1. They speak Spanish in Bolivia.	_____
2. _____	Soccer is played in Bolivia.
3. _____	The photo was taken by Reza Deghati.
4. They translated the articles into Spanish.	_____
5. They grow quinoa in the mountains.	_____
6. _____	The main street was named El Prado.

Ⓑ Complete the sentences with the correct passive form of the verbs in parentheses.

1. Jamaica _____ by Europeans in the sixteenth century.
(discover)

2. Today, Creole, a mixture of languages, _____ by many Jamaicans.
(speak)

3. Some of the best coffee in the world _____ on the island.
(grow)

4. Sugar _____ to many countries.
(export)

5. Many people _____ by the sugar industry.
(employ)

6. Reggae music originated in Jamaica. It _____ popular by Bob Marley.
(make)

7. Since the summer of 1992, it _____ at the Sumfest festival on the island.
(perform)

8. Every year, the festival _____ by music lovers from around the world.
(attend)

Ⓒ Find and correct six mistakes.

Photojournalist Alexandra Avakian was born and raise in New York. Since she began

her career, she has covered many of the world's most important stories. Her work have

been published in many newspapers and magazines including *National Geographic*, and her

photographs have being exhibited around the world. Avakian has also written a book, *Window*

of the Soul: My Journey in the Muslim World, which was been published in 2008. It has not yet been

translated by translators into other languages, but the chapter titles appear in both English and

Arabic. Avakian's book have be discussed on international TV, radio, and numerous websites.

Now check your answers on page 479.

The Passive with Modals and Similar Expressions
INTERNATIONAL COOPERATION

OUTCOMES
- Express certainty, ability, possibility, impossibility, advice, or necessity with passive modals and similar expressions
- Identify key information in a social science article
- Identify details in a science-fiction movie dialog
- Discuss rules for group living in close quarters
- Discuss pros and cons of investing money in space projects
- Write about the ideal school for diplomacy

STEP 1   GRAMMAR IN CONTEXT

BEFORE YOU READ

Look at the article and at the photos on this page and on pages 288–289. Discuss the questions.

1. What do you know about the International Space Station?

2. What are some problems that can occur when people from different cultures must live and work together?

READ

▶ 18|01   Read this article about an international space project.

Close Quarters[1]

"Will decisions be made too fast?" the Japanese astronauts wondered. "Can they be made quickly enough?" the Americans wanted to know. "Is dinner going to be taken seriously?" was the question worrying the French and the Dutch, while the Italians were nervous about their personal space: "How can privacy be maintained in such very close quarters?"

The year was 2000. It was the beginning of the new millennium,[2] and the focus of all these concerns was the International Space Station (ISS), the largest and most complex international project ever. At the time, many were asking themselves: "Can this huge undertaking really be accomplished by a multicultural group living in close quarters?"

In addition to their other concerns, all the astronauts were worrying about language. In the beginning, English was the official language on the ISS, and a great number of technical terms had to be learned by everyone on board. (Today, both English and Russian must be

---

1 *close quarters:* a small, crowded place where people live or work together
2 *millennium:* a time when a new 1,000-year period begins

learned by all astronauts before they go into space.) Another major concern was food. What time should meals be served? How should preparation and cleanup be handled?

Those worries had to be tested in space before anyone would know for sure. But by now the answer is clear. For almost two decades, ISS astronauts have been proving that great achievements in technology and science can be made by an international group working together. Since November 2000, when the first crew boarded the ISS, the station has been operated by astronauts from fifteen countries, including Brazil, Canada, Japan, Russia, the United States, and members of the European Union.

How did this international group of astronauts manage to work together and assemble the space station in just about ten years? How were they able to cooperate with one another to achieve their research goals during long periods in a "trapped environment"? All astronauts receive cross-cultural training, but often sensitivity and tolerance can't be taught from a textbook. They must be observed and experienced personally.

Two researchers suggested that a model for space station harmony[3] might be found in an unusual place—the popular TV series *Star Trek*, in which a multicultural crew has been getting along for eons.[4] However, real-life astronauts have found a more down-to-earth solution: the family dinner. Astronaut Nicole Stott reported, "... we always spend mealtimes together ... it's a lot like bringing your family together." The dinner table is where the world's (and each other's) problems can be solved, and where the astronauts "listen to good music, eat good food, improve our vocabulary in other languages, and laugh a lot."

Astronauts also benefit from their unique perspective of Earth. They like to point out that national borders can't be seen from space. As Indian-American astronaut Sunita Williams says, "I consider myself a citizen of the universe. When we go up in space, all we can see is a beautiful Earth where there are no borders of nations and religions." Russian cosmonaut[5] Sergey Ryazansky says, "The ISS can't exist without international cooperation." This spirit of cooperation may turn out to be the project's greatest achievement.

---

3 *harmony:* a situation in which people are friendly and peaceful together
4 *eons:* very long immeasurable periods of time
5 *cosmonaut:* the Russian word for *astronaut*

AFTER YOU READ

A **VOCABULARY** Complete the sentences with the words from the box.

assemble	benefit	concern	cooperate	perspective	undertaking

1. It took years to _____ the many parts of the space station.

2. Money is a big _____. There has to be enough for this expensive project.

3. This book changed my _____. I see the problem differently now.

4. If we all _____ and work together, we'll get the job done quickly.

5. This is a big _____, and it requires a lot of planning.

6. How do we _____ from this change? How will it help us?

B **COMPREHENSION** Read the statements. Check (✓) *True* or *False*.

	True	False
1. Japanese and American astronauts worried about decision making.	☐	☐
2. Dutch astronauts worried about privacy.	☐	☐
3. The time of meals was also a big concern.	☐	☐
4. At first, all ISS astronauts had to learn technical language in English.	☐	☐
5. Today, English is the only official language on the ISS.	☐	☐
6. The ISS was completely assembled in around ten years.	☐	☐
7. Astronauts learn cross-cultural understanding most effectively from textbooks.	☐	☐
8. The astronauts can see individual countries from the ISS.	☐	☐

C **DISCUSSION** Work with a partner. Compare your answers to the questions in B. Why did you choose *True* or *False*?

THE PASSIVE WITH MODALS AND SIMILAR EXPRESSIONS

Statements

Subject	Modal	*Be*	Past Participle	
The decision	will (not) should (not) ought (not) to must (not) can (not) might (not) had better (not)	be	made	quickly.

Subject	*Have (got) to/Be going to*	*Be*	Past Participle	
The problem	has (got) to doesn't have to had to is (not) going to	be	solved	quickly.

Yes/No Questions

Modal	Subject	*Be*	Past Participle	
Will				
Should	it	be	made	quickly?
Must				
Can				

Short Answers

Affirmative			Negative		
Yes,	it	will.	No,	it	won't.
		should.			shouldn't.
		must.			doesn't have to be.
		can.			can't.

Yes/No Questions

Auxiliary Verb	Subject	*Have to/ Going to*	*Be*	Past Participle	
Does	it	have to	be	solved?	
Is		going to			

Short Answers

Affirmative			Negative		
Yes,	it	does.	No,	it	doesn't.
		is.			isn't.

GRAMMAR NOTES

1 Passive Modals and Similar Expressions: Forms

Use **modal/expression** + *be* + **past participle** to form passive modals or expressions.

You can use all modals and similar expressions in the passive. For example:

• *will*	The labs *will* **be used** for experiments.
• *can*	The Earth *can* **be seen** from the ISS.
• *have to*	Sometimes decisions *have to* **be made** quickly.

CONTINUED ▶

Remember to use *by* before the **agent** if the agent is mentioned. However, only mention the agent when it is important information.	The repairs will be made **by a robot**.
IN WRITING The passive with modals is not common in conversation. It is more common in academic writing, especially with *may*, *must*, and *should*.	Lessons in cross-cultural understanding **should be introduced** early in the program. *(textbook)*

2 Certainty in the Future

Use *will* or a form of *be going to* with the passive to express **certainty in the future**.	
• *will*	The ISS *will* **be used** for several more years.
• *be going to*	The ISS *is going to* **be used** for several more years.

3 Ability or Possibility

Use a form of *can* with the passive to express **ability or possibility**.	
• **present ability**	Russian *can* **be understood** by all the astronauts.
• **present possibility**	Many languages *can* **be heard** aboard the ISS.
• **past ability**	Problems *could* **be solved** by the crew.
• **past possibility**	Last month, the ISS *could* **be seen** from Earth.

4 Future Possibility or Impossibility

Use *could*, *may*, *might*, and *can't* with the passive to express **future possibility or impossibility**.	
• **future possibility**	The equipment *could* **be replaced** very soon. Some anxiety *may* **be experienced** on takeoff. New discoveries *might* **be made**.
• **future impossibility**	The job *can't* **be handled** by just one person.

5 Advice or Necessity

Use *should*, *ought to*, *had better*, *must*, and *have (got) to* with the passive to express **advice or necessity**.	
• **advice**	The crew *should* **be told** to leave now. They *ought to* **be given** more training. Privacy *had better* **be taken** seriously.
• **necessity**	Everyone *must* **be treated** with respect. Technical language *has got to* **be learned**. The equipment *had to* **be repaired**.

REFERENCE NOTES

For a review of **modals and similar expressions**, see Unit 14 on page 222.
For information about **modals and their functions**, see Appendix 18 on page 461.

EXERCISE 1   DISCOVER THE GRAMMAR

Ⓐ GRAMMAR NOTES 1–5   Read the interview with scientist Dr. Bernard Kay (BK) by *Comet Magazine* (CM). Underline the passive with modals and similar expressions. Circle *by* when it is used before the agent in a passive sentence.

CM: I understand that some parts of the ISS could not be built, and the building of other parts was delayed (by) various problems. But the whole station has finally been assembled. What an undertaking this has been! When was it completed?

BK: It was finished at the end of 2010. In February of that year, the last major sections—Tranquility and the Cupola—were attached. In Tranquility, oxygen can be produced and waste water can be recycled.[1] And life in the ISS will be supported by Tranquility's equipment if communication with Earth can't be maintained for a period of time.

CM: And the Cupola? I understand it was built by the European Space Agency.

BK: Yes, it was. It's amazing. It should be considered one of the most important parts of the station. It's got seven huge windows, and the views of Earth and space are spectacular.

CM: Why the big windows?

BK: Because maintenance outside the space station has to be performed by robots. The windows allow astronauts to observe and control them more easily. But I think that the perspective of Earth and space that we gain from these views might be considered just as important.

CM: Why is that?

BK: Observing the Earth and space keeps the astronauts in touch with the importance of their mission. Originally the station was going to include sleeping cabins with windows, but that part of the project couldn't be accomplished for a number of reasons. Now the sleeping cabins are windowless, and the Cupola is everyone's favorite hangout.[2]

---

1 *recycled:* cleaned or treated (such as water or paper) so that it can be used again
2 *hangout:* a place where people like to spend free time, especially with friends

CM: Now that the station is complete, will more scientific work be done on the ISS?

BK: Yes, it will. The ISS is the first step to further exploration of our solar system. On the ISS, ways to grow food in space can be developed, and new materials can be tested, for example. But most important of all, human interactions have got to be understood better. An international crew from fifteen different countries makes the ISS a wonderful laboratory for cross-cultural understanding. This could be one of the great benefits of the ISS.

CM: I guess we don't know what might be discovered, right?

BK: Right. That's what makes it so exciting.

B Answer the questions.

1. What will support life in the ISS if there's a problem? _____

2. Who built the Cupola? _____

3. Who performs maintenance outside the space station? _____

EXERCISE 2 AFFIRMATIVE AND NEGATIVE STATEMENTS

GRAMMAR NOTES 1–5 Complete this article about zero-G (zero gravity or weightlessness) with the correct form of the words in parentheses.

Living in Zero-G

Some tasks _____*can be accomplished*_____ more easily in zero-G. Inside the station,
        1. (can / accomplish)

astronauts _____ from the deadly conditions of space—but life in
        2. (can / protect)

almost zero-G still _____ normal. What's it like to live on the ISS?
        3. (can't / consider)

Getting Rest: Sleeping _____ to floating in water. It's
        4. (can / compare)

relaxing, but sleeping bags _____ to the walls of the cabins.
        5. (must / attach)

Otherwise, astronauts will drift around as they sleep.

Keeping Clean: Showers _____ because in zero-G, water from
        6. (can't / use)

a shower flies in all directions and sensitive equipment _____ .
        7. (might / damage)

Instead, astronauts take sponge baths, and they use no-rinse soap and shampoo to wash their

hands and hair. Used bath water _____ into a container by a
        8. (have to / suck)

vacuum machine. Clothes _____ by putting them into a bag with
        9. (can / wash)

water and soap, but astronauts really _____ with laundry. They
                                          10. (not have to / concern)

usually put dirty clothes into a trash container which _____ back
                                                            11. (can / send)

toward Earth and _____ in Earth's atmosphere.
                      12. (burn up)

Eating Good Meals: From the beginning of the project, ISS planners have known that food

_____ very seriously. Unlike meals on early space missions, food
    13. (should / take)

on the ISS _____ out of tubes. Frozen, dried, canned, and fresh
                14. (not have to / squeeze)

food _____ and _____ at a
          15. (can / heat)   **16.** (eat)

table. Regular utensils are used, but meals are packed into containers that

_____ to a tray so they don't float away.
    17. (must / attach)

Taking It Easy: Not surprisingly, a stressed astronaut is a grouchy astronaut. Free time

_____ for relaxing and enjoying views from the Cupola. All crew
    18. (have got to / provide)

members have laptops that _____ for listening to music, reading
                                19. (can / use)

e-books, and accessing the Internet. Before, the Internet _____
                                                                20. (could / access)

only for work, but now a direct Internet connection is available for astronauts' personal use. Emails

and texts _____ easily with friends and family. And blogs,
              21. (can / exchange)

tweets, and videos from the astronauts _____ by millions of
                                            22. (be going to / enjoy)

people back on Earth.

Staying Fit: Time also _____ for exercise. In low-gravity
                                23. (must / allow)

environments, muscle and bone _____ quickly without exercise.
                                    24. (will / lose)

Astronauts spend two hours a day, five to six days a week, exercising.

EXERCISE 3 AFFIRMATIVE AND NEGATIVE STATEMENTS

A GRAMMAR NOTES 1–5 Some scientists who are going to join the space station have just completed a simulation¹ of life on the station. Complete each conversation using the modals or expressions in parentheses and correct verbs from the boxes.

Conversation 1

accept	do	~~keep~~	reject	send	train

CESAR: This simulation was great, but it was too warm in there. I think the temperature on the ISS

_____*should be kept*_____ at 20 degrees Celsius—no warmer than that.
1. (should)

GINA: Shorts and T-shirts _____ to the station for you. That's what
2. (can)

most astronauts ask for.

CESAR: By the way, you know that woman who wants to visit the space station? I hear that she

_____ on our mission. They're considering her application
3. (might not)

now. Her company wants her to do a spacewalk, and so far only astronauts have done that.

GINA: Her application _____ just for that. But she ought to
4. (shouldn't)

complete a simulation first.

LYLE: Absolutely. She _____ to work while wearing a spacesuit.
5. (have got to)

That _____ except underwater in one of the space labs.
6. (can't)

Conversation 2

approve	do	send	share	surprise

HANS: Did you fill in your food-preference forms? They _____ to the
7. (should)

Food Systems Lab today.

HISA: I did. I'm glad the new dishes _____ by everyone.
8. (have to)

HANS: You'll find that the food _____ by everyone, too. Everyone
9. (will)

enjoys trying different things, and we all benefit from the variety.

LUIS: That's great. But I have a concern about shaving in zero-G. The whisker dust from my beard

and mustache keep flying back into my face. It's uncomfortable. I also wonder if it could be

dangerous and if something _____ about it.
10. (could)

HANS: I have a feeling we _____ by a lot of unexpected problems.
11. (be going to)

▶18|02 **B** LISTEN AND CHECK **Listen to the conversations and check your answers in A.**

---

1 *simulation:* something you do in order to practice what you would do in a real situation

EXERCISE 4 EDITING

GRAMMAR NOTES 1–5 Read an astronaut's journal notes. There are seven mistakes in the use of the passive with modals and similar expressions. The first mistake is already corrected. Find and correct six more.

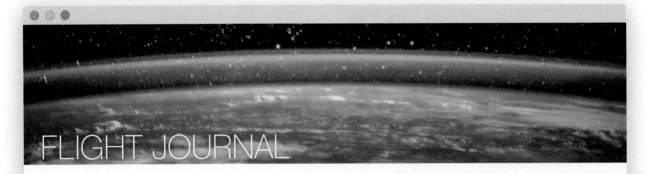

FLIGHT JOURNAL

October 4

6:15 a.m. In the past, astronauts used sleeping restraints, so their feet and hands didn't float around while they were sleeping. It was clear that sleeping arrangements had to be ~~make~~ *made* more comfortable. Luckily, things have improved a lot. Last night, I slept in a soft sleeping bag that's attached to the wall of my sleeping "pod." It seemed very natural. But maybe the sleeping quarters could designed differently. They're too small— it's kind of like sleeping in a closet.

1:00 p.m. Lunch was pretty good. Chicken teriyaki. It's nice and spicy, and the sauce can actually taste, even at zero gravity. More had better be fly in for us soon. It's the most popular dish in the freezer and will all be eaten up soon!

4:40 p.m. I'm worried about my daughter. Just before I left on this mission, she said she was planning to quit school at the end of the semester. That's only a month away. I want to call her and discuss it. But I worry that I might get angry and yell. I might overheard by the others. We really could use a little more privacy here.

10:30 p.m. The view of Earth is unbelievably breathtaking! Tonight I spent a long time just looking out the window and watching Earth pass below. At night, a halo of light surrounds the horizon. It's so bright that the tops of the clouds can see. It can't be described. It simply have to be experienced.

EXERCISE 5 LISTENING

▶18|03 (A) Some crew members aboard the ISS are watching a science-fiction movie. Listen to the conversations from the movie. Listen again and circle the words that you hear the movie characters say.

1. "It can / (can't) be repaired out here."

2. "Our messages could / should be misunderstood."

3. "We know that Lon will / won't be taken seriously down there."

4. "Oxygen must / mustn't be used in this situation."

5. "They can / can't be grown in space."

6. "As you know, we have to help / be helped with the repairs."

▶18|03 (B) Work with a partner. Listen again. Discuss the answers. Why do you think the movie characters made those statements?

EXAMPLE: A: For number 1, the answer is *can't*. The captain said "It can't be repaired out here."
B: Right. Why do you think the spaceship can't be repaired in space?
A: I don't know. Maybe they don't have the parts they need.
B: That's possible. Maybe the parts have to be sent from Earth or another planet.

EXERCISE 6 IN CLOSE QUARTERS

(A) REACHING AGREEMENT Work in a group. Imagine that in preparation for a space mission, your group is going to spend a week together in a one-room apartment. Discuss the rules that should be made for living in close quarters. Consider some of the issues listed below.

EXAMPLE: A: I think dinner should be served at 6:00 every night.
B: 6:00? Isn't that a little early?
C: Well, do meals always have to be eaten together? Perhaps people should be given a choice of time.
A: Good idea. And what about choice of food? I think we should be given several choices.

- food
- clothes
- room temperature
- noise
- neatness
- cleanliness
- privacy
- language
- Other: _____
- entertainment
- sleep time

(B) Make a list of rules that you've agreed on. Use the passive with modals and similar expressions.

Dinner will be served at 6:00 and 8:00 p.m.

A choice of at least two menus should be given for each meal.

C Compare your list with another group's list.

EXAMPLE: **A:** We decided that dinner should be served at 6:00 and then again at 8:00.
            B: And we also thought that a choice of at least two menu items should be given for each meal.

EXERCISE 7 A LOT SHOULD BE DONE HERE

PROBLEM SOLVING **Work in a group. Look at the picture of an international student lounge. You are responsible for getting it in order, but you have limited time and money. Agree on five things that should be done.**

EXAMPLE: **A:** The window has to be replaced.
            B: No. That'll cost too much. It can just be taped.
            C: That'll look terrible. It's really got to be replaced.
            A: OK. What else should be done?

EXERCISE 8 FOR OR AGAINST

DISCUSSION **Sending people to the International Space Station costs millions of dollars. Should money be spent for these space projects, or could it be spent better on Earth? If so, how should it be spent? Discuss these questions with your classmates.**

EXAMPLE: **A:** I think space projects are useful. A lot of new products are going to be developed in space.
            B: I don't agree. Some of that money should be spent on public housing.

FROM GRAMMAR TO WRITING

A BEFORE YOUR WRITE Diplomats are people who officially represent their country in a foreign country. Imagine that you are going to attend a school for future diplomats. Complete the information about some of the features of your ideal school.

Courses required: _____

Language(s) spoken: _____

Living quarters provided: _____

Food offered: _____

Trips taken: _____

Electronic devices provided: _____

B WRITE Use your information to write one or two paragraphs about your ideal school for diplomacy. Use the passive with modals and similar expressions. Try to avoid some of the common mistakes in the chart.

EXAMPLE: I think the ideal school for diplomacy should teach a lot about cross-cultural understanding. Courses should be required in . . . More than one official language should be spoken. Classes could be offered in . . .

Common Mistakes in Using the Passive with Modals and Similar Expressions

Use *be* + **past participle after the modal**. Do not leave out *be*.	Language classes **should *be* required**. NOT Language classes ~~should required~~.
Use the **past participle after *be***. Do not use the base form of the verb after *be*.	A lot **could *be* learned**. NOT A lot could be ~~learn~~.

C CHECK YOUR WORK Read your paragraph(s). Underline the passive with modals and similar expressions. Use the Editing Checklist to check your work.

Editing Checklist

Did you use . . . ?

☐ *be* + past participle to form the passive after modals or similar expressions

☐ *will* or *be going to* for certainty in the future

☐ *can* for present ability

☐ *could* for past ability or future possibility

☐ *may*, *might*, and *can't* for future possibility or impossibility

☐ *should*, *ought to*, and *had better* for advice

☐ *must* and *have (got) to* for necessity

D REVISE YOUR WORK Read your paragraph(s) again. Can you improve your writing? Make changes if necessary. Give your writing a title.

UNIT 18 REVIEW

Test yourself on the grammar of the unit.

Ⓐ Circle the correct words to complete the sentences.

1. What should be <u>did / done</u> about the student lounge?

2. I think the furniture should <u>be replaced / replaced</u>.

3. Maybe some computer workstations <u>could / have</u> be provided.

4. The air conditioning <u>has / had</u> better be repaired.

5. It might not <u>be / being</u> fixed by the summer.

6. The lounge <u>don't / won't</u> be used by students while it's being painted.

7. The school office <u>has / had</u> got to be told about these problems.

8. In the future, problems will be <u>handle / handled</u> faster.

Ⓑ Complete the sentences with the correct form of the verbs in parentheses.

1. Astronauts _____ in zero gravity.
   (should / train)

2. They _____ the chance to work in those conditions.
   (have to / give)

3. Equipment _____ in conditions similar to space.
   (must / test)

4. Zero gravity _____ underwater as well as on the ISS.
   (can / experience)

5. Underwater living space _____ by Aquatics Laboratory.
   (will / provide)

6. A lot more astronauts _____ there for training.
   (may / send)

7. Skills for Moon missions _____ also _____ underwater.
   (could / develop)

Ⓒ Find and correct five mistakes.

   The new spacesuits are going to be testing underwater today. They've got to been improved before they can be used on the Moon or Mars. Two astronauts are going to be wearing them while they're working, and they'll watched by the engineers. This morning, communication was lost with the Earth's surface, and all decisions had to be make by the astronauts themselves. It was a very realistic situation. This crew will got to be very well prepared for space travel. They're going to the Moon in a few years.

Now check your answers on page 480.

The Passive Causative
PERSONAL SERVICES

STEP 1   GRAMMAR IN CONTEXT

BEFORE YOU READ

Look at the photos on this page and on pages 302–303. Discuss the questions.

1. Which forms of body art do you think are attractive?

2. Does body art have any disadvantages? What are they?

READ

▶ 19|01   Read this article from a fashion magazine.

Body Art

Each culture has a different ideal of beauty, and throughout the ages,[1] men and women have done amazing things to achieve the ideal. They have had their hair shaved, cut, colored, straightened, and curled; and they have had their bodies decorated with painting and tattoos. Here are some of today's many options:

Hair

Getting your hair done is the easiest way to change your appearance. Today, both men and women have their hair permed. This chemical procedure[2] can curl hair or just give it more body.[3]

---

1 *throughout the ages:* during different periods of time
2 *chemical procedure:* a technique that uses chemicals (for example, hydrogen peroxide) to change the appearance or texture of something
3 *body:* hair thickness

If your hair is long, you can, of course, get it cut. But did you know that you can also have short hair lengthened with hair extensions?[4] Of course you can have your hair colored and become a blonde, brunette, or redhead. But you can also have it bleached white or get it dyed blue, green, or orange!

Tattoos

This form of body art was created many thousands of years ago. Today, tattoos have again become popular. More and more people are having them done. However, caution is necessary. Although nowadays you can get a tattoo removed with less pain and scarring[5] than before, getting a tattoo is still a big decision.

Piercing

Pierced ears are an old favorite, but lately the practice of piercing has expanded. Many people now are getting their noses, lips, or other parts of the body pierced for jewelry. Piercing requires even more caution than tattooing, and aftercare is very important to avoid infection.

Body Paint

If a tattoo is not for you, you can have ornaments painted on your skin instead. Some people have necklaces and bracelets painted on their neck and arms or get a butterfly mask applied to their face for a special event. Sports fans often get their face painted with their team's colors or the name of their favorite player. Body paintings can be large, but unlike tattoos, they can be washed off.

---

4 *hair extensions:* pieces of hair (natural or synthetic) that people have attached to their own hair to make it longer
5 *scarring:* the creation of a permanent mark on the skin as a result of an accident, or a cosmetic or medical procedure

Cosmetic Surgery

You can get your nose shortened, or have your chin lengthened. You can even have the shape of your body changed. There is always some risk involved, so the decision to have cosmetic surgery requires a lot of thought.

Some of the ways of changing your appearance may be cheap and temporary. However, others are expensive and permanent. So, think before you act, and don't let today's choice become tomorrow's regret.

AFTER YOU READ

A VOCABULARY **Complete the sentences with the words from the box.**

caution	expand	option	permanent	risk	temporary

1. Buying a new car isn't a(n) _____ for us now. It's much too expensive.

2. Miguel's job is just _____. He's leaving next month.

3. Be careful! _____ is always necessary when crossing the street.

4. My salon is small, but they are going to _____ next month.

5. Carly hates her new hair color. It's a good thing it isn't _____.

6. Piercing can be attractive, but there is always the _____ of infection.

B COMPREHENSION **Read the statements. Check (✓) *True* or *False*.**

	True	False
1. Changing your hair is an easy way to change your appearance.	☐	☐
2. Only women perm their hair.	☐	☐
3. It's possible to lengthen short hair.	☐	☐
4. Tattoos are very popular.	☐	☐
5. Tattoos are permanent.	☐	☐
6. People usually pierce only their ears for jewelry.	☐	☐
7. You can have surgery to make your chin longer.	☐	☐

C DISCUSSION **Work with a partner. Compare your answers in B. Why did you check *True* or *False*?**

THE PASSIVE CAUSATIVE

Statements

Subject	*Have/Get*	Object	Past Participle	(*By* + Agent)	
She	has	*her hair*	cut	*by André*	every month.
He	has had	*his beard*	trimmed		before.
I	get	*my nails*	done		at André's.
They	are going to get	*their ears*	pierced.		

Yes/No Questions

Auxiliary Verb	Subject	*Have/Get*	Object	Past Participle	(*By* + Agent)	
Does	she	have	*her hair*	cut	*by André?*	
Has	he	had	*his beard*	trimmed		before?
Do	you	get	*your nails*	done		at André's?
Are	they	going to get	*their ears*	pierced?		

Wh- Questions

Wh- Word	Auxiliary Verb	Subject	*Have/Get*	Object	Past Participle	(*By* + Agent)	
How often	does	she	have	*her hair*	cut	*by André?*	
Where	did	he	get	*his beard*	trimmed		before?
When	do	you	get	*your nails*	done		at André's?
Why	are	they	going to get	*their ears*	pierced?		

GRAMMAR NOTES

1 Forms of the Passive Causative

Form the **passive causative** with the appropriate form of *have* or *get* + **object** + **past participle**. *Have* and *get* have the same meaning.

• *have*	I **have** *my hair* **cut** by André.
• *get*	I **get** *my hair* **cut** by André.

CONTINUED ▶

You can use the **passive causative** with:

- **all verb tenses**
  (simple present, simple past, etc.)

- **all modals**
  (*can, could, must, should, will*, etc.)

- **gerunds**

- **infinitives**

I **get** *my car* **checked** every year.	
I **had** *it* **washed** yesterday.	
I **can get** *the oil* **changed** tomorrow.	
You **should have** *the tires* **checked**, too.	
I love **having** *my hair* **done**.	
I want **to get** *it* **colored**.	

BE CAREFUL! The **object** always goes right **after** *have* or *get*. Do not put the object after the past participle.

She **gets** *her nails* **done**.
NOT She ~~gets done her nails~~.

2 Meaning of the Passive Causative

Use the **passive causative** to describe services that you arrange for someone to do for you.

There is a big difference in meaning between an active sentence and a passive causative sentence.

- **active**

- **passive causative**

I **color** my hair.
  (*I do it myself.*)

I **have** *my hair* **colored**.
  (*Someone does it for me.*)

BE CAREFUL! Do not confuse the passive causative with *had* with the past perfect. The meaning is very different.

PASSIVE CAUSATIVE WITH *HAD*
I **had** *it* **colored** last week.
  (*Someone did it for me.*)

PAST PERFECT
I **had colored** it before.
  (*I did it myself.*)

IN WRITING The regular passive is more common in writing. The **passive causative** is more common in **conversation**.

REGULAR PASSIVE
The operation **was done** on Monday. *(report)*

PASSIVE CAUSATIVE
She **had it done** on Monday. *(conversation)*

3 The Passive Causative with *By* + Agent

Use *by* when it is necessary to mention the **agent** (the person doing the service).

When it is new or important information, use *by* + **agent** to express who is doing the service.

This week, Lee **is getting her hair done** *by a new stylist*.

BE CAREFUL! Do not use *by* + agent when it is clear who is doing the service or when it is not important information.

NOT When does Lee get her hair done ~~by a stylist~~?
  (*Because of the causative, it is already clear that a stylist does her hair.*)

STEP 3 FOCUSED PRACTICE

EXERCISE 1 DISCOVER THE GRAMMAR

GRAMMAR NOTES 1–3 **Read the conversations. Decide if the statement that follows each conversation is *True* (*T*) or *False* (*F*).**

1. DEBRA: We should start planning for our party.
   JAKE: OK. In fact, I'm going to get my hair cut by Roberto tomorrow for the big event.

   _F_ Jake cuts his own hair.

2. JAKE: Speaking about hair—Amber, *your* hair's getting awfully long.
   AMBER: I know, Dad. I'm going to cut it tomorrow.

   _____ Amber cuts her own hair.

3. DEBRA: And what about your party dress? Are you going to have it shortened?
   AMBER: Yes, Mom. But not until next week.

   _____ Amber is going to shorten her dress herself.

4. AMBER: Mom, why didn't you get your nails done last time you went to the hair salon?
   DEBRA: Because I did them just before my appointment.

   _____ Debra did her own nails.

5. AMBER: I was thinking of painting a butterfly on my forehead for the party.
   DEBRA: A butterfly! Well, OK. At least paint is just temporary.

   _____ Someone is going to paint a butterfly on Amber's forehead for her.

6. DEBRA: Jake, do you think we should get the floors waxed before the party?
   JAKE: I think they look OK. We'll get them done afterward.

   _____ Debra and Jake are going to hire someone to wax their floors after the party.

7. DEBRA: I'm going to watch some TV and then go to bed. What's on the agenda for tomorrow?
   JAKE: I have to get up early. I'm getting the car washed before work.

   _____ Jake is going to wash the car himself.

8. DEBRA: You know, I think it's time to change the oil, too.
   JAKE: You're right. I'll do it this weekend.

   _____ Jake is going to change the oil himself.

EXERCISE 2 STATEMENTS

GRAMMAR NOTES 1–2 Today is February 15. Look at the Santanas' calendar and write sentences about when they *had/got things done* and when they *are going to have/get things done*. Use the correct form of the words in parentheses.

FEBRUARY

SUNDAY	MONDAY	TUESDAY	WEDNESDAY	THURSDAY	FRIDAY	SATURDAY
1	2	3	4	5	6	7 Deb – hair salon
8	9	10	11	12 Jake – haircut	13 carpets	14 dog groomer
15 TODAY	16 windows	17	18	19	20 food and drinks	21 party!! family pictures
22	23	24	25 Amber – ears pierced	26	27	28

1. <u>The Santanas are going to have family pictues taken on the 21st.</u>
   (The Santanas / have / family pictures / take)

2. _____
   (Debra / get / her hair / perm)

3. _____
   (Amber / have / the dog / groom)

4. _____
   (They / get / the windows / wash)

5. _____
   (They / have / the carpets / clean)

6. _____
   (Amber / have / her ears / pierce)

7. _____
   (Jake / get / his hair / cut)

8. _____
   (They / have / food and drinks / deliver)

EXERCISE 3 STATEMENTS AND QUESTIONS

GRAMMAR NOTES 1–3 Debra and Jake are going to have a party. Complete the
conversations with the passive causative of the appropriate verbs in the box.

color	cut	dry clean	paint	remove	repair	~~shorten~~	wash

1. AMBER: I bought a new dress for the party, Mom. What do you think?

   DEBRA: It's pretty, but it's a little long. Why don't you _____ *get or have it shortened* _____?

   AMBER: OK. They do alterations at the cleaners. I'll take it in tomorrow.

2. AMBER: By the way, what are *you* planning to wear?

   DEBRA: Me? My white silk suit. But I have to _____. It has a stain on

   the sleeve. I hope it's not permanent.

   AMBER: I can drop it off at the cleaners with my dress.

3. JAKE: The house is ready, except for the windows. They look pretty dirty.

   DEBRA: Don't worry. We _____ tomorrow.

4. DEBRA: Amber, your hair is getting really long. I thought you were going to cut it.

   AMBER: I decided not to do it myself this time. I _____ by André.

5. DEBRA: My hair's getting a lot of gray in it. Should I _____?

   JAKE: Well, I guess that's an option. But it looks fine to me the way it is.

6. AMBER: Mom, I've been thinking about getting a butterfly tattoo instead of having one painted. I

   can always _____ if I decide I don't like it.

   DEBRA: No! That's *not* an option! There are too many risks involved in the procedure.

7. AMBER: Someone's at the door, and it's only 6 o'clock!

   DEBRA: No, it's not. I guess my mother's antique clock stopped again.

   JAKE: Oh no, not again. I don't believe it! I _____ twice this

   year, and it's only February!

8. GUEST: The house looks really beautiful, Jake. I love the colors you chose. _____ you

   _____?

   JAKE: No, actually we did it ourselves last summer.

EXERCISE 4 EDITING

GRAMMAR NOTES 1–3 Read Amber's Facebook post. There are seven mistakes in the use of the passive causative. The first mistake is already corrected. Find and correct six more.

● ● ●

Amber's thoughts...

February 21: The party was tonight. It went really well! The house looked

great. Last week, Mom and Dad had the floors waxed and all the windows ~~clean~~ *cleaned*

professionally so everything sparkled. And of course we had the whole house

painted ourselves last summer. (I'll never forget that. It took us two weeks!) I wore

my silver dress that I have shortened by Bo; and my best friend, Alicia, wore her

new black gown. Right before the party, I got cut my hair by André. He did a great

job. There were a lot of guests at the party. We had almost fifty people invited,

and they almost all showed up for our

family event! The food was great, too.

Mom made most of the main dishes

herself, but she had the rest of the

food prepare by a caterer. Mom

and Dad had hired a professional

photographer, so at the end of

the party we took our pictures.

Here's one of me and Alicia.

EXERCISE 5 LISTENING

▶ 19|02 **A** Ji-woo has just gone away to college. Read the list of tasks. Then listen to the phone call between Ji-woo and her father. Listen again and check (✓) *Does the Job Herself* or *Hires Someone to Do the Job*.

	Does the Job Herself	Hires Someone to Do the Job
1. change the oil in her car	☑	☐
2. change the locks	☐	☐
3. paint the apartment	☐	☐
4. put up bookshelves	☐	☐
5. bring new furniture to the apartment	☐	☐
6. paint her hands	☐	☐
7. cut her hair	☐	☐
8. color her hair	☐	☐

▶ 19|02 **B** Listen again. Then work with a partner. What do you think? Answer the questions and give reasons for your opinions. Do you and your partner agree?

1. Is Ji-woo handy? (good at making, maintaining, and repairing things)

    EXAMPLE: **A:** I think she's pretty handy. She changed the oil in her car by herself.
    B: Right. She didn't have to have it done for her. And she...

2. Why does Ji-woo tell her father not to worry?
3. Why does Ji-woo turn down her father's offer to paint her apartment?
4. Why didn't Ji-woo have to get her new desk and lamps delivered?
5. Why does Ji-woo's father ask, "Will we be able to recognize you?"

EXERCISE 6 GETTING READY

A ROLE PLAY Work in a group. Imagine that you are taking a car trip together to another country. You'll be gone for several weeks. Decide where you're going. Then make a list of things you have to do and arrange before the trip. Use the ideas below and ideas of your own.

EXAMPLE: **A:** I have to get my passport renewed.
    B: Me too. And we should apply for visas right away.

- passport and visa
- car (oil, gas, tires, brake fluid)
- home (pets, plants, mail, newspaper delivery)
- personal (clothing, hair, nails)
- medical (teeth, eyes, prescriptions)
- Other: _____

B Now compare your list with that of another group. Did you forget anything?

EXERCISE 7 BEFORE AND AFTER

Ⓐ PICTURE DISCUSSION Work with a partner. Look at the *Before* and *After* pictures of a fashion model. Discuss all the things the model had done to change her appearance.

EXAMPLE: A: Well, her nose looks different.
 B: You're right. She had it shortened! And look at her . . .

Before   After

Ⓑ Do you think the woman looks better? Why or why not?

EXAMPLE: A: I don't know why she had her nose fixed.
 B: Neither do I. I think it looked fine before.

EXERCISE 8 BODY ART AROUND THE WORLD

CROSS-CULTURAL COMPARISON Work in a group. Think about other cultures. Discuss the types of things men and women do or get done in order to change or improve their appearance. Report back to your class.

EXAMPLE: A: In India, women get their hands painted for special occasions. I think it looks nice.
 B: In Japan, . . .

Some procedures to think about:

- **hands/feet:** painting nails, painting hands or bottom of feet
- **eyes:** lengthening eyelashes, coloring eyebrows
- **teeth:** straightening, whitening
- **face:** shortening nose, plumping lips
- **hair:** coloring, lengthening, styling, curling, straightening, braiding
- **skin:** whitening, tanning, tattooing, painting

A BEFORE YOU WRITE Think about an event in your life (a party, a wedding, moving into a new home, looking for a job, a trip). What did you do to prepare for it? What did you have done to prepare for it? Complete the outline.

The Event: _____

Things I did myself	Things I had done
_____	_____
_____	_____
_____	_____

B WRITE Use your outline to write one or two paragraphs about the preparations for your event. Try to avoid the mistakes in the chart.

EXAMPLE: Last month, I moved into a new apartment. It's an old apartment, and it needed a lot of work. Because the apartment is small, I was able to do quite a few things myself. For example, before I moved in, I painted the kitchen and living room, but I had to have carpet installed and some windows replaced. I didn't have any furniture, so I bought a bed and a couch and had them delivered. I also got . . . Although I've already been there a month, there are still a lot of things I have to get done!

Common Mistakes in Using the Passive Causative

Use the correct word order, *have something done*. Do not use *have done something*.	I had *the apartment* painted by Colorama. NOT I had painted the apartment by Colorama.
Use *by* + **agent** only when it is important to mention the agent. Do not mention the agent when it is obvious or unimportant information.	I had *the apartment* painted by Colorama. NOT I had the apartment painted by a painter.

C CHECK YOUR WORK Read your paragraph(s). Underline once the words that express things you did yourself. Underline twice the words that express things someone did for you. Circle the *by* + agent if you used it. Use the Editing Checklist to check your work.

Editing Checklist

Did you use . . . ?

☐ the passive causative for services someone did for you

☐ the passive causative with the appropriate form of *have* or *get* + object + past participle

☐ the correct word order for the passive causative

☐ *by* only when it was important to mention the agent

D REVISE YOUR WORK Read your paragraph(s) again. Can you improve your writing? Make changes if necessary. Give your paragraph(s) a title.

UNIT 19 **REVIEW**

Test yourself on the grammar of the unit.

Ⓐ Circle the correct words to complete the sentences.

1. I don't cut my own hair. I have it cut / have cut it.

2. My friend has her hair did / done every week.

3. We should get / gotten the house painted again this year.

4. Did you have painted your house / your house painted?

5. I want to have the job done by / from a professional.

Ⓑ Complete each sentence with the correct passive causative form of the verbs in parentheses and a pronoun.

1. My computer stopped working. I have to _____ .
   (get / repair)

2. I don't clean the windows myself. I _____ once a year.
   (have / clean)

3. Your pants are too long. You should _____ .
   (have / shorten)

4. Does Monica color her own hair or does she _____ ?
   (get / color)

5. I can't fix this vacuum cleaner myself. I'll have to _____ .
   (get / fix)

6. Todd used to have a tattoo, but he _____ last year.
   (have / remove)

7. My passport is going to expire soon. I need to _____ .
   (get / renew)

8. The car has been making a strange noise. I _____ tomorrow.
   (have / check)

Ⓒ Find and correct seven mistakes.

I'm going on vacation next week. I'd like to have done some work in my office, and this seems like a good time for it. Please have my carpet clean while I'm gone. And could you have my computer and printer looked at? It's been quite a while since they've been serviced. Ted wants to have my office painted by a painter while I'm gone. Please tell him any color is fine except pink! Last week, I had designed some new brochures by Perfect Print. Please call the printer and have them delivered directly to the sales reps. And could you also get made up more business cards? When I get back, it'll be time to plan the holiday party. I think we should have it catered this year from a professional. While I'm gone, why don't you call around and get some estimates from caterers? Has the estimates sent to Ted. Thanks.

Now check your answers on page 480.

Conditional Sentences

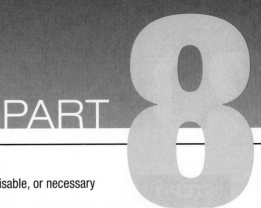

PART 8

OUTCOMES

- Describe present real conditions and results that are certain, possible, advisable, or necessary
- Express instructions, commands, or invitations that depend on a condition
- Identify specific information in an article about shopping online
- Infer correct information from announcements
- Discuss different types of shopping
- Write about things to do in one's city or town

OUTCOMES

- Describe future real conditions and results that will be certain, possible, advisable, or necessary
- Identify specific information in a magazine article
- Identify and discuss details in an interview
- Discuss common problems and possible solutions
- Discuss superstitions, giving opinions and making cross-cultural comparisons
- Write a speech about what one will do if elected class or school president

OUTCOMES

- Describe present or future unreal conditions and results that are untrue, impossible, or possible
- Give advice with *If I were you*
- Express wishes about the present or the future
- Identify key details in a written and a recorded fairy tale
- Discuss hypothetical questions and wishes
- Write about a wish one has for oneself or society

OUTCOMES

- Describe past unreal conditions and results that are untrue, imagined, impossible, or possible
- Express regret about things that happened or didn't happen in the past
- Extract specific information from an article
- Infer correct information from conversations
- Speculate about past events or hypothetical situations
- Discuss a past decision one regrets
- Write about an event that changed one's life

Present Real Conditional Sentences

SHOPPING

OUTCOMES
- Describe present real conditions and results that are certain, possible, advisable, or necessary
- Express instructions, commands, or invitations that depend on a condition
- Identify specific information in an article about shopping online
- Infer correct information from announcements
- Discuss different types of shopping
- Write about things to do in one's city or town

STEP 1   GRAMMAR IN CONTEXT

BEFORE YOU READ

Look at the photo and at the title of the article. Discuss the questions.

1. What is a cyber mall?

2. Have you ever purchased something online? If *yes*, what?

3. What are some steps people should take to shop safely online?

READD

20|01   Read this article about cyber malls.

Pick and Click: Shopping@Home

Where is the largest mall[1] in the world? If you think it's in Dubai or China, you're wrong! It's in cyberspace![2] And you can get there from home on your very own computer.

Cyber shopping is fast, convenient, and often less expensive. It doesn't matter if it's a book or a diamond necklace—with just a click of your mouse, you can buy anything without getting up from your chair. If you're looking for the best price, you can easily compare prices and read other buyers' reviews of products. Shopping online can save you time and money—but

---

1 *mall:* a very large building or outdoor area with a lot of stores in it
2 *cyberspace:* all the connections between computers in different places (people think of it as a real place where information, messages, pictures, etc., exist)

you need to surf³ and shop safely. Here are some tips to make your trip to the cyber mall a good one:

- You are less likely to have a problem if you shop with well-known companies.
- If you don't know the company, ask them to send you information. What is their address? Their phone number?
- Always pay by credit card if you can. If you are unhappy with the product (or if you don't receive it), then you can dispute the charge.
- Only enter your credit card information on a secure site. If you see a closed lock 🔒 or complete key 🗝 symbol at the bottom of your screen, the site is secure. Also, the web address will change from `http://www` to `https://www`. This means that your credit card number will be encrypted (changed so that others can't read it). If the site isn't secure, don't enter your credit card information.
- If you have kids, don't let them give out personal information.
- If you have any doubts about a site's security, contact the store by phone or email.
- Find out the return policy. What happens if you don't like the product?
- Print out and save a record of your purchase. If there is a problem, the receipt gives you proof of purchase.
- If you change your mind about an order, contact the company immediately.

As you can see, many of these steps are similar to the ones you follow in a "store with doors." Just use common sense. If you take some basic precautions, you shouldn't have any problems.

Internet shopping has literally⁴ brought a world of opportunity to consumers. Today, we can shop 24 hours a day, 7 days a week in stores that are halfway around the globe without ever having to leave home or stand in line. As with many things in life, there are some risks. Just remember that online or off, if an offer seems too good to be true, it probably is. Happy cyber shopping!

---

3 *surf:* go quickly from one website to another in order to find information that interests you
4 *literally:* according to the most basic meaning of a word or expression

AFTER YOU READ

Ⓐ VOCABULARY **Complete the sentences with the words from the box.**

consumer	dispute	policy	precaution	secure	site

1. You should ask about a store's return _____.

2. A smart _____ always compares prices before making a purchase.

3. As a safety _____, you should never give your password to anyone.

4. My friend never shops online. He doesn't think it's _____ enough.

5. I don't like that store's online _____. It's very confusing.

6. I need to _____ that charge. I ordered one shirt, but they charged me for two.

B COMPREHENSION Choose the word or phrase that best completes each sentence.

1. The largest mall in the world is in _____ .
   a. China
   b. Dubai
   c. cyberspace

2. The process of shopping for a book online is _____ shopping for a diamond necklace.
   a. the same as
   b. faster than
   c. different from

3. It's a good idea to shop with a company that has _____ .
   a. a nice website
   b. a name you know
   c. products for children

4. If possible, you should pay for Internet purchases _____ .
   a. by credit card
   b. by check
   c. with cash

5. A closed lock at the bottom of the computer screen means _____ .
   a. you can't shop there
   b. the site is safe
   c. the product is sold out

6. You can avoid problems by _____ .
   a. shopping in "real" stores
   b. using cash
   c. being careful

7. An offer that seems unbelievably good is probably not _____ .
   a. safe
   b. expensive
   c. cheap

C DISCUSSION Work with a partner. Compare your answers in B. Why did you choose each answer?

STEP 2 GRAMMAR PRESENTATION

PRESENT REAL CONDITIONAL SENTENCES

Statements

If-Clause	Result Clause
If I **shop** online,	I **save** time.
If the mall **is** closed,	I **can shop** online.

Statements

Result Clause	If-Clause
I **save** time	*if* I **shop** online.
I **can shop** online	*if* the mall **is** closed.

Yes/No Questions

Result Clause	If-Clause
Do you **save** time	*if* you **shop** online?
Can you **shop** online	*if* the mall **is** closed?

Short Answers

Affirmative		Negative	
Yes,	I do.	No,	I don't.
	I can.		I can't.

Wh- Questions

Result Clause	If-Clause
What **happens**	*if* I **don't like** it?

GRAMMAR NOTES

1 Present Real Conditional Sentences

Use present real conditional sentences to describe **real conditions** and **results** that are **certain**. When these conditions happen, the results are always the same.

The *if-clause* describes a **real** or **true condition**. The **result clause** describes **what always happens** when this condition occurs.	*IF-CLAUSE* RESULT CLAUSE *If* it's a holiday, the store is closed. *(When there is a holiday, the store is always closed.)*

You can use present real conditional sentences to express:

• **general truths**	*If* you use a credit card, it's faster. *(When you use a credit card, it's always faster.)*
• **habits** or things that happen again and again	*If* Bill shops online, he spends a lot of money. *(Every time Bill shops on line, he always spends a lot of money.)*
For **general truths**, use the **simple present** in both clauses.	PRESENT PRESENT *If* you **see** a closed lock symbol, the site **is** secure.
For **habits** or things that happen again and again, use the **simple present or present progressive** in the *if-clause*. Use the **simple present** in the result clause.	PRESENT PRESENT *If* I **surf** the Web, I **use** Google. PRESENT PROG. PRESENT *If* I'm **surfing** the Web, I **use** Google.
USAGE NOTE We often use *even if* when the **result is surprising**.	*Even if* it's a holiday, this store stays open.

2 With a Modal in the Result Clause

You can use **modals** or similar expressions in the **result clause** to express **possibility** (*can, may, could*), **advice** (*should, ought to*), or **necessity** (*must, have to*).

	IF-CLAUSE RESULT CLAUSE
• *can*	If you don't like the gift, you *can* **return** it.
• *should*	If it's not too expensive, you *should* **buy** it.
• *must*	If you use their website, you *must* **have** a password.
USAGE NOTE We sometime use *then* to **emphasize the result** in present real conditional sentences with modals or similar expressions.	If you don't like the gift, *then* you **can return** it.

3 With an Imperative in the Result Clause

Use an **imperative** in the result clause to give **instructions**, **commands**, and **invitations** that depend on a condition.

	IF-CLAUSE	RESULT CLAUSE
• **instructions**	If you change your mind,	**call** the company.
• **command**	If you get home very late,	**don't make** noise.
• **invitation**	If you want to come along,	**meet** us at noon.

USAGE NOTE We sometimes use *then* to **emphasize the result** in present real conditional sentences with imperatives.

If you change your mind, ***then* call** the company.

4 Position of the *If*-Clause

The *if*-clause can come **at the beginning or the end** of the sentence. The meaning is the same.

- at the **beginning**

  If **I shop online**, I save time.

- at the **end**

  I save time *if* **I shop online**.

IN WRITING Use a **comma after the *if*-clause** when it comes at the **beginning** of the sentence. Do not use a comma after the result clause when the result clause comes first.

If **I shop online,** I use my credit card.

NOT I use my credit card͓ if I shop online.

5 Present Real Conditional Sentences with *When* Instead of *If*

In present real conditional sentences, you can often use *when* instead of *if*. The meaning is the same.

- **general truths**

  If you **use** a credit card, it**'s** faster.
  When you **use** a credit card, it**'s** faster.

- **habits** or things that happen again and again

  If Bill **shops** online, he **spends** a lot of money.
  When Bill **shops** online, he **spends** a lot of money.

USAGE NOTE We sometimes use *when* with the **present progressive** in both clauses to describe actions that happen **at the same time**.

When stores **are opening** in Los Angeles, they **are closing** in Johannesburg.

USAGE NOTE We sometimes use *whenever* instead of *when*. It means *every time*.

Whenever Bill shops online, he spends a lot of money.
  (Every time Bill shops online, he spends a lot of money.)

EXERCISE 1   DISCOVER THE GRAMMAR

GRAMMAR NOTES 1–5   Read these shopping tips. In each present real conditional sentence, underline once the result clause. Underline twice the clause that talks about the condition.

SHOP Smart

YOU'RE SHOPPING in a foreign city. Should you pay full price, or should you bargain? If you don't know the answer, you can pay too much or miss a fun experience. Bargaining is one of the greatest shopping pleasures if you know how to do it. The strategies are different in different places. Check out these tips before you go.

HONG KONG   Hong Kong is one of the world's greatest shopping cities. If you like to bargain, you can do it anywhere except the larger department stores. The trick is not to look too interested. If you see something you want, pick it up along with some other items and ask the prices. Then make an offer below what you are willing to pay. If the seller's offer is close to the price you want, then you should be able to reach an agreement quickly.

ITALY   When Italians shop at outdoor markets, they often bargain. You can try this, too, if you want to get a better price. In stores, you can politely ask for a discount if you want to bargain. Take your time. Make conversation if you speak Italian. Show your admiration for the object by picking it up and pointing out its wonderful features. When you hear the price, look sad. Make your own offer. Then end the bargaining politely if you don't agree.

MEXICO   In Mexico, people truly enjoy bargaining. There are some clear rules, though. You should bargain only if you really are interested in buying the object. If the vendor's price is far more than you want to pay, then politely stop the negotiation. If you know your price is truly reasonable, walking away often brings a lower offer.

Remember, bargaining is always a social interaction, not an argument. And it can still be fun even if you don't get the item you want at the price you want to pay.

EXERCISE 2 PRESENT REAL CONDITIONAL SENTENCES

(A) GRAMMAR NOTES 1–2, 4 Complete the interview with Claudia Leggett, a fashion buyer. Combine the two sentences in parentheses to make a present real conditional sentence. Keep the same order and decide which clause begins with *if*. Make necessary changes in capitalization and punctuation.

INTERVIEWER: Is understanding fashion the most important thing for a career as a buyer?

LEGGETT: It is. *If you don't understand fashion, you don't belong in this field.*
1. (You don't understand fashion. You don't belong in this field.)

But buyers need other skills, too.

INTERVIEWER: Such as?

LEGGETT: _____
2. (You can make better decisions. You have good business skills.)

INTERVIEWER: "People skills" must be important, too.

LEGGETT: True. _____
3. (A buyer needs great interpersonal skills. She's negotiating prices.)

INTERVIEWER: Do you travel in your business?

LEGGETT: A lot! _____
4. (There's a big international fashion fair. I'm usually there.)

INTERVIEWER: Why fashion fairs?

LEGGETT: Thousands of professionals attend. _____
5. (I go to a fair. I can see hundreds of products in a few days.)

_____

INTERVIEWER: You just got back from the Milan fair, didn't you?

LEGGETT: Yes, and I went to Paris and Madrid, too. _____
6. (I usually stay two weeks. I'm traveling to Europe.)

_____

INTERVIEWER: Does your family ever go with you?

LEGGETT: Often. _____
7. (My husband has the time to come. He and our son, Pietro, do things together.)

_____
8. (Pietro comes to the fair with me. My husband doesn't have time.)

Next week, we're all going to Hong Kong.

INTERVIEWER: What do you do when you're not at a fashion fair?

LEGGETT: _____
9. (I always go shopping. I have free time.)

● 20|02 (B) LISTEN AND CHECK Listen to the interview and check your answers in A.

EXERCISE 3 PRESENT REAL CONDITIONAL SENTENCES WITH MODALS AND IMPERATIVES

GRAMMAR NOTES 1–3 Read this Q & A about shopping around the world. Write conditional sentences to summarize the advice. Start with the *if*-clause and use appropriate punctuation.

1. **Hong Kong**

   Q: I want to buy some traditional crafts. Any ideas?

   A: You ought to visit the Western District on Hong Kong Island. It's famous for its crafts.

   If you want to buy some traditional crafts, (then)

   you ought to visit the Western District on Hong

   Kong Island.

2. **Barcelona**

   Q: I want to buy some nice but inexpensive clothes. Where can I go?

   A: Take the train to outdoor markets in towns *outside* of the city. They have great stuff.

   _____

   _____

   _____

3. **Istanbul**

   Q: I want to go shopping in the Grand Bazaar. Is it open on Sunday?

   A: No. You have to go during the week.

   _____

   _____

   _____

4. **Bangkok**

   Q: My son wants to buy computer games. Where should he go?

   A: He should try the Pantip Plaza. The selection is huge.

   _____

   _____

   _____

5. **Mexico City**

   Q: I plan to buy some silver jewelry in Mexico. Any tips?

   A: Try bargaining. That way, you may get something nice at a very good price.

   _____

   _____

   _____

6. **London**

   Q: I want to find some nice secondhand clothing shops. Can you help me?

   A: Try Portobello Market on the weekend. Happy shopping!

   _____

   _____

   _____

EXERCISE 4 PRESENT REAL CONDITIONAL SENTENCES WITH *WHEN*

GRAMMAR NOTE 5 Look at the map. Write sentences about the cities with clocks. Use the words in parentheses and *when*. The white clocks show daylight hours; the gray clocks show evening or nighttime hours.

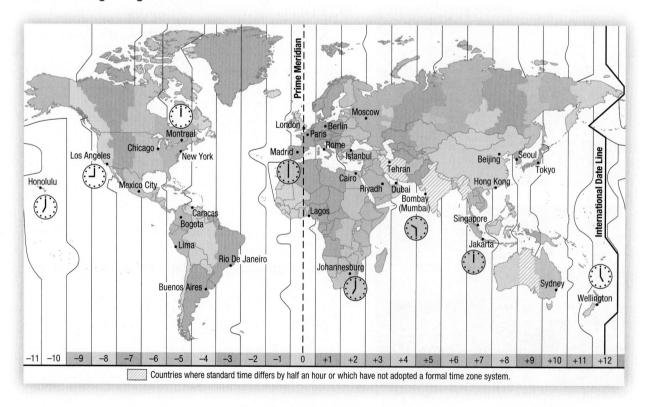

1. <u>When it's noon in Montreal, it's midnight in Jakarta.</u>
   (be noon / be midnight)

2. <u>When stores are opening in Los Angeles, they're closing in Johannesburg.</u>
   (stores open / stores close)

3. _____
   (people watch the sunrise / people watch the sunset)

4. _____
   (be midnight / be 6:00 p.m.)

5. _____
   (people eat lunch / people eat dinner)

6. _____
   (people get up / people go to bed)

7. _____
   (be 7:00 a.m. / be 7:00 p.m.)

8. _____
   (be 5:00 a.m. / be 9:00 a.m.)

EXERCISE 5 EDITING

GRAMMAR NOTES 1–5 Read Claudia's email message. There are seven mistakes in the use of present real conditional sentences. The first mistake is already corrected. Find and correct six more. Don't forget to check punctuation.

Tomorrow, I'm flying to Hong Kong for a fashion show! My son, Pietro, is flying

with me, and my husband is already there. When Pietro's off from school, I

like
~~liked~~ to take him on trips with me. If my husband comes too, they are going

sightseeing during the day. Our plane leaves Los Angeles around midnight. If

we flew at night, we can sleep on the plane. (At least that's the plan!)

I love Hong Kong. We always have a great time, when we will go there. The

shopping is really fantastic. When I'm not working I'm shopping.

I'll be arriving at the hotel around 7:00 a.m. When it will be 7:00 a.m. in Hong

Kong, it's midnight in London. That's probably too late to call you, so I'll just

text. OK?

EXERCISE 6   LISTENING

▶20|03   (A) Claudia Leggett and her son, Pietro, are flying from Los Angeles to Hong Kong. Listen to the announcements they hear in the airport and aboard the plane. Read the statements. Then listen again and check (✓) *True* or *False*.

		True	False
Announcement 1:	Claudia has two pieces of carry-on luggage, and Pietro has one. They can take them all on the plane.	☐	☑
Announcement 2:	Look at their boarding passes. They can board now.	☐	☐

UPAir *Boarding Pass*
01 of 02

NAME OF PASSENGER
LEGGETT/PIETRO

FROM X/O   Los Angeles

TO X/O   Hong Kong

CARRIER
UPAIR

CODE	FLIGHT	CLASS	DATE	TIME
UP	398	V	13Aug	11:45P

GATE	BOARDING TIME	SEAT
8C	11:15PM	16A

1   037   2171281950   2

UPAir *Boarding Pass*
02 of 02

NAME OF PASSENGER
LEGGETT/CLAUDIA

FROM X/O   Los Angeles

TO X/O   Hong Kong

CARRIER
UPAIR

CODE	FLIGHT	CLASS	DATE	TIME
UP	398	V	13Aug	11:45P

GATE	BOARDING TIME	SEAT
8C	11:15PM	16B

1   037   2171281950   2

		True	False
Announcement 3:	Look at their boarding passes again. They can board now.	☐	☐
Announcement 4:	Pietro is only ten years old. Claudia should put his oxygen mask on first.	☐	☐
Announcement 5:	Claudia is sitting in a left-hand window seat. She can see the lights of Tokyo.	☐	☐
Announcement 6:	Passengers who are taking connecting flights can get this information on the plane.	☐	☐

▶20|03   (B) Work with a partner. Listen again to the announcements. Discuss your answers.

EXAMPLE: **A:** OK. So, why is the answer to number 1 *False*?

     B: The announcement says if you have more than one piece of carry-on luggage, you must check the extra pieces at the gate.

     A: Right. And they have three pieces, so they can't take them all on the plane with them. Now, what did you choose for number 2?

Passengers on Flight 398 to Hong Kong

EXERCISE 7 WHAT SHOULD WE GET?

Ⓐ REACHING AGREEMENT Work with a partner. You are going to buy some T-shirts for a friend—an eighteen-year-old male or female. Look at part of a store's website and discuss the selections. Agree on a purchase. Think about the following issues.

• color   • size   • style   • quantity   • price   • shipping

EXAMPLE: **A:** Let's get a cherry red, short-sleeve, V-neck T-shirt.
B: But what if she doesn't like red?
A: Well, if she doesn't like it, she can always exchange it for another color.
B: OK. And, if we order it today, ...

Unisex
T-Shirts

| short-sleeves, crew neck $15.00 | short-sleeves, V-neck $15.00 | long-sleeves, crew neck $18.00 | long-sleeves, V-neck $18.00 |

Available in:

tangerine   hot pink   cherry red   ivory   ebony   ink blue   turquoise

All T-shirts available in Small, Medium, Large

Buy 1, get the second at *50% off* **! Buy today, take another** *10% off* **!**

Return/Exchange Policy: Return by mail (within 45 days of purchase): $6.00 fee
Exchange by mail (within 45 days of purchase): free

Ⓑ Work with your partner. Complete the order form for the item(s) you decided on.

	QUANTITY	COLOR	SIZE
short-sleeved, crew neck T			○ S ○ M ○ L
short-sleeved, V-neck T			○ S ○ M ○ L
long-sleeved, crew neck T			○ S ○ M ○ L
long-sleeved, V-neck T			○ S ○ M ○ L

Shipping Method   ○ Standard: 5–9 business days **$5.00**
○ Express: 2 business days **$10.00**

EXERCISE 8 SHOPPING HERE AND THERE

CROSS-CULTURAL COMPARISON **Work with a partner. Compare shopping in a place you've lived in or one you have visited. Choose two different places and consider the questions below.**

EXAMPLE: **A:** If you're in a small city or town in Mexico, stores are usually open from Monday to Friday between 9:00 a.m. and 2:00 or 4:00 p.m.

B: In South Korean cities, stores usually stay open until 10:00 p.m. And if you want to go shopping after that, you can find many stores that are open 24 hours.

- What days and hours are stores open?
- What kinds of stores are there: malls? small stores? indoor or outdoor markets?
- Do people bargain?
- How do people pay?
- What are some special products sold in that country?
- Is there a sales tax for clothing? If *yes*, how much is it?
- Do stores allow refunds or exchanges?

EXERCISE 9 AN IMPORTANT PURCHASE

CONVERSATION **Work in a group. Talk about what you do when you want to make an important purchase (a gift, a camera, a car).**

EXAMPLE: **A:** If I want to buy a camera, I check prices online.

B: When I buy a camera, I always ask friends for recommendations.

C: I always . . .

EXERCISE 10 OFF-LINE AND ON

PICTURE DISCUSSION **Work with a partner. Look at the cartoon. What are some of the differences between shopping in a "store with doors" and shopping online? What are the advantages and disadvantages of each?**

EXAMPLE: **A:** If you shop for clothes in a store, you can try them on first.

B: But you have a lot more choices if you shop online.

A BEFORE YOU WRITE Work with a partner. Brainstorm information for tourists visiting your city or town. Then complete the list of tips for visitors.

What to Do if You Visit _____
(name of city or town)

Shopping _____   Weather _____

Food _____   Interesting Sights _____

Transportation _____   Outdoor Activities _____

B WRITE Use your list to write a short article about things to do in your city or town. Use present real conditional sentences. Try to avoid the mistakes in the chart.

EXAMPLE: There are many things to do if you visit Jamestown. If you enjoy swimming, you can go to one of the many beautiful beaches in and around town. The weather is great in the summer, but remember to bring a sweater if you plan to go out in the evening. If you forget to pack one, don't worry. You can go shopping for one at . . .

Common Mistakes in Using Present Real Conditional Sentences

Use the **simple present** in both clauses for **general truths**. Do not use the future in the _if/when_ clause.	**If** you **shop** online, **it's** faster. NOT If you ~~will shop~~ online, it's faster.
Use the **simple present or present progressive** in the _if/when_ clause for **habits** and things that happen again and again. Do not use the future in the _if/when_ clause.	**When** I **visit** Jamestown, I always eat at Joe's. NOT When I ~~will visit~~ Jamestown, I always eat at Joe's.
Use a **comma after the** _if/when_ **clause** when it comes first. Do not use a comma after the result clause when the result clause comes first.	**If** **it's** nice out**,** go to the beach. NOT Go to the beach_x if it's nice out.

C CHECK YOUR WORK Read your article. Underline the _if_ or _when_ clauses once and the result clauses twice. Circle _if_ or _when_. Use the Editing Checklist to check your work.

Editing Checklist

Did you use . . . ?

☐ the simple present in both clauses for general truths

☐ the simple present or present progressive in the _if/when_ clause for habits and things that happen again and again

☐ a comma after the _if/when_ clause when it comes first

D REVISE YOUR WORK Read your article again. Can you improve your writing? Make changes if necessary. Give your article a title.

UNIT 20 REVIEW

Test yourself on the grammar of the unit.

A Complete the present real conditional sentences in the conversation with the correct form of the verbs in parentheses.

A: What _____ you _____ when you _____ too busy
                                    1. (do)   **2.** (be)

   to shop?

B: It depends. If a store _____ open late, I _____ in the evening.
                          3. (be)   **4.** (shop)

A: What _____ if a store _____ open late?
        5. (happen)   **6.** (not stay)

B: If it _____ early, I _____ to its website. It's really easy.
         7. (close)   **8.** (go)

A: Great idea! When I _____ rushed, I never _____ of that.
                      9. (feel)   **10.** (think)

B Combine each pair of sentences to make a present real conditional sentence. Keep the same order.

1. It's 7:00 a.m. in Honolulu. What time is it in Mumbai?

   _____

2. You love jewelry. You should visit an international jewelry show.

   _____

3. A tourist may have more fun. She tries bargaining.

   _____

4. You're shopping at an outdoor market. You can always bargain for a good price.

   _____

5. But don't try to bargain. You're shopping in a big department store.

   _____

C Find and correct five mistakes. Remember to check punctuation.

1. If I don't like something I bought online, then I returned it.

2. Don't buy from an online site, if you don't know anything about the company.

3. When he'll shops online, Frank always saves a lot of time.

4. I always fell asleep if I fly at night. It happens every time.

5. Isabel always has a wonderful time, when she visits Istanbul.

Now check your answers on page 480.

Future Real Conditional Sentences
CAUSE AND EFFECT

OUTCOMES
- Describe future real conditions and results that will be certain, possible, advisable, or necessary
- Identify specific information in a magazine article
- Identify and discuss details in an interview
- Discuss common problems and possible solutions
- Discuss superstitions, giving opinions and making cross-cultural comparisons
- Write a speech about what one will do if elected class or school president

STEP 1   GRAMMAR IN CONTEXT

BEFORE YOU READ

Look at the pictures on this page and on page 332. Discuss the questions.

1. What is a superstition? Can you give an example of one?

2. Do you believe in any superstitions?

3. Do you wear or carry things that make you feel lucky?

READ

21|01 Read this magazine article about superstitions.

Knock on Wood!

- If you knock on wood, you'll keep bad luck away.

- You'll get a good grade on the test if you wear your shirt inside out.

- You'll get a bad grade unless you use your lucky pen.

Superstitions may sound silly to some, but millions of people all over the world believe in their power to bring good luck or prevent bad luck. In fact, different cultures share many similar superstitions:

- If you break a mirror, you'll have seven years of bad luck.

- If the palm of your hand itches, you're going to get some money.

- If it rains when you move to a new house, you'll get rich.

All superstitions are based on a cause-and-effect relationship: If X happens, then Y will also happen. However, in superstitions, the cause is magical and unrelated to the effect. In our scientific age, why are these beliefs so powerful and widespread? The Luck Project, an online survey of superstitious behaviors, gives us some fascinating insight. Read some of their findings on the next page.

- Emotions can influence superstitions, especially in uncertain situations where people do not have control. People will react in a more superstitious way if they are worried. They will react in a less superstitious way if they don't feel a strong need for control.

- We make our own luck. If you believe you're lucky, you will carry out rituals[1] that make you feel good (crossing your fingers for luck, for example). As a result, you probably won't fear bad luck signs (such as breaking a mirror), and you might perform better in stressful situations. In contrast, if you think you're unlucky, you will anticipate the worst and look for signs of bad luck that confirm your belief. Your attitude makes a difference.

- More people than you might think believe in superstitions. Of the 4,000 people surveyed, 84 percent knocked on wood for good luck. Almost half feared walking under a ladder. And 15 percent of the people who studied or worked in the sciences feared the number 13.

Clearly, higher education doesn't eliminate[2] superstition—college students are among the most superstitious people. Other superstitious groups are performers, athletes, gamblers,[3] and stock traders. People in these groups often have lucky charms[4] or personal good luck rituals.

Deanna McBrearty, a New York City Ballet member, has lucky hair bands. "If I have a good performance when I'm wearing one, I'll keep wearing it," she says. Baseball player Wade Boggs would only eat chicken before a game. Brett Gallagher, a stock trader, believes he'll be more successful if he owns pet fish. "I had fish for a while, and after they died, the market didn't do so well," he points out.

Will you do better on the test if you use your lucky pen? Maybe. If the pen makes you feel more confident, you might improve your score. So go ahead and use it. But don't forget: Your lucky pen will be powerless unless you study. The harder you work, the luckier you'll get.

---

1 *rituals:* sets of actions always done in the same way
2 *eliminate:* get rid of something completely
3 *gamblers:* people who risk money in a game or race (cards, horse race) because they might win more money
4 *lucky charms:* very small objects worn on a chain that will bring good luck (horseshoes, four-leaf clovers, etc.)

AFTER YOU READ

A VOCABULARY **Match the words with their definitions.**

_____ 1. **widespread**   **a.** to expect that something will happen

_____ 2. **insight**   **b.** sure

_____ 3. **percent**   **c.** the usual way someone thinks or feels about something

_____ 4. **confident**   **d.** the ability to understand something clearly

_____ 5. **anticipate**   **e.** happening in many places

_____ 6. **attitude**   **f.** equal to a certain amount in every hundred

COMPREHENSION Read the statements. Check (✓) *True* or *False*.

	True	False
1. A superstition expresses a cause and effect.	☐	☐
2. If you are worrying about something, you might act less superstitiously.	☐	☐
3. If you feel lucky, you'll have more good luck rituals.	☐	☐
4. If you feel unlucky, you won't believe in superstitions.	☐	☐
5. If you study science, you won't be superstitious.	☐	☐
6. If you don't study, your good luck pen won't work.	☐	☐

C **DISCUSSION** Work with a partner. Compare your answers in B. Why did you check *True* or *False*?

STEP 2 GRAMMAR PRESENTATION

FUTURE REAL CONDITIONAL SENTENCES

Statements

If-Clause: Present	Result Clause: Future
If she **studies**,	she **won't fail** the test. she **'s going to pass** the test. she **might get** an A.
If she **doesn't study**,	she**'ll fail** the test. she **isn't going to pass** the test. she **might not get** an A.

Yes/No Questions

Result Clause: Future	*If*-Clause: Present
Will she **pass** the test	*if* she **studies**?
Is she **going to pass** the test	

Short Answers

Affirmative		Negative	
Yes,	she **will**.	No,	she **won't**.
	she **is**.		she **isn't**.

Wh- Questions

Result Clause: Future	*If*-Clause: Present
What **will** she **do** What **is** she **going to do**	*if* she doesn't **pass** the test?

GRAMMAR NOTES

1 Future Real Conditional Sentences

Use future real conditional sentences to describe **real conditions** and **results** that are **certain**.

The *if*-clause describes a **real or true condition**. The **result clause** describes the **certain result**.	IF-CLAUSE / RESULT CLAUSE **If** I use this pen, I'll pass the test. *(If I use this pen, I'll certainly pass the test.)*
Use the **simple present** in the *if*-clause. Use the **future** with *will* or *be going to* in the **result clause**.	PRESENT / FUTURE **If** you **feel** lucky, you**'ll expect** good things. **If** you **feel** unlucky, you**'re going to expect** bad things to happen.
BE CAREFUL! Even though the *if*-clause refers to the future, use the simple present. Do not use the future.	**If** she **gets** an A on her test, she **will stop** worrying. NOT If she ~~will get~~ an A on her test, she will stop worrying.

2 With a Modal in the Result Clause

You can use **modals** or similar expressions in the **result clause** to express **possibility** (*may, might, could*), **advice** (*should, ought to*), or **necessity** (*must, have to*).

• *may*	IF-CLAUSE / RESULT CLAUSE If they have time tomorrow, they ***may* go** to the park.
• *should*	If you want to pass that test, you ***should* study** more.
• *must*	If she wants to do well here, she ***must* work** harder.
USAGE NOTE We sometimes use *then* to **emphasize the result** in future real conditional sentences with **modals** or similar expressions or with *will*.	If she studies hard, ***then*** she **might get** an A. If she studies hard, ***then*** she**'ll get** an A.

3 Position of the *If*-Clause

The *if*-clause can come **at the beginning or the end** of the sentence. The meaning is the same.

• at the **beginning**	**If** she **uses that pen**, she'll feel lucky.
• at the **end**	She'll feel lucky **if** she **uses that pen**.
IN WRITING Use a **comma after the *if*-clause** when it comes at the **beginning** of the sentence. Do not use a comma after the result clause when the result clause comes first.	**If** she **gets a good grade,** she'll be happy. NOT She'll be happy_x if she gets a good grade.

You can use *if* or *unless* in future real conditional sentences, but their **meanings are very different**.

Use *if* to express an **affirmative condition**.	**If** he studies, he will pass the test.
Use *unless* to express a **negative condition**.	**Unless** he studies, he will fail the test. *(If he doesn't study, he will fail the test.)*
Unless often means *if . . . not*.	**Unless** you're superstitious, you won't be afraid of black cats. or **If** you aren't superstitious, you won't be afraid of black cats.

STEP 3   FOCUSED PRACTICE

EXERCISE 1   DISCOVER THE GRAMMAR

Ⓐ GRAMMAR NOTES 1–2, 4 **Match each condition with its result.**

Condition

_d_ **1.** If I lend someone my baseball bat,

____ **2.** Unless you take an umbrella,

____ **3.** If I give my boyfriend a new pair of shoes,

____ **4.** If the palm of your hand itches,

____ **5.** If I use my lucky pen,

____ **6.** If you wear your sweater backwards,

Result

a. you'll want to scratch it.

b. people might laugh at you.

c. I'll get 100 percent on the test.

~~**d.**~~ I won't hit a home run.

e. you're going to get wet.

f. he'll walk out of the relationship.

Ⓑ **Now write the sentences that describe superstitions.**

1. *If I lend someone my baseball bat, I won't hit a home run.*

2. _____

3. _____

EXERCISE 2 *IF* OR *UNLESS*

A GRAMMAR NOTE 4 **Two students are talking about a test. Complete their conversations with *if* or *unless*.**

Conversation 1

YUKI: It's midnight. _____*Unless*_____ we get some sleep, we won't do well tomorrow.
1.

EVA: But I won't be able to sleep _____ I stop worrying about the test.
2.

YUKI: Here's my lucky charm. _____ you wear it, you'll do fine!
3.

Conversation 2

EVA: I found my blue shirt! _____ I wear it, I'm sure I'll pass!
4.

YUKI: Great. Now _____ we just clean up the room, we can leave for school.
5.

EVA: We can't clean up! There's a Russian superstition that says _____ you clean
6.

your room, you'll get a bad test grade!

Conversation 3

YUKI: _____ we finish the test by noon, we can go to the job fair.
7.

EVA: I want to get a job, but nobody is going to hire me _____ I pass this test.
8.

Conversation 4

EVA: I'm looking for my lucky pen. _____ I find it, I won't pass the test!
9.

YUKI: Don't worry. _____ you use the same pen that you used to study with, you'll
10.

do great! The pen will remember the answers.

Conversation 5

EVA: I was so nervous without my lucky pen. It'll be a miracle[1] _____ I pass.
11.

YUKI: That's the wrong attitude! There aren't any miracles. _____ you study, you'll
12.

do well. It's that simple.

Conversation 6

EVA: Do you think a company like ZY3, Inc. will offer me a job _____ I fill out
13.

an application?

YUKI: Only _____ you use your lucky pen. I'm kidding! You won't know
14.

_____ you try!
15.

▶ 21|02 **B** LISTEN AND CHECK **Listen to the conversations and check your answers in A.**

---

1 *miracle:* something lucky that happens when you didn't think it was possible

EXERCISE 3 SIMPLE PRESENT OR FUTURE

GRAMMAR NOTE 1 Complete these sentences describing superstitions from around the world. Use the correct form of the verbs in parentheses.

1. If you _____*spill*_____ salt at the table,

a. (spill)
   you _____'*ll have*_____ an argument. *(Russia)*

b. (have)

2. If a cat _____ behind its ears, it

a. (wash)
   _____. *(England)*

b. (rain)

3. If you _____ under a ladder, you

a. (walk)
   _____ bad luck. *(Canada)*

b. (have)

4. If you _____ the dirt and dust

a. (sweep)
   out of your house through the front door, you
   _____ away your family's good

b. (sweep)
   luck. *(China)*

5. If your right hand _____ itchy, you _____ money. If your left hand

a. (be)   b. (get)
   _____, you _____ someone money. *(Greece)*

c. (itch)   d. (give)

6. If somebody _____ away a dead mouse, the wind _____ to blow

a. (throw)   b. (start)
   from that direction. *(Iceland)*

7. If you _____ at the corner of the table, then you _____

a. (sit)   b. (not get)
   married. *(Slovakia)*

8. If you _____ red beans at a newly married couple, they _____ good

a. (throw)   b. (have)
   luck. *(Mexico)*

9. If you _____ food on your clothing while you're eating, you _____

a. (drop)   b. (have)
   guests that day. *(Turkey)*

10. If you _____ a broom behind the front door, you _____ bad

a. (put)   b. (keep away)
    visitors. *(Brazil)*

11. If you _____ a snake skin in your wallet, you _____ rich. *(Japan)*

a. (put)   b. (become)

12. If you _____ your hair, you _____ taller. *(Korea)*

a. (cut)   b. (grow)

EXERCISE 4 AFFIRMATIVE AND NEGATIVE SENTENCES

Ⓐ GRAMMAR NOTES 1, 3 Eva is thinking of working for a company called ZY3, Inc. Her best friend Don, who used to work there, thinks it's a terrible idea and is explaining to her the consequences. Write his responses. Use the words in parentheses and future real conditional sentences. Begin with the *if*-clause.

1. EVA: If I work for ZY3, I'm going to be happy. I'm sure of it.

   DON: *If you work for ZY3, you're not going to be happy. You're going to be miserable.*
   (miserable)

2. EVA: You have such a pessimistic attitude! I'll have the chance to travel a lot if I take this job.

   DON: Not true. _____
   (never leave the office)

3. EVA: But I'll get a raise every year if I stay at ZY3.

   DON: _____
   (every two years)

4. EVA: Well, if I join ZY3, I'm going to have wonderful health care benefits.

   DON: Stay healthy! _____
   (terrible health care benefits)

5. EVA: I don't believe you! If I accept ZY3's offer, it'll be the best career move of my life.

   DON: Believe me, _____
   (the worst)

🔊 21|03 Ⓑ LISTEN AND CHECK Listen to the conversation and check your answers in A.

EXERCISE 5 SENTENCES WITH *WILL* AND MODALS

GRAMMAR NOTES 1–3 Yuki Tamari is not sure if she should go to law school or not. She made a decision tree to help her decide. In the tree, arrows connect the conditions and the results. Write future real conditional sentences about her decision. Use *will* if the result is certain. Use *may*, *might*, or *could* if the result is possible. Remember to use commas where necessary.

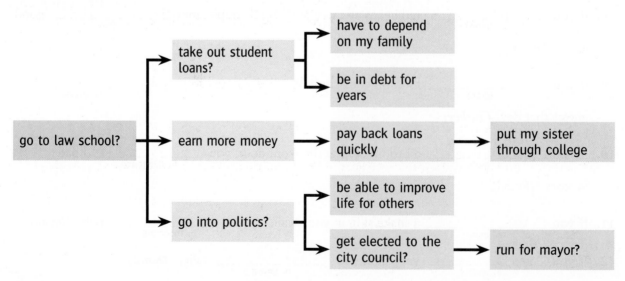

1. _If I go to law school, I might take out students loans._ _____

2. _I'll be in debt for years if I take out student loans._ _____

3. _____

4. _____

5. _____

6. _____

7. _____

8. _____

9. _____

10. _____

EXERCISE 6 EDITING

GRAMMAR NOTES 1–4 Read Yuki's blog. There are seven mistakes in the use of future real conditional sentences. The first mistake is already corrected. Find and correct six more. Don't forget to check punctuation.

OCTOBER 1

Should I campaign for student council president? I'll have to decide soon if I ~~wanted~~ *want*

to run. If I'll be busy campaigning, I won't have much time to study. That's a problem

because I'm not going to get into law school if I get good grades this year. On the

other hand, the problems in this school are widespread, and nothing is getting done

if Todd Laker becomes president again. I'm 100 percent certain of that, and most

people agree with me. But will I know what to do if I'll get the job? Never mind. I

shouldn't anticipate difficulties. I really need to have a better attitude. I'll deal with

that problem, if I win. I know what I'll do. If I become president, I cut my hair. That

always brings me good luck!

EXERCISE 7 LISTENING

▶21|04 **A** Yuki is talking about her campaign platform. Read the list of issues. Then listen to the interview. Listen again and check (✓) the things that Yuki promises to work for if she is elected.

- ☑ **1.** have contact with a lot of students
- ☐ **2.** improve the student council's newsletter
- ☐ **3.** publish teacher evaluations on the student council's website
- ☐ **4.** get the college to provide a bus service between the airport and the college
- ☐ **5.** get the college to offer a major in environmental science
- ☐ **6.** reduce tuition costs

▶21|04 **B** Listen again to the interview. Work with a partner. Discuss Yuki's platform. Do you think she is a good candidate for student council president? Why or why not?

EXAMPLE: **A:** I think she'll improve things if she gets elected.
   B: I agree. I like the fact that she thinks communication is very important. If she's elected, she'll communicate more with students. For example, she'll have . . .

EXERCISE 8
IT'S A REAL PROBLEM!

PROBLEM SOLVING Work in a group. Read this list of problems. Discuss possible solutions for each one. Use *if*, *if . . . not*, or *unless*.

1. Your neighbors are always playing music so loudly that you can't fall asleep.

   EXAMPLE: **A:** What will you do if they don't stop?
      B: If they don't stop, I'll call the police.
      C: Unless they stop, I'll call the landlord.
      D: I'll consider moving if they continue to bother me.

2. You've had a headache every day for a week. You can't concentrate.

3. You keep phoning your parents, but there's no answer. It's now midnight, and you're worried.

4. You like your job, but you just found out that other workers are making much more money than you are.

5. You live in an apartment building. It's winter, and the building hasn't had any heat for a week. You're freezing.

6. You're ten pounds overweight. You've been trying for months to lose weight, but so far you haven't lost a single pound.

7. You bought a phone at a local store. It doesn't work, but when you tried to return it, the salesperson refused to take it back.

8. Your roommates don't clean up after they cook. You've already reminded them several times, but they always "forget."

9. You paid for a parking space near school or work. For the past week, the same car has taken your space.

EXERCISE 9 LUCK AROUND THE WORLD

CROSS-CULTURAL COMPARISON Work in a group. Read the list of superstitions below. Compare each one with a similar superstition in a country or culture you know well.

EXAMPLE: A: In Germany, people press the thumbs of both their hands to wish themselves or another person good luck.
B: In Mexico, . . .
C: In Russia, . . .

- If you cross your fingers, you'll have good luck.
- If you touch blue, your dreams will come true.
- If you break a mirror, you will have seven years of bad luck.
- If you put a piece of clothing on inside out, you will have good luck.
- If your palm itches, you're going to find some money soon.

EXERCISE 10 IT'S HOW YOU LOOK AT IT

DISCUSSION Work with a partner. What is your attitude about superstitions? Are superstitions good or bad? Discuss and give examples to support your opinions.

EXAMPLE: A: I think some superstitions are bad. For example, if you think a lucky pen will help you do well on a test, you may not study enough. And if you don't study enough, you probably won't get a good grade.
B: I don't know about that. If you believe a special pen will give you good luck, you may have more confidence. If you have more confidence, you might actually do better on the test.

A BEFORE YOU WRITE Imagine you are running for class or school president. Make a list of five things you will do if you become president.

1. _____

2. _____

3. _____

4. _____

5. _____

B WRITE Use your list to write a short speech. What will you do if you become class or school president? What may, might, or could happen if you don't win the election? Try to avoid the common mistakes in the chart.

EXAMPLE: We have a wonderful school, but there are always opportunities for improvement. If I become school president, I will ask for ten new computers.... If I'm not elected, classroom conditions might ...

Common Mistakes in Using Future Real Conditional Sentences

Use the **simple present** in the *if*-clause. Do not use the future in the *if*-clause.	*If* I **become** president, I will ask for more money. NOT If I ~~will become~~ president, I will ask for more money.
Use *unless* or *if . . . not* to state a **negative condition**. Do not use *if*.	*Unless* you **vote** for me, I won't get the job done. *If* you **don't vote** for me, I won't get the job done. NOT ~~If you vote~~ for me, I won't get the job done.
Use a **comma after the *if/unless* clause** when it comes first. Do not use a comma after the result clause when the result clause comes first.	*If* I **win,** I will make changes. NOT I will make changes_x if I win.

C CHECK YOUR WORK Read your speech. Underline the *if* or *unless* clauses once and the result clauses twice. Circle *if* or *unless*. Use the Editing Checklist to check your work.

Editing Checklist

Did you use . . . ?

☐ the simple present in the *if*-clause

☐ the future with *will* or *be going to* in the result clause for results that are certain

☐ *may*, *might*, or *could* in the result clause for results that are possible

☐ *unless* or *if not* to express a negative condition

☐ a comma after the *if/unless* clause when it comes first

D REVISE YOUR WORK Read your speech again. Can you improve your writing? Make changes if necessary. Give your speech a title.

UNIT 21 REVIEW

Test yourself on the grammar of the unit.

Ⓐ Match each condition with its result.

Condition	Result
_____ **1.** If it rains,	**a.** you might have good luck.
_____ **2.** Unless you study,	**b.** I could pay you back tomorrow.
_____ **3.** If you cross your fingers,	**c.** I may not buy it.
_____ **4.** Unless they lower the price,	**d.** I'll take an umbrella.
_____ **5.** If you lend me $10,	**e.** you could rent one.
_____ **6.** If you don't own a car,	**f.** you won't pass.

Ⓑ Complete the future real conditional sentences in these conversations with the correct form of the verbs in parentheses.

1. A: Are you going to take the bus?

    B: No. If I _____ the bus, I _____ late.
                a. (take)   **b. (be)**

2. A: What _____ you _____ if you _____ the job?
                               a. (do)   **b. (not get)**

    B: I _____ in school unless I _____ the job.
             c. (stay)   **d. (get)**

3. A: If I _____ the test, I _____.
             a. (pass)   **b. (celebrate)**

    B: Good luck, but I'm sure you'll pass. You've studied really hard for it.

    A: Thanks!

Ⓒ Find and correct six mistakes. Remember to check punctuation.

It's been a hard week, and I'm looking forward to the weekend. If the weather will be nice tomorrow Marco and I are going to go to the beach. The ocean is usually too cold for swimming at this time of year, so I probably don't go in the water unless it's really hot outside. But I love walking along the beach and breathing in the fresh sea air.

If Marco has time, he might makes some sandwiches to bring along. Otherwise, we'll just get some pizza. I hope it'll be a nice day. I just listened to the weather report, and there may be some rain in the afternoon. Unless it rains, we probably go to the movies instead. That's our Plan B. But I really want to go to the beach, so I'm keeping my fingers crossed!

Now check your answers on page 480.

UNIT 22

Present and Future Unreal Conditional Sentences

WISHES

STEP 1   GRAMMAR IN CONTEXT

BEFORE YOU READ

Read the first sentence of the story and look at the picture. Discuss the questions.

1. Is this a true story? What makes you think so?

2. How do fairy tales begin in your culture?

READ

▶ 22|01   Read this version of a famous fairy tale.

The Fisherman and His Wife

O nce upon a time, there was a poor fisherman and his wife who lived in a pigpen[1] near the sea. Every day, the man went to fish. One day, after waiting a very long time, he caught a very big fish. To his surprise, the fish spoke and said, "Please let me live. I'm not a regular fish. If you knew my real identity, you wouldn't kill me. I'm an enchanted prince."

"Don't worry. I won't kill you," responded the kind-hearted fisherman. With these words, he threw the fish back into the clear water and went home to his wife.

"Husband," said the wife, "didn't you catch anything today?"

"I caught a fish, but it said it was an enchanted prince, so I let it go."

"You mean you didn't wish for anything?" asked the wife.

"No," said the fisherman. "What do I need to wish for?"

---

1 *pigpen:* a small building where pigs are kept

"Just look around you," said the wife. "We live in a pigpen. I wish we had a nice little cottage.² If we had a cottage, I would be a lot happier. You saved the prince's life. He's sure to grant your wish. Go back and ask him."

"I'm not going to ask for a cottage! If I asked for a cottage, the fish might get angry." But in the end, he consented because he was much more afraid of his wife's anger.

When he got to the sea, it was all green and yellow. "My wife wishes we had a cottage," said the fisherman. "Just go on back," said the fish. "She already has it."

When he returned home, the fisherman found his wife sitting outside a lovely little cottage. The kitchen was filled with food and all types of cooking utensils.³ Outside was a little garden with vegetables, fruit trees, hens, and ducks.

Things were fine for a week or two. Then the wife said, "This cottage is much too crowded. I wish we lived in a bigger house. If we lived in a big stone castle, I would be much happier. Go and ask the fish for it."

The fisherman didn't want to go, but he did. When he got to the sea, it was dark blue and gray. "My wife wishes we lived in a big stone castle," he said to the fish.

"Just go on back. She's standing in front of the door," said the fish.

When he returned home, the fisherman found his wife on the steps of a great big stone castle. The inside was filled with beautiful gold furniture, chandeliers,⁴ and carpets. There were servants everywhere.

The next morning, the wife woke up and said, "I wish I were king of all this land."

"What would you do if you were king?" asked her husband.

"If I were king, I would own all this land. Go on back and ask the fish for it."

This time, the sea was all blackish gray, and the water was rough and smelled terrible. "What does she want now?" asked the fish.

"She wants to be king," said the embarrassed fisherman.

"Just go on back. She already is."

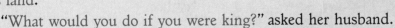

2 *cottage:* a small house, usually in the country
3 *cooking utensils:* tools used for cooking or preparing food
4 *chandeliers:* large structures that hang from the ceiling and hold many lights or candles

When the fisherman returned home, he found an enormous palace.[5] Everything inside was made of marble and pure gold, and it was surrounded by soldiers with drums and trumpets. His wife was seated on a throne, and he said to her, "How nice for you that you are king. Now we won't need to wish for anything else."

But his wife was not satisfied. "I'm only king of *this* country," she said. "I wish I were emperor of the whole world. If I were emperor, I would be the most powerful ruler on Earth."

"Wife, now be satisfied," responded the fisherman. "You're king. You can't be anything more."

The wife, however, wasn't convinced. She kept thinking and thinking about what more she could be. "If I were emperor, I could have anything—and you wouldn't have to ask the fish for anything more. Go right now and tell the fish that I want to be emperor of the whole world."

"Oh, no," said the fisherman. "The fish can't do that. If I were you, I wouldn't ask for anything else." But his wife got so furious that the poor fisherman ran back to the fish. There was a terrible storm, and the sea was pitch black[6] with waves as high as mountains.

"Well, what does she want now?" asked the fish.

"She wishes she were emperor of the whole world," said the fisherman.

"Just go on back. She's sitting in the pigpen again."

And they are still sitting there today.

---

5 *palace:* a very large house where the ruler of a country lives
6 *pitch black:* very dark black; the color of coal or tar

AFTER YOU READ

A VOCABULARY **Choose the word or phrase that best completes each sentence.**

1. If something is **enchanted**, it has been _____.
   a. changed by magic   **b.** broken   **c.** stolen

2. When you **consent**, you _____ to do something.
   a. refuse   **b.** agree   **c.** like

3. Someone who is **furious** is very _____.
   a. kind-hearted   **b.** poor   **c.** angry

4. Someone who is **embarrassed** feels _____.
   a. uncomfortable   **b.** powerful   **c.** frightened

5. If you **grant** someone's request, you say _____ to it.
   a. yes   **b.** maybe   **c.** no

6. If you have a **regular** day, your day is _____.
   a. special   **b.** ordinary   **c.** surprising

	True	False
1. Before the fisherman caught the fish, he and his wife lived in a nice little cottage.	☐	☐
2. As soon as he caught the fish, the fisherman knew its real identity.	☐	☐
3. The wife wanted to have a cottage.	☐	☐
4. The fisherman didn't want to ask for a cottage because he didn't want to make the fish angry.	☐	☐
5. The wife was satisfied with the stone castle.	☐	☐
6. The man advised his wife not to ask to be emperor of the whole world.	☐	☐

C DISCUSSION Work with a partner. Discuss your answers in B. Why did you check *True* or *False*?

STEP 2 GRAMMAR PRESENTATION

PRESENT AND FUTURE UNREAL CONDITIONAL SENTENCES

Statements

If-Clause: Simple Past	Result Clause: *Would (not)* + Base Form
If Mia **had** money, *If* she **were*** rich,	she **would live** in a palace. she **wouldn't live** in a cottage.
If Mia **didn't have** money, *If* she **weren't** rich,	she **wouldn't live** in a palace. she **would live** in a cottage.

*With the verb *be*, use *were* for all subjects.

Contractions

I would	=	**I'd**
you would	=	**you'd**
he would	=	**he'd**
she would	=	**she'd**
it would	=	**it'd**
we would	=	**we'd**
they would	=	**they'd**
would not	=	**wouldn't**

Yes/No Questions

Result Clause	*If*-Clause
Would she **live** here	*if* she **had** money?
	if she **were** rich?

Short Answers

Affirmative	Negative
Yes, she **would**.	**No**, she **wouldn't**.

Wh- Questions

Result Clause	*If*-Clause
What **would** she **do**	*if* she **had** money?
	if she **were** rich?

GRAMMAR NOTES

1 Present and Future Unreal Conditional Sentences

Use present and future unreal conditional sentences to describe **unreal conditions and their results**. A condition and its result may be untrue, imagined, or impossible.

The *if-clause* describes an **unreal or untrue condition**. The result clause describes the **unreal or untrue result** of that condition.

IF-CLAUSE	RESULT CLAUSE
If I had more time, I would read fairy tales.	
(But I don't have time, so I don't read fairy tales.)	

The sentence can be about:

• the **present**

If I lived in a palace **now**, I would give parties.
(I don't live in a palace. I don't give parties.)

• the **future**

If I moved **next month**, I would buy a car.
(I won't move. I won't buy a car.)

2 Verb Forms in Present and Future Unreal Conditional Sentences

Use the **simple past** in the *if-clause*. Use *would* + **base form** of the verb in the **result clause**.

SIMPLE PAST	WOULD + BASE FORM
If he **had** a nice house, he **wouldn't move**.	

BE CAREFUL! The *if-clause* uses the simple past, but it's **not about the past**. It's about the present or the future. Do not use the simple present or *will* in the *if-clause*.

If I **had** more money *now*, I would take a big trip.
NOT If I ~~have~~ more money now, . . .
If I **got** money *tomorrow*, I would take a big trip.
NOT If I ~~I'll get~~ money tomorrow, . . .

BE CAREFUL! Use *would* only in the **result clause**. Do not use *would* in the *if-clause*.

If I **lived** there, I **would move**.
NOT If I ~~would live~~ there, I would move.

Use *were* for **all subjects** when the verb in the *if-clause* is a form of *be*. Do not use *was*.

If I **were** king, I would solve the problem.
NOT If I ~~was~~ king, . . .

USAGE NOTE Some people use *was* with *I*, *he*, *she*, and *it*. However, this is usually considered incorrect, especially in formal or written English.

3 With a Modal in the Result Clause

You can use the **modals *might*** or ***could*** in the **result clause** to express **possibility**.

• *might*

• *could*

IF-CLAUSE	RESULT CLAUSE
If they took a trip, they *might* **go** to China.	
If I knew Chinese, I *could* **translate** for them.	

BE CAREFUL! Do not use *may* or *can* in unreal conditional sentences.

If they had time, they *might* **take** a trip.
NOT If they had time, they ~~may~~ take a trip.
If they went there, they *could* **see** the Great Wall.
NOT If they went there, they ~~can~~ see . . .

4 Position of the *If*-Clause

The *if*-clause can come **at the beginning or the end** of the sentence. The meaning is the same.

• at the **beginning**	***If* I had more money**, I would move.
• at the **end**	I would move ***if* I had more money**.

IN WRITING Use a **comma after the *if*-clause** when it comes at the **beginning** of the sentence. Do not use a comma after the result clause when the result clause comes first.

***If* I had time,** I would go fishing.
NOT I would go fishing~~,~~ if I had time.

5 With *If I Were You* to Give Advice

Use ***If I were you*** to **give advice**.

If I were you, I wouldn't ask for more.
(My advice is: Don't ask for more.)

BE CAREFUL! Use *were* in the *if*-clause. Do not use *was*.

If I were you, I'd try harder.
NOT If I ~~was~~ you, I'd try harder.

6 With *Wish* to Express Wishes

Use ***wish* + simple past** to express things that you **want to be true now**, but that are **not true**.

I ***wish* I lived** in a castle.
(I don't live in a castle now, but I want to.)

BE CAREFUL! Use *were* after *wish*. Do not use *was*.

I **wish** I *were* a child again.
NOT I wish I ~~was~~ a child again.

Use ***wish* + *would*/*could* + base form** of the verb for **wishes about the future**.

I **wish** she *would* **visit** us next summer.
She **wishes** she *could* **travel** around the world.

USAGE NOTE We often use *wish* + *would*/*could* to express a **wish for change**.

My neighbors are loud. I **wish** they *would* **be** quiet.
I don't like my apartment, I **wish** I *could* **move**.

BE CAREFUL! Use *would* or *could* after *wish*. Do not use *will* or *can*.

I **wish** she *would* **call** me.
NOT I wish she ~~will~~ call me.
I **wish** I *could* **buy** a car.
NOT I wish I ~~can~~ buy a car.

EXERCISE 1 DISCOVER THE GRAMMAR

GRAMMAR NOTES 1–3, 5–6 **Read the numbered statements. Decide if the sentences that follow are *True (T)* or *False (F)*.**

1. If I had time, I would read fairy tales in English.
   _F_ **a.** I have time.
   _F_ **b.** I'm going to read fairy tales in English.

2. If it weren't so cold, I would go fishing.
   _____ **a.** It's cold.
   _____ **b.** I'm going fishing.

3. If I caught an enchanted fish, I would make three wishes.
   _____ **a.** I believe I'm going to catch an enchanted fish.
   _____ **b.** I'm going to make three wishes.

4. If I had three wishes, I wouldn't ask for a palace.
   _____ **a.** I have three wishes.
   _____ **b.** I don't want a palace.

5. If my house were too small, I would try to find a bigger one.
   _____ **a.** My house is big enough.
   _____ **b.** I'm not looking for a bigger house right now.

6. I could buy a new car if I got a raise.
   _____ **a.** I recently got a raise.
   _____ **b.** I want a new car.

7. If I didn't earn enough money babysitting, I might look for a regular job.
   _____ **a.** I don't earn enough money.
   _____ **b.** I'm looking for a regular job.

8. Your friend tells you, "If I were you, I wouldn't change jobs."
   _____ **a.** Your friend is giving you advice.
   _____ **b.** Your friend thinks you shouldn't change jobs.

9. I wish I were a princess.
   _____ **a.** I'm a princess.
   _____ **b.** I want to be a princess.

10. I wish I could live in a big house.
    _____ **a.** I want to live in a big house.
    _____ **b.** I don't live in a big house.

EXERCISE 2 VERB FORMS IN THE *IF* AND RESULT CLAUSES

GRAMMAR NOTES 1–3, 6 Complete this article from a popular psychology magazine. Use the correct form of the verbs in parentheses to form unreal conditional sentences.

Marty Hadad has always wanted to invite his whole family over for the holidays, but his apartment is small, his family is very large, and he doesn't want to feel embarrassed. "If I

___*invited*___ them all for dinner, there ___*wouldn't be*___ enough
 1. (invite)   2. (not be)

room for everyone to sit down," he told a friend. If Marty _____ a
                                                             3. (be)

complainer, he _____ about the size of his apartment and spend the
                   4. (moan)

holiday at his parents' house. But Marty is a problem solver. This year he is hosting an open house.

People can drop in at different times during the day, and there will be room for everyone.

   "If life _____ a fairy tale, we _____
              5. (be)   6. (can / wish)

problems away," noted psychologist Joel Grimes. "What complainers are really saying is, 'If I

_____ a magical solution, I _____ with this
       7. (have)   8. (not have to deal)

myself.' I wish it _____ that easy," says Grimes. He gives an example of a
                      9. (be)

very wealthy client who is convinced that he has almost no time for his family. "He's waiting for a

miracle to give him the time he needs. But he _____ the time if he
                                                  10. (can / find)

_____ about the problem creatively," says Grimes.
    11. (think)

   Even very wealthy people have limited time, money, and space. If complainers

_____ this, then they _____
      12. (realize)   13. (understand)

that there will always be problems. Then they could stop complaining and try to

find possible solutions. Marty, who is still a student in college,

_____ for years before inviting his
    14. (may / have to wait)

family over if he _____ on a bigger
                     15. (insist)

apartment for his party. Instead, he is creatively solving his

problems right now.

   There is an old sixteenth-century English saying: "If

wishes _____ horses, then beggars
          16. (be)

_____." But wishes aren't horses. We
    17. (will / ride)

have to learn to create our own good fortune and not wait for a

genie with three wishes to come along and solve our problems.

EXERCISE 3 STATEMENTS

GRAMMAR NOTES 1–4 Psychologist Joel Grimes hears all types of excuses from his clients. Rewrite each excuse as a present unreal conditional statement. Keep the same order and decide which clause begins with *if*. Use commas where necessary.

1. I'm so busy. That's why I don't read bedtime stories to my little girl.

   If I weren't so busy, I would read bedtime stories to my little girl.

2. My husband won't ask for a raise. It's because he's not ambitious.

   _____

3. I don't play sports. But only because I'm not in shape.

   _____

4. I don't have enough time. That's why I'm not studying for the exam.

   _____

5. I'm too old. That's why I'm not going back to school.

   _____

6. I can't do my job. The reason is, my boss doesn't explain things properly.

   _____

7. I'm not good at math. That's why I don't balance my checkbook.

   _____

8. I can't stop smoking. The problem is, I feel nervous all the time.

   _____

9. I'm so tired. That's why I get up so late.

   _____

EXERCISE 4 WISHES ABOUT THE PRESENT OR FUTURE

GRAMMAR NOTE 6 Remember the fish from the fairy tale on pages 344–346? Read the things the fish would like to change. Then write sentences with *wish*.

1. I'm a fish. *I wish I weren't a fish.*

2. My life doesn't change. *I wish my life would change.*

3. I'm not a handsome prince. _____

4. I live in the sea. _____

5. I don't live in a castle. _____

6. The fisherman comes here every day. _____

7. He'll return tomorrow. _____

8. His wife always wants more. _____

9. She'll ask for a bigger house. _____

10. She can't be satisfied. _____

11. They don't leave me alone. _____

12. I can't grant my own wishes. _____

EXERCISE 5
QUESTIONS

GRAMMAR NOTES 1–4

Marty is having his open-house holiday party. His nieces and nephews are playing a fantasy question game. Use the words in parentheses to write present and future unreal conditional questions. Use commas where necessary. Keep the same order.

1. _What would you do if you were a millionaire?_
(what / you / do / if / you / be a millionaire)

2. _____
(if / you / be the leader of this country / what / you / do)

3. _____
(how / you / feel / if / you / never need to sleep)

4. _____
(what / you / do / if / you / have more free time)

5. _____
(if / you / have three wishes / what / you / ask for)

6. _____
(what / you / do / if / you / not have to work)

7. _____
(if / you / have a ticket for anywhere in the world / where / you / travel)

8. _____
(if / you / can build anything / what / it / be)

9. _____
(if / you / can meet a famous person / who / you / want to meet)

10. _____
(who / you / have dinner with / if / you can invite three famous people)

EXERCISE 6 EDITING

GRAMMAR NOTES 1–6 Read part of a book report that Marty's niece wrote. There are eight mistakes in the use of present and future unreal conditional sentences. The first mistake is already corrected. Find and correct seven more.

NAME: Laila Hadad   CLASS: English 4

The Disappearance

What would happen to the women if all the men in the world ~~would disappear~~ *disappeared*?

What would happen to the men when there were no women in the world?

Philip Wylie's 1951 science-fiction novel, *The Disappearance*, addresses these

fascinating questions. The answers show us how society has changed since

the 1950s.

According to Wylie, if men and women live in different worlds, the results

would be a disaster. In Wylie's vision, men are too aggressive to survive on

their own, and women are too helpless. If women didn't control them, men

will start more wars. If men aren't there to pump gas and run the businesses,

women wouldn't be able to manage.

If Wylie is alive today, would he write the same novel? Today, a lot of men

take care of their children, and a lot of women run businesses. In 1951, Wylie

couldn't imagine these changes because of his opinions about men and women.

I wish that Wylie was here today. If he were, then he might learns that men are

not more warlike than women, and women are not more helpless than men.

His story might be very different.

EXERCISE 7 LISTENING

22|02 **A** Listen to a modern fairly tale about Cindy, a clever young girl. Then read the statements. Listen again to the fairy tale and check (✓) *True* or *False*.

	True	False
1. Cindy wishes she had a new soccer ball.	☐	☑
2. The toad wishes Cindy would marry him.	☐	☐
3. If Cindy married the toad, he would become a prince again.	☐	☐
4. Cindy wishes she could become a beautiful princess.	☐	☐
5. If Cindy became a princess, she'd have plenty of time to study science.	☐	☐
6. The toad doesn't know how to use his powers to help himself.	☐	☐
7. Cindy wants to become a scientist and help the prince.	☐	☐
8. Cindy wishes she didn't have to work.	☐	☐

B Work with a partner. Discuss your answers in A. Why did you check *True* or *False*?

EXAMPLE: **A:** Number 1 is false. Cindy doesn't wish she had a new soccer ball.
  B: Right. She already has one, but she can't find it.
  A: She just wishes she could find it.

EXERCISE 8 WHAT ABOUT YOU?

CONVERSATION Work in a group. Answer the questions in Exercise 5 on page 353. Then talk about your answers with the whole class.

EXAMPLE: **A:** What would you do if you were a millionaire?
  B: If I were a millionaire, I'd donate half my money to charity.
  C: With half the money, you could...

EXERCISE 9 IF I WERE YOU . . .

PROBLEM SOLVING Work in a group. One person describes a problem. Group members give advice with *If I were you, I would / wouldn't . . .* Use the problems below and write three more.

1. You need $500 to pay this month's rent. You only have $300.

    EXAMPLE: **A:** I can't pay the rent this month. I only have $300, and I need $500. I wish I knew what to do.
    B: If I were you, I'd try to borrow the money.
    C: If I were you, I'd call the landlord right away.

2. You're lonely. You work at home and never meet new people.

3. You never have an opportunity to practice English outside of class.

4. You've been invited to dinner. The main dish is going to be shrimp. You hate shrimp.

5. _____

6. _____

7. _____

EXERCISE 10 JUST THREE WISHES

A CONVERSATION In fairy tales, people are often given three wishes. Imagine that you had just three wishes. What would they be? Write them down.

1. *I wish I were famous.*
2. *I wish I spoke perfect English.*
3. *I wish I knew how to fly a plane.*

B Talk about your wishes with a partner.

EXAMPLE: **A:** I wish I were famous.
B: What would you do if you were famous?
A: I would . . .

C There is an old saying: "Be careful what you wish for; it may come true." Look at your wishes again. Work with a partner. Talk about the results—negative as well as positive— that might happen if they came true.

EXAMPLE: **A:** If I were famous, I might not have enough free time to do regular things. I wouldn't have a private life because . . .
B: Yes, but if you were famous, maybe you could travel a lot and meet a lot of interesting people.

FROM GRAMMAR TO WRITING

A BEFORE YOUR WRITE Think about a wish you have for yourself or for society. Then think about both positive and negative results if your wish came true. Complete the outline.

Your Wish: _____

Positive Results	Negative Results
_____	_____
_____	_____

B WRITE Use your outline to write a paragraph about your wish. First, state your wish and describe its positive results. Then, describe its possible negative results. Use present and future unreal conditional sentences. Try to avoid the common mistakes in the chart.

EXAMPLE: I wish people lived forever and didn't have to die. If people lived forever, they would be able to accomplish much more. . . . On the other hand, if people lived forever, there might be some serious problems. For example, . . .

Common Mistakes in Using Present and Future Unreal Conditional Sentences

Use the **simple past** in the *if*-clause. Do not use the simple present or the future in the *if*-clause.	*If* I **lived** forever, I would be happy. **NOT** If I ~~live~~ forever, I would be happy. **NOT** If I ~~will live~~ forever, I will be happy.
Use *would* + **base form** of the verb in the **result clause**. Do not use *would* in the *if*-clause.	If I lived forever, I **would get** a lot more done. **NOT** If I ~~would live~~ forever . . .
Use *wish* + **simple past** for wishes about the **present**. Do not use *would* after *wish*.	I **wish** I **had** more friends. **NOT** I wish I ~~would have~~ more friends.
Use a **comma after the *if*-clause** when it comes first. Do not use a comma after the result clause when the result clause comes first.	*If* **I had more time,** I would travel. **NOT** I would travel, if I had more time.

C CHECK YOUR WORK Read your paragraph. Underline the *if*-clauses once and the result clauses twice. Circle *wish*. Use the Editing Checklist to check your work.

Editing Checklist

Did you use . . . ?

- [ ] the simple past in the *if*-clause
- [ ] *would/might/could* + base form of the verb in the result clause
- [ ] *wish* + simple past for wishes about the present
- [ ] a comma after the *if*-clause when it comes first

D REVISE YOUR WORK Read your paragraph again. Can you improve your writing? Make changes if necessary. Give your paragraph a title.

UNIT 22 REVIEW

Test yourself on the grammar of the unit.

Ⓐ Circle the correct words to complete the conversation.

A: If I lived in another city, <u>I'd feel / I'm feeling</u> much happier.
     1.

B: Then if I <u>am / were</u> you, I'd move.
          2.

A: I wish I <u>can / could</u> move, but that's just impossible right now.
         3.

B: Would it be impossible if <u>you found / you'll find</u> a job somewhere else?
                              4.

A: No, I think Harry <u>can / could</u> help me find a job if I asked him. But I hate to ask.
                  5.

B: If he <u>isn't / weren't</u> an old friend, he might not want to help. But he's been your friend for ages.
         6.

A: That's true. You know, I thought that if I talked to you, <u>I'll / I'd</u> get some good ideas. Thanks!
                                                          7.

Ⓑ Complete the present and future unreal conditional sentences in this paragraph with the correct form of the verbs in parentheses.

What _____ you _____ if you _____ a wallet
                      1. (do)   **2. (find)**

lying in the middle of the street? _____ you _____ the money if
                                                      3. (take)

you _____ no one would ever find out? When Lara faced that situation, she first
    4. (know)

said to herself, "Our life _____ a lot easier if I just _____ this
                          5. (become)   **6. (put)**

money in my pocket." Then she brought the wallet to the police. Her family needed the money,

but she's not sorry. "If we _____ bad choices, our kids _____ the
                            7. (make)   **8. (learn)**

wrong lessons," she told reporters. "So we always try to do the right thing."

Ⓒ Find and correct five mistakes.

1. Pablo wishes he can speak German.

2. If he had the time, he'll study in Germany. But he doesn't have the time right now.

3. He could get a promotion when he spoke another language.

4. His company may pay the tuition if he took a course.

5. What would you do if you are in Pablo's situation?

Now check your answers on page 481.

Past Unreal Conditional Sentences

ALTERNATE HISTORIES

OUTCOMES
- Describe past unreal conditions and results that are untrue, imagined, impossible, or possible
- Express regret about things that happened or didn't happen in the past
- Extract specific information from an article
- Infer correct information from conversations
- Speculate about past events or hypothetical situations
- Discuss a past decision one regrets
- Write about an event that changed one's life

STEP 1 GRAMMAR IN CONTEXT

BEFORE YOU READ

Look at the title of the article and at the pictures on this page and on page 360. Discuss the questions.

1. What is an example of a *What if* question?

2. Do you think *What if* questions are useful?

READ

23|01 Read this article about alternate histories.

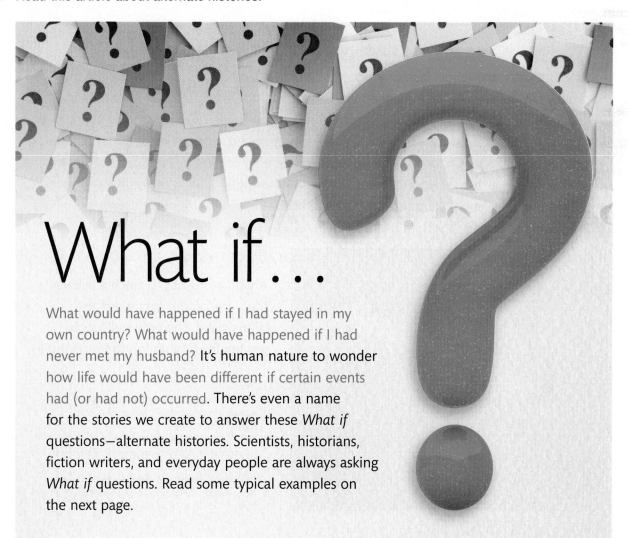

What if...

What would have happened if I had stayed in my own country? What would have happened if I had never met my husband? It's human nature to wonder how life would have been different if certain events had (or had not) occurred. There's even a name for the stories we create to answer these *What if* questions—alternate histories. Scientists, historians, fiction writers, and everyday people are always asking *What if* questions. Read some typical examples on the next page.

Science

More than 65 million years ago, dinosaurs roamed[1] our planet. Then a meteor[2] hit the Earth, changing the climate, causing the complete extinction[3] of most types of dinosaurs, and making the development of other kinds of animals possible. But what if the meteor had missed? Phil Currie, a scientist from the University of Alberta, Canada, believes that if the meteor had not struck the Earth, some types of dinosaurs would have become even more intelligent and would have

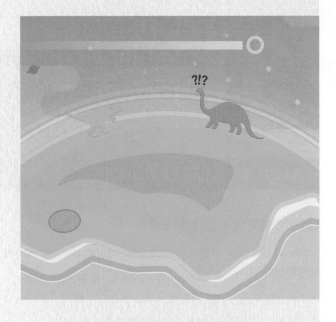

continued dominating the world, the way humans do today. Would humans have been able to develop alongside these "supersaurs"? If yes, what would our lives have been like if most types of dinosaurs had survived?

History

The seventeenth-century French philosopher Blaise Pascal said, "If Cleopatra's nose had been shorter, the whole face of the world would have been changed." Like Cleopatra, many famous people have changed the course of history,[4] and there has been much speculation on what would have occurred if they hadn't lived. One of the most common questions, for example, is "What would have happened if Adolf Hitler had never been born or if the assassination[5] attempt on his life had been successful?" Many people believe that World War II could have been avoided or at least might have been shortened, saving tens of millions of lives and countless cities from destruction.

Everyday Life

A woman rushes to catch a subway train. Just as she gets there, the doors close. The train pulls away, leaving the woman on the platform.

---

1 *roamed:* traveled freely over a wide area
2 *meteor:* a rock that falls from space into the Earth's atmosphere
3 *extinction:* the disappearance of a whole group of animals so that no more animals of that kind exist any more
4 *the course of history:* the direction history takes
5 *assassination:* the murder of an important person, usually for political reasons

What would have happened if she had gotten on the train? The film *Sliding Doors* explores this question by showing us two parallel stories: the life of the woman if she had gotten on the train, and the life of the same woman if she had missed the train. In one version of the story, the woman meets a man on the train, and the two end up falling in love. In the other, she gets mugged[6] while running to catch a taxi and has to go to the hospital. The outcomes of this everyday occurrence—catching or missing a train—show us how a single ordinary moment can change the direction of our lives.

Some people argue that there is no way of ever really knowing what would have happened if a single event had been different. To those people, speculating about the past is just a game, an amusing way to pass the time. Yet to others, it is obvious that alternate histories have a lot to offer. To them, while we can never know exactly how a small change could have affected an outcome, exploring the results of an alternate past—in books, movies, or our own lives—can teach us important lessons.

---

6 *gets mugged:* is attacked and robbed in a public place

AFTER YOU READ

A VOCABULARY **Match the words with their definitions.**

____ 1.	**alternate**	**a.**	to happen
____ 2.	**dominate**	**b.**	one person's description of an event
____ 3.	**occur**	**c.**	a result
____ 4.	**outcome**	**d.**	happening at the same time
____ 5.	**parallel**	**e.**	different
____ 6.	**version**	**f.**	to have power and control over other people or things

B COMPREHENSION **Check (✓) the events which, according to the article, can lead to an alternate history.**

☐ **1.** staying in one's own country

☐ **2.** a meteor hitting the Earth

☐ **3.** missing one's train

☐ **4.** reading fiction

☐ **5.** the survival of an animal species

☐ **6.** a person's appearance

☐ **7.** playing a game

C DISCUSSION **Work with a partner. Compare your answers in B. Why did you choose each answer?**

PAST UNREAL CONDITIONAL SENTENCES

Statements

If-Clause: Past Perfect	Result Clause: Would (not) have + Past Participle
If I **had missed** the train,	I **would have been** late. I **wouldn't have come** on time.
If I **had not gotten** that job,	I **would have felt** very bad. I **wouldn't have met** my wife.

Yes/No Questions

Result Clause	If-Clause
Would you **have walked**	if you **had had** the time?

Short Answers

Affirmative	Negative
Yes, I **would have**.	**No**, I **wouldn't have**.

Wh- Questions

Result Clause	If-Clause
What **would** you **have done**	if you **had missed** the train?

Contractions

would have	= **would've**
would not have	= **wouldn't have**

GRAMMAR NOTES

1 Past Unreal Conditional Sentences

Use past unreal conditional sentences to describe **past unreal conditions and their results**. A condition and its result may be untrue, imagined, or impossible.

The *if-clause* describes the **unreal** or **untrue condition**. The **result clause** describes the **unreal** or **untrue result** of that condition.

IF-CLAUSE   RESULT CLAUSE
If I had missed the train, I would have been late.
(But I didn't miss the train, so I wasn't late.)
If I hadn't taken that job, I wouldn't have met my wife.
(But I took the job, so I met my wife.)

2 Verb Forms in Past Unreal Conditional Sentences

Use the **past perfect** in the *if-clause*. Use *would have* + **past participle** of the verb in the **result clause**.

PAST PERFECT   WOULD HAVE + PAST PART.
If it **had won** an award, it **would have become** a famous movie.

BE CAREFUL! Sometimes speakers use *would have* in the *if*-clause. However, this is usually considered incorrect, especially in formal or written English.

If I **had had** time, I **would have watched** the movie.
NOT If I ~~would have had~~ time . . .

3 With a Modal in the Result Clause

You can use the **modals** *might have* or *could have* in the **result clause** to express **possibility**.

	IF-CLAUSE RESULT CLAUSE
• *might have*	If Ed had studied hard, he *might have* become a teacher.
• *could have*	If Ed had studied hard, he *could have* become a teacher.

> **BE CAREFUL!** Use *might have* or *could have* if the result is **not certain**. Do not use *may have* or *can have*.
>
> If I had known about the party, I *might have* gone.
> NOT . . . I ~~may have~~ gone . . .
> If I had gone, I *could have* seen you there.
> NOT . . . I ~~can have~~ seen . . .

4 Position of the *If*-Clause

The *if*-clause can come **at the beginning or the end** of the sentence. The meaning is the same.

• at the **beginning**	*If he had won a million dollars*, he would have traveled around the world.
• at the **end**	He would have traveled around the world *if he had won a million dollars*.

> **IN WRITING** Use a **comma after the *if*-clause** when it comes at the **beginning** of the sentence. Do not use a comma after the result clause when the result clause comes first.
>
> *If* I had known, I would have told you.
> NOT I would have told you, if I had known.

5 Past Unreal Conditional Sentences to Express Regret

Past unreal conditional sentences are often used to express **regret** about what really **happened in the past**.	*If* I had been free, I would have gone with you. *(I regret that I didn't go with you.)*

6 With *Wish* to Express Regret or Sadness

Use *wish* + **past perfect** to express **regret or sadness** about things in the past that you **wanted to happen but didn't**, or about things you **didn't want to happen but happened**.	Glen *wishes* he **had studied** history. *(He didn't study history, and now he thinks that was a mistake.)* He *wishes* he **hadn't taken** that job. *(He took that job, and now he regrets it.)*

EXERCISE 1   DISCOVER THE GRAMMAR

GRAMMAR NOTES 1–3, 5–6   **Read the numbered statements. Decide if the sentences that follow are *True (T)* or *False (F)*.**

1. If a girl hadn't stepped in front of her, Helen wouldn't have missed her train.

   __T__   **a.** A girl stepped in front of Helen.

   __T__   **b.** Helen missed her train.

2. If she had gotten on the train, she would've met James.

   ____   **a.** She met James.

   ____   **b.** She got on the train.

3. She wouldn't have gotten her new job if James hadn't told her about it.

   ____   **a.** She got a new job.

   ____   **b.** James didn't tell her about it.

4. If I had gotten home before 10:00, I could've watched the movie *Sliding Doors*.

   ____   **a.** I got home before 10:00.

   ____   **b.** I regret missing the movie.

5. I would have called you if I hadn't fallen asleep.

   ____   **a.** I called you.

   ____   **b.** I fell asleep.

6. If I hadn't had a history test the next day, I wouldn't have gone to bed so late.

   ____   **a.** I had a history test the next day.

   ____   **b.** I went to bed late.

7. I wish I had studied hard for the test.

   ____   **a.** I studied hard for the test.

   ____   **b.** I feel bad about not studying hard.

8. Ana would've helped me if I had asked.

   ____   **a.** Ana helped me.

   ____   **b.** I asked Ana for help.

9. If I had studied more, I might have gotten a good grade.

   ____   **a.** I definitely would have gotten a good grade.

   ____   **b.** I possibly would have gotten a good grade.

10. If I had gotten a good grade, I would've been happy.

    ____   **a.** I didn't get a good grade.

    ____   **b.** I wasn't happy.

EXERCISE 2 VERB FORMS IN *IF* AND RESULT CLAUSES

GRAMMAR NOTES 1–3 George is a character from the movie *It's a Wonderful Life* by Frank Capra. Circle the correct form of the verbs to complete George's thoughts about the past.

1. I didn't go into business with my friend Sam. If I went / (had gone) into business with him, I might become / (might have become) a success.

2. I couldn't go into the army because I was deaf in one ear. I would have gone / would go into the army if I hadn't lost / didn't lose the hearing in that ear.

3. Mary and I weren't able to go on a honeymoon. We could have gone / could go away if my father had gotten / hadn't gotten sick.

4. My uncle lost $8,000 of the company's money. I would have felt / wouldn't have felt so desperate if he had found / hadn't found the money.

5. I'm really feeling depressed. So many things seem to be going wrong. Sometimes I wish I had / would never been / would be born.

6. Clarence showed me how the world would look without me. I didn't know / wouldn't have known that I was so important to a lot of people if Clarence had shown / hadn't shown me.

7. If I hadn't rescued / wouldn't have rescued my little brother Harry from drowning in a pond, Harry would have saved / wouldn't have saved all those lives, later on, when he was a soldier.

8. My old boss once almost made a terrible mistake in his shop. If I didn't help / hadn't helped him, my boss might have gone / might go to jail.

George with his angel, Clarence

9. My wife, Mary, hadn't been / wouldn't have been happy if she hadn't met / had met me.

10. Clarence showed me that life here in Bedford Falls really were / would have been worse if I hadn't been / wouldn't have been born.

EXERCISE 3 STATEMENTS

GRAMMAR NOTES 1–3 Complete this article about a two-car accident. Use the correct form of the verbs in parentheses. Use contractions when possible.

Accidents Happen

"Everything _____ *could've turned out* _____ very differently if just one small thing
                  1. (can / turn out)

_____ different." That's what Officer Rosa Ortiz said about
            2. (be)

yesterday's collision between a Honda Civic and a Volkswagen Jetta at 6:15 p.m. on Route 1.

"I guess that can be said about all accidents," she added. This is what other first responders,

eyewitnesses, and the drivers themselves said:

■ "If the accident _____ a little earlier in the day, there
                              3. (happen)

_____ many more cars on the road." —*Jake O'Neill, police officer*
            4. (be)

■ "If the ambulance _____ a little earlier, the victims
                                  5. (arrive)

_____ medical treatment sooner." —*Angela DuBois, witness*
            6. (can / receive)

■ "If the driver of the VW _____ his seatbelt on, his injuries
                                        7. (not have)

_____ much worse." —*Lucy Chen, emergency medical technician*
            8. (be)

■ "If the driver of the Honda _____ the speed limit, she
                                          9. (not ignore)

_____ to stop in time." —*Luke Adams, witness*
            10. (may / be able to)

■ "If I _____ this morning, I _____
                11. (not oversleep)   **12.** (take)

the train. And if I _____ the train, I _____
                          13. (take)   **14.** (not be)

on the road when the VW got to the intersection." —*Michelle Johnson, driver of the Honda*

■ "If I _____ for a donut and cup of coffee on the way home,
                15. (not stop)

I _____ the accident. I was just in the wrong place at the wrong
          16. (may / avoid)

time." —*Jason Hill, driver of the VW*

"Accidents happen," said Officer Ortiz. "Sometimes just a little thing like stopping for a cup

of coffee can determine the outcome of events. But there *are* things we can do to help avoid

accidents or reduce their seriousness, such as obeying the speed limit and wearing a seatbelt.

Luckily, in this case both drivers are going to be fine."

EXERCISE 4 AFFIRMATIVE AND NEGATIVE STATEMENTS

GRAMMAR NOTES 1–4 Read these stories from an Internet message board about how people met their wives, husbands, boyfriends, or girlfriends. Using the words in parentheses, combine each pair of sentences to make one past unreal conditional sentence.

My temp became permanent. I'd already planned this great vacation to Jamaica when my boss canceled my time off. "Sorry," she told me, "I'm going to be away, but I'll hire a temp to help you out." I was so furious that I almost quit right on the spot. I thought,

<u>if she had planned ahead, we wouldn't have needed that temp</u>.
1. She didn't plan ahead. We needed that temp. (would)

Now I know that _____
2. She didn't plan ahead. I met the love of my life. (might)

When Vlad, the temp, walked in that first morning, I nearly ran into her office to thank her.

_____
3. She was so disorganized. My next trip to Jamaica was for my honeymoon. (would)

She knocked me off my feet.[1] I was skiing with some friends in Colorado. I met my wife when she knocked me down on a ski slope. It's a good thing I was OK because

_____
4. I didn't break my leg. I accepted her dinner invitation. (could)

Actually, I only accepted because she felt so bad about the accident. But after the first few minutes, I knew I had to see her again. She was pretty, funny, and really intelligent.

_____
5. I went skiing that day. She knocked me over. (would)

And _____!
6. She knocked me over. We got married. (would)

Best in the universe. I met my boyfriend online. We write stories on a *Star Trek* fan site.

_____
7. He was such a good writer. I thought about contacting him. (would)

because I'm very careful about online privacy. In fact, I didn't even know he was a guy!

_____
8. I didn't know. I was brave enough to write to him. (might)

But I thought he was another Isaac Asimov,[2] so I wanted to discuss his writing. We just emailed for a long time. Then we decided to meet at a *Star Trek* conference. I'm really glad we waited. He isn't the most handsome Klingon[3] in the universe, but to me he's Mr. Right.

_____
9. We didn't meet right away. I realized that. (might)

---

1 *knocked me off my feet:* made a very big impression on me
2 *Isaac Asimov:* a famous science-fiction writer
3 *Klingon:* in *Star Trek* stories, a race of people from another planet

EXERCISE 5 REGRETS ABOUT THE PAST

A GRAMMAR NOTE 6 These characters from the movie *Sliding Doors* feel bad about some things that occurred. Read the facts. Then write their regrets about the past. Use *wish*.

Helen and James after
their first meeting

1. **HELEN:** I took supplies from my office. My boss fired me.

   I wish I hadn't taken supplies from my office. I wish my boss hadn't fired me.

2. **HELEN:** I didn't catch my train. I had to find a taxi.

   _____

3. **TAXI DRIVER:** She got mugged near my taxi. She needed to go to the hospital.

   _____

4. **GERRY** *(Helen's old boyfriend):* Helen saw me with Lydia. Helen left me.

   _____

5. **LYDIA** *(Gerry's old girlfriend):* I started seeing Gerry again. I didn't break up with him.

   _____

6. **JAMES** *(Helen's new boyfriend):* I didn't tell Helen about my wife. I lost her trust.

   _____

7. **HELEN:** James didn't call me. I got so depressed.

   _____

8. **ANNA** *(Helen's best friend):* James lied to Helen. He hurt her.

   _____

⏵23|02 **B** LISTEN AND CHECK Listen to the characters' regrets and check your answers in A.

EXERCISE 6 EDITING

GRAMMAR NOTES 1–6   Read this student's journal essay. There are ten mistakes in the use of past unreal conditional sentences. The first mistake is already corrected. Find and correct nine more.

It Changed My Life

Have you ever made a small decision that changed the rest of your life? Has an unimportant event, like missing a bus, ever altered the course of your personal history? What would have happened if you had ~~decide~~ *decided* to do something different? How would your life had been different if you hadn't missed your bus? Will your life have been better or worse?

Several years ago, I went to see *Sliding Doors*, a movie about parallel lives. At first, I wasn't going to go because I had too much school work to do. But, at the last minute, my friend convinced me to take a break. I rushed out of the house just in time to see my bus pull away. I was upset with myself. "I wish I have left earlier!" I thought. I got to the movie theater late, and in my rush, I dropped my jacket. A friendly-looking guy picked it up and handed it to me. We started talking, met for coffee after the movie, and, five months later, we were married.

I often think of that day. When I hadn't gone to the movies, I wouldn't have met my husband-to-be. Also, if I had missed my bus, I probably won't have met him, either. And, if I haven't dropped my jacket, he might not have noticed me. (Of course in *his* version of the story, he says he would have noticed me even if there were a hundred other people in the theater lobby that day!)

The movie *Sliding Doors* is about alternate histories. It is ironic that a film about alternate histories ended up changing *my* history. If I hadn't went to see *Sliding Doors*, my life would have been very different.

EXERCISE 7 LISTENING

▶ 23|03 Ⓐ Read the statements. Listen again to the conversations and check (✓) *True* or *False*.

	True	False
Conversation 1		
1. The man missed his train.	✓	☐
2. The train was in an accident.	☐	☐
3. The man was injured in the accident.	☐	☐
Conversation 2		
1. The woman always wanted to be an English teacher.	☐	☐
2. The woman's friend got sick one day and couldn't teach a class.	☐	☐
3. The woman became a teacher as a result of her friend's illness.	☐	☐
Conversation 3		
1. The man was having trouble finding an apartment.	☐	☐
2. One day, he saw a For Rent sign in front of a building.	☐	☐
3. The man found an apartment when he got lost.	☐	☐
Conversation 4		
1. The woman went to the movies with the man.	☐	☐
2. The man really liked the movie.	☐	☐
3. The woman regrets that she missed the movie.	☐	☐
Conversation 5		
1. The man lost his wallet.	☐	☐
2. The man got a call from the police.	☐	☐
3. The man had definitely planned to call the police.	☐	☐
Conversation 6		
1. The man used to work at a bank.	☐	☐
2. On the day that he lost his job, he went to a café.	☐	☐
3. The man doesn't regret losing his job.	☐	☐

▶ 23|03 Ⓑ Work with a partner. Listen again. Discuss your answers in A. Each conversation describes a bad event that led to a good result. What was the bad event? What would have happened differently if that event hadn't happened?

EXAMPLE: A: In the first conversation, the man missed his train and was late for his meeting. Usually missing a train is bad luck.

B: But in this case, it turned out to be good luck. The train he missed was in an accident. If he had been on that train, he could have been injured.

EXERCISE 8 THINGS WOULD HAVE BEEN VERY DIFFERENT!

CONVERSATION Work in a group. Tell your classmates how a single decision or event changed your life or the life of someone you know. What would have happened if that decision or event hadn't occurred?

EXAMPLE: A: Four years ago, I was going to take a 5:15 train home from work, but I was two minutes late, and I missed the train.

B: Oh. And what happened as a result?

A: Well, the train was in an accident. If I had been on it, I could have been injured, or worse.

C: Something like that happened to me, too. Ten years ago, . . .

EXERCISE 9 WHAT WOULD *YOU* HAVE DONE?

PROBLEM SOLVING Work in a group. Read the following situations. Did the person make the right decision? What would *you* have done in each situation? Why? What *might have* or *could have* happened as a result?

1. Zeke started his business making and selling energy bars[1] when he was a teenager. Ten years later, a large company offered to buy the business. Zeke turned the offer down because he wanted to make sure Zeke's Bars were always very high quality. If he had accepted, he could have retired rich by age thirty-five. What would you have done?

EXAMPLE: A: I wouldn't have rejected the offer. I would've sold the business.

B: If he'd sold the business, he could've started a new one.

C: He might've . . .

2. A man was walking down the street when he found ten $100 bills lying on the ground. There was no one else around. He picked them up and put them in his pocket.

3. A woman came home late and found her apartment door unlocked. She was sure she had locked it. No one else had the keys. She went inside.

---

1 *energy bars:* food that gives you energy and that is in the shape of candy bars

EXERCISE 10 A REGRET

CONVERSATION Work with a partner. Talk about a decision you made at one point in your life and that you now regret. Describe the situation and talk about what you wish had happened and why.

EXAMPLE: A: Someone asked me to go to a party the night before a test. I didn't like the course, and I didn't really feel like studying, so I decided to go.

B: And what happened? Did you do OK on the test?

A: No. I failed it.

B: Oh, that's too bad.

A: It's even worse than that. I had to repeat the course! I wish I hadn't gone to the party. If I'd stayed home, I'd have studied for the test. If I'd been prepared, I would've passed.

B: But you shouldn't let regrets dominate your life. Everyone makes mistakes.

FROM GRAMMAR TO WRITING

A BEFORE YOU WRITE Think about an event that changed your life (or the life of someone you know). Answer these questions.

1. What was the event? _____

2. When did it happen? _____

3. What happened as a result of the event? _____

B WRITE Use your answers to write one or two paragraphs about the event. If the event hadn't happened, what would have been different? Would the result have been better or worse? Use past unreal conditional sentences. Try to avoid the common mistakes in the chart.

EXAMPLE: Two years ago, I was in a serious car accident that changed my life. I was in the hospital for a long time, and my friends and family were always there for me. If I hadn't been so badly injured, I might never have realized what good friends and family I had....

Common Mistakes in Using Past Unreal Conditional Sentences

Use the **past perfect** in the *if*-clause. Do not use *would have* in the *if*-clause.	*If* I **hadn't been** in that accident, I wouldn't have known how great my friends are. NOT If I ~~wouldn't have been~~ in that accident . . .
Use *wish* + **past perfect**. Do not use the simple past or *would have* after *wish*.	I *wish* I **had known** you in 2015. NOT I wish I ~~knew~~ you in 2015. NOT I wish I ~~would have known~~ you in 2015.
Use a **comma after the *if*-clause** when it comes first. Do not use a comma after the result clause when the result clause comes first.	*If* I **had had more time,** I would have traveled. NOT I would have traveled~~,~~ if I had had more time.

C CHECK YOUR WORK Read your paragraph(s). Underline the *if*-clauses once and the result clauses twice. Circle *wish*. Use the Editing Checklist to check your work.

Editing Checklist

Did you use . . . ?

☐ the past perfect in the *if*-clause

☐ *would have, might have,* or *could have* + past participle in the result clause

☐ *wish* + past perfect to express regret or sadness

☐ a comma after the *if*-clause when it comes first

D REVISE YOUR WORK Read your paragraph(s) again. Can you improve your writing? Make changes if necessary. Give your paragraph(s) a title.

UNIT 23 REVIEW

Test yourself on the grammar of the unit.

Ⓐ Circle the correct words to complete the sentences.

1. If you <u>didn't tell</u> / <u>hadn't told</u> us about the movie, we wouldn't have seen it.

2. I wish I <u>had</u> / <u>hadn't</u> gone to the movie, too. I hear it's great.

3. We <u>had been</u> / <u>would have been</u> late if we had taken the bus.

4. <u>If</u> / <u>When</u> you had called me, I might have driven you there.

5. I would've <u>gone</u> / <u>went</u> to the movies if I had had the time.

Ⓑ Complete the past unreal conditional sentences in these conversations with the correct form of the verbs in parentheses.

1. **A:** Sorry I'm late. I _____ on time if I _____ my train.
                 a. (be)   **b. (not miss)**

   B: Well, if you _____ on time, I _____ that great café.
                 c. (be)   **d. (not discover)**

2. **A:** I wish I _____ this job offer.
              a. (not accept)

   B: But, if you _____ another job instead, we _____!
               b. (take)   **c. (not meet)**

3. **A:** It's hard to believe that birds are a type of dinosaur!

   B: I know. If I _____ that science program on TV, I _____ it.
            a. (not see)   **b. (not believe)**

Ⓒ Find and correct six mistakes.

     Tonight, we watched the movie *Back to the Future* starring Michael J. Fox. I might never had seen it if I hadn't read his autobiography, *Lucky Man*. His book was so good that I wanted to see his most famous movie. Now, I wish I saw it in the theater when it first came out, but I hadn't even been born yet! It would have been better if we would have watched it on a big screen. Fox was great. He looked really young—just like a teenager. But I would have recognized him even when I hadn't known he was in the film.

     In real life, when Fox was a teenager, he was too small to become a professional hockey player. But if he hadn't looked so young, he can't have gotten his role in the TV hit series *Family Ties*. In Hollywood, he had to sell his furniture to pay his bills, but he kept trying to find an acting job. If he would have given up, he might never have become a star.

Now check your answers on page 481.

Indirect Speech and Embedded Questions

PART 9

OUTCOMES
- Report what others said, using direct or indirect speech
- Identify key information in a social science article
- Identify and discuss details in conversations
- Discuss lying and telling the truth
- Discuss and interpret literary quotes and international proverbs
- Write about a past conversation, reporting what was said, using direct and indirect speech

OUTCOMES
- Report other people's statements using indirect speech, making necessary tense and time-word changes
- Match quotations with speakers, based on information in a scientific article
- Identify specific information in a conversation
- Discuss extreme weather events and report other people's statements
- Write about an extreme weather event, reporting another person's experience

OUTCOMES
- Report other people's instructions, commands, advice, requests, and invitations, using indirect speech
- Identify specific information in an interview transcript
- Identify medical advice reported in a conversation
- Discuss health issues and possible home remedies
- Report how someone followed instructions
- Write about a health problem one had and about the health advice one received

OUTCOMES
- Report other people's questions, using indirect speech
- Identify specific information in a business article
- Identify and discuss details in a conversation
- Role-play and discuss a job interview
- Complete a questionnaire about work values, discuss the answers, and report conversations
- Write a report on a job interview

OUTCOMES
- Ask for information or express something you don't know, using embedded questions
- Extract key information from an interview transcript
- Identify and discuss details in a call-in radio show
- Discuss tipping around the world, giving opinions
- Discuss problems one had during a first-time experience
- Role-play a conversation between a hotel clerk and a guest asking for information
- Write about a confusing or surprising situation

Direct and Indirect Speech

TRUTH AND LIES

STEP 1 GRAMMAR IN CONTEXT

BEFORE YOU READ

Look at the title of the article and at the photo, and read what the woman is saying. Discuss the questions.

1. Do you think the woman's hair looks great?

2. Is it ever all right to tell a lie? If *yes*, in what situations?

READ

▶ 24|01 Read this article about lying.

The Truth About Lying

At 9:00, Rick Spivak's landlord[1] called and said Rick's rent was late. "The check is in the mail," Rick replied quickly. At 11:45, Rick left for a 12 o'clock meeting across town. Arriving late, Rick told his client that traffic had been bad. That evening, Rick's wife, Ann, came home with a new hairstyle. Rick hated it. "It looks great," he said.

Three lies in one day! Does Rick have a problem? Or is he just an ordinary guy? Each time, he told himself that sometimes the truth causes too many problems. Like Rick, most of us tell white lies— harmless untruths that help us avoid trouble. In fact, one social psychologist[2] estimates that the average American tells about 200 lies a day! He says that lying is a habit, and we are often not even aware that we are doing it. When we do notice, we justify the lie by telling ourselves it was for a good purpose.

He said my hair looked great this way!

---

1 *landlord:* someone who owns a building or other property and rents it to other people

2 *social psychologist:* a psychologist who studies how social groups affect the way people behave

These are our six most common excuses:

- To be polite: "I'd love to go to your party, but I have to work."

- To protect someone else's feelings: "Your hair looks great that way!"

- To feel better about yourself: "I'm looking good these days."

- To appear more interesting to others: "I run five miles every day."

- To get something more quickly: "I have to have that report today."

- To avoid uncomfortable situations: "I was going to call you, but my phone battery was dead."

How do we get away with all those white lies? First of all, it's difficult to recognize a lie because body language usually doesn't reveal dishonesty. But even when we suspect[3] someone is lying, we often don't want to know the truth. If an acquaintance says she's fine, but she clearly isn't, a lot of people find it easier to take her statement at face value.[4] And when someone tells you, "You did a great job!" you probably don't want to question the compliment!

Is telling lies a new trend? In one survey, the majority of people who answered said that people were more honest in the past. Nevertheless, lying wasn't really born yesterday. In the eighteenth century, the French philosopher[5] Vauvenargues told the truth about lying when he wrote, "All men are born truthful and die liars."

---

3 *suspect:* think that something—usually something bad—is probably true
4 *take her statement at face value:* accept what she says without looking for hidden meanings
5 *philosopher:* someone who thinks a lot and questions the meaning of life and ideas about the world

AFTER YOU READ

A VOCABULARY Choose the word or phrase that best completes each sentence.

1. I enjoy reading **survey** results. It's interesting learning other people's _____.
   a. stories   **b.** opinions   **c.** secrets

2. Ed was **aware** that Sid lost his job. He _____ it.
   a. suspected   **b.** didn't know about   **c.** knew about

3. Some people **justify** lying. They _____ it.
   a. always avoid   **b.** find good reasons for **c.** never recognize

4. The **majority** of people are honest. _____ of them don't tell lies.
   a. None   **b.** All   **c.** Most

5. Hamid **revealed** his plans yesterday. He _____ about them.
   a. refused to say anything **b.** told everyone **c.** didn't tell the truth

6. I really didn't like the meal. **Nevertheless**, I said that the food was _____.
   a. delicious   **b.** terrible   **c.** healthy

COMPREHENSION Read the statements. Check (✓) *True* or *False*.

		True	False
1.	Rick's rent check is in the mail.	☐	☐
2.	Rick likes Ann's new hairstyle.	☐	☐
3.	Rick thinks some lies are all right.	☐	☐
4.	We often lie to avoid hurting another person.	☐	☐
5.	It's easy to know when a person is lying.	☐	☐
6.	Lying is a new trend.	☐	☐
7.	Vauvenargues thinks people get more dishonest with age.	☐	☐

C DISCUSSION Work with a partner. Compare your answers in B. Why did you choose *True* or *False*?

STEP 2 GRAMMAR PRESENTATION

DIRECT AND INDIRECT SPEECH

Direct Speech

Direct Statement	Subject	Reporting Verb	Noun/Pronoun
"The check **is** in the mail," "Your hair **looks** great," "The traffic **was** bad,"	he	**told**	the bank. Ann. her.
		said.	

Indirect Speech

Subject	Reporting Verb	Noun/Pronoun	Indirect Statement	
He	**told**	the bank Ann her	**(that)**	the check **was** in the mail. her hair **looked** great. the traffic **had been** bad.
	said			

GRAMMAR NOTES

1 Direct Speech

Direct speech states the exact words that the speaker used.	**"I always pay on time,"** he said. **"I like that tie,"** she told him.
Put **quotation marks** before and after the speech you are quoting. That speech (called the **quotation**) can go at the **beginning** or at the **end** of the sentence.	**"The traffic is bad,"** he said. He said, **"The traffic is bad."**
Use a **comma** to separate the quotation from the rest of the sentence.	Rick said, "It looks great." "It looks great," Rick said.
After a **quotation at the beginning**, the word order is **verb + subject** or **subject + verb**. With pronouns, verb + subject is rare.	"That's great," **said Chen**. *(more common)* "That's great," **Chen said**. *(less common)* "That's great," **said he**. *(rare)*

2 Indirect Speech

Indirect speech (also called *reported speech*) **reports** what a speaker **said without using the exact words** that the speaker used.	Rick said **he always paid on time**.
	  (Rick: "I always pay on time.")
	Ann told him **she liked that tie**.
	  (Ann: "I like that tie.")

The word *that* can introduce the indirect speech statement.	He said *that* **he always paid on time**. He said **he always paid on time**.
Do not use quotation marks or a comma in indirect speech.	She said **that she had to work**. NOT She said that_x [×]she had to work.[×]

3 Reporting Verbs

We use **reporting verbs** (such as *say* and *tell*) with both direct and indirect speech. The reporting verb is usually in the simple past tense.

• **direct speech**	"It looks great," he **said**. "I'm sorry to be late," Rick **told** Ann.
• **indirect speech**	He **said** it looked great. He **told** Ann that he was sorry to be late.
Use *say* when you **do not mention the listener.**	"It looks great," he **said**. He **said** it looked great.
Use *tell* or *say to* when you **mention the listener.**	"It looks great," he **told** *Ann*. "It looks great," he **said to** *Ann*. He **told** *her* that it looked great. He **said to** *Ann* that it looked great.
Do not confuse *say* and *tell*. Do not use *say* without *to* when you mention the listener. Do not use *tell* with *to* when you mention the listener.	He **said to me** it was great. NOT He said me it was great. He **told me** it was great. NOT He told to me it was great.

4 Change of Tense in Indirect Speech

When the **reporting verb** is in the **simple past** (*said*, *told*), we often **change the verb tense** in the indirect speech statement.

The **simple present** in direct speech becomes the **simple past** in indirect speech. Notice that the indirect speech uses the simple past, but the meaning is present.	She **said**, "I only *buy* shoes on sale." She **said** that she only *bought* shoes on sale. *(She only buys shoes on sale.)*
The **simple past** in direct speech becomes the **past perfect** in indirect speech.	She **said**, "I *found* a great store." She **said** she **had found** a great store.
BE CAREFUL! When the **reporting verb** is in the **simple present**, do **not change the verb tense** in the indirect speech statement.	Ann **says**, "I *run* a mile every day." Ann **says** that she *runs* a mile every day. NOT Ann says that she ~~ran~~ a mile every day.

5 Optional Change of Tense in Indirect Speech

You do not always have to change the tense in indirect speech.

The tense in indirect speech can **remain the same** when you report:

• something that was **just said**	A: **I'm** tired from all this shopping. B: What did you say? A: I **said** I**'m** tired. **or** I **said** I *was* tired.
• something that is **still true**	Rick **said** the bank *wants* a check. Rick **said** the bank *wanted* a check.
• a **general truth** or **scientific law**	He **told** us that water *freezes* at 0° Celsius. He **told** us that water *froze* at 0° Celsius.

6 Other Changes in Indirect Speech

We often make changes in indirect speech to **keep the speaker's original meaning**.

To keep the original meaning, change:

• **subject pronouns**	Ann told her boss, "**I** love the job." Ann told the boss that *she* loved the job.
• **object pronouns**	Ann said, "Jon texts **me** all the time." Ann told us that Jon texts *her* all the time.
• **possessive adjectives**	Ann said, "**Your** new tie is great!" Ann told me that *my* new tie was great.

REFERENCE NOTES

For **punctuation rules for direct speech**, see Appendix 28 on page 466.

For **additional tense changes in indirect speech**, see Unit 25 on page 395.

For a list of **reporting verbs**, see Appendix 19 on page 462.

EXERCISE 1 DISCOVER THE GRAMMAR

A GRAMMAR NOTES 1–6 Read this magazine article about lying at a job interview. Circle the reporting verbs. Underline once the examples of direct speech. Underline twice the examples of indirect speech.

"Lying during a job interview is risky business," says Martha Toledo, director of the management consulting firm Maxwell. "The truth has a funny way of coming out." Toledo tells the story of one woman, Jane, applying for a job as an office manager. The woman told the interviewer that she had a B.A. degree. Actually, she was eight credits short. She also said that she had made $50,000 at her last job. The truth was $10,000 less. "Many firms really do check facts," warns Toledo. In this case, a call to the applicant's company revealed the truth. "She was a strong applicant," says Toledo, "and most of the information on the résumé was true. Nevertheless, those details cost her the job."

Toledo relates a story about another job applicant, George. During an interview, George reported that he had quit his last job. George got the new job and was doing well until the company hired another employee, Pete. George and Pete had worked at the same company. Pete later told his boss that his old company had fired George. After George's supervisor became aware of the lie, he stopped trusting George, and their relationship became difficult. Eventually, George quit.

B Choose the correct answer to complete each statement.

1. _____ Jane told the job interviewer.
   a. "I had a B.A. degree,"
   b. "I have a B.A. degree,"

2. She said, _____
   a. "She had made $50,000 at her last job."
   b. "I made $50,000 at my last job."

3. George said, _____
   a. "He had quit his last job."
   b. "I quit my last job."

4. _____ Pete told his boss.
   a. "My old company fired George,"
   b. "His old company fired George,"

EXERCISE 2 *SAID* AND *TOLD*; VERB AND PRONOUN CHANGES

GRAMMAR NOTES 2–6 **Complete this student's essay with the correct words.**

The Broken Bowl

Once when I was a teenager, I went to my Aunt Leah's house. Aunt Leah

collected pottery, and as soon as I got there, she <u>said / (told)</u> me she <u>wants / wanted</u>
1. 2.

to show me <u>my / her</u> lovely new bowl. She <u>said / told</u> she <u>has / had</u> just bought it. I
3. 4. 5.

admired it and <u>said / told</u> her it <u>is / was</u> very beautiful.
6. 7.

When Aunt Leah left the room, she handed me the bowl. To my horror, as I was

looking at it, it slipped from my hands and broke into pieces on the floor. When she

came back, I <u>said / told</u> the cat had broken <u>her / your</u> bowl. Aunt Leah gave me a
8. 9.

strange look, but <u>said / told</u> me that it <u>isn't / wasn't</u> important. She <u>said / told</u> that
10. 11. 12.

people were much more important than things.

I didn't sleep at all that night, and the next morning I called my aunt and

<u>said / told</u> her that I <u>have / had</u> broken the bowl. I apologized and <u>said / told</u> that
13. 14. 15.

I <u>feel / felt</u> really terrible about it. She laughed and said that <u>I / she</u> had known all
16. 17.

along. We still laugh about it today. The bowl broke that day, but my relationship

with my aunt is stronger than ever.

EXERCISE 3 INDIRECT SPEECH

GRAMMAR NOTES 1–4, 6 Look at the pictures. Rewrite the statements as indirect speech.
Use *said* as the reporting verb and make all necessary changes in the verbs and pronouns.

1. a. <u>She said it was her own recipe.</u>

   b. <u>He said it looked great.</u>

2. a. <u>He said his car had broken down.</u>

   b. <u>He said he had missed the meeting, Mr. Brown</u>

3. a. <u>He said he had to drive his aunt to...</u>

   b. <u>Tina said she had already bought...</u>

4. a. <u>She said she exercised every day.</u>

   b. <u>He said she looked very fit.</u>

5. a. <u>He told Mr Morgan that his bill was overdue</u>

   b. <u>He told Mr Morgan that he had just mailed the checked</u>

6. a. <u>He said he was 35</u> is

   b. <u>She said he didn't look 35</u> don't?

EXERCISE 4 INDIRECT SPEECH

GRAMMAR NOTE 2–4, 6 Rewrite Lisa and Ben's conversation using indirect speech. Use the reporting verbs in parentheses. Make necessary changes in the verbs and pronouns.

1. **LISA:** I just heard about a job at a scientific research company.

   (tell) <u>She told him she had just heard about a job at a scientific research company.</u>

2. **BEN:** Oh, I majored in science at Florida State.

   (say) <u>He said that he had majored in science at Florida State.</u>

3. **LISA:** They didn't mention the starting salary.

   (say) _____

4. **BEN:** I need a lot of money to pay off my student loans.

   (say) _____

5. **LISA:** They want someone with some experience as a programmer.

   (say) _____

6. **BEN:** Well, I work as a programmer for Data Systems.

   (tell) _____

7. **LISA:** Oh—they need a college graduate.

   (say) _____

8. **BEN:** Well, I graduated from Florida State.

   (tell) _____

9. **LISA:** But they don't want a recent graduate.

   (say) _____

10. **BEN:** I got my degree four years ago.

    (tell) _____

11. **LISA:** Great—I wasn't aware of that.

    (tell) _____

12. **BEN:** I really appreciate the information.

    (say) _____

13. **LISA:** My boss just came in, and I have to go.

    (tell) _____

EXERCISE 5 EDITING

GRAMMAR NOTES 2-4 Read the article. There are ten mistakes in the use of direct and indirect speech. The first mistake is already corrected. Find and correct nine more. Mistakes with quotation marks count as one mistake for the sentence.

WARNING!!!! THIS MESSAGE IS A HOAX!!!!!

Everyone gets urgent email messages. They tell you that billionaire Bill

wants
Gates now ~~wanted~~ to give away his money—to YOU! They say you that

a popular floor cleaner kills family pets. They report that your computer

monitor had taken photographs of you. Before I became aware of Internet

hoaxes, I used to forward these emails to all my friends. Not long ago,

a very annoyed friend explains that the story about killer bananas was

a hoax (an untrue story). He said me "that the majority of those scary

emails were hoaxes." He told me about these common signs of hoaxes:

- The email always says that it was very urgent. It has lots of

  exclamation points.

- It tells that it is not a hoax and quotes important people.

  (The quotations are false.)

- It urges you to send the email to everyone you know.

He also told that a lot of Internet sites reveal information about Internet

hoaxes. With this information, you can avoid forwarding all your friends a

false warning. So, before *you* announce that sunscreen had made people

blind, check out the story on a reliable website.

EXERCISE 6   LISTENING

▶ 24|02   **A**   Read the sentences. Then listen to Lisa's conversations. Listen again and circle the correct word or phrase to complete each sentence.

Conversation 1

1. Lisa said to Alex, "I didn't / (don't) like to eat meat."

2. Lisa told Alex, "My parents are / were in town."

Conversation 2

3. Ben told Lisa, "I used to like / like to go to the gym."

4. Lisa told Ben, "I take / took aerobics on Sunday."

Conversation 3

5. Lisa told Mark that her boss said it wasn't / was urgent.

6. Lisa told Mark the staff meeting wasn't / was on Monday.

Conversation 4

7. Katy told Lisa, "I want / wanted to make something special for you."

8. Katy's mother said, "I always use / used two kinds of meat."

▶ 24|02   **B**   Work with a partner. Read Lisa's weekly planner. Lisa wasn't always honest in her conversations. Listen to the conversations again and notice the differences between what Lisa said and the truth. Discuss the differences with your partner.

EXAMPLE: **A:** Lisa said her parents were in town for the weekend, but that's not true.
           B: Right. She said she wanted to spend time with her parents on Saturday night, but she really had a date with Ben on Saturday night.

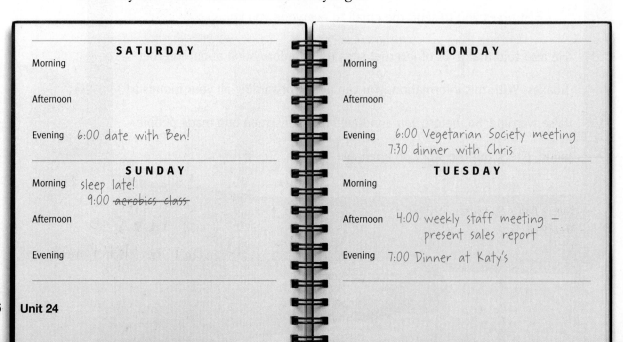

SATURDAY
Morning
Afternoon
Evening   6:00 date with Ben!

SUNDAY
Morning   sleep late!
          9:00 ~~aerobics class~~
Afternoon
Evening

MONDAY
Morning
Afternoon
Evening   6:00 Vegetarian Society meeting
          7:30 dinner with Chris

TUESDAY
Morning
Afternoon   4:00 weekly staff meeting –
          present sales report
Evening   7:00 Dinner at Katy's

EXERCISE 7 TO LIE OR NOT TO LIE?

DISCUSSION Review the six excuses for lying described in "The Truth About Lying" on page 377. Then work in a group. Is it OK to lie in these circumstances? Give examples from your own experience to support your ideas.

- To be polite
- To protect someone else's feelings
- To feel better about yourself
- To appear more interesting to others
- To get something more quickly
- To avoid uncomfortable situations

EXAMPLE: A: Once, my friend told me that my haircut looked great, but it really looked awful. I know she wanted to protect my feelings, but I think she should have told me the truth. Now it's hard for me to believe anything she says.

B: I think at times it's OK to lie to protect someone's feelings. Once, I told my best friend that . . .

C: I think . . .

EXERCISE 8 QUOTABLE QUOTES

DISCUSSION Work in a group. Discuss these famous quotations about lying. Do you agree with them? Give examples to support your opinion. Use *says* to report the proverbs and *said* to report the ideas of individuals.

1. All men are born truthful and die liars.
   —*Vauvenargues (French philosopher, 1715–1747)*

   EXAMPLE: A: Vauvenargues said that all men are born truthful and die liars.
   B: I agree because babies don't lie, but children and adults do.
   C: I don't believe that *everyone* lies. . . .

2. A half-truth is a whole lie.
   —*Jewish proverb*

3. A little inaccuracy saves tons of explanation.
   —*Saki (British short story writer, 1870–1916)*

4. A liar needs a good memory.
   —*Quintilian (first-century Roman orator)*

5. The man who speaks the truth is always at ease.
   —*Persian proverb*

6. The cruelest lies are often told in silence.
   —*Robert Louis Stevenson (Scottish novelist, 1850–1894)*

Robert Louis Stevenson

EXERCISE 9 HONESTLY SPEAKING

A QUESTIONNAIRE Complete the questionnaire. Check (✓) your answers.

	Always	Usually	Sometimes	Rarely	Never
1. I tell the truth to my friends.	☐	☐	☐	☐	☐
2. I tell the truth to my family.	☐	☐	☐	☐	☐
3. It's OK to lie on the job.	☐	☐	☐	☐	☐
4. "White lies" protect people's feelings.	☐	☐	☐	☐	☐
5. Most people are honest.	☐	☐	☐	☐	☐
6. It's best to tell the truth.	☐	☐	☐	☐	☐
7. I tell people my real age.	☐	☐	☐	☐	☐
8. My friends are honest with me.	☐	☐	☐	☐	☐
9. It's difficult to tell a convincing lie.	☐	☐	☐	☐	☐
10. Politicians are honest.	☐	☐	☐	☐	☐
11. Doctors tell patients the whole truth.	☐	☐	☐	☐	☐
12. I answer questionnaires honestly.	☐	☐	☐	☐	☐

B Work in a group. Compare your answers to the questionnaire. Summarize your group's results and report them to the rest of the class.

EXAMPLE: A: Five of us said that we usually told the truth.
　　　　　 B: Only one of us said it was always best to tell the truth.
　　　　　 C: Everyone in our group said that they tell people their real age.

EXERCISE 10 TO TELL THE TRUTH

A GAME Work in a group of three. Each student tells the group an interesting fact about his or her life. The fact can *only* be true for this student.

EXAMPLE: A: Once I climbed a mountain that was 7,000 meters high.
B: I speak four languages.
C: I scored the winning goal for my soccer team at a big tournament.

B The group chooses a fact and goes to the front of the class. Each student states the same fact, but, remember: Only one student is telling the truth.

EXAMPLE:

Once I climbed a mountain that was 7,000 meters high.

Once I climbed a mountain that was 7,000 meters high.

Once I climbed a mountain that was 7,000 meters high.

C The class asks the three students questions to find out who is telling the truth.

EXAMPLE: A: Alice, how long did it take you to climb the mountain?
B: Justin, who did you climb the mountain with?
C: Kate, did you train for a long time?

D As a class, decide who was telling the truth. Explain your reasons.

EXAMPLE: A: I didn't believe Alice. She said it had taken two weeks to climb the mountain.
B: I think Justin was lying. He told us he'd climbed the mountain alone.
C: I think Kate was telling the truth. She said that she'd trained for several months.

A BEFORE YOU WRITE Think about a short conversation you once had when you thought someone was not telling the truth. When and where was it? Who were you speaking to? What were you speaking about? Write three direct quotations from the conversation.

1. _____

2. _____

3. _____

B WRITE Use the situation and the direct quotations in A to write one or two paragraphs about your conversation. Use both direct and indirect speech. Try to avoid the common mistakes in the chart.

EXAMPLE: Two years ago, I wanted to buy a used car. I was talking to a woman who owned a Honda Civic, and we were discussing the price. She told me that it was a great car and that it had only 10,000 miles on it. She also said, "It was brand new when I bought it." I didn't believe her because . . .

Common Mistakes in Using Direct and Indirect Speech

Use **quotations marks** with direct speech, before and after the speech you are quoting. Do not use quotation marks with indirect speech.	She said, "The car is new." **NOT** She said that "the car is new."
Use a **comma** to separate a direct quotation from the rest of the sentence. Do not use a comma before the statement in indirect speech.	She said, "It's a great car." **NOT** She said, that it's a great car.
Change the verb tenses and the pronouns in indirect speech to keep the speaker's original meaning.	"I love your new car," he told Ina. He told Ina that he loved her new car. **NOT** He told Ina that I love your new car.

C CHECK YOUR WORK Read your paragraph(s). Underline once all the examples of direct speech. Underline twice all the examples of indirect speech. Circle all the reporting verbs. Use the Editing Checklist to check your work.

Editing Checklist

Did you use . . . ?

☐ quotation marks before and after the quotation in direct speech

☐ a comma to separate a direct quotation from the rest of the sentence

☐ the verb *say* when you didn't mention the listener

☐ the verb *tell* when you mentioned the listener

☐ the correct verb tenses and pronouns in indirect speech

D REVISE YOUR WORK Read your paragraph(s) again. Can you improve your writing? Make changes if necessary. Give your writing a title.

UNIT 24 **REVIEW**

Test yourself on the grammar of the unit.

Ⓐ Circle the correct words to complete the sentences.

1. My friend Ryan always <u>says / tells</u> that white lies are OK.

2. When Talia invited him to dinner last month, he said, <u>"I'd love to." / "That he'd love to."</u>

3. Then Talia told him that she <u>plans / planned</u> to cook a Chinese meal.

4. Ryan said that <u>he / I</u> loved Chinese food. That was a white lie—he really dislikes it.

5. Talia served a wonderful meal. She told Ryan that <u>she'd cooked / I cooked</u> it all herself.

6. Ryan really liked it! When he finished dinner, he <u>told / said</u> Talia, "That was great."

7. After they got married, Talia told Ryan that the Chinese meal <u>is / had been</u> takeout.

8. Today, Ryan always says it was the best meal of <u>my / his</u> life—and that's the truth.

Ⓑ Rewrite each direct statement as an indirect statement. Keep the original meaning. (The direct statement was said one week ago.)

Direct Speech	**Indirect Speech**
1. "I always get up early."	She said _____.
2. "Water boils at 100 degrees Celsius."	He told them _____.
3. "I like your haircut."	He told me _____.
4. "I loved the pasta."	She said _____.
5. "It's my own recipe."	He said _____.
6. "I mailed you the check."	She told him _____.
7. "My boss liked my work."	He said _____.

Ⓒ Find and correct five mistakes. Remember to check punctuation.

1. A psychologist I know often tells me "that people today tell hundreds of lies every day."

2. Yesterday, Mia's boyfriend said her that he liked her new dress.

3. When she heard that, Mia said she didn't really believe you.

4. I didn't think that was so bad. I said that her boyfriend tells her a little white lie.

5. But Mia hates lying. She said that to me, all lies were wrong.

Now check your answers on page 481.

Tense Changes in Indirect Speech
EXTREME WEATHER

OUTCOMES
• Report other people's statements using indirect speech, making necessary tense and time-word changes
• Match quotations with speakers, based on information in a scientific article
• Identify specific information in a conversation
• Discuss extreme weather events and report other people's statements
• Write about an extreme weather event, reporting another person's experience

STEP 1 GRAMMAR IN CONTEXT

BEFORE YOU READ

Look at the photos and at the title of the article. Discuss the questions.

1. What do you think a *force of nature* is?

2. What is another example of a force of nature?

READ

▶ 25|01 Read this article about tornadoes.

Force of Nature

It was March 18, 1925. The weather forecaster said that there was going to be rain and strong winds. No one, however, was prepared for the extreme weather event that killed almost 700 people and destroyed 15,000 homes in the region of the United States known as the Midwest. The cause of this mass destruction? A tornado.

Tornadoes are extremely violent storms. They spin very quickly in the shape of a funnel.[1] Tornadoes occur mostly in North America and strike without much warning. They move quickly across both land and water, and their powerful winds, which often exceed 60 mph (96.5 kph), can destroy entire towns. Sadly, that's what happened in 1925, when the "Great Tri-State Tornado" hit the states of Missouri, Illinois, and Indiana, leaving death and destruction in its path.
The tornado took everyone by surprise.

Judith Cox was having lunch in Gorham, Illinois, when the twister reached the town. She told a local newspaper that there had been a great roar[2] like a train, but much louder. She said that the air had been full of everything—boards, tree branches, clothing, pans, stoves, and even parts of houses.

Tornado destruction

---

1 *funnel:* a tube with a wide top and a narrow bottom, used for pouring liquids into a container
2 *roar:* a deep and loud continuous sound

Lela Hartman was just a four-year-old child on March 18, 1925, but she remembered that day well. She had been visiting her grandmother's farm in Illinois. Years later, she recounted the events of that terrible day. She said that the day had started out nice, but that then it had kept getting darker and darker. The worried family found shelter in the basement of the house. When they came out afterwards, the world looked very different to the young girl. As usual, her father had parked his car in the barn. Hartman said the storm had totally destroyed the barn, had taken the roof off her father's car, and had moved the car closer to the house. The house itself had been turned around on its foundation.[3] At the end of her account, when asked if she had anything else to say, Hartman replied simply that she hoped they would never have another tornado.

Tri-State Tornado 1925 Statistics	
Duration:	3½ hours
Distance Traveled:	219 miles (352 km)
Average Speed:	62 mph (99.7 kph)
Highest Speed:	73 mph (117.5 kph)
Deaths:	695 people
Injuries:	more than 2,000
Homes Destroyed:	15,000
Financial Loss:	$1.5 billion

---

3 *foundation:* the solid base that is built underground to support a building

In May, 2011, almost ninety years after the Tri-State Tornado, a tornado hit the state of Missouri again. This time, however, things were different. Whereas it took days for the world to learn about the 1925 disaster, this time news traveled much faster. Newspaper editor Joe Hadsall reported that it had taken only minutes for people to find out about the tornado through sites like Facebook and Twitter. He said that people's friends and family had known instantly about the disaster and that his newspaper had used these sites to spread more information.

Can a tornado like the Tri-State hit again? When asked this question, one meteorologist[4] answered that not only could one strike again, but that one would strike again. He said that it was not a question of *if*, it was a question of *when*. In other words, it is inevitable. However, thanks to advances in science, technology, and communication, the devastation of this force of nature will probably not be as great as on that tragic day in 1925.

---

4 *meteorologist:* a scientist who studies weather

AFTER YOU READ

A VOCABULARY **Complete the sentences with the words from the box.**

devastation	exceed	extreme	inevitable	shelter	whereas

1. A tornado can cause enormous _____.

2. It was _____. It had to happen. Nothing could stop it.

3. The damage may _____ last year's damage. In fact, it could be much worse.

4. The amount of destruction was _____. No one expected it to be so bad.

5. The basement provided _____ from the storm. They were much safer there.

6. Tornadoes start over land; _____ hurricanes begin over water.

B COMPREHENSION **Read the quotations. Which of the following people said each one?**

a. Judith Cox   **b.** Lela Hartman   **c.** Joe Hadsall

d. the weather forecaster   **e.** the meteorologist

_____ **1.** "There's going to be rain and strong winds."

_____ **2.** "The air was full of everything."

_____ **3.** "A tornado will strike again."

_____ **4.** "The day started out nice."

_____ **5.** "It only took minutes for people to find out about the tornado."

_____ **6.** "It kept getting darker and darker."

_____ **7.** "There was a great roar."

_____ **8.** "I hope we'll never have another tornado."

C DISCUSSION **Work with a partner. Discuss your answers in B. Why did you choose your answers?**

TENSE CHANGES IN INDIRECT SPEECH

Direct Speech			Indirect Speech				
Subject	Reporting Verb	Direct Statement	Subject	Reporting Verb	Noun/ Pronoun	*(that)*	Indirect Statement
He	said,	"I **live** in Indiana."	He	told	Jim me you him her us them		he **lived** in Indiana.
		"I **moved** here in June."					he **had moved** there in June.
		"I**'m looking** for an apartment."					he **was looking** for an apartment.
		"I**'ve started** a new job."					he **had started** a new job.
		"I**'m going to stay** here."					he **was going to stay** there.
		"I**'ll invite** you for the holidays."					he **would invite** me for the holidays.
		"We **can go** to the park."		said		*(that)*	we **could go** to the park.
		"I **may look** for a roommate."					he **might look** for a roommate.
		"I **should get back** to work."					he **should get back** to work.
		"I **have to finish** my report."					he **had to finish** his report.
		"You **must come** to visit."					I **had to come** to visit.
		"We **ought to see** each other more."					we **ought to see** each other more.

GRAMMAR NOTES

1 Change of Verb Tense in Indirect Speech

When the **reporting verb** is in **the simple past**, we often change the verb tense in the indirect speech statement.

DIRECT SPEECH		INDIRECT SPEECH	
simple present	→	simple past	He said, "It**'s** cloudy." *(direct)* He said it **was** cloudy. *(indirect)*
present progressive	→	past progressive	She said, "A tornado **is coming**." *(direct)* She said that a tornado **was coming**. *(indirect)*
simple past	→	past perfect	He said, "Ken **called**." *(direct)* He said that Ken **had called**. *(indirect)*
present perfect	→	past perfect	She told him, "I**'ve heard** the news." *(direct)* She told him that she**'d heard** the news. *(indirect)*

Notice that the verb in indirect speech often uses the **past**, but the meaning is **present**.

I just spoke to John. He said it **was** cloudy in Miami.
 *(It is cloudy **now** in Miami.)*

2 Modals and Indirect Speech

Modals often change in indirect speech.

DIRECT SPEECH		INDIRECT SPEECH	
will	→	*would*	I said, "The winds **will be** strong." *(direct)* I said the winds **would be** strong. *(indirect)*
can	→	*could*	"You **can stay** with me," he told us. *(direct)* He told us that we **could stay** with him. *(indirect)*
may	→	*might*	He said, "The storm **may cause** damage." *(direct)* He said the storm **might cause** damage. *(indirect)*
must	→	*had to*	"You **must leave**," he told us. *(direct)* He told us that we **had to leave**." *(indirect)*

Some verbs do not change in indirect speech.

• the modals *could, might, should, ought to,* and *would*	"You **should leave**," he told us. *(direct)* He told us that we **should leave**. *(indirect)*
• past modals *could have, might have, should have, ought to have,* and *would have*	"We **couldn't have known**." *(direct)* They said they **couldn't have known**. *(indirect)*
• verbs in the past perfect	"I **had moved** a week before," he said. *(direct)* He said he **had moved** a week before. *(indirect)*
• present conditional verbs	Jim said, "If I **knew**, I **would tell** you." *(direct)* Jim said if he **knew**, he **would tell** me. *(indirect)*
• past unreal conditional verbs	Ana said, "If I **had known**, I **would have told** you." *(direct)* Ana said if she **had known**, she **would have told** me. *(indirect)*
USAGE NOTE We often do not change the tense when we report something that was **just said**, something that is **still true**, or a **general truth** or **scientific law**.	"Tornadoes **are** worse than a bad storm." She said that tornadoes **are** worse than a bad storm.

Change time words in indirect speech to keep the speaker's **original meaning**. This is especially important when reporting something that was said at a much earlier date.

DIRECT SPEECH		INDIRECT SPEECH	
tomorrow	→	*the next day*	Jim said, "I'll start **tomorrow**." *(June 5)* He said he would start **the next day**. *(Jim's friend reported July 5.)*
yesterday	→	*the day before*	Jim said, "I arrived **yesterday**." *(June 5)* He said he had arrived **the day before**. *(Jim's friend reported July 5.)*
now	→	*then*	"I'll call Mom **now**." She said she'd call Mom **then**.
today	→	*that day*	"**Today** has been terrible." They said **that day** had been terrible.
this week / month	→	*that week / month*	"There has been so much damage **this week**." He said there had been so much damage **that** week.
last week / year	→	*the week / year before*	"They left town **last week**." She said they had left town **the week before**.
next week / year	→	*the following week / year*	"Our electricity won't be restored until **next week**." Luisa reported that their electricity wouldn't be restored until **the following week**.

Change *here* and *this* in indirect speech to keep the speaker's **original meaning**.

DIRECT SPEECH		INDIRECT SPEECH	
here	→	*there*	"I love it **here**. **This** California climate is great." *(Jim is saying this in California.)*
this	→	*that*	Jim said he loved it *there*. He told me *that* California climate was great. *(Jim's friend in Ohio is reporting what Jim said in California.)*

REFERENCE NOTES

For a list of **reporting verbs**, see Appendix 19 on page 462.

For **punctuation rules for direct speech**, see Appendix 28 on page 466.

STEP 3   FOCUSED PRACTICE

EXERCISE 1 DISCOVER THE GRAMMAR

GRAMMAR NOTES 1–5 Read the indirect speech statements. Then choose the direct speech statement that is similar in meaning.

1. The local weather forecaster said that it was going to be a terrible storm.
   a. "It was going to be a terrible storm."
   b. "It's going to be a terrible storm."
   c. "It was a terrible storm."

2. She said the winds might exceed 45 miles (28 kilometers) per hour.
   a. "The winds exceeded 45 miles per hour."
   b. "The winds would exceed 45 miles per hour."
   c. "The winds may exceed 45 miles per hour."

3. She said there would be more rain the next day.
   a. "There will be more rain the next day."
   b. "There would be more rain tomorrow."
   c. "There will be more rain tomorrow."

4. She told people that they should try to leave the region.
   a. "You should try to leave the region."
   b. "You should have tried to leave the region."
   c. "You would leave the region."

5. She reported that people were evacuating the city.
   a. "People are evacuating the city."
   b. "People were evacuating the city."
   c. "People evacuated the city."

6. She said that they could expect the damage to be extreme.
    a. "We could expect the damage to be extreme."
    b. "We could have expected the damage to be extreme."
    c. "We can expect the damage to be extreme."

7. She said that the winds were the strongest they had had there.
    a. "The winds are the strongest we have here."
    b. "The winds are the strongest we have had here."
    c. "The winds are the strongest we have had there."

8. She told them that the emergency relief workers had arrived the day before.
    a. "Emergency relief workers arrived the day before."
    b. "Emergency relief workers arrived yesterday."
    c. "Emergency relief workers arrived today."

9. She said that if they hadn't had time to prepare, the damage would have been even greater.
    a. "If we hadn't had time to prepare, the damage would have been even greater."
    b. "If we don't have time to prepare, the damage will be even greater."
    c. "If we didn't have time to prepare, the damage would be even greater."

EXERCISE 2 INDIRECT STATEMENTS AND TENSE CHANGES

GRAMMAR NOTES 1–5 Imagine you heard these statements last week. They were about a storm that happened in another part of the country. Use *They said* to report the statements. Be careful to keep the original meaning of the direct speech.

1. "The storm changed direction last night."

    They said that the storm had changed direction the night before.

2. "It's going to pass north of here."

    _____

3. "The bridge collapsed this afternoon."

    _____

4. "It's not really a tornado. It's just a very big storm."

    _____

5. "People are leaving town."

    _____

6. "They won't be able to restore the electricity until tomorrow."

    _____

7. "Cars can't use the highway because of the flooding."

    _____

8. "People ought to use bottled water for a few days."

    _____

EXERCISE 3 INDIRECT STATEMENTS AND TENSE CHANGES

GRAMMAR NOTES 1–3 Read this interview between radio station WWEA and meteorologist Dr. Andrea Meyers. Then for each statement following the interview, write *That's right* or *That's wrong* and report what Dr. Meyers said about each item. Change the tense when possible.

WWEA: Where do tornadoes occur? Do they only occur in the United States and Canada?

MEYERS: No. Whereas it *is* true that tornadoes are most common in North America, they occur in all seven continents except Antarctica.

WWEA: Is there a time of year when tornadoes are more common?

MEYERS: Yes. They are most common in the spring.

WWEA: What was the largest tornado in history?

MEYERS: The Tri-State Tornado in the United States. And that took place in the spring of 1925.

WWEA: How strong are the winds during a tornado?

MEYERS: Tornado winds can reach a speed between 261 and 318 miles per hour. That's between about 420 and 512 kilometers an hour.

WWEA: And how quickly do they travel across land?

MEYERS: Not as fast. They travel at a speed of 70 miles per hour or less. In kilometers, that's about 112 kilometers or less. However, the Tri-State Tornado reached a traveling speed of 73 miles per hour, or 117.5 kilometers an hour.

WWEA: How long does a tornado typically last?

MEYERS: Usually just a few minutes. The Tri-State, however, lasted three and a half hours.

WWEA: Has North America suffered the most deaths as a result of tornadoes?

MEYERS: No. North America has the *most* tornadoes, but the most deaths have occurred in Bangladesh, in Southeast Asia.

WWEA: One last question. Can tornadoes be prevented?

MEYERS: No. We can't prevent them. They are inevitable. But we can predict tornadoes much better now than in the past. We've made a lot of progress, but we still must improve our ability to predict this force of nature.

1. Tornadoes only occur in North America.
   That's wrong. She said that tornadoes occurred in all seven continents except Antarctica.

2. Tornadoes are most common in the summer.

   _____

3. The largest tornado in history was the Tri-State Tornado.

   _____

4. Tornado winds can reach a speed of 318 mph (about 512 kph).

   _____

5. Tornadoes usually travel at a speed of 70 mph (about 112 kph).

   _____

6. The Tri-State Tornado lasted just a few minutes.

   _____

7. North America has the most tornadoes.

   _____

8. Most deaths from tornadoes have occurred in North America.

   _____

9. We can prevent tornadoes.

   _____

10. We still must improve our ability to predict this force of nature.

    _____

EXERCISE 4 DIRECT SPEECH

GRAMMAR NOTES 1–5 Filip and Lena live in Poland. In 2010, there were terrible floods as the result of heavy rainstorms. Read the information and advice that Filip received on the day of the storm. Then write what people said. Use direct speech. Change words to keep the speakers' original meaning.

Filip's mother called. She told him that she was listening to the weather report. She said that she was worried about Filip and Lena. She told him that if they weren't so stubborn, they'd pack up and leave right then.

1. "*I'm listening to the weather report.*"

2. "_____"

3. "_____"

Filip's father gave him some good advice. He said he'd had some experience with floods. He said Filip and Lena had to put sandbags in front of their doors. He also told Filip that they ought to fill the sinks and the bathtub with clean water. He said they should buy a lot of batteries.

4. "_____"

5. "_____"

6. "_____"

7. "_____"

Filip's brother, Adam, called. He and his wife, Zofia, are worried. Their place is very close to the river. Adam said that they couldn't stay there. He told Filip that they wanted to stay with him and Lena. He said they were leaving that night. Adam told Filip that he and Zofia should have called sooner.

8. "_____"

9. "_____"

10. "_____"

11. "_____"

Filip listened to the storm warning in the afternoon. The forecaster said the storm would hit that night. She warned that the rainfall was going to be very heavy, and she said that the storm might last for several hours.

12. "_____"

13. "_____"

14. "_____"

EXERCISE 5 EDITING

GRAMMAR NOTES 1–5 Read this student's report. There are eleven mistakes in the use of indirect speech. The first mistake is already corrected. Find and correct ten more.

What is it like to live through a flood? For my report, I interviewed the Nemec family, who experienced last month's floods in our city. They reported that ~~we~~ *they* had experienced fear and sadness. On September 14, the family went to a movie. Jerzy, a high school student, said they can't drive the car home because their street was flooded. He said it had happened in only three hours. Mrs. Nemec said that all their belongings are ruined, but that their cat has escaped to an upstairs bedroom. They were sad about losing so many valuable items, but she said she will have been much sadder to lose the family pet. Jerzy's father also said their home had been a complete mess and that the family had worked all this week to clean out the house. Anna, who is in junior high school, wanted to keep her old dollhouse. It had belonged to her mother and her mother's mother. At first, her father said her that she wouldn't be able to keep it because seeing it would just make her sad. Anna replied that she saw memories in this dollhouse—not just broken wood. She said she couldn't bear to throw it away. In the end, they kept it. Mr. Nemec said he and Anna are able to restore the dollhouse a few weeks later. Mrs. Nemec said that Anna had taught them something important today. She also said that if they had known about the flood in advance, they would had left the city.

EXERCISE 6 LISTENING

▶25|02 **A** Listen to a couple discuss the weather report about a winter storm. Then read the information. Listen again and check (✓) the correct information.

Schools

1. Today schools:	✓ closed at 10:00	☐ will close at 1:00
2. Students and teachers:	☐ should stay at school	☐ should go home immediately
3. Tomorrow schools:	☐ will open	☐ may stay closed

Roads

4. Road conditions:	☐ are safe	☐ are dangerous
5. Drivers must:	☐ drive slowly	☐ pick up passengers
6. Everyone should:	☐ avoid driving	☐ continue driving

Public Offices

7. Government offices:	☐ will close today	☐ will remain open tomorrow
8. Libraries:	☐ will stay open	☐ will close at 1:00
9. Post offices:	☐ will stay open until 5:00	☐ will be closed tomorrow

Businesses

10. Banks:	☐ will close at noon	☐ will stay open until 3:00
11. Gas stations:	☐ will close at noon	☐ will stay open until evening
12. Supermarkets:	☐ are open now	☐ are closed now

B Work with a partner. Compare your answers in A.

EXAMPLE: A: They said that schools would close at 1:00.
　　　　　B: That's not right. They said that schools had closed at 10:00, not at 1:00.
　　　　　A: Well, let's listen again and check.

EXERCISE 7 WHAT ABOUT YOU?

A CONVERSATION Work with a partner. Find out about his or her experience with a weather event.

EXAMPLE: A: Have you ever experienced an extreme weather event?
　　　　　B: Yes. I was living in Toronto, Canada, and we had several blizzards in one week.
　　　　　A: Did you have to go to a shelter?
　　　　　B: Actually, we couldn't even get out of the house that week because all the roads were blocked. They had to call in the army to clear the roads.
　　　　　A: What did you do? Did you have enough food and water at home?

B Report your conversation to the rest of the class.

EXAMPLE: Peter told me that he had experienced an extreme weather event when he was living in Canada. He said they had several blizzards in one week and that he couldn't leave the house that week. He said...

EXERCISE 8 EXTREME WEATHER

A GROUP PROJECT Work in a group. Choose an extreme weather event from the list in the box. Do an online search to find the answers to the questions below.

1. What is the definition of the extreme weather event?
2. In what parts of the world does it take place?
3. When does it take place?
4. How common is it?
5. What is a historic example of the event?
6. Can the event be predicted?
7. Can the event be prevented?

| Drought |
| Heat Wave |
| Flood |
| Wildfire |
| Blizzard |
| Winter Storm |
| Sandstorm |
| Other: _____ |

B Report your findings to the rest of the class.

EXAMPLE: A: We researched droughts. A drought is...
B: We looked at the National Weather site. It said that droughts took place mostly in...
C: It said that they happened when...

EXERCISE 9 THAT'S NOT WHAT I HEARD!

GAME Work in a group. Play "Telephone." Student A whispers a statement in the ear of Student B. Student B reports (in a whisper) to Student C what he or she heard. Each student reports to the next student in a whisper and may only say the information once. The last student tells the group what he or she heard. Expect surprises!

EXAMPLE: A: There won't be any class tomorrow.
B: He said that there wouldn't be any class tomorrow.
C: She said that there wouldn't be any gas tomorrow.
D: He said that there wouldn't be any cash tomorrow!

FROM GRAMMAR TO WRITING

(A) BEFORE YOU WRITE Work with a partner. Interview your partner about a weather event he or she or someone your partner knows experienced. Answer the questions below.

1. What type of weather event did he or she experience?
2. When and where did it happen?
3. What was it like?
4. How did he or she feel?
5. What did he or she do?
6. What advice would he or she give someone in the same situation?

(B) WRITE Use your answers to write two paragraphs reporting your partner's (or another person's) experience of a weather event. Use indirect speech. Try to avoid the common mistakes in the chart.

EXAMPLE: Julie told me about a dust storm in Australia several years ago. She said that the sky had gotten very dark and the wind had started to blow hard. Her mother told her they all had to go inside and close the windows. Then . . .

Common Mistakes in Using Indirect Speech with Tense Changes

Change the tense of the verb in indirect speech when the reporting verb is in the simple past and you are reporting something that is no longer true. Do not keep the same tense as in the direct speech.	"It**'s raining** hard." *(said two weeks ago)* He **told** me that it **was raining** hard. NOT He told me that it is raining hard.
Do not change *should, could, might, ought to* in the indirect sentence.	"We **should buy** water." *(said two weeks ago)* He said they **should buy** water. NOT He said that they should have bought water.
Use the correct time and place words in indirect speech to **keep the original meaning** of the direct speech. Do not use the same time or place words in indirect speech if they change the meaning.	"I'll leave **now**." *(said two weeks ago)* She said she would leave **then**. NOT She said she would leave now.

(C) CHECK YOUR WORK Read your paragraphs. Underline all the examples of indirect speech. Circle all the verbs and time and place words in the indirect speech. Use the Editing Checklist to check your work.

Editing Checklist

Did you use . . . ?

☐ the correct verb tenses

☐ time and place words to keep the speaker's original meaning

(D) REVISE YOUR WORK Read your paragraphs again. Can you improve your writing? Make changes if necessary. Give your paragraphs a title.

UNIT 25 REVIEW

Test yourself on the grammar or the unit.

A Circle the correct words to complete the indirect speech sentences.

Direct Speech	Indirect Speech
"It's cloudy."	She said it <u>was / were</u> cloudy. **1.**
"You should take a coat."	He told me <u>she / I</u> should <u>take / have taken</u> a coat. **2.** **3.**
"The temperature may drop."	She said the temperature <u>must / might</u> drop. **4.**
"Tomorrow will be nice."	Yesterday, you said that <u>tomorrow / today</u> <u>will / would</u> be nice. **5.** **6.**
"We can expect a lot of damage here in Florida."	She said they <u>can / could</u> expect a lot of damage <u>here / there</u> **7.** **8.** in Florida. *(reported a week later in Texas)*

B Rewrite each direct statement as an indirect statement. Keep the original meaning. (The direct statement was said to you two months ago.)

Direct Speech	Indirect Speech
1. "It's going to rain."	She said _____.
2. "It could be the worst storm this year."	He said _____.
3. "It's going to start soon."	She said _____.
4. "We should buy water."	He said _____.
5. "We must leave right now."	He told me _____.
6. "I'll call you tomorrow."	She said _____.

C Find and correct six mistakes.

What a storm! They said it is going to be bad, but it was terrible. They said it will last two days, but it lasted four. On the first day of the storm, my mother called and told me that we should have left the house right now. (I still can hear her exact words: "You should leave the house *right now!*") We should have listened to her! We just didn't believe it was going to be so serious. I told her last night that if we had known, we would had left right away. We're lucky we survived. I just listened to the weather forecast. Good news! They said tomorrow should have been sunny.

Now check your answers on page 482.

Indirect Instructions, Commands, Advice, Requests, Invitations

HEALTH ISSUES

OUTCOMES
- Report other people's instructions, commands, advice, requests, and invitations, using indirect speech
- Identify specific information in an interview transcript
- Identify medical advice reported in a conversation
- Discuss health issues and possible home remedies
- Report how someone followed instructions
- Write about a health problem one had and about the health advice one received

---

STEP 1   GRAMMAR IN CONTEXT

BEFORE YOU READ

Look at the photo. Discuss the questions.

1. What time is it? Where is the woman?

2. How does the woman feel? Why does she feel that way?

READ

26|01   Read this transcript of a radio interview with the director of a sleep clinic.

Here's to Your Health

SUNG: Good morning! This is Connie Sung, bringing you "Here's to Your Health," a program about today's health issues. This morning, we've invited Dr. William Ray, director of the Sleep Disorders[1] Clinic, to talk to us about insomnia. As you probably know, insomnia is a problem with getting to sleep or staying asleep. Welcome to the show, Doctor!

RAY: Thanks, Connie. It's great to be here.

SUNG: Your book *Night Shift*[2] will be coming out soon. In it, you tell people to pay more attention to sleep disorders. But why is losing a little sleep such a big problem?

RAY: Good question. I always tell people to think of the worst industrial disaster[3] they've ever heard about. Usually, it was caused at least in part by fatigue due to sleep

---

1 *disorders:* physical or mental problems that can affect health for a long period of time
2 *shift:* a work period, especially in a factory (the night shift is often midnight to 8:00 a.m.)
3 *industrial disaster:* an accident in a factory that causes a great deal of damage and loss of life

deprivation.[4] Then I ask them to think about what can happen if they drive when they're tired. Every year, more than 100,000 automobile accidents in this country are caused by sleepy drivers.

SUNG: A hundred thousand! That's astonishing!

RAY: And costly, too. Recently, a large study of workers' fatigue reported that the problem costs U.S. employers around $136.4 billion a year in lost work time.

SUNG: So, how can people deal with this problem? If I came to your clinic, for example, what would you advise me to do?

RAY: First, I would find out about some of your habits. If you drank coffee or cola late in the day, I would tell you to stop. The caffeine in these drinks interferes with sleep.

SUNG: What about old-fashioned remedies like warm milk?

RAY: Actually, a lot of home remedies make sense. We tell patients to have a snack before they go to bed. High-carbohydrate[5] foods like bananas are good. Warm milk helps, too. But I'd advise you not to eat a heavy meal before bed.

SUNG: My doctor told me to get more exercise, but when I run at night, I have a hard time getting to sleep.

RAY: It's true that if you exercise regularly, you'll sleep better. But we always tell patients not to exercise too close to bedtime.

SUNG: Suppose I try these remedies and they don't help?

RAY: If the problem persists, we often ask patients to come and spend a night at our sleep clinic. Our equipment monitors the patient through the night. In fact, if you're really interested, we can invite you to come to the clinic for a night.

SUNG: Maybe I should do that.

---

4 *deprivation:* not having something that you need or want
5 *high-carbohydrate:* containing a great deal of sugar or starch (for example fruit, potatoes, and rice)

AFTER YOU READ

A VOCABULARY Choose the word or phrase that best completes each sentence.

1. An **astonishing** fact is very _____.
   a. frightening   **b.** surprising   **c.** uninteresting

2. **Fatigue** is a feeling of extreme _____.
   a. excitement   **b.** pain   **c.** tiredness

3. Something that **interferes** with your sleep _____ it.
   a. helps   **b.** prevents   **c.** causes

4. Marta **monitors** the amount of carbohydrates she eats by taking _____ every day.
   a. notes   **b.** pills   **c.** sugar

5. My grandparents use traditional **remedies**. Those old _____ fascinate me.
   a. recipes   **b.** stories   **c.** treatments

6. After Ethan took pain medication, his headache **persisted**. It _____ for days.
   a. stopped   **b.** continued   **c.** improved

B COMPREHENSION Check (✓) the things Dr. Ray advises people with insomnia to do.

- ☐ **1.** Stop drinking coffee and cola late in the day.
- ☐ **2.** Eat a heavy meal before bed.
- ☐ **3.** Get more exercise.
- ☐ **4.** Exercise right before bedtime.
- ☐ **5.** Have a banana before bed.
- ☐ **6.** Spend the night at a sleep clinic.

C DISCUSSION Work with a partner. Compare your answers to the questions in B. Why did you or didn't you check each item?

STEP 2 GRAMMAR PRESENTATION

INDIRECT INSTRUCTIONS, COMMANDS, ADVICE, REQUESTS, INVITATIONS

Direct Speech

Subject	Reporting Verb	Direct Speech
He	said,	"**Drink** warm milk." "**Don't drink** coffee." "Can you **turn out** the light, please?" "Why don't you **visit** the clinic?"

Indirect Speech

Subject	Reporting Verb	Noun/ Pronoun	Indirect Speech
He	told advised asked	Connie her	**to drink** warm milk. **not to drink** coffee. **to turn out** the light.
	said		
	invited	her	**to visit** the clinic.

GRAMMAR NOTES

1 Infinitives in Indirect Speech

In **indirect speech**, use an **infinitive** (*to* + **base form of the verb**) for instructions, commands, advice, requests, and invitations.

• **instructions**	"**Come** early," said the doctor. *(direct)* The doctor said **to come** early. *(indirect)*
• **commands**	The doctor told her, "**Lie down.**" *(direct)* The doctor told her **to lie down**. *(indirect)*
• **advice**	She said, "**Drink** more water." *(direct)* She advised her **to drink** more water. *(indirect)*
• **requests**	"Could you please **arrive** by 8:00?" *(direct)* He asked her **to arrive** by 8:00. *(indirect)*
• **invitations**	"Will you **join** me for lunch?" *(direct)* He invited us **to join** him for lunch. *(indirect)*

2 Negative Infinitives

In **indirect speech**, use a **negative infinitive** (*not* + **infinitive**) for negative instructions, commands, advice, and requests.

• **negative instructions**	"**Don't eat** after 9:00 p.m.," he said. *(direct)* He said **not to eat** after 9:00 p.m. *(indirect)*
• **negative commands**	Ms. Tan told me, "**Don't wake** Lee." *(direct)* Ms. Tan told me **not to wake** Lee. *(indirect)*
• **negative advice**	"**Don't eat** so much sugar," he said. *(direct)* He advised me **not to eat** so much sugar. *(indirect)*
• **negative requests**	Jan said, "Please **don't set** the alarm." *(direct)* Jan asked me **not to set** the alarm. *(indirect)*

REFERENCE NOTES

For general information on **direct and indirect speech**, see Unit 24 on page 378.

For a list of **reporting verbs**, see Appendix 19 on page 462.

For **punctuation rules for direct speech**, see Appendix 28 on page 466.

EXERCISE 1   DISCOVER THE GRAMMAR

A   GRAMMAR NOTES 1–2   Connie Sung decided to write an article about her recent visit to Dr. Ray's clinic. Read her notes for the article. Underline the indirect instructions, commands, advice, requests, and invitations. Circle the reporting verbs that introduce them.

A Dream Job

2/18   **11:00 a.m.**   The clinic called and (asked) me to arrive at 8:30 tonight. They told me to bring my pajamas and toothbrush. They told me people also like to bring their own pillow.

8:30 p.m.   I arrived on schedule. My room was small but cozy. Only the video camera and cable told me I was in a sleep clinic. Juan Estrada, the technician for the night shift, told me to relax and watch TV for an hour. Then he left me alone in the room.

9:30 p.m.   Juan came back and got me ready for the test. He pasted twelve small metal disks to my face, legs, and stomach. I asked him to explain, and he told me that the disks, called electrodes, would be connected to a machine that records electrical activity in the brain.

11:30 p.m.   Juan came back and asked me to get into bed. After he hooked me up to the machine, he instructed me not to leave the bed that night. I fell asleep easily.

2/19   **7:00 a.m.**   Juan came to awaken me and to disconnect the wires. I told him that I didn't think insomnia was my problem–those electrodes hadn't interfered with my sleep at all! He invited me to join him in the next room, where he had spent the whole night monitoring the equipment. I looked at the pages of graphs and asked myself aloud whether Juan and Dr. Ray would be able to read my weird dream of the night before. Juan laughed and told me not to worry. "Those just show electrical impulses," he assured me.

8:00 a.m.   Dr. Ray reviewed my data with me. He told me I had healthy sleep patterns, except for some leg movements. He told me to get more exercise, and I promised I would.

B   Look at the underlined words in A. Then check (✓) the clinic's and Juan's exact words.

☑   **1.** "Arrive at 8:30 tonight."   ☐   **5.** "Don't get into bed."

☐   **2.** "Bring your pajamas and toothbrush."   ☐   **6.** "Don't leave the bed."

☐   **3.** "Relax."   ☐   **7.** "Join him in the next room."

☐   **4.** "Don't watch TV."   ☐   **8.** "Get more exercise."

EXERCISE 2 INDIRECT INSTRUCTIONS

GRAMMAR NOTES 1–2   Helen is a nurse who people call for health advice. Read each question for Helen and report her instructions (affirmative and negative), using the verbs in parentheses.

MIKE: Do you have a remedy for insomnia? I suffer from constant fatigue.

HELEN: Try exercising regularly, early in the day. And don't drink anything with caffeine after 2:00 p.m.

1. (say) _She said to try exercising regularly, early in the day._

2. (tell) _She told him not to drink anything with caffeine after 2:00 p.m._

ANNE: What can I do to soothe a sore throat? I never take medicine unless I have to.

HELEN: One remedy is to drink hot herbal tea with honey. But don't drink black tea. It will make your throat dry.

3. (say) _____

4. (tell) _____

LOU: I get leg cramps at night. They wake me up, and I can't get back to sleep.

HELEN: The next time you feel a cramp, do this: Pinch the place between your upper lip and your nose. The cramp should stop right away. Sounds simple, but it's astonishing how well this works.

5. (say) _____

PETE: Do you know of an inexpensive way to remove stains on teeth?

HELEN: Make a toothpaste of one tablespoon of baking soda and a little water. Brush as usual.

6. (tell) _____

7. (say) _____

MARLA: What can I do to ease an itchy poison ivy rash?

HELEN: Spread cool, cooked oatmeal over the rash. Also, try soaking the rash in a cool bath with a quarter cup of baking soda. Don't scratch the rash. That will make it worse.

8. (tell) _____

9. (say) _____

10. (tell) _____

LISA: Help! Bugs love me. They bite me all the time. Is there anything I can do to stop them?

HELEN: There are a few things you can do to keep bugs away. Eat onions or garlic every day. Your skin will have a slight odor that bugs hate. Or ask your doctor about a vitamin B supplement.

11. (say) _____

12. (tell) _____

EXERCISE 3 DIRECT AND INDIRECT SPEECH

A GRAMMAR NOTES 1–2 Connie had a dream at the sleep clinic. She wrote about it in her journal. Read her account of the dream and underline the indirect instructions, commands, advice, requests, and invitations.

I dreamed that an extraterrestrial came into my room. He told me <u>to get up</u>. Then he said to follow him. There was a spaceship outside the clinic. It was an astonishing sight! The creature from outer space invited me to come aboard. I asked him to lead the way! Juan, the lab technician, was on the ship. Suddenly, Juan told me to pilot the ship. He ordered me not to leave the controls. Then he went to sleep. Next, Dr. Ray was at my side giving me instructions. He told me to slow down. Then he said to point the ship toward the Earth. There was a loud knocking noise as we hit the ground, and I told everyone not to panic. Then I heard Juan tell me to wake up. I opened my eyes and saw him walking into my room at the sleep clinic.

B Complete the comic strip by writing what each character said.

1. Get up.
2.
3.
4.
5.
6.
7.
8.
9.
10.

EXERCISE 4 EDITING

GRAMMAR NOTES 1–2 Read this entry in a student's journal. There are eight mistakes in the use of indirect instructions and advice. The first mistake is already corrected. Find and correct seven more. Don't forget to check punctuation. Mistakes with quotation marks count as one mistake for the sentence.

○ ○ ○

MY POSTS

I am SO tired! I hardly got any sleep at all last night. That makes three sleepless nights in a row, so I decided to call one of those health lines that gives you advice. The nurse I spoke
to
to told me ⌃ exercise every day. But, and this is important, she also said no to exercise late in the day. That can interfere with sleep. I'll try that. She asked me about what I eat and drink. When she heard about all the coffee I drink, she told me to not drink any in the evening. No coffee! I need coffee to stay awake! She said having milk at night instead because there is a chemical in milk that can make you sleepy. She had some other good tips for me, too. She told to keep the bedroom cool. People sleep better when the room isn't warm. Oh, and she said that not to look at a computer, e-book, or cell phone screen for an hour before bedtime. The "blue" light from these screens also interferes with sleep. I didn't know that! And I told her what my mother used to say. Mom always told me "to getting up and scrub the floor when I couldn't sleep." The nurse agreed that sometimes works. She advised one of her patients balance his checkbook. He went right to sleep just to escape from the task! By the way, look at this funny cartoon about insomnia!

"I couldn't sleep."

Anyhow, the nurse was very helpful and all her ideas sound good. In fact, I want to try them out right away. The only problem is, I'm so excited about them, I'm not sure I'll be able to fall asleep tonight!

EXERCISE 5 LISTENING

▶26|02 (A) Marta is telling a friend about her experience at a headache clinic. Listen to their conversation. Read the list. Then listen again and check (✓) the correct column to show what the doctors at the clinic told Marta to do, what they told her not to do, and what they didn't mention.

	Do	Don't Do	Not Mentioned
1. Monitor the headaches.	✓	☐	☐
2. Get regular exercise.	☐	☐	☐
3. Get eight hours of sleep.	☐	☐	☐
4. Take painkillers.	☐	☐	☐
5. Use an ice pack.	☐	☐	☐
6. Massage around the eyes.	☐	☐	☐
7. Eat three big meals a day.	☐	☐	☐
8. Eat chocolate.	☐	☐	☐
9. Avoid cheese.	☐	☐	☐

▶26|02 (B) Work with a partner. Listen again. Discuss your answers in A. Why did you choose each answer?

EXAMPLE: A: For number 1, the answer is "Do." They told her to monitor her headaches.
B: That's right. They told her to write down when she got a headache.
A: They also told her to write down what she was doing before she got the headache. What about number 2?

EXERCISE 6 HOME REMEDIES

PROBLEM SOLVING Work with a partner. What advice have you heard for the following problems? Discuss what to do and what not to do for them.

EXAMPLE: A: My mother always told me to hold a burn under cold water.
B: They say not to put butter on a burn.

- minor burns
- insomnia
- insect bites
- headaches
- snoring
- hiccups

- a cold
- blisters
- poison ivy
- a sore throat
- a toothache
- Other: _____

EXERCISE 7 HOME ALONE

PICTURE DISCUSSION Jeff's parents went out for the evening and left a list of instructions for him. Work in pairs. Read the list and look at the picture. Talk about which instructions Jeff followed and which ones he didn't follow. Use indirect instructions.

EXAMPLE: A: His parents told him not to stay up after 10:00, but it's 11:30 now and he's not in bed—he's asleep on the couch and having a nightmare.
B: They also said to . . .

Dear Jeff,
We'll be home late. Here are a few things to remember:

- Don't stay up after 10:00. You need to get more sleep.

- Don't drink any cola — all that sugar keeps you awake. Drink some milk instead.

- Have some cake, but please save some for us!

- Please take the garbage out. Also, wash the dishes and put them away.

- And please don't let the cat in — You know that you're allergic to cats!

- Keep the back door closed.

- Do your homework.

- Don't watch any horror movies. (They give you nightmares — remember?)

- Don't invite your friends over tonight.

Love,
Mom and Dad

FROM GRAMMAR TO WRITING

A BEFORE YOU WRITE Think about a health problem you (or someone you know) had. Answer the questions.

What was the problem? _____

Who did you (or the person) ask for advice? _____

What advice did you (or the person) receive? Use direct speech with quotation marks.

Things to do	Things not to do
_____	_____
_____	_____
_____	_____

Did the advice work? _____

B WRITE Use your answers in A to write one or two paragraphs about the advice you or someone you know received. Use indirect speech to report the advice. Try to avoid the common mistakes in the chart below.

EXAMPLE: Four years ago, I got a bad rash from poison ivy. It really itched, and I felt miserable. My friend had had a lot of experience with this annoying health problem, so I asked him for advice. He told me to put some cucumber slices on the rash. But, most importantly, he told me not to scratch. That advice was easier said than done! My friend also advised me to . . .

Common Mistakes in Using Indirect Instructions and Advice

Use an **infinitive** to report indirect instructions and advice. Do not leave out *to*.	He told me **to drink** a lot of water. **NOT** He told me ~~drink~~ a lot of water.
Use *not* + **infinitive** to report indirect negative instructions and advice. Do not use *don't*.	He told me ***not to scratch*** the rash. **NOT** He told me ~~don't scratch~~ the rash.

C CHECK YOUR WORK Read your paragraph(s). Underline all the examples of indirect instructions and advice. Circle *not*. Use the Editing Checklist to check your work.

Editing Checklist

Did you use . . . ?

☐ infinitives to report indirect instructions and advice

☐ negative infinitives to report indirect negative instructions and advice

D REVISE YOUR WORK Read your paragraph(s) again. Can you improve your writing? Make changes if necessary. Give your paragraph(s) a title.

UNIT 26 REVIEW

Test yourself on the grammar of the unit.

A Circle the correct punctuation mark or words to complete the sentences.

1. I arrived at 8:00 because the doctor asked me to come early <u>. / ?</u>

2. The assistant asked me to <u>give / gave</u> her my health insurance card.

3. The doctor said, <u>"To lie down." / "Please lie down."</u>

4. She advised me <u>don't / not to</u> drink so much coffee.

5. Some experts <u>say / tell</u> to eat a snack before bedtime.

6. At the sleep clinic, the technician <u>told / said</u> me to relax and watch TV.

7. The doctor <u>invited / advised</u> me not to have a late dinner.

B Rewrite the direct speech as an indirect instruction, command, request, invitation, or as advice. Use an appropriate reporting verb (*tell*, *ask*, *invite*, or *advise*). Use pronouns.

1. Officer David Zhu to Anita: "Please show me your license."

   _____

2. Doctor Sue Rodriguez to Sam: "You ought to get more exercise."

   _____

3. Ms. Carson to her students: "Please come to the English Department party."

   _____

4. Robert to Nina: "Could you turn on the light, please?"

   _____

5. Lisa to Nina and Paulo: "Why don't you hang out at my house?"

   _____

C Find and correct eight mistakes. Remember to check punctuation.

    Too much stress is bad for your health. So, I asked my doctor give me some tips on how to reduce everyday stress. First of all, she told me exercising every day. She also told me to don't work too long without taking a break. She advised me doing things to relax. For example, she said that to listen to music. She also said me to sit with my eyes closed and to concentrate on my breathing. That helps lower blood pressure. She also advised me no drink too many beverages with caffeine. Finally, she said to "get enough sleep"—at least seven hours a night!

Now check your answers on page 482.

Indirect Questions
JOB INTERVIEWS

OUTCOMES
• Report other people's questions, using indirect speech
• Identify specific information in a business article
• Identify and discuss details in a conversation
• Role-play and discuss a job interview
• Complete a questionnaire about work values, discuss the answers, and report conversations
• Write a report on a job interview

STEP 1   GRAMMAR IN CONTEXT

BEFORE YOU READ

Look at the photo and at the title of the article. Discuss the questions.

1. What are the people doing?

2. Are the man's questions typical in this situation? What is the woman's reaction?

3. What do you think a *stress interview* is?

READ

27|01   Read this article about job interviews.

The Stress Interview

A few weeks ago, Melissa Morrow had an unusual job interview. First, the interviewer asked why she couldn't work under pressure. Before she could answer, he asked if she had cleaned out her car recently. Right after that, he wanted to know who had written her application letter for her. Melissa was shocked, but she handled herself well. She asked the interviewer whether he was going to ask her any serious questions. Then she politely ended the interview.

Melissa had had a *stress interview*, a type of job interview that asks tough, tricky questions, with long silences and negative evaluations of the job candidate. To the

Why can't you work under pressure?
Have you cleaned out your car recently?
Who wrote your application letter for you?

Do I really want this job?

unhappy candidate, this may seem unnecessarily nasty on the interviewer's part. However, some positions require an ability to handle just this kind of pressure. If there is an accident in an oil well near the coast, for example, the oil company's public relations officer[1] must remain calm when hostile[2] reporters ask how the accident could have occurred.

The uncomfortable atmosphere[3] of a stress interview gives the potential employer a chance to watch a candidate react to pressure. In one case, the interviewer ended each interview by saying, "We're really not sure that you're the right person for this job." One excellent candidate asked the interviewer angrily if he was sure he knew how to conduct an interview. She clearly could not handle the pressure she would encounter as a TV news reporter—the job she was interviewing for.

Stress interviews may be appropriate for some jobs, but they can also work against a company. Some excellent candidates may refuse the job after a hostile interview. Melissa Morrow handled her interview extremely well, but she later asked herself if she really wanted to work for that company. Her answer was *no*.

A word of warning to job candidates: Not all tough questioning is legitimate.[4] In some countries, certain questions are illegal unless the answers are directly related to the job. If an interviewer asks how old you are, whether you are married, or how much money you owe, you can refuse to answer. If you think a question isn't appropriate, then ask the interviewer how the answer specifically relates to that job. If you don't get a satisfactory explanation, you don't have to answer the question. And remember: Whatever happens, don't lose your cool.[5] The interview will be over before you know it!

---

1 *public relations officer:* someone hired by a company to explain to the public what the company does so that the public will understand it and approve of it
2 *hostile:* angry and unfriendly
3 *atmosphere:* the feeling that you get from a situation or a place
4 *legitimate:* proper and allowable
5 *lose your cool:* get excited and angry

AFTER YOU READ

A VOCABULARY Choose the word or phrase that best completes each sentence.

1. A job **evaluation** gives a worker _____.
   a. more money **b.** more vacation time **c.** comments on his or her work

2. A bad way to **handle** an interview is to _____.
   a. say the right things **b.** get angry **c.** ask good questions

3. A **candidate** for a job promotion _____ get a better position.
   a. may **b.** will **c.** can't

4. A job with a lot of **pressure** _____.
   a. pays well **b.** is easy **c.** is difficult

5. Sara's behavior was **appropriate**. She did the _____ thing.
   a. right **b.** wrong **c.** easiest

6. A **potential** problem is one that _____.
   a. is very serious **b.** may happen **c.** has an easy solution

COMPREHENSION **Read the statements. Check (✓) *True* or *False*.**

	True	False
1. Melissa told the interviewer she couldn't work under pressure.	☐	☐
2. Melissa asked, "Are you going to ask me any serious questions?"	☐	☐
3. One candidate asked if the interviewer knew how to interview.	☐	☐
4. Melissa asked herself how long she wanted to work for the company.	☐	☐
5. You should always answer the interview question, "Are you married?"	☐	☐
6. It's OK to ask an interviewer, "How does the answer relate to this job?"	☐	☐

C DISCUSSION **Work with a partner. Compare your answers in B. Why did you check *True* or *False*?**

STEP 2   GRAMMAR PRESENTATION

INDIRECT QUESTIONS

Direct Speech: *Yes/No* Questions

Subject	Reporting Verb	Direct Question
He	asked,	"**Do you have** any experience?" "**Can you create** spreadsheets?" "**Will you stay** for a year?"

Indirect Speech: *Yes/No* Questions

Subject	Reporting Verb	(Noun/ Pronoun)	Indirect Question	
He	asked	(Melissa) (her)	*if* *whether (or not)*	**she had** any experience. **she could create** spreadsheets. **she would stay** for a year.

Direct Speech: *Wh-* Questions About the Subject

Subject	Reporting Verb	Direct Question
He	asked,	"*Who* **told** you about the job?" "*What* **happened** on your last job?" "*Which company* **hired** you?"

Indirect Speech: *Wh-* Questions About the Subject

Subject	Reporting Verb	(Noun/ Pronoun)	Indirect Question	
He	asked	(Bob) (him)	*who*	**had told** him about the job.
			what	**had happened** on his last job.
			which company	**had hired** him.

Direct Speech: *Wh-* Questions About the Object

Subject	Reporting Verb	Direct Question
He	asked,	"*Who* **do you work** for?" "*What* **do you do** there?" "*Which job* **did you accept**?"

Indirect Speech: *Wh-* Questions About the Object

Subject	Reporting Verb	(Noun/ Pronoun)	Indirect Question	
He	asked	(Melissa) (her)	*who*	**she worked** for.
			what	**she did** there.
			which job	**she had accepted**.

Direct Speech: *Wh-* Questions with *When, Where, Why,* and *How*

Subject	Reporting Verb	Direct Question
He	asked,	"*When* **did you start** your new job?" "*Where* **do you work** now?" "*Why* **have you changed** jobs?" "*How much* **did you earn** there?"

Indirect Speech: *Wh-* Questions with *When, Where, Why,* and *How*

Subject	Reporting Verb	(Noun/ Pronoun)	Indirect Question	
He	asked	(Melissa) (her)	*when*	**she had started** her new job.
			where	**she worked** now.
			why	**she had changed** jobs.
			how much	**she had earned** there.

GRAMMAR NOTES

1 Indirect Questions

We often use indirect speech to **report questions**.

The most common **reporting verb** for both direct and indirect questions is **ask**.	"Did you find a new job?" she **asked**. *(direct)* She **asked if I had found a new job**. *(indirect)*

As in indirect statements, when the reporting verb is in the **simple past**, the **verb tense in the indirect question often changes**. For example:

• simple present becomes simple past	"**Do** you **like** your new job?" he asked. *(direct)* He **asked** me if I **liked** my new job. *(indirect)*
• simple past becomes past perfect	"**Did** you **find** it online?" he wanted to know. *(direct)* He **asked** if I **had found** it online. *(indirect)*
• present perfect becomes past perfect	"How long **have** you **been** there?" he asked. *(direct)* He **asked** me how long I **had been** there. *(indirect)*

BE CAREFUL! When the reporting verb is in the **simple present**, the verb tense in the indirect question **does not change**.	He asked me, "Where **do** you **work**?" *(direct)* He always **asks** me where I **work**. *(indirect)* **NOT** He always asks me where I ~~worked~~.
Remember to make **pronoun changes** and other changes to keep the speaker's original meaning.	He asked, "Why do **you** want to work **here**?" *(direct)* He asked me why **I** wanted to work **there**. *(indirect)*
IN WRITING Do not end an indirect question with a question mark. End it with a period.	She asked me where I had worked before**.** **NOT** She asked me where I had worked before~~?~~

2 Indirect *Yes/No* Questions

Use **if** or **whether** in indirect *yes/no* questions.

	She asked, "Can you type?" *(direct)*
• *if*	She asked me **if I could type**. *(indirect)*
• *whether*	She asked me **whether I could type**. *(indirect)*

USAGE NOTE *Whether* is more formal than *if*.	My boss wants to know **whether** the report **is ready**.
We can also use **whether or not** to report *yes/no* questions.	He wants to know **whether or not** the report **is ready**.

3 Indirect *Wh-* Questions

Use **question words** in indirect *wh-* questions.

You can use any question word in an indirect question. For example:

• *where*	"**Where** is your office?" *(direct)* I asked **where his office was**. *(indirect)*
• *how much*	"**How much** is the salary?" *(direct)* I asked **how much the salary was**. *(indirect)*

Use **statement word order (subject + verb)**, not question word order, for all **indirect questions**. Do not use the auxiliaries *do, does,* or *did.*

The word order in the indirect question is the same word order as in a **statement**.

SUBJECT + VERB
Samantha is sure.

- **indirect** *yes/no* **questions**

  "**Is Samantha** sure?" *(direct)*
  He asked me **if Samantha is** sure. *(indirect)*
  "**Did he hire** Li?" *(direct)*
  I asked **if he had hired** Li. *(indirect)*

- **indirect** *wh-* **questions** about the **subject**

  "**Who is** late?" *(direct)*
  She asked **who was** late. *(indirect)*
  "**Who hired** Li?" *(direct)*
  I asked **who had hired** Li. *(indirect)*

- **indirect** *wh-* **questions** about the **object**

  "Who **did he hire**?" *(direct)*
  I asked who **he had hired**. *(indirect)*

- **indirect** *wh-* **questions** with *when, where, why* and *how* or *how much/many*

  "Why **did they hire** Li?" *(direct)*
  I asked why **they had hired** Li. *(indirect)*

BE CAREFUL! Do not use question word order or the auxiliaries *do, does, did* in indirect questions.

"Where **do you live**?" *(direct)*
She asked me where **I lived**. *(indirect)*
NOT She asked me ~~where do you live~~.

BE CAREFUL! If a direct question about the subject has the form **question word + *be* + noun**, then the indirect question has the form **question word + noun + *be***.

"**Who *is* the boss**?" *(direct)*
I asked them **who the boss *was***. *(indirect)*
NOT I asked them ~~who was the boss~~.

REFERENCE NOTES

For more information about **indirect speech**, see Unit 24 on page 378 and Unit 25 on page 395.

For a list of **reporting verbs in questions**, see Appendix 19 on page 462.

For **punctuation rules for direct speech**, see Appendix 28 on page 466.

EXERCISE 1   DISCOVER THE GRAMMAR

Ⓐ GRAMMAR NOTES 1–4   Bruno Lopez is telling a friend about his job interview. Underline the indirect questions in the conversation.

ANDREA: So, how did the interview go?

BRUNO: It went well! The interviewer, Mr. Chen, asked me a lot of good questions.

ANDREA: Great. Tell me about it.

BRUNO: Well, first, he asked me how much experience I'd had, and I told him I'd been a sales manager for ten years. Let's see.... He also asked what I would change about my current job. I thought that was a good question.

ANDREA: It was. What did you say?

BRUNO: Well, I didn't want to say anything negative, so I told him that I was ready to take on a lot more responsibility.

ANDREA: Good answer! What else did he ask?

BRUNO: Oh, you know, the usual things. He asked what my greatest success had been, and how much I was making at my current job. He also asked me how I handled on-the-job stress.

ANDREA: Did you tell him you have no problems handling stress?

BRUNO: Of course! Then he asked me what my goals were. Oh, and he asked me if *I* had any questions for *him*.

ANDREA: Did you?

BRUNO: Yes. I had researched the company online and had several questions. Mr. Chen seemed pleased with them.

ANDREA: So, do you think you'll get a job offer?

BRUNO: I already did! At the end of the interview, he asked me when I could start!

Ⓑ Check (✓) the direct questions that the interviewer asked Bruno in A.

☑ **1.** "How much experience have you had?"

☐ **2.** "What would I change about my current job?"

☐ **3.** "What was your greatest success?"

☐ **4.** "How much are you making at your current job?"

☐ **5.** "How have you handled on-the-job stress?"

☐ **6.** "What were your goals?"

☐ **7.** "Do you have any questions for me?"

☐ **8.** "When can you start?"

EXERCISE 2 WORD ORDER

GRAMMAR NOTES 1–4 **Jason has an interview next week. His neighbor, Claire, wants to know all about it. Report Claire's questions. Put the words in parentheses in the correct order.**

1. **CLAIRE:** I heard you're going on an interview next week. What kind of job is it?
   JASON: It's for an accounts-assistant job.

   She asked what kind of job it was.
   (asked / kind of job / what / was / it / she)

2. **CLAIRE:** Oh, really? When is the interview?
   JASON: It's on Tuesday at 9:00.

   _____
   (the interview / she / was / when / asked)

3. **CLAIRE:** Where's the company?
   JASON: It's downtown on the west side.

   _____
   (was / where / she / the company / asked)

4. **CLAIRE:** Do you need directions?
   JASON: No, I know the way.

   _____
   (asked / needed / she / if / he / directions)

5. **CLAIRE:** How long does it take to get there?
   JASON: About half an hour.

   _____
   (asked / to get there / it / she / takes / how long)

6. **CLAIRE:** Are you going to drive?
   JASON: I think so. It's probably the fastest way.

   _____
   (was going to / asked / if / he / drive / she)

7. **CLAIRE:** Who's going to interview you?
   JASON: Um. I'm not sure. Probably the manager of the department.

   _____
   (she / was going to / him / who / interview / asked)

8. **CLAIRE:** Well, good luck. When will they let you know?
   JASON: It will take a while. They have a lot of candidates.

   _____
   (him / they / would / asked / she / when / let / know)

EXERCISE 3 INDIRECT QUESTIONS WITH NO TENSE CHANGES

GRAMMAR NOTES 1–4 Read the information in the box. Write sentences about questions employers cannot ask during an interview in many countries. Use indirect questions, and do not change the tense in the indirect questions.

You Can't Ask That!

In some countries, employers must hire only on the basis of skills and experience. In Canada, most countries in Europe, and in the United States, for example, an interviewer cannot ask an applicant certain questions unless the information is related to the job. Here are some questions an interviewer may *not* ask:

- How old are you?
- Have you ever been arrested?
- What is your religion?
- How many children do you have?
- Are you married?
- How tall are you?
- What does your husband (or wife) do?
- Where were you born?

1. *They can't ask how old you are.*

2. _____

3. _____

4. _____

5. _____

6. _____

7. _____

8. _____

EXERCISE 4
INDIRECT QUESTIONS WITH VERB AND PRONOUN CHANGES

GRAMMAR NOTES 1–4 Read the questions that were asked during Jason's interview. Jason asked some of the questions, and the manager, Ms. Suarez, asked others. Decide who asked each question. Then rewrite each question as indirect speech. Make verb and pronoun changes if necessary.

1. "What type of training is available for the job?"

   Jason asked Ms. Suarez what type of training was available for the job.

2. "What kind of experience do you have?"

   Ms. Suarez...

3. "Is there opportunity for promotion?"

   _____

4. "Why did you apply for this position?"

   _____

5. "Are you interviewing with other companies?"

   _____

6. "Did you get along well with your last employer?"

   _____

7. "How is job performance rewarded?"

   _____

8. "What was your salary at your last job?"

   _____

9. "What will my responsibilities be?"

   _____

10. "When does the job start?"

    _____

EXERCISE 5 EDITING

GRAMMAR NOTES 1–4 Read this memo an interviewer wrote after an interview. There are seven mistakes in the use of indirect questions. The first mistake is already corrected. Find and correct six more. Don't forget to check punctuation. Mistakes with quotation marks count as one mistake for the sentence.

May 15, 2017

TO: Francesca Giuffrida
FROM: Ken Marley
SUBJECT: Interview with Alex Kaminski

This morning I interviewed Alex Kaminski for the administrative assistant position.

Since this job requires a lot of contact with the public, I thought it was appropriate to

do some stress questioning. I asked Mr. Lopez why ~~couldn't he~~ *he couldn't* work under pressure.

I also told him, "Why does your supervisor dislike you?" Finally, I inquired when he

would quit the job with our company?

Mr. Kaminski remained calm throughout the interview. He answered all my questions,

and he had some excellent questions of his own. He asked "if we expected changes

in the job." He also asked how often do we perform employee evaluations. I was

quite impressed when he asked why did I decide to join this company.

Mr. Kaminski is an excellent candidate for the job, and I believe he will handle the

responsibilities well. At the end of the interview, Mr. Kaminski inquired when we

could let him know our decision. I asked him if or not he was considering another job,

and he said he was. I think we should act quickly in order not to lose this excellent

potential employee.

EXERCISE 6   LISTENING

⏵27|02 **A** You are going to hear a conversation about a job interview that took place in Canada. Read the checklist. Then listen to the conversation. Listen again and check (✓) the topics that the interviewer asked about.

POSSIBLE JOB INTERVIEW TOPICS	
OK to Ask	**Not OK to Ask**
☐ Name	☑ Age
☐ Address	☐ Race
☐ Work experience	☐ Sex
☑ Reason for leaving job	☐ Religion
☐ Reason for seeking position	☐ National origin
☐ Salary	☐ Height or weight
☐ Education	☐ Marital status
☐ Professional affiliations	☐ Information about spouse
☐ Convictions[1] for crimes	☐ Arrest record
☐ Skills	☐ Physical disabilities
☐ Job performance	☐ Children
☐ Permission to work in Canada	☐ Citizenship
	☐ English language skill
	☐ Financial situation

1 *convictions:* a court's decisions that a person is guilty of a crime

⏵27|02 **B** Work with a partner. Listen again and discuss the seven illegal questions the interviewer asks.

EXAMPLE: **A:** He asked her how old she was.

   B: That's right. In Canada, you can't ask about age. It's illegal.

How old are you?

Indirect Questions   **431**

EXERCISE 7 A JOB INTERVIEW

A ROLE PLAY You are going to role-play a job interview. Before you role-play, work with a partner. Student A is the interviewer. Student B is the job candidate. Read the résumé and the job-listings advertisement. Write at least three questions to ask each other.

EXAMPLE: Questions to ask the candidate: *Why did you leave your job at Union Hospital?*

Questions to ask the interviewer: *How many doctors work here?*

Pat Rogers

215 West Hill Drive
Baltimore, MD 21233
Telephone: (410) 555-7777
progers@email.com

EDUCATION

Taylor Community College
Associate's degree (Business) 2015

Middlesex High School
High school diploma, 2013

JOB LISTINGS

MEDICAL RECEPTIONIST

For busy doctor's office. Mature individual needed to answer phones, greet patients, make appointments. Some filing and billing. Similar experience preferred. Computer skills necessary.

EXPERIENCE

2015–Present Medical receptionist
Patients Plus, Baltimore, MD
Responsibilities: Greet patients, make appointments, answer telephones, update computer records

2013–2015 Admitting clerk, hospital admissions office
Union Hospital, Baltimore, MD
Responsibilities: Interviewed patients for admission, input information in computer, answered telephones

B Work in a group. With your partner in A, use your questions to role-play your interview for the group.

EXAMPLE: A: Why did you leave your job at Union Hospital?

B: I liked my job, but I wanted more responsibility.

Ⓒ Discuss each role-play interview with your group. Use the questions below to guide your discussion. Support your ideas by reporting questions that were asked during the interview.

1. Was it a stress interview? Why or why not?

   EXAMPLE: A: I think it was a stress interview because the interviewer asked him why he couldn't find a new job.
   B: Yes. And he also asked him why he didn't have good computer skills. . . .

2. Did the interviewer ask any illegal questions? Which ones were illegal?

3. Which of the candidate's questions were the most useful in evaluating the job? Why do you think so?

4. Which of the interviewer's questions gave the clearest picture of the candidate? Why do you think so?

5. If you were the interviewer, would you hire this candidate? Why or why not?

6. If you were the candidate, would you want to work for this company? Why or why not?

EXERCISE 8 WHAT ABOUT YOU?

CONVERSATION Work in a group. Talk about a personal experience with a school or job interview. (If you do not have a personal experience, use the experience of someone you know.) Answer the questions below.

1. What did the interviewer ask?

   EXAMPLE: A: The interviewer asked me if I was married.
   B: That isn't legal, is it?
   A: I don't think so.
   C: What did you say?
   A: I asked him . . .

2. What was the most difficult question to answer? Why?

3. Were there any questions that you didn't think were appropriate? What did you say?

4. What did you ask the interviewer?

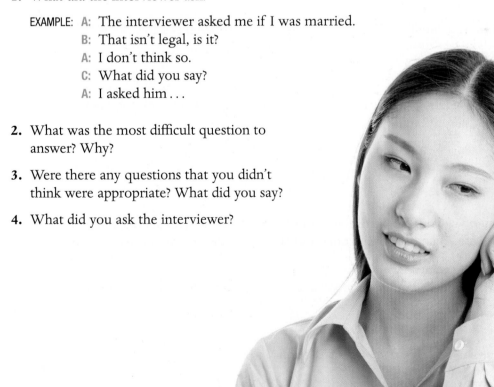

EXERCISE 9 WORK VALUES

A DISCUSSION You are going to have a discussion about values. Your values are the things that are most important to you. Before your discussion, complete this work values questionnaire on your own. (If none of the answers match your values, add your own.)

Work Values Questionnaire

1. Why do you want to work?
- ○ To make a lot of money.
- ○ To help people.
- ○ To become well known.
- ○ Other: _____

2. Where do you prefer to work?
- ○ I'd like to travel.
- ○ In an office.
- ○ At home.
- ○ Other: _____

3. When do you want to work?
- ○ 9–5 every day.
- ○ On a changing schedule.
- ○ On my own schedule.
- ○ Other: _____

4. What kind of routine do you like?
- ○ The same type of task all day.
- ○ A variety of tasks every day.
- ○ Tasks that change often.
- ○ Other: _____

5. How much job pressure can you handle?
- ○ I like a high-pressure job.
- ○ I can handle some, but not a lot.
- ○ Just enough to keep me awake.
- ○ Other: _____

6. Who would you like to work with?
- ○ I work best with a team.
- ○ I like to work by myself.
- ○ I enjoy working with the public.
- ○ Other: _____

B Work with a partner. Ask your partner three of the questions in the questionnaire in A and discuss your answers. Then answer the other questions and discuss your answers.

EXAMPLE: A: So, why do you want to work?
B: I like working. I find it interesting. What about you? Why do you want to work?
A: Well, I need to make money to . . .

C Work with another pair and report your conversations in B.

EXAMPLE: A: I asked Sami why he wanted to work. He told me . . .
B: I asked Lisa why she wanted to work. She said that . . .

A BEFORE YOU WRITE Before you look for work, it's a good idea to talk to people who are already working in jobs that might interest you. In these kinds of "informational interviews," you can ask what the tasks in that job are, why people like or dislike the work, or how much you can expect to be paid. Write a list of questions to ask in an informational job interview. Then interview a classmate and write his or her answers.

Questions	Answers
_____	_____
_____	_____
_____	_____

B WRITE Use your questions and answers in A to write a report on an informational interview. Use indirect questions and answers. Try to avoid the common mistakes in the chart.

EXAMPLE: I interviewed Pete Ortiz, who is an assistant in the computer lab. I wanted to talk to him because I'm interested in applying for a job there. I asked Pete if he liked working there, and he told me he liked it most of the time. I also asked him how long . . .

Common Mistakes in Using Indirect Questions

Use *if* or **whether** in an indirect *yes/no* question. Do not use the auxiliaries *do*, *does*, or *did*.	She asked me *if* I like my present job. **NOT** She asked me ~~do~~ I like my present job.
Use **statement word** order in indirect questions. Do not use question word order. Do not use the auxiliaries *do*, *does*, or *did*.	She asked me **how fast** I typed. **NOT** She asked me how fast ~~do I type~~.
Use a **period** at the end of an indirect question. Do not use a question mark.	He asked me where I lived**.** **NOT** He asked me where I lived~~?~~

C CHECK YOUR WORK Read your report. Underline the indirect *yes/no* questions once. Underline the indirect *wh-* questions twice. Use the Editing Checklist to check your work.

Editing Checklist

Did you use . . . ?

- [ ] *if* or *whether* in indirect *yes/no* questions
- [ ] question words in indirect *wh-* questions
- [ ] statement word order for all indirect questions
- [ ] a period at the end of indirect questions

D REVISE YOUR WORK Read your report again. Can you improve your writing? Make changes if necessary. Give your report a title.

UNIT 27 REVIEW

Test yourself on the grammar or the unit.

A Circle the correct punctuation mark or words to complete the sentences.

1. She asked what my name was <u>. / ?</u>

2. He asked me <u>if / do</u> I had work experience.

3. I asked them where <u>was their office / their office was</u>.

4. They asked where <u>I lived / did I live</u>.

5. They asked me why <u>had I / I had</u> left my last job.

B Rewrite the direct questions in parentheses as indirect questions. (The direct questions were asked last year.)

1. They asked _____
   (Who did the company hire?)

2. He asked me _____
   (Did you take the job?)

3. She asked _____
   (Do you like your job?)

4. He asked me _____
   (How long have you worked there?)

5. I asked _____
   (How many employees work here?)

6. They asked _____
   (Why do you want to work for us?)

7. I asked _____
   (What's the starting salary?)

8. They asked _____
   (Can you start soon?)

C Find and correct seven mistakes. Remember to check punctuation.

They asked me so many questions! They asked me where did I work. They asked who was my boss. They asked why I did want to change jobs. They asked how much money I made. They ask me who I have voted for in the last election. They even asked me what my favorite color was? Finally, I asked myself whether or no I really wanted that job!

Now check your answers on page 482.

Embedded Questions
TIPPING AROUND THE WORLD

OUTCOMES
• Ask for information or express something you don't know, using embedded questions
• Extract key information from an interview transcript
• Identify and discuss details in a call-in radio show
• Discuss tipping around the world, giving opinions
• Discuss problems one had during a first-time experience
• Role-play a conversation between a hotel clerk and a guest asking for information
• Write about a confusing or surprising situation

STEP 1   GRAMMAR IN CONTEXT

BEFORE YOU READ

Look at the cartoon. Discuss the questions.

1. What is unusual about the vending machine?

2. What is the man worried about?

READ

28|01   Read this interview about tipping from *World Travel (WT)* magazine.

The Tip:
Who? When? and How much?

In China, it used to be illegal. In New Zealand, it's uncommon. In Germany, it's included in the restaurant bill. In the United States and Canada, it's common, but it isn't logical: You tip the person who delivers flowers, but not the person who delivers a package.

Do *you* often wonder what to do about tipping? *We* do, so to help us through the tipping maze[1] we interviewed author Irene Frankel. Her book, *Tips on Tipping: The Ultimate Guide to Who, When, and How Much to Tip*, answers all your questions about this complicated practice.

WT: Tell me why you decided to write a book about tipping.

IF: I began writing it for people from

"I wonder how much we should give."

---
1 *maze:* something that is complicated and hard to understand

cultures where tipping isn't a custom. But when I started researching, I found that Americans were also unsure how to tip, so *Tips* became a book to clarify tipping practices for people traveling to the United States *and* for people living here.

WT: Does your book explain who to tip?

IF: Oh, absolutely. It tells you who to tip, how much to tip, and when to tip. And equally important, it tells you when not to tip.

WT: That *is* important. Suppose[2] I don't know whether to tip someone, and I left your book at home. Is it OK to ask?

IF: Sure. If you don't know whether to leave a tip, the best thing to do is ask. People usually won't tell you what to do, but they *will* tell you what most customers do.

WT: I always wonder what to do when I get bad service. Should I still tip?

IF: Don't tip the ordinary amount, but tip *something* so that the service person doesn't think that you just forgot to leave a tip.

WT: That makes sense. Here's another thing I've always wondered about. Is there any reason why we tip a restaurant server but we don't a flight attendant?

IF: Not that I know. The rules for tipping in the United States aren't very logical, and there are often contradictions in who we tip.

WT: Another thing—I've never really understood why a restaurant tip depends on the amount of the bill rather than on the amount of work involved in serving the meal. After all, bringing out a $20 dish of food involves the same amount of work as carrying out a $5 plate.

IF: You're right. It makes no sense. That's just the way it is.

WT: One last question. Suppose I'm planning a trip to Egypt. Tell me how I can learn about tipping customs in that country.

IF: There are a number of Internet sites where you can learn what the rules are for tipping in each country. The *World Travel* site is always reliable. You can also find that information in travel books for the country you're planning to visit.

WT: Well, thanks for all the good tips! I know our readers will find them very helpful. *I* certainly did.

IF: Thank *you*.

---

2 *suppose:* imagine that something is true and its possible results; a way to ask "What if...?"

AFTER YOU READ

A VOCABULARY **Match the words with their definitions.**

_____ 1. clarify   **a.** not unusual

_____ 2. custom   **b.** reasonable and sensible

_____ 3. ultimate   **c.** a traditional way of doing something

_____ 4. logical   **d.** to make clear

_____ 5. ordinary   **e.** to be affected by

_____ 6. depend on   **f.** best

COMPREHENSION Check (✓) the questions that the interviewer *(WT)* wants the author *(IF)* to answer.

☐ **1.** When did you decide to write a book about tipping?

☐ **2.** Who do I tip?

☐ **3.** Is it OK to ask someone whether I should leave a tip?

☐ **4.** How much should I tip if I get bad service?

☐ **5.** What Internet sites should I use to find out more?

☐ **6.** How can I learn about tipping customs in other countries?

C **DISCUSSION** Work with a partner. Compare your answers in B. Why did you or didn't you check each item?

STEP 2 GRAMMAR PRESENTATION

EMBEDDED QUESTIONS

Direct *Yes/No* Question
Did I leave the right tip?
Was five dollars enough?
Should we leave a tip?

Main Clause	Embedded *Yes/No* Question
I don't know	*if* **I left** the right tip.
Can you tell me	*if* **I left** the right tip?
I wonder	*whether (or not)* **five dollars was** enough.
Do you know	*whether (or not)* **five dollars was** enough?
We're not sure	*whether (or not)* **to leave** a tip.

Direct *Wh-* Question
Who **is our server?**
Why **didn't he leave** a tip?
How much **should we give?**

Main Clause	Embedded *Wh-* Question
I don't know	*who* **our server is.**
Can you tell me	*who* **our server is?**
I wonder	*why* **he didn't leave** a tip.
Do you know	*why* **he didn't leave** a tip?
We're not sure	*how much* **to give.**

GRAMMAR NOTES

1 Embedded Questions

Embedded questions are **questions** that are **inside another sentence**.

• inside a **statement**	I don't know **who our server is.**
• inside **another question**	Do you remember **who our server is?**

IN WRITING If the embedded question is inside a **statement**, use a **period** at the end of the sentence.	I wonder **if that's our server.** NOT I wonder if that's our server?
If the embedded question is inside a **question**, use a **question mark** at the end of the sentence.	Do you know **if that's our server?**

2 Use of Sentences with Embedded Questions

Sentences with embedded questions have **two main uses**:

• to **express** something you **do not know**	*I don't know if the tip is included.* *(statement)*
• to **ask for information**	*Do you know if the tip is included?* *(question)*

The **phrase introducing the embedded question** (for example, *I don't know* or *Do you know*) shows if the sentence expresses something you do not know or asks for information.

USAGE NOTE We use **sentences with embedded questions** instead of direct questions to be **more polite**, especially when we speak to people we don't know well.	Where should I leave the tip? *(less polite)* *Can you tell me where I should leave the tip?* *(more polite)*

3 Common Phrases That Introduce Embedded Questions

Embedded questions always **follow certain phrases**.

Use these phrases in **statements**:

I don't know . . .	*I'm not sure . . .*	*I don't know* what the name of the café is.
I don't understand . . .	*I wonder . . .*	*I wonder* what time the restaurant closes.
I'd like to know . . .	*Let's ask . . .*	*Let's ask* what today's specials are.

Use these phrases in **questions**:

Do you know . . . ?	*Can you tell me . . . ?*	*Do you know* how much the shrimp is?
Can you remember . . . ?	*Could you explain . . . ?*	*Could you explain* what that sign means?

4 Embedded *Yes/No* Questions

A direct *yes/no* question can be embedded in a statement or question.	**Do they sell pizza?** *(direct question)*
	I wonder **if they sell pizza.** *(embedded question in a statement)*
	Do you know **if they sell pizza?** *(embedded question in a question)*
Begin embedded *yes/no* questions with *if,* **whether**, or **whether or not**.	Do you know **if they ordered it?**
USAGE NOTE *Whether* is more **formal** than *if.*	Do you know **whether they ordered it?** Do you know **whether or not they ordered it?**

5 Embedded *Wh-* Questions

A direct **wh- question** can be embedded in a statement or question.	**Who delivered it?** *(direct question)*
	I wonder **who delivered it.** *(embedded question in a statement)*
	Do you know **who delivered it?** *(embedded question in a question)*
Begin embedded *wh-* questions with a *wh- word* (*who, what, which, whose, when, where, why, how, how much, how many*).	I wonder **who our server is.** Do you know **when the restaurant closes?** People wonder **how much they should tip.**

6 Word Order in Embedded Questions

Use **statement word order (subject + verb)**, not question word order, for all **embedded questions**.

The word order in the embedded question is the same word order as in a **statement**.	SUBJECT + VERB **Eva ordered** pizza.
• embedded *yes/no* questions	Did Eva order pizza? *(direct)* Do you know **if Eva ordered** pizza? *(embedded)*
• embedded *wh-* questions about the **subject**	Who ordered pizza? *(direct)* I can't remember **who ordered** pizza. *(embedded)*
• embedded *wh-* questions about the **object**	What does it cost? *(direct)* Can you tell me **what it costs**? *(embedded)*
• embedded *wh-* questions with *when, where, why, how, how much,* or *how many*	When do they open? *(direct)* Do you know **when they open**? *(embedded)*

CONTINUED ▶

BE CAREFUL! Do not use question word order and the auxiliaries *do*, *does*, or *did* in embedded questions. Also, do not leave out *if* or *whether* in embedded *yes/no* questions.	I wonder **why they ordered** pizza. **NOT** I wonder why ~~did they order~~ pizza. I don't know **if they ordered** pizza. **NOT** I don't know ~~did they order~~ pizza.
BE CAREFUL! If a direct question about the subject has the form *be* + **noun**, then the embedded question has the form **noun** + *be*.	Who *is* **our server**? *(direct)* Do you know who **our server** *is*? *(embedded)* **NOT** Do you know who ~~is our server~~? *Is* **our order** ready? *(direct)* Do you know if **our order** *is* ready? *(embedded)* **NOT** Do you know ~~is our order~~ ready?

7 Infinitives in Embedded Questions

In embedded questions, you can also use **infinitives** after a **question word or** *whether*.	
• **question word + infinitive**	Let's ask **where to leave** the tip. *(Let's ask where we should leave the tip.)*
• *whether* + infinitive	Can you tell me **whether to leave** a tip? *(Can you tell me whether I should leave a tip?)*
BE CAREFUL! Do not use the infinitive after *if* or *why*.	I don't understand **why I should tip**. **NOT** I don't understand why ~~to tip~~.

REFERENCE NOTE

For a list of **phrases introducing embedded questions**, see Appendix 21 on page 463.

EXERCISE 1   DISCOVER THE GRAMMAR

GRAMMAR NOTES 1–7   Read this advertisement for *Tips on Tipping*. Underline the embedded questions.

TIPS ON TIPPING

This book is for you if . . .

- you've ever avoided a situation just because you didn't know <u>how much to tip</u>.

- you've ever realized (too late) that you were supposed to offer a tip.

- you've ever given a huge tip and then wondered if a tip was necessary at all.

- you've ever needed to know how to calculate the right tip instantly.

- you're new to the United States and you're not sure who you should tip here.

- you'd like to learn how tipping properly can get you the best service for your money.

What readers are saying . . .

"Essential, reliable information—I can't imagine how I got along without it."

—Chris Sarton, Minneapolis, Minnesota

"Take *Tips* along if you want a stress-free vacation."

—Midori Otaka, Osaka, Japan

"I took my fiancée to dinner at Deux Saisons and knew exactly how to tip everyone!"

—S. Prasad, San Francisco, California

"You need this book—whether you stay in hostels or five-star hotels."

—Cuno Pumpin, Bern, Switzerland

Do you want to learn who to tip, when to tip, and how much to tip? Get the ultimate guide to tipping and get all the answers to your tipping questions!

EXERCISE 2 EMBEDDED QUESTIONS

GRAMMAR NOTES 1–6 Complete this travel column about tipping customs around the world.
Change the direct questions in parentheses to embedded questions. Use correct punctuation.

Tipping customs vary, so travelers should find out who, where, and how much to tip. Here are some frequently asked questions.

Q: Can you tell me whether *I should tip in Canada?*

                                                     1. (Should I tip in Canada?)

A: Yes. Tipping practices in Canada are similar to those in the United States.

Q: I know that most restaurants and cafés in France include a service charge. I don't understand
how I can tell if the tip is included in the bill.

                                         2. (How can I tell if the tip is included in the bill?)

A: Look for the phrase *service compris* (service included) on the bill.

Q: I'm going to China next month. I understand that tipping used to be illegal there. Do you know

_____
3. (Will restaurant servers accept tips now?)

A: It depends on where you are. In large cities with a lot of tourists, you can leave a small tip in a restaurant
if there isn't already a service charge on the check. In small cities, your tip may not be accepted.

Q: On a recent trip to Iceland, I found that most service people refused tips. I don't know

_____
4. (Why did this happen?)

A: In Iceland, people often feel insulted by tips. Just say thank you—that's enough.

Q: I'll be in Dubai on business next month, and I'll be taking a lot of taxis. Can you tell me

_____
5. (Should I tip the driver?)

A: You don't really have to, but many people leave a small tip of 5 to 10 AED (Arab Emirate Dirhams).
Or you can round the fare up to the nearest paper bill.

Q: My husband and I are planning a trip to several cities in Australia and New Zealand. Please tell us

_____
6. (Who expects a tip and who doesn't?)

A: Restaurant servers expect a tip of 10 percent, but you don't need to tip taxi drivers.

Q: I'm moving to Japan, and I have a lot of luggage. I'm finding some contradictions on travel

websites. One says not to tip in Japan, but another says to tip airport porters. Could you tell me

_____
7. (Is it the custom to tip airport and train porters?)

A: There's a fixed fee[1] per bag for airport porters, not a tip. Most train stations don't have porters.
We recommend shipping your luggage from the airport. I hope that clarifies things!

---

1 *fixed fee:* a price that does not change

EXERCISE 3 EMBEDDED QUESTIONS

GRAMMAR NOTES 1–6 Two foreign exchange students are visiting Rome, Italy. Complete their conversations. Choose the appropriate questions from the list and change them to embedded questions. Use correct punctuation.

- ~~How much are we supposed to tip the driver?~~
- Could we rent a car and drive there?
- Do they have tour buses that go there?
- How much does the subway cost?
- How far are you going?
- How are we going to choose?
- How much does a bus tour cost?
- What did they put in the sauce?
- Where is the Forum?
- ~~Where is it?~~

Rome: The Forum

Conversation 1

DRIVER: Where do you want to go? The airport?

MARTINA: The Hotel Forte. Do you know _where it is?_
                                                    1.

DRIVER: Sure. Get in and I'll take you there.

MARTINA: *(whispering)* I wonder _how much we're supposed to tip the driver._
                                                                        2.

MIUKI: According to the book, the custom is to leave 10 to 15 percent. I've got it.

Conversation 2

MARTINA: There's so much to see in Rome. I don't know _____
                                                            3.

MIUKI: We could take a bus tour of the city first, and then decide.

MARTINA: Does the guidebook say _____
                                        4.

MIUKI: Yeah. About $15 per person, plus tips for the guide and the driver.

Conversation 3

MARTINA: That was delicious.

MIUKI: Let's try to find out _____
                                    5.

MARTINA: It tasted like it had a lot of garlic and basil. I'll ask the server.

Conversation 4

MARTINA: Excuse me. Can you tell me _____
                                            6.

OFFICER: Sure. Just turn right and go straight.

Conversation 5

MIUKI: Let's take the subway. Do you know _____
  7.

MARTINA: It's not expensive. I don't think it depends on _____
  8.

Conversation 6

MARTINA: I'd like to visit Ostia Antica. It's supposed to be like the ruins at Pompeii.

MIUKI: I wonder _____
  9.

MARTINA: I really don't want to go with a big group of people. What about you? Do you know

_____
  10.

MIUKI: Sure! It would be nice to drive around and see some of the countryside, too.

EXERCISE 4 QUESTION WORD + INFINITIVE

GRAMMAR NOTE 7 **Complete the conversation between Martina and Miuki. Use a question word and the infinitive form of the verbs from the box.**

figure out	get	go	invite	leave	~~wear~~

MARTINA: I can't decide _____*what to wear*_____ Friday night.
  1.

MIUKI: Your red dress. You always look great in it. By the way, where are you going?

MARTINA: Trattoria da Luigi. It's Janek's birthday, so I wanted to take him someplace special—not just

the ordinary places we usually go to. We're meeting there at 8:00.

MIUKI: Great! You know _____ there, don't you?
  2.

MARTINA: Yes, but I'm not sure _____.
  3.

MIUKI: Leave at 7:30. That'll give you enough time.

MARTINA: I'd like to take Janek someplace for dessert afterward. He loves desserts, but I don't know

_____.
  4.

MIUKI: The desserts at da Luigi's are supposed to be pretty good.

MARTINA: Oh. By the way, since it's Janek's birthday, I'm paying. But I'm still not quite sure

_____ the tip.
  5.

MIUKI: Service is usually included in Italy. The menu should tell you. So, who else is going?

MARTINA: Well, I thought about asking a few people to join us, but I really didn't know

_____.
  6.

MIUKI: Don't worry. I'm sure it will be fine with just the two of you.

EXERCISE 5 EDITING

GRAMMAR NOTES 1–7   Read this post to a travelers' website. There are ten mistakes in the use of embedded questions. The first mistake is already corrected. Find and correct nine more. Don't forget to check punctuation.

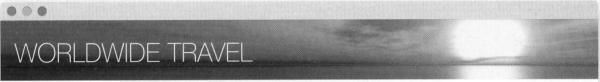

WORLDWIDE TRAVEL

Email this page to someone!   New Topic   Post a Poll   Post Reply

Subject: Tipping at the Hair Salon in Italy

Posted April 10 by Jenna Thompson

I wonder *if or whether* you can help clarify some tipping situations for me. I never know what doing at the

hair salon. I don't know if I should tip the person who washes my hair? What about the person

who cuts it, and the person who colors it? And what happens if the person is the owner.

Do you know do I still need to tip him or her? That doesn't seem logical. (And often I'm not

even sure who is the owner!) Then I never know how much to tip or where should I leave

the tip? Do I leave it on the counter or in the person's hands? What if somebody's hands are

wet or have hair color on them? Can I just put the tip in his or her pocket? It all seems so

complicated! I can't imagine how do customers figure all this out? What's the custom? I really

need to find out what to do—and FAST! My hair is getting very long and dirty.

Please help!

I wonder how much I should tip.

EXERCISE 6 LISTENING

▶ 28|02 **Ⓐ** A call-in radio show is taking questions from callers about tipping. Listen to the callers' questions. Listen again and choose the appropriate response to each caller's question.

1. **Caller One**
   a. between 15 and 20 percent of the bill
   b. the server

2. **Caller Two**
   a. about 15 percent of the fare
   b. only if you are happy with the ride

3. **Caller Three**
   a. before you leave
   b. on the table

4. **Caller Four**
   a. the manager
   b. don't leave a tip

5. **Caller Five**
   a. one dollar
   b. with the cashier

6. **Caller Six**
   a. look it up on the Internet
   b. It's included in the bill.

7. **Caller Seven**
   a. at least three dollars
   b. the person who delivers your food

▶ 28|02 **Ⓑ** Work with a partner. Listen to each conversation again. Discuss your answers. Why did you, or didn't you, choose each response? Do you agree with the advice in each response?

EXAMPLE: **A:** Caller number one wants to know how much to tip in a restaurant. She asked how much to tip—she didn't ask *who* to tip.
B: Right. So, the answer is "a"—between 15 and 20% of the bill.
A: Do you agree with that advice?
B: I don't know. I think it depends on how good the service is.

EXERCISE 7 TO TIP OR NOT TO TIP?

DISCUSSION Work in a group. Discuss these questions.

1. Do you think tipping is a good system? Why or why not?

   EXAMPLE: **A:** I'm not sure whether tipping is good or not. I think people should get paid enough so that they don't have to count on tips to live.
   B: I wonder if you would still get good service if the tip were included.
   C: Sure you would. A service charge is included in a lot of countries, and the service is still good.

2. Were you ever in a situation where you didn't know what to do about a tip? What did you do?

3. How do people tip in your country and in other countries you know?

EXERCISE 8 WHAT ABOUT YOU?

CONVERSATION Think about the first time you did something. Use one of the situations below or an idea of your own. Then work with a partner. Talk about what problems you had.

EXAMPLE: A: I remember the first time I went to Italy. I was at a restaurant and I didn't know how to get the server's attention.
B: When I was in Austria, I didn't know whether to tip or not.

- traveled to a foreign country
- went on a job interview
- drove a car
- became a parent
- Other: _____

EXERCISE 9 INFORMATION PLEASE!

ROLE PLAY Work with a partner. Student A is a desk clerk at a hotel. Student B is a guest at the hotel. The guest asks the clerk for information about some of the things in the list below. Use embedded questions.

EXAMPLE: A: Can I help you?
B: Yes. Could you tell me where to find a good, inexpensive restaurant around here?
A: There are some nice restaurants around the university.

- restaurants
- interesting sights
- transportation
- entertainment
- banks
- shopping
- tipping
- laundry

FROM GRAMMAR TO WRITING

A BEFORE YOUR WRITE Think about a situation that confused or surprised you such as a new job or being in a new country. Answer the questions.

Where were you? _____

What confused or surprised you? _____

What questions did you ask yourself? (Use direct questions, for example: *Should I leave a tip?*)

_____

_____

B WRITE Use your answers to write a paragraph about the situation that surprised you. Use embedded questions. Try to avoid some of the common mistakes in the chart.

EXAMPLE: When I was an exchange student in China, my Chinese friends always wanted to know how old I was. I couldn't understand why . . . I wasn't sure whether . . .

Common Mistakes in Using Embedded Questions

Use **statement word order** for embedded questions. Do not use question word order.	Do you know ***what* I should do**? **NOT** Do you know what ~~should I do~~?
You can use **an infinitive** after a **question word** or ***whether***. Do not use an infinitive after *why* or *if*.	Can you tell me ***how* to do** it? **NOT** Can you tell me ~~why to do~~ it? I'm not sure ***whether* to go**. **NOT** I'm not sure ~~if to go~~.
Use a **period** at the end of a **statement** with an embedded question. Do not use a question mark.	I don't know ***who* I can ask**. **NOT** I don't know who I can ask~~?~~
Use a **question mark** at the end of a **question** with an embedded question. Do not use a period.	Do you know ***where* to leave the tip?** **NOT** Do you know where to leave the tip~~.~~

C CHECK YOUR WORK Read your paragraph. Underline the embedded questions. Circle the question words, *whether*, or *if*. Use the Editing Checklist to check your work.

Editing Checklist

Did you use . . . ?

☐ *if, whether (or not)*, or a *wh-* word to begin an embedded question

☐ an infinitive after a question word or *whether*

☐ statement word order (subject + verb) for embedded questions

☐ a period at the end of statements with embedded questions

☐ a question mark at the end of questions with embedded questions

D REVISE YOUR WORK Read your paragraph again. Can you improve your writing? Make changes if necessary. Give your paragraph a title.

UNIT 28 **REVIEW**

Test yourself on the grammar of the unit.

A Circle the correct words and punctuation marks to complete the sentences.

1. I wonder whether <u>should we</u> / <u>we should</u> tip the driver.

2. Do you remember who <u>is our server</u> / <u>our server is</u>?

3. I don't know why she ordered pizza <u>?</u> / <u>.</u>

4. Let's ask how <u>can we</u> / <u>to</u> get to the museum.

5. I wonder if <u>to</u> / <u>I should</u> take a taxi.

6. Can you tell me whether I need to tip the owner of a hair salon <u>?</u> / <u>.</u>

7. I'm not sure <u>whether</u> / <u>did</u> they read the book on tipping.

B Rewrite the questions in parentheses to complete the embedded questions. Use correct punctuation.

1. Can you remember _____
(Where is the restaurant?)

2. I don't know _____
(Does the subway go to the museum?)

3. We're not sure _____
(Should we tip the porter?)

4. I can't imagine _____
(Why didn't we buy the book on tipping?)

5. Let's ask _____
(How much should we tip the tour guide?)

6. I'd like to know _____
(Do you have any travel books?)

7. Could you explain _____
(What does this sign say?)

C Find and correct six mistakes. Remember to check punctuation.

A: Hi. Is this a good time to call? I wasn't sure what time you have dinner?

B: This is fine. I didn't know were you back from your trip.

A: We got back two days ago. I can't remember if I email you some photographs.

B: Yes. They were great. Can you tell me where took you that picture of the lake? I want to go!

A: Hmm. I'm not sure which one was that. We saw a lot of lakes in Switzerland.

B: I'll show it to you. I'd really like to find out where is it.

Now check your answers on page 483.

Appendices

1 Irregular Verbs

When two forms are listed, the more common form is listed first.

BASE FORM	SIMPLE PAST	PAST PARTICIPLE	BASE FORM	SIMPLE PAST	PAST PARTICIPLE
arise	arose	arisen	go	went	gone
awake	awoke	awoken	grind	ground	ground
be	was or were	been	grow	grew	grown
beat	beat	beaten/beat	hang	hung*/hanged**	hung*/hanged**
become	became	become	have	had	had
begin	began	begun	hear	heard	heard
bend	bent	bent	hide	hid	hidden
bet	bet	bet	hit	hit	hit
bite	bit	bitten	hold	held	held
bleed	bled	bled	hurt	hurt	hurt
blow	blew	blown	keep	kept	kept
break	broke	broken	kneel	knelt/kneeled	knelt/kneeled
bring	brought	brought	knit	knit/knitted	knit/knitted
build	built	built	know	knew	known
burn	burned/burnt	burnt/burned	lay	laid	laid
burst	burst	burst	lead	led	led
buy	bought	bought	leap	leaped/leapt	leaped/leapt
catch	caught	caught	leave	left	left
choose	chose	chosen	lend	lent	lent
cling	clung	clung	let	let	let
come	came	come	lie (lie down)	lay	lain
cost	cost	cost	light	lit/lighted	lit/lighted
creep	crept	crept	lose	lost	lost
cut	cut	cut	make	made	made
deal	dealt	dealt	mean	meant	meant
dig	dug	dug	meet	met	met
dive	dove/dived	dived	pay	paid	paid
do	did	done	prove	proved	proven/proved
draw	drew	drawn	put	put	put
dream	dreamed/dreamt	dreamed/dreamt	quit	quit	quit
drink	drank	drunk	read /rid/	read /rɛd/	read /rɛd/
drive	drove	driven	ride	rode	ridden
eat	ate	eaten	ring	rang	rung
fall	fell	fallen	rise	rose	risen
feed	fed	fed	run	ran	run
feel	felt	felt	say	said	said
fight	fought	fought	see	saw	seen
find	found	found	seek	sought	sought
fit	fit/fitted	fit	sell	sold	sold
flee	fled	fled	send	sent	sent
fling	flung	flung	set	set	set
fly	flew	flown	sew	sewed	sewn/sewed
forbid	forbid/forbade	forbidden	shake	shook	shaken
forget	forgot	forgotten	shave	shaved	shaved/shaven
forgive	forgave	forgiven	shine (intransitive)	shone/shined	shone/shined
freeze	froze	frozen	shoot	shot	shot
get	got	gotten/got	show	showed	shown
give	gave	given	shrink	shrank/shrunk	shrunk/shrunken

* hung = *hung an object such as a painting*
** hanged = *executed by hanging*

BASE FORM	SIMPLE PAST	PAST PARTICIPLE	BASE FORM	SIMPLE PAST	PAST PARTICIPLE
shut	shut	shut	swear	swore	sworn
sing	sang	sung	sweep	swept	swept
sink	sank/sunk	sunk	swim	swam	swum
sit	sat	sat	swing	swung	swung
sleep	slept	slept	take	took	taken
slide	slid	slid	teach	taught	taught
speak	spoke	spoken	tear	tore	torn
speed	sped/speeded	sped/speeded	tell	told	told
spend	spent	spent	think	thought	thought
spill	spilled/spilt	spilled/spilt	throw	threw	thrown
spin	spun	spun	understand	understood	understood
spit	spit/spat	spat	upset	upset	upset
split	split	split	wake	woke	woken
spread	spread	spread	wear	wore	worn
spring	sprang	sprung	weave	wove/weaved	woven/weaved
stand	stood	stood	weep	wept	wept
steal	stole	stolen	win	won	won
stick	stuck	stuck	wind	wound	wound
sting	stung	stung	withdraw	withdrew	withdrawn
stink	stank/stunk	stunk	wring	wrung	wrung
strike	struck	struck/stricken	write	wrote	written

2 Non-Action Verbs

APPEARANCE	EMOTIONS	MENTAL STATES		POSSESSION AND RELATIONSHIP	SENSES AND PERCEPTIONS	WANTS AND PREFERENCES
appear	admire	agree	imagine	belong	feel	desire
be	adore	assume	know	come from (origin)	hear	hope
look (seem)	appreciate	believe	mean	contain	hurt	need
represent	care	consider	mind	have	notice	prefer
resemble	detest	disagree	presume	own	observe	want
seem	dislike	disbelieve	realize	possess	perceive	wish
signify	doubt	estimate	recognize		recognize	
	envy	expect	remember		see	
VALUE	fear	feel (believe)	see (understand)		seem	
cost	forgive	find (believe)	suppose		smell	
equal	hate	forget	suspect		sound	
weigh	like	guess	think (believe)		taste	
	love	hesitate	understand			
	miss	hope	wonder			
	regret					
	respect					
	trust					

3 Verbs and Expressions Used Reflexively

allow yourself	behave yourself	feel proud of yourself	kill yourself	see yourself
amuse yourself	believe in yourself	feel sorry for yourself	look after yourself	take care of yourself
ask yourself	blame yourself	forgive yourself	look at yourself	talk to yourself
avail yourself of	buy yourself	help yourself	prepare yourself	teach yourself
be hard on yourself	cut yourself	hurt yourself	pride yourself on	tell yourself
be pleased with yourself	deprive yourself of	imagine yourself	push yourself	treat yourself
be proud of yourself	dry yourself	introduce yourself	remind yourself	wash yourself
be yourself	enjoy yourself	keep yourself (busy)		

(s.o. = someone   s.t. = something)

Separable phrasal verbs show the object between the verb and the particle: **call** s.o. **up.**
Verbs that must be separated have an asterisk (*): **do** s.t. **over*.**
Inseparable phrasal verbs show the object after the particle: **carry on** s.t.
Phrasal verbs that can have a **gerund as object** are followed by *doing*: **put off** doing s.t.

PHRASAL VERB	MEANING
ask s.o. **over***	*invite to one's home*
block s.t. **out**	*stop from passing through (light/noise)*
blow s.t. **out**	*stop burning by blowing air on it*
blow s.t. **up**	*make explode*
bring s.t. **about**	*make happen*
bring s.o. **or** s.t. **back**	*return*
bring s.o. **down***	*depress*
bring s.t. **out**	*introduce (a new product/book)*
bring s.o. **up**	*raise (a child)*
bring s.t. **up**	*bring attention to*
build s.t. **up**	*increase*
burn s.t. **down**	*burn completely*
call s.o. **back***	*return a phone call*
call s.o. **in**	*ask for help with a problem*
call s.t. **off**	*cancel*
call s.o. **up**	*contact by phone*
calm s.o. **down**	*make less excited*
carry on s.t.	*continue*
carry s.t. **out**	*complete (a plan)*
cash in on s.t.	*profit from*
charge s.t. **up**	*charge with electricity*
check s.t. **out**	*examine*
cheer s.o. **up**	*cause to feel happier*
clean s.o. **or** s.t. **up**	*clean completely*
clear s.t. **up**	*explain*
close s.t. **down**	*close by force*
come from s.o. **or** s.t.	*have been born in a particular family or place*
come off s.t.	*become unattached*
come up with s.t.	*invent*
count on s.t. **or** s.o.	*depend on*
cover s.o. **or** s.t. **up**	*cover completely*
cross s.t. **out**	*draw a line through*
cut s.t. **down**	*1. bring down by cutting (a tree)*
	2. reduce
cut s.t. **off**	*1. stop the supply of*
	2. remove by cutting
cut s.t. **out**	*remove by cutting*
cut s.t. **up**	*cut into small pieces*
deal with s.t.	*handle*
do s.t. **over***	*do again*
do s.o. **or** s.t. **up**	*make more beautiful*
draw s.t. **together**	*unite*
dream s.t. **up**	*invent*
drink s.t. **up**	*drink completely*
drop s.o. **or** s.t. **off**	*take someplace in a car and leave there*
drop out of s.t.	*quit*
empty s.t. **out**	*empty completely*
end up doing s.t.	*do something you didn't plan to do*
end up with s.t.	*have an unexpected result*
fall for s.o.	*feel romantic love for*

PHRASAL VERB	MEANING
fall for s.t.	*be tricked by, believe*
figure s.o. **out**	*understand (the behavior)*
figure s.t. **out**	*solve, understand after thinking about it*
fill s.t. **in**	*complete with information*
fill s.t. **out**	*complete (a form)*
fill s.t. **up**	*fill completely*
find s.t. **out**	*learn information*
fix s.t. **up**	*redecorate (home)*
follow through with s.t.	*complete*
get s.t. **across**	*get people to understand an idea*
get off s.t.	*leave (a bus/train)*
get on s.t.	*board (a bus/train)*
get out of s.t.	*leave (a car/taxi)*
get s.t. **out of** s.t.*	*benefit from*
get over s.t.	*recover from*
get through with s.t.	*finish*
get to s.o. **or** s.t.	*1. reach s.o. or s.t.*
	2. upset s.o.
get together with s.o.	*meet*
give s.t. **away**	*give without charging money*
give s.t. **back**	*return*
give s.t. **out**	*distribute*
give s.t. **up**	*quit, abandon*
give up doing s.t.	*quit, stop*
go after s.o. **or** s.t.	*try to get or win, pursue*
go along with s.t.	*support*
go on doing s.t.	*continue*
go over s.t.	*review*
hand s.t. **in**	*give work (to a boss/teacher), submit*
hand s.t. **out**	*distribute*
hand s.t. **over**	*give*
hang s.t. **up**	*put on a hook or hanger*
help s.o. **out**	*assist*
hold s.t. **on**	*keep attached*
keep s.o. **or** s.t. **away**	*cause to stay at a distance*
keep s.t. **on***	*not remove (a piece of clothing/ jewelry)*
keep on doing s.t.	*continue*
keep s.o. **or** s.t. **out**	*not allow to enter*
keep up with s.o. **or** s.t.	*go as fast as*
lay s.o. **off**	*end employment*
lay s.t. **out**	*1. arrange according to plan*
	2. spend money
leave s.t. **on**	*1. not turn off (a light/radio)*
	2. not remove (a piece of clothing/ jewelry)
leave s.t. **out**	*not include, omit*
let s.o. **down**	*disappoint*
let s.o. **or** s.t. **in**	*allow to enter*
let s.o. **off**	*1. allow to leave (from a bus/car)*
	2. not punish

PHRASAL VERB	MEANING	PHRASAL VERB	MEANING
light s.t. **up**	*illuminate*	**stick with/to** s.o. or s.t.	*not quit, not leave, persevere*
look after s.o. or s.t.	*take care of*	**straighten** s.o. **out**	*change bad behavior*
look for s.o. or s.t.	*try to find*	**straighten** s.t. **up**	*make neat*
look into s.t.	*research*	**switch** s.t. **on**	*start (a machine/light)*
look s.o. or s.t. **over**	*examine*	**take** s.t. **away**	*remove*
look s.t. **up**	*try to find (in a book/on the Internet)*	**take** s.o. or s.t. **back**	*return*
make s.t. **up**	*create*	**take** s.t. **down**	*remove*
miss out on s.t.	*lose the chance for something good*	**take** s.t. **in**	1. *notice, understand, and remember*
move s.t. **around***	*change the location*		2. *earn (money)*
pass s.t. **on**	*give to others*	**take** s.t. **off/out**	*remove*
pass s.t. **out**	*distribute*	**take** s.o. **on**	*hire*
pass s.o. or s.t. **over**	*decide not to use*	**take** s.t. **on**	*agree to do*
pass s.o. or s.t. **up**	*decide not to use, reject*	**take over** s.t.	*get control of*
pay s.o. or s.t. **back**	*repay*	**take** s.t. **up**	*begin a job or activity*
pick s.o. or s.t. **out**	1. *choose*	**talk** s.o. **into***	*persuade*
	2. *identify*	**talk** s.t. **over**	*discuss*
pick s.o. or s.t. **up**	1. *lift*	**team up with** s.o.	*start to work with*
	2. *go get someone or something*	**tear** s.t. **down**	*destroy*
pick s.t. **up**	1. *buy, purchase*	**tear** s.t. **off**	*remove by tearing*
	2. *get (an idea/a new book)*	**tear** s.t. **up**	*tear into small pieces*
	3. *answer the phone*	**think about** doing s.t.	*consider*
point s.o. or s.t. **out**	*indicate*	**think back on** s.t.	*remember*
put s.t. **away**	*put in an appropriate place*	**think** s.t. **over**	*consider*
put s.t. **back**	*return to its original place*	**think** s.t. **up**	*invent*
put s.o. or s.t. **down**	*stop holding*	**throw** s.t. **away/out**	*put in the trash, discard*
put s.o. **off**	*discourage*	**touch** s.t. **up**	*improve by making small changes*
put s.t. **off**	*delay*	**try** s.t. **on**	*put clothing on to see if it fits*
put off doing s.t.	*delay*	**try** s.t. **out**	*use to see if it works*
put s.t. **on**	*cover the body (with clothes/lotion)*	**turn** s.t. **around***	*make it work well*
put s.t. **together**	*assemble*	**turn** s.o. or s.t. **down**	*reject*
put s.t. **up**	*erect*	**turn** s.t. **down**	*lower the volume (a TV/radio)*
run into s.o.	*meet accidentally*	**turn** s.t. **in**	*give work (to a boss/teacher), submit*
see s.t. **through***	*complete*	**turn** s.o. or s.t. **into***	*change from one form to another*
send s.t. **back**	*return*	**turn** s.o. **off***	*[slang] destroy interest in*
send s.t. **out**	*mail*	**turn** s.t. **off**	*stop (a machine/light), extinguish*
set s.t. **up**	1. *prepare for use*	**turn** s.t. **on**	*start (a machine/light)*
	2. *establish (a business/ an organization)*	**turn** s.t. **over**	*turn so the top side is at the bottom*
		turn s.t. **up**	*make louder (a TV/radio)*
settle on s.t.	*choose after thinking about many possibilities*	**use** s.t. **up**	*use completely, consume*
		wake s.o. **up**	*awaken*
show s.o. or s.t. **off**	*display the best qualities*	**watch out for** s.o. or s.t.	*be careful about*
show up on s.t.	*appear*	**work** s.t. **off**	*remove by work or activity*
shut s.t. **off**	*stop (a machine/light)*	**work** s.t. **out**	*solve, find a solution to a problem*
sign s.o. **up (for** s.t.**)**	*register*	**write** s.t. **down**	*write on a piece of paper*
start s.t. **over***	*start again*	**write** s.t. **up**	*write in a finished form*

PHRASAL VERB	MEANING
act up	cause problems
blow up	explode
break down	stop working (a machine)
break out	happen suddenly
burn down	burn completely
call back	return a phone call
calm down	become less excited
catch on	1. begin to understand
	2. become popular
cheer up	make happier
clean up	clean completely
clear up	become clear
close down	stop operating
come about	happen
come along	come with, accompany
come around	happen
come back	1. return
	2. become fashionable again
come by	visit
come down	become less (prices)
come in	enter
come off	become unattached
come on	1. do as I say
	2. let's go
come out	appear
come up	arise
dress up	wear special clothes
drop in	visit by surprise
drop out	quit
eat out	eat in a restaurant
empty out	empty completely
end up	reach a final place or condition
fall off	become detached
find out	learn information
fit in	be accepted in a group
follow through	complete
fool around	act playful
get ahead	make progress, succeed
get along	have a good relationship
get away	go on vacation
get back	return
get by	survive
get through	1. finish
	2. succeed in reaching s.o. by phone
get together	meet
get up	1. get out of bed
	2. stand

PHRASAL VERB	MEANING
give up	quit
go ahead	begin or continue to do something
go away	leave
go back	return
go down	become less (price, number), decrease
go off	explode (a gun/fireworks)
go on	continue
go out	leave
go over	succeed with an audience
go up	1. be built
	2. become more (price, number), increase
grow up	become an adult
hang up	end a phone call
help out	assist
hold on	1. wait
	2. not hang up the phone
keep away	stay at a distance
keep out	not enter
keep up	go as fast
lie down	recline
light up	illuminate
look out	be careful
make up	end a disagreement, reconcile
miss out	lose the chance for something good
pass away	die
pay off	be worthwhile
pick up	improve
play around	have fun
run out	not have enough
set out	begin an activity or a project
show up	appear
sign up	register
sit down	take a seat
slip up	make a mistake
stand up	rise
start over	start again
stay up	remain awake
straighten up	make neat
take off	depart (a plane)
tune in	1. watch or listen to (a show)
	2. pay attention
turn up	appear
wake up	stop sleeping
watch out	be careful
work out	1. be resolved
	2. exercise
	3. understand

6 Irregular Plural Nouns

SINGULAR	PLURAL		SINGULAR	PLURAL		SINGULAR	PLURAL		SINGULAR	PLURAL
analysis	analyses		half	halves		man	men		deer	deer
basis	bases		knife	knives		woman	women		fish	fish
crisis	crises		leaf	leaves		child	children		sheep	sheep
hypothesis	hypotheses		life	lives		foot	feet			
			loaf	loaves		tooth	teeth			
			shelf	shelves		goose	geese			
			wife	wives		mouse	mice			
						person	people			

7 Adjectives That Form the Comparative and Superlative in Two Ways

The more common form of the comparative and the superlative is listed first.

ADJECTIVE	COMPARATIVE	SUPERLATIVE
common	more common/commoner	most common/commonest
cruel	crueler/more cruel	cruelest/most cruel
deadly	deadlier/more deadly	deadliest/most deadly
friendly	more friendly/friendlier	most friendly/friendliest
handsome	more handsome/handsomer	most handsome/handsomest
happy	happier/more happy	happiest/most happy
lively	livelier/more lively	liveliest/most lively
lonely	lonelier/more lonely	loneliest/most lonely
lovely	lovelier/more lovely	loveliest/most lovely
narrow	narrower/more narrow	narrowest/most narrow
pleasant	more pleasant/pleasanter	most pleasant/pleasantest
polite	more polite/politer	most polite/politest
quiet	quieter/more quiet	quietest/most quiet
shallow	shallower/more shallow	shallowest/most shallow
simple	simpler/more simple	simplest/most simple
sincere	more sincere/sincerer	most sincere/sincerest
stupid	stupider/more stupid	stupidest/most stupid
true	truer/more true	truest/most true

8 Irregular Comparisons of Adjectives, Adverbs, and Quantifiers

ADJECTIVE	ADVERB	COMPARATIVE	SUPERLATIVE
bad	badly	worse	the worst
far	far	farther/further	the farthest/furthest
good	well	better	the best
little	little	less	the least
many/a lot of	—	more	the most
much*/a lot of	much*/a lot	more	the most

* *Much* is usually only used in questions and negative statements.

9 Participial Adjectives

-ED	-ING	-ED	-ING	-ED	-ING
alarmed	alarming	disturbed	disturbing	moved	moving
amazed	amazing	embarrassed	embarrassing	paralyzed	paralyzing
amused	amusing	entertained	entertaining	pleased	pleasing
annoyed	annoying	excited	exciting	relaxed	relaxing
astonished	astonishing	exhausted	exhausting	satisfied	satisfying
bored	boring	fascinated	fascinating	shocked	shocking
confused	confusing	frightened	frightening	surprised	surprising
depressed	depressing	horrified	horrifying	terrified	terrifying
disappointed	disappointing	inspired	inspiring	tired	tiring
disgusted	disgusting	interested	interesting	touched	touching
distressed	distressing	irritated	irritating	troubled	troubling

10 Verbs Followed by Gerunds (Base Form of Verb + -ing)

acknowledge	delay	escape	imagine	postpone	report
admit	deny	excuse	justify	practice	resent
advise	detest	explain	keep (continue)	prevent	resist
allow	discontinue	feel like	keep on*	prohibit	risk
appreciate	discuss	finish	limit	propose	suggest
avoid	dislike	forgive	mention	put off*	support
ban	end up*	give up*	mind (object to)	quit	think about* (consider)
can't help	endure	go	miss	recall	tolerate
celebrate	enjoy	go on*	permit	recommend	understand
consider					

*These phrasal verbs can be followed by a gerund.

11 Verbs Followed by Infinitives (To + Base Form of Verb)

afford	can't wait	grow	mean (intend)	pretend	threaten
agree	claim	help*	need	promise	volunteer
aim	choose	hesitate	neglect	refuse	wait
appear	consent	hope	offer	rush	want
arrange	decide	hurry	pay	seem	wish
ask	deserve	intend	plan	struggle	would like
attempt	expect	learn	prepare	swear	yearn
can('t) afford	fail	manage			

* Help is often followed by the base form of the verb (example: I helped paint the kitchen).

12 Verbs Followed by Gerunds or Infinitives

begin	forget*	like	prefer	regret*	stop*
can't stand	hate	love	remember*	start	try
continue					

*These verbs can be followed by either a gerund or an infinitive, but there is a big difference in meaning (see Unit 9).

13 Verbs Followed by Object + Infinitive

advise	choose*	get	order	promise*	tell
allow	convince	help**	pay*	remind	urge
ask*	encourage	hire	permit	request	want*
beg*	expect*	instruct	persuade	require	warn
cause	forbid	invite	prefer*	teach	would like*
challenge	force	need*			

*These verbs can also be followed by an infinitive without an object (example: *ask to leave* or *ask someone to leave*).

** *Help* is often followed by the base form of the verb, with or without an object (example: *I helped (her) paint the kitchen*).

14 Adjectives Followed by Infinitives

afraid	delighted	eager	happy	ready	sorry
alarmed	depressed	easy	hesitant	relieved	surprised
amazed	determined	embarrassed	likely	reluctant	touched
angry	difficult	encouraged	lucky	right	upset
anxious	disappointed	excited	pleased	sad	willing
ashamed	distressed	fortunate	prepared	shocked	wrong
curious	disturbed	glad	proud		

15 Nouns Followed by Infinitives

attempt	desire	offer	plan	reason	time
chance	dream	opportunity	price	request	trouble
choice	failure	permission	promise	right	way
decision	need				

16 Adjective + Preposition Combinations

accustomed to	bored with/by	disappointed with	happy about	responsible for	sorry for/about
afraid of	capable of	excited about	known for	sad about	surprised at/
amazed at/by	careful of	famous for	interested in	safe from	about/by
angry at	certain about	fed up with	nervous about	satisfied with	terrible at
ashamed of	concerned about	fond of	opposed to	shocked at/by	tired of
aware of	content with	glad about	pleased about	sick of	used to
awful at	curious about	good at	ready for	slow at/in	worried about
bad at	different from				

17 Verb + Preposition Combinations

admit to	believe in	dream about/of	pay for	succeed in	think about
advise against	choose between	feel about	plan on	talk about	wonder about
apologize for	complain about	insist on	rely on	thank someone for	worry about
approve of	decide on	object to	resort to		

1 SOCIAL MODALS AND EXPRESSIONS

FUNCTION	MODAL OR EXPRESSION	TIME	EXAMPLES
Ability	can can't	Present	Sam **can swim**. He **can't skate**.
	could couldn't	Past	We **could swim** last year. We **couldn't skate**.
	be able to* not be able to*	All verb forms	Lea **is able to run** fast. She **wasn't able to run** fast last year.
Possibility	can can't	Present or future	I **can help** you now. I **can't help** you tomorrow.
Permission	can can't could may may not	Present or future	**Can** I **sit** here? **Can** I **call** tomorrow? Yes, you **can**. No, you **can't**. Sorry. **Could** he **leave** now? **May** I **borrow** your pen? Yes, you **may**. No, you **may not**. Sorry.
Requests	can can't could will would	Present or future	**Can** you **close** the door, please? Sure, I **can**. Sorry, I **can't**. **Could** you please **answer** the phone? **Will** you **wash** the dishes, please? **Would** you please **mail** this letter?
Advice	should shouldn't ought to had better** had better not**	Present or future	You **should study** more. You **shouldn't miss** class. We **ought to leave**. We**'d better go**. We**'d better not stay**.
Advisability in the Past and Regret or Criticism	should have shouldn't have ought to have could have might have	Past	I **should have become** a doctor. I **shouldn't have wasted** time. He **ought to have told** me. She **could have gone** to college. You **might have called**. I waited for hours.
Necessity	have to* not have to*	All verb forms	He **has to go** now. I **had to go** yesterday. I **will have to go** soon. He **doesn't have to go** yet.
	have got to* must	Present or future	He**'s got to leave**! You **must use** a pen for the test.
Prohibition	must not can't	Present or future	You **must not drive** without a license. You **can't drive** without a license.

*The meaning of this expression is similar to the meaning of a modal. Unlike a modal, the verb changes for present tense third-person singular.

**The meaning of this expression is similar to the meaning of a modal. Like a modal, it has no -s for third-person singular.

FUNCTION	MODAL OR EXPRESSION	TIME	EXAMPLES
Conclusions and Possibility	must must not have to* have got to*	Present	This **must be** her house. Her name is on the door. She **must not be** home. I don't see her car. She **has to know** him. They went to school together. He**'s got to be** guilty. We saw him do it.
	may may not might might not could	Present or future	She **may be** home now. It **may not rain** tomorrow. Lee **might be sick** today. He **might not come** to class. They **could be** at the library. It **could rain** tomorrow.
	may have may not have might have might not have could have	Past	They **may have left** already. I don't see them. They **may not have arrived** yet. He **might have called**. I'll check my phone messages. He **might not have left** a message. She **could have forgotten** to mail the letter.
Impossibility	can't	Present or future	That **can't be** Ana. She left for France yesterday. It **can't snow** tomorrow. It's going to be too warm.
	couldn't	Present or future	He **couldn't be** guilty. He wasn't in town when the crime occurred. The teacher **couldn't give** the test tomorrow. Tomorrow's Saturday.
	couldn't have	Past	You **couldn't have failed**. You studied too hard.

*The meaning of this expression is similar to the meaning of a modal. Unlike a modal, the verb changes for present tense third-person singular.

19 Reporting Verbs

STATEMENTS

acknowledge	claim	explain	remark	state
add	comment	indicate	repeat	suggest
admit	complain	maintain	reply	tell
announce	conclude	mean	report	warn
answer	confess	note	respond	whisper
argue	declare	observe	say	write
assert	deny	promise	shout	yell
believe	exclaim			

INSTRUCTIONS, COMMANDS, ADVICE, REQUESTS, INVITATIONS

advise	invite
ask	order
caution	say
command	tell
demand	urge
instruct	warn

QUESTIONS

ask
inquire
question

20 Time Word Changes in Indirect Speech

DIRECT SPEECH		INDIRECT SPEECH
now	→	then
today	→	that day
tomorrow	→	the next day or the following day or the day after
yesterday	→	the day before or the previous day
this week/month/year	→	that week/month/year
last week/month/year	→	the week/month/year before
next week/month/year	→	the following week/month/year

21 Phrases Introducing Embedded Questions

I don't know …	I'd like to know …	Do you know …?
I don't understand …	I need to know …	Do you understand …?
I wonder …	I want to know …	Can you tell me …?
I'm not sure …	I want to understand …	Could you explain …?
I can't remember …	I'd like to find out …	Can you remember …?
I can't imagine …	We need to find out …	Would you show me …?
It doesn't say …	Let's ask …	Who knows …?

22 Spelling Rules for the Simple Present: Third-Person Singular (*He*, *She*, *It*)

1 Add **-s** for most verbs.

work	work**s**
buy	buy**s**
ride	ride**s**
return	return**s**

2 Add **-es** for verbs that end in **-ch**, **-s**, **-sh**, **-x**, or **-z**.

watch	watch**es**
pass	pass**es**
rush	rush**es**
relax	relax**es**
buzz	buzz**es**

3 Change the **y** to **i** and add **-es** when the base form ends in **consonant + y**.

study	stud**ies**
hurry	hurr**ies**
dry	dr**ies**

4 Do not change the **y** when the base form ends in **vowel + y**. Add **-s**.

play	play**s**
enjoy	enjoy**s**

5 A few verbs have **irregular forms**.

be	**is**
do	**does**
go	**goes**
have	**has**

23 Spelling Rules for Base Form of Verb + *-ing* (Progressive and Gerund)

1 Add **-ing** to the base form of the verb.

read	read**ing**
stand	stand**ing**

2 If the verb ends in a **silent -e**, drop the final **-e** and add **-ing**.

leave	leav**ing**
take	tak**ing**

3 In **one-syllable** verbs, if the last three letters are a consonant-vowel-consonant combination (CVC), double the last consonant and add **-ing**.

```
C V C
↓ ↓ ↓
s i t      sit**ting**
```

```
C V C
↓ ↓ ↓
p l a n    plan**ning**
```

EXCEPTION: Do not double the last consonant in verbs that end in **-w**, **-x**, or **-y**.

sew	sew**ing**
fix	fix**ing**
play	play**ing**

4 In verbs of **two or more syllables** that end in a consonant-vowel-consonant combination, double the last consonant only if the last syllable is stressed.

admít	admit**ting**	*(The last syllable is stressed, so double the -**t**.)*
whísper	whisper**ing**	*(The last syllable is not stressed, so don't double the -**r**.)*

5 If the verb ends in **-ie**, change the **ie** to **y** before adding **-ing**.

die	d**ying**
lie	l**ying**

> **Stress**
> ' shows main stress.

24 Spelling Rules for Base Form of Verb + -ed (Simple Past and Past Participle of Regular Verbs)

1 If the verb ends in a **consonant**, add *-ed*.

return	return**ed**
help	help**ed**

2 If the verb ends in *-e*, add *-d*.

live	live**d**
create	create**d**
die	die**d**

3 In **one-syllable** verbs, if the last three letters are a consonant-vowel-consonant combination (CVC), double the last consonant and add *-ed*.

```
C V C
↓ ↓ ↓
h o p          hop**ped**
```

```
C V C
↓ ↓ ↓
g r a b        grab**bed**
```

EXCEPTION: Do not double the last consonant in **one-syllable** verbs that end in *-w*, *-x*, or *-y*.

bow	bow**ed**
mix	mix**ed**
play	play**ed**

4 In verbs of **two or more syllables** that end in a consonant-vowel-consonant combination, double the last consonant only if the last syllable is stressed.

prefér	prefer**red**	*(The last syllable is stressed, so double the -r.)*
vísit	visit**ed**	*(The last syllable is not stressed, so don't double the -t.)*

5 If the verb ends in **consonant + y**, change the *y* to *i* and add *-ed*.

worry	worr**ied**
carry	carr**ied**

6 If the verb ends in **vowel + y**, add *-ed*. (Do not change the *y* to *i*.)

play	play**ed**
annoy	annoy**ed**

EXCEPTIONS:

lay	la**id**
pay	pa**id**
say	sa**id**

> **Stress**
> ´ shows main stress.

25 Spelling Rules for the Comparative (-er) and Superlative (-est) of Adjectives

1 With **one-syllable** adjectives, add *-er* to form the comparative. Add *-est* to form the superlative.

cheap	cheap**er**	cheap**est**
bright	bright**er**	bright**est**

2 If the adjective ends in *-e*, add *-r* or *-st*.

nice	nice**r**	nice**st**

3 If the adjective ends in **consonant + y**, change *y* to *i* before you add *-er* or *-est*.

pretty	prett**ier**	prett**iest**

EXCEPTION:

shy	shy**er**	shy**est**

4 In **one-syllable** adjectives, if the last three letters are a consonant-vowel-consonant combination (CVC), double the last consonant before adding *-er* or *-est*.

```
C V C
↓ ↓ ↓
b i g          big**ger**        big**gest**
```

EXCEPTION: Do not double the last consonant in adjectives that end in *-w* or *-y*.

slow	slow**er**	slow**est**
gray	gray**er**	gray**est**

26 Spelling Rules for Adverbs Ending in -ly

1 Add **-ly** to the corresponding adjective.

nice	nice**ly**
quiet	quiet**ly**
beautiful	beautiful**ly**

EXCEPTION:

true	tru**ly**

2 If the adjective ends in **consonant + y**, change the **y** to **i** before adding **-ly**.

easy	eas**ily**

3 If the adjective ends in **-le**, drop the **e** and add **-y**.

possible	possib**ly**

4 If the adjective ends in **-ic**, add **-ally**.

basic	basic**ally**
fantastic	fantastic**ally**

27 Capitalization and Punctuation Rules

	USE FOR . . .	EXAMPLES
capital letter	• the first-person pronoun *I*	Tomorrow **I** will be here at 2:00.
	• proper nouns	His name is **Karl**. He lives in **Germany**.
	• the first word of a sentence	**When** does the train leave? **At** 2:00.
apostrophe (')	• possessive nouns	Is that **Marta's** coat?
	• contractions	**That's** not hers. **It's** mine.
comma (,)	• after items in a list	He bought **apples, pears, oranges,** and **bananas**.
	• before sentence connectors *and*, *but*, *or*, and *so*	They watched TV**, and** she played video games. She's tired**, so** she's going to bed now.
	• after the first part of a sentence that begins with *because*	*Because* it's raining**,** we're not walking to the office.
	• after the first part of a sentence that begins with a preposition	*Across from* the post office**,** there's a good restaurant.
	• after the first part of a sentence that begins with a time clause or an *if*-clause	*After* he arrived**,** we ate dinner. *If* it rains**,** we won't go.
	• before and after a nonidentifying adjective clause in the middle of a sentence	Tony**, who lives in Paris,** emails me every day.
	• before a nonidentifying adjective clause at the end of a sentence	I get emails every day from Tony**, who lives in Paris**.
exclamation point (!)	• at the end of a sentence to show surprise or a strong feeling	You're here! That's great! Stop! A car is coming!
period (.)	• at the end of a statement	Today is Wednesday**.**
question mark (?)	• at the end of a question	What day is today**?**

28 Direct Speech Punctuation Rules

Direct speech can either come **after or before** the reporting verb.

1 When direct speech comes **after** the reporting verb:

EXAMPLES: He said**, "I had a good time."**
She asked**, "Where's the party?"**
They shouted**, "Be careful!"**

a. Put a comma after the reporting verb.

b. Use opening quotation marks (") before the first word of the direct speech.

c. Begin the quotation with a capital letter.

d. Use the appropriate end punctuation for the direct speech:
If the direct speech is a statement, use a period (.).
If the direct speech is a question, use a question mark (?).
If the direct speech is an exclamation, use an exclamation point (!).

e. Put closing quotation marks (") after the end punctuation of the quotation.

2 When direct speech comes **before** the reporting verb:

EXAMPLES: **"I had a good time,"** he said**.**
"Where's the party?" she asked**.**
"Be careful!" they shouted**.**

a. Begin the sentence with opening quotation marks (").

b. Use the appropriate end punctuation for the direct speech:
If the direct speech is a statement, use a comma (,).
If the direct speech is a question, use a question mark (?).
If the direct speech is an exclamation, use an exclamation point (!).

c. Use closing quotation marks after the end punctuation for the direct speech (").

d. Begin the reporting clause with a lowercase letter.

e. Use a period at the end of the main sentence (.).

29 Pronunciation Table

▶ A|01 These are the pronunciation symbols used in this text. Listen to the pronunciation of the key words.

VOWELS				CONSONANTS			
SYMBOL	KEY WORD	SYMBOL	KEY WORD	SYMBOL	KEY WORD	SYMBOL	KEY WORD
i	beat, feed	ə	banana, among	p	pack, happy	z	zip, please, goes
ɪ	bit, did	ɚ	shirt, murder	b	back, rubber	ʃ	ship, machine, station,
eɪ	date, paid	aɪ	bite, cry, buy, eye	t	tie		special, discussion
ɛ	bet, bed	aʊ	about, how	d	die	ʒ	measure, vision
æ	bat, bad	ɔɪ	voice, boy	k	came, key, quick	h	hot, who
ɑ	box, odd, father	ɪr	beer	g	game, guest	m	men
ɔ	bought, dog	ɛr	bare	tʃ	church, nature, watch	n	sun, know, pneumonia
oʊ	boat, road	ɑr	bar	ʤ	judge, general, major	ŋ	sung, ringing
ʊ	book, good	ɔr	door	f	fan, photograph	w	wet, white
u	boot, food, student	ʊr	tour	v	van	l	light, long
ʌ	but, mud, mother			θ	thing, breath	r	right, wrong
				ð	then, breathe	y	yes, use, music
				s	sip, city, psychology	ţ	butter, bottle

30 Pronunciation Rules for the Simple Present: Third-Person Singular (*He, She, It*)

1 The third-person singular in the simple present always ends in the letter *-s*. There are, however, three different pronunciations for the final sound of the third-person singular.

/s/	/z/	/ɪz/
talk**s**	lov**es**	danc**es**

2 The final sound is pronounced /s/ after the voiceless sounds /p/, /t/, /k/, and /f/.

top	top**s**	take	take**s**
get	get**s**	laugh	laugh**s**

3 The final sound is pronounced /z/ after the voiced sounds /b/, /d/, /g/, /v/, /m/, /n/, /ŋ/, /l/, /r/, and /ð/.

describe	describ**es**	remain	remain**s**
spend	spend**s**	sing	sing**s**
hug	hug**s**	tell	tell**s**
live	liv**es**	lower	lower**s**
seem	seem**s**	bathe	ba**thes**

4 The final sound is pronounced /z/ after all **vowel sounds**.

agree	agr**ees**	stay	sta**ys**
try	tri**es**	know	kn**ows**

5 The final sound is pronounced /ɪz/ after the sounds /s/, /z/, /ʃ/, /ʒ/, /tʃ/, and /dʒ/. /ɪz/ adds a syllable to the verb.

miss	mi**sses**	massage	massa**ges**
freeze	free**zes**	watch	wa**tches**
rush	ru**shes**	judge	ju**dges**

6 *Do* and *say* have a change in vowel sound.

do /du/	does /dʌz/
say /seɪ/	says /sɛz/

31 Pronunciation Rules for the Simple Past and Past Participle of Regular Verbs

1 The regular simple past and past participle always end in the letter *-d*. There are three different pronunciations for the final sound of the regular simple past and past participle.

/t/	/d/	/ɪd/
race**d**	live**d**	attend**ed**

2 The final sound is pronounced /t/ after the voiceless sounds /p/, /k/, /f/, /s/, /ʃ/, and /tʃ/.

hop	hop**ped**	address	addre**ssed**
work	wor**ked**	publish	publi**shed**
laugh	lau**ghed**	watch	wat**ched**

3 The final sound is pronounced /d/ after the voiced sounds /b/, /g/, /v/, /z/, /ʒ/, /dʒ/, /m/, /n/, /ŋ/, /l/, /r/, and /ð/.

rub	ru**bbed**	rhyme	rhy**med**
hug	hu**gged**	return	retur**ned**
live	live**d**	bang	ba**nged**
surprise	surpri**sed**	enroll	enro**lled**
massage	massa**ged**	appear	appea**red**
change	chan**ged**	bathe	ba**thed**

4 The final sound is pronounced /d/ after all **vowel sounds**.

agree	agr**eed**	enjoy	enj**oyed**
die	di**ed**	snow	sn**owed**
play	pla**yed**		

5 The final sound is pronounced /ɪd/ after /t/ and /d/. /ɪd/ adds a syllable to the verb.

start	start**ed**	decide	decid**ed**

Glossary of Grammar Terms

action verb A verb that describes an action.

> Alicia **ran** home.

active sentence A sentence that focuses on the agent (the person or thing doing the action).

> **Ari kicked** the ball.

addition A clause or a short sentence that follows a statement and expresses similarity or contrast with the information in the statement.

> Pedro is tall, **and so is Alex.**
> Trish doesn't like sports. **Neither does her sister.**

adjective A word that describes a noun or pronoun.

> It's a **good** plan, and it's not **difficult.**

adjective clause A clause that identifies or gives additional information about a noun.

> The woman **who called you** didn't leave her name.
> Samir, **who you met yesterday**, works in the lab.

adverb A word that describes a verb, an adjective, or another adverb.

> She drives **carefully.**
> She's a **very** good driver.
> She drives **really** well.

affirmative A statement without a negative, or an answer meaning *Yes*.

> He **works.** *(affirmative statement)*
> **Yes**, he **does.** *(affirmative short answer)*

agent The person or thing doing the action in a sentence. In passive sentences, the word *by* is used before the agent.

> This article was written ***by* my teacher.**

article A word that goes before a noun.
The indefinite articles are *a* and *an*.

> I ate **a** sandwich and **an** apple.

The definite article is *the*.

> I didn't like **the** sandwich. **The** apple was good.

auxiliary verb (also called **helping verb**) A verb used with a main verb. *Be*, *do*, and *have* are often auxiliary verbs. Modals (*can, should, may, must . . .*) are also auxiliary verbs.

> I **am** exercising right now.
> **Do** you like to exercise?
> I **should** exercise every day.

base form The simple form of a verb without any endings (*-s, -ed, -ing*) or other changes.

> **be, have, go, drive**

clause A group of words that has a subject and a verb. A sentence can have one or more clauses.

> **We are leaving now.** *(one clause)*
> **If it rains, we won't go.** *(two clauses)*

common noun A word for a person, place, or thing (but not the name of the person, place, or thing).

> Teresa lives in a **house** near the **beach.**

comparative The form of an adjective or adverb that shows the difference between two people, places, or things.

> Alain is **shorter** than Brendan. *(adjective)*
> Brendan runs **faster** than Alain. *(adverb)*

conditional sentence A sentence that describes a condition and its result. The sentence can be about the past, the present, or the future. The condition and result can be real or unreal.

> If it **rains, I won't go.** *(future real)*
> If it **had rained, I wouldn't have gone.** *(past unreal)*

continuous See **progressive.**

contraction A short form of a word or words. An apostrophe (') replaces the missing letter or letters.

> **she's** = she is
> **can't** = cannot

count noun A noun that you can count. It has a singular and a plural form.

> one **book**, two **books**

definite article *the*
This article goes before a noun that refers to a specific person, place, or thing.

>Please bring me **the book** on **the table**.

dependent clause (also called **subordinate clause**) A clause that needs a main clause for its meaning.

>**When it's hot out,** I go to the beach.

direct object A noun or pronoun that receives the action of a verb.

>Marta kicked **the ball**. Ian caught **it**.

direct speech (also called **quoted speech**) Language that gives the exact words a speaker used. In writing, quotation marks come before and after the speaker's words.

>**"I saw Bob yesterday,"** she said.
>**"Was he in school?"** he asked.

embedded question A question that is inside another sentence.

>I don't know **where the restaurant is**.
>Do you know **if it's on Tenth Street**?

formal Language used in business situations or with adults you do not know.

>Good afternoon, Mr. Rivera. Please have a seat.

gerund A noun formed with verb + *-ing* that can be used as a subject or an object.

>**Swimming** is great exercise.
>I enjoy **swimming**.

helping verb See **auxiliary verb**.

identifying adjective clause (also called **restrictive adjective clause**) A clause that identifies which member of a group the sentence is about.

>There are ten students in the class. The student **who sits in front of me** is from Russia.

***if*-clause** The clause that states the condition in a conditional sentence.

>**If I had known you were here,** I would have called you.

imperative A sentence that gives a command or instructions.

>**Hurry!**
>**Turn left on Main Street.**

indefinite article *a* or *an*
These articles go before a noun that does not refer to a specific person, place, or thing.

>Can you bring me **a book**? I'm looking for something to read.

indefinite pronoun A pronoun such as *someone*, *something*, *anyone*, *anything*, *anywhere*, *no one*, *nothing*, *nowhere*, *everyone*, and *everything*. An indefinite pronoun does not refer to a specific person, place, or thing.

>**Someone** called you last night.
>Did **anything** happen?

indirect object A noun or pronoun (often a person) that receives something as the result of the action of the verb.

>I told **John** the story.
>He gave **me** some good advice.

indirect question Language that reports what a speaker asked without using the exact words.

>He asked **what my name was**.
>He asked **if he had met me before**.

indirect speech (also called **reported speech**) Language that reports what a speaker said without using the exact words.

>Ann said **she had seen Bob the day before**.
>She asked **if he was in school**.

infinitive *to* + base form of the verb

>I want **to leave** now.

infinitive of purpose *(in order) to* + base form
This form gives the reason for an action.

>I go to school **(in order) to learn** English.

informal Language used with family, friends, and children.

>Hi, Pete. Sit down.

information question See *wh-* **question**.

inseparable phrasal verb A phrasal verb whose parts must stay together.

>We **ran into** Tomás at the supermarket.
>NOT We ran Tomás into . . .

intransitive verb A verb that does not have an object.

> She **paints**.
> We **fell**.

irregular A word that does not change its form in the usual way.

> good → well
> bad → worse
> go → went

main clause A clause that can stand alone as a sentence.

> **I called my friend Tom**, who lives in Chicago.

main verb A verb that describes an action or state. It is often used with an auxiliary verb.

> Jared is **calling**.
> Does he **call** every day?
> Paulo is **studying** in Barcelona this semester.
> Do you **know** him?

modal A type of auxiliary verb. It goes before a main verb or stands alone as a short answer. It expresses ideas such as ability, advice, permission, and possibility. *Can, could, will, would, may, might, should,* and *must* are modals.

> **Can** you swim?
> Yes, I **can**.
> You really **should** learn to swim.

negative A statement or answer meaning *No*.

> He **doesn't** work. *(negative statement)*
> **No**, he **doesn't**. *(negative short answer)*

non-action verb (also called **stative verb**) A verb that does not describe an action. It describes such things as thoughts, feelings, and senses.

> I **remember** that word.
> Chris **loves** ice cream.
> It **tastes** great.

non-count noun A noun you usually do not count (*air, water, rice, love*...). It has only a singular form.

> The **rice** is delicious.

nonidentifying adjective clause (also called **nonrestrictive adjective clause**) A clause that gives additional information about the noun it refers to. The information is not necessary to identify the noun. It is separated from the rest of the sentence by commas.

> My sister Diana**, who usually hates sports,** recently started tennis lessons.

nonrestrictive adjective clause See **nonidentifying adjective clause**.

noun A word for a person, place, or thing.

> My **sister**, **Anne**, works in an **office**.
> She uses a **computer**.

object A noun or a pronoun that receives the action of a verb. Sometimes a verb has two objects.

> Layla threw **the ball**.
> She threw **it** to **Tom**.
> She threw **him the ball**.

object pronoun A pronoun (*me, you, him, her, it, us, them*) that receives the action of the verb.

> I gave **her** a book.
> I gave **it** to **her**.

object relative pronoun A relative pronoun that is an object in an adjective clause.

> I'm reading a book **that** I really like.

paragraph A group of sentences, usually about one topic.

particle A word that looks like a preposition and combines with a main verb to form a phrasal verb. It often changes the meaning of the main verb.

> He looked the word **up**.
> *(He looked for the meaning of the word in the dictionary.)*

passive causative A sentence formed with *have* or *get* + object + past participle. It is used to talk about services that you arrange for someone to do for you.

> She **had the car checked** at the service station.
> He's going to **get his hair cut** by André.

passive sentence A sentence that focuses on the object (the person or thing receiving the action). The passive is formed with *be* + past participle.

> **The ball was kicked** by Ari.

past participle A verb form (verb + *-ed*). It can also be irregular. It is used to form the present perfect, past perfect, and future perfect. It can also be an adjective.

> We've **lived** here since April.
> They had **spoken** before.
> She's **interested** in math.

phrasal verb (also called *two-word verb*) A verb that has two parts (verb + particle). The meaning is often different from the meaning of its separate parts.

> He **grew up** in Texas. *(became an adult)*
> His parents **brought** him **up** to be honest. *(raised)*

phrase A group of words that form a unit without a main verb. Many phrases give information about time or place.

> **Last year**, we were living **in Canada**.

plural A form that means *two or more*.

> There **are** three **people** in the restaurant.
> **They are** eating dinner.
> **We** saw **them**.

possessive Nouns, pronouns, or adjectives that show a relationship or show that someone owns something.

> Zach is **Megan's** brother. *(possessive noun)*
> Is that car **his**? *(possessive pronoun)*
> That's **his** car. *(possessive adjective)*

predicate The part of a sentence that has the main verb. It tells what the subject is doing or describes the subject.

> My sister **works for a travel agency**.

preposition A word or phrase that goes before a noun or a pronoun to show time, place, or direction.

> Amy and I went **to** the cafeteria **on** Friday. She sits **next to** me **in** class.

progressive (also called **continuous**) The verb form *be* + verb + *-ing*. It focuses on the continuation (not the completion) of an action.

> She**'s reading** the paper.
> We **were watching** TV when you called.

pronoun A word used in place of a noun.

> That's my brother. You met **him** at my party.

proper noun A noun that is the name of a person, place, or thing. It begins with a capital letter.

> **Maria** goes to **Central High School**.
> It's on **High Street**.

punctuation Marks used in writing (period, comma, . . .) that make the meaning clear. For example, a period (**.**) shows the end of a sentence and that the sentence is a statement, not a question.

> "Come in**,**" she said**.**

quantifier A word or phrase that shows an amount (but not an exact amount). It often comes before a noun.

> Josh bought **a lot of** books last year.
> He doesn't have **much** money.

question See *yes/no* question, *wh-* question, **tag question**, **indirect question**, and **embedded question**.

question word See *wh-* word.

quoted speech See **direct speech**.

real conditional sentence A sentence that talks about general truths, habits, or things that happen again and again if a condition occurs. It can also talk about things that will happen in the future under certain circumstances.

> If it rains, he takes the bus.
> If it rains tomorrow, we'll take the bus with him.

regular A word that changes its form in the usual way.

> play → played
> fast → faster
> quick → quickly

relative pronoun A word that connects an adjective clause to a noun in the main clause.

> He's the man **who** lives next door.
> I'm reading a book **that** I really like.

reported speech See **indirect speech**.

reporting verb A verb such as *said*, *told*, or *asked*. It introduces direct and indirect speech. It can also come after the quotation in direct speech.

> Li **said**, "I'm going to be late." or "I'm going to be late," Li **said**. or "I'm going to be late," **said** Li.
> She **told** me that she was going to be late.

restrictive adjective clause See **identifying adjective clause**.

result clause The clause in a conditional sentence that talks about what happens if the condition occurs.

> If it rains, **I'll stay home**.
> If I had a million dollars, **I would travel**.
> If I had had your phone number, **I would have called you**.

sentence A group of words that has a subject and a main verb.

> **Computers are** very useful.

separable phrasal verb A phrasal verb whose parts can separate.

> Tom **looked** the word **up** in a dictionary.
> He **looked** it **up**.

short answer An answer to a *yes/no* question.

> A: Did you call me last night?
> B: **No, I didn't.** or **No.**

singular A form that means *one*.

> They have **a sister**.
> **She works** in **a hospital**.

statement A sentence that gives information. In writing, it ends in a period.

> Today is Monday.

stative verb See **non-action verb**.

subject The person, place, or thing that the sentence is about.

> **Ms. Chen** teaches English.
> **Her class** is interesting.

subject pronoun A pronoun that shows the person (*I, you, he, she, it, we, they*) that the sentence is about.

> **I** read a lot.
> **She** reads a lot, too.

subject relative pronoun A relative pronoun that is the subject of an adjective clause.

> He's the man **who** lives next door.

subordinate clause See **dependent clause**.

superlative The form of an adjective or adverb that is used to compare a person, place, or thing to a group of people, places, or things.

> Cindi is **the oldest** dancer in the group. *(adjective)*
> She dances **the most gracefully**. *(adverb)*

tag question A statement + tag. The **tag** is a short question at the end of the statement. Tag questions check information or comment on a situation.

> You're Jack Thompson, **aren't you?**
> It's a nice day, **isn't it?**

tense The form of a verb that shows the time of the action.

> **simple present:** Fabio **talks** to his friend every day.
> **simple past:** Fabio **talked** to his teacher yesterday.

third-person singular The pronouns *he, she,* and *it* or a singular noun. In the simple present, the third-person-singular verb ends in *-s*.

> Tomás **works** in an office. *(Tomás = he)*

three-word verb A phrasal verb + preposition.

> Slow down! I can't **keep up with** you.

time clause A clause that begins with a time word such as *when, before, after, while,* or *as soon as*.

> I'll call you **when I get home**.

transitive verb A verb that has an object.

> She **likes** apples.

two-word verb See **phrasal verb**.

unreal conditional sentence A sentence that talks about unreal conditions and their unreal results. The condition and its result can be untrue, imagined, or impossible.

> If I were a bird, I would fly around the world.
> If you had called, I would have invited you to the party.

verb A word that describes what the subject of the sentence does, thinks, feels, senses, or owns.

> They **run** two miles every day.
> She **loved** that movie.
> He **has** a new camera.

wh- question (also called **information question**) A question that begins with a *wh-* word. You answer a *wh-* question with information.

> A: **Where** are you going?
> B: To the store.

wh- word (also called **question word**) A word such as *who, what, when, where, which, why, how,* and *how much*. It can begin a *wh-* question or an embedded question.

> **Who** is that?
> **What** did you see?
> **When** does the movie usually start?
> I don't know **how much** it costs.

yes/no question A question that begins with a form of *be* or an auxiliary verb. You can answer a *yes/no* question with *yes* or *no*.

> A: **Are** you a student?
> B: **Yes**, I am. **or No**, I'm not.
> A: **Do** you come here often?
> B: **Yes**, I do. **or No**, I don't.

Unit Review Answer Key

Note: In this answer key, where a short or contracted form is given, the full or long form is also correct (unless the purpose of the exercise is to practice the short or contracted forms).

UNIT 1

A 1. studies
   2. are coming
   3. do
   4. understand
   5. use

B 1. 'm looking for
   2. think
   3. 's not **or** isn't carrying
   4. need
   5. see
   6. 's standing
   7. 's waiting
   8. sounds
   9. don't believe
   10. wants

C Hi Leda,

How <s>do you do</s> *are you doing* these days? We're all fine. I'm writing to tell you that <s>we</s> *we're* not living in California anymore. We just moved to Oregon. Also, <s>we expect</s> *we're expecting* a baby! We're looking for an interesting name for our new daughter. Do you have any ideas? Right now, we're thinking about *Gabriella* because <s>it's having</s> *it has* good nicknames. For example, *Gabby*, *Bree*, and *Ella* all seem good to us. How <s>are</s> *do* those nicknames sound to you?

We hope you'll write soon and tell us your news.

Love,
Samantha

UNIT 2

A 1. met
   2. was working
   3. saw
   4. had
   5. When
   6. was thinking
   7. gave

B 1. were…doing
   2. met
   3. were waiting
   4. met
   5. were studying
   6. noticed
   7. entered

C It was 2005. I <s>studied</s> *was studying* French in Paris <s>while</s> *when* I met Paul. Like me, Paul was from California. We were both taking the same 9:00 a.m. conversation class. After class, we always <s>were going</s> *went* to a café with some of our classmates. One day, while we <s>was</s> *were* drinking café au lait, Paul <s>was asking</s> *asked* me to go to a movie with him. After that, we started to spend most of our free time together. We really got to know each other well, and we discovered that we had a lot of similar interests. When the course was over, we left Paris and <s>were going</s> *went* back to California together. The next year, we got married!

UNIT 3

A 1. has been
   2. took
   3. has been reading
   4. started
   5. has gone
   6. for
   7. have become

B 1. has been working **or** has worked
   2. discovered
   3. didn't know
   4. found out
   5. got
   6. has been going **or** has gone
   7. hasn't found
   8. has been having **or** has had

C A: How long <s>did</s> *have* you been doing adventure sports?

B: <s>I've gotten</s> *I got* interested five years ago, and I haven't stopped since then.

A: You're lucky to live here in Colorado. It's a great place for adventure sports. <s>Did you live</s> *Have you lived* **or** *Have you been living* here long?

B: No, not long. <s>I've</s> *I* moved here last year. I used to live in Alaska.

A: I haven't <s>go</s> *gone* there yet, but I've heard it's great.

B: It *is* great. When you go, be sure to visit Denali National Park.

UNIT 4

A 1. had gotten
   2. had been studying
   3. had graduated
   4. moved
   5. hadn't given

B 1. had…been playing
2. joined
3. 'd decided
4. 'd been practicing
5. 'd taught
6. Had…come
7. 'd…moved
8. 'd…been living
9. hadn't been expecting

C   When five-year-old Sarah Chang enrolled in the Juilliard School, she ~~has~~ *had* already been playing the violin for more than a year. Her parents, both musicians, had ~~been moving~~ *moved* from Korea to further their careers. They had ~~gave~~ *given* their daughter a violin as a fourth birthday present, and Sarah had been ~~practiced~~ *practicing* hard since then. By seven, she ʌ already performed with several local orchestras. A child prodigy, Sarah became the youngest person to receive the Hollywood Bowl's Hall of Fame Award. She had already ~~been receiving~~ *received* several awards including the Nan Pa Award—South Korea's highest prize for musical talent.

UNIT 5

A 1. turn
2. Are
3. doing
4. is
5. is going to
6. you're
7. finishes

B 1. will…be doing **or** are…going to be doing
2. 'll be leaving
3. 'll…be going
4. won't be coming **or** 're not going to be coming
5. Is…going to cause **or** Will…cause
6. No…it isn't. **or** No…it won't.
7. 'll be **or** 's going to be
8. 'll see

C A: How long are you going to ~~staying~~ *stay or be staying* in Beijing?

B: I'm not sure. I'll let you know as soon as ~~I'll~~ find out, OK?

A: OK. It's going to be a long flight. What will you ~~doing~~ *do or be doing* to pass the time?

B: I'll ~~be work~~ *work or be working* a lot of the time. And I'm going to try to sleep.

A: Good idea. Have fun, and ~~I'm emailing~~ *I'll email* you all the office news. I promise.

UNIT 6

A 1. have been selling
2. we get
3. have been exercising
4. I'll have read
5. By

B 1. 'll have been living
2. 'll have been studying
3. 'll have graduated
4. graduate
5. 'll have found
6. 'll have made
7. 'll have earned

C   I'm so excited about your news! By the time you read this, you'll already have ~~moving~~ *moved* into your new house! And I have some good news, too. By the end of this month, I'll have ~~save~~ *saved* $5,000. That's enough for me to buy a used car! And that means that by this time next year, ~~I drive~~ *I'll have driven* to California to visit you! I have more news, too. By the time I ~~will~~ graduate, I will have ~~been~~ started my new part-time job. I hope that by this time next year, I'll also ~~had~~ *have* finished working on my latest invention—a solar-powered flashlight.

    It's hard to believe that in June, we will have been ~~being~~ friends for ten years. Time sure flies! And we'll have ~~been stayed~~ *stayed or been staying* in touch even though we are 3,000 miles apart. Isn't technology a great thing?

UNIT 7

A 1. isn't
2. Didn't
3. You've
4. it
5. has
6. she
7. Shouldn't

B 1. have
2. No, I haven't
3. Aren't
4. No, I'm not
5. are
6. won't
7. Yes, you will

C A: Ken hasn't come back from Korea yet, has ~~Ken~~ *he*?

B: ~~No~~ *Yes*, he has. He got back last week. Didn't he call you when he got back?

A: No, he didn't. He's probably busy. There are a lot

of things to do when you move, ~~isn't~~ _aren't_ there?

B: Definitely. And I guess his family ~~wanted~~ _will want_ to spend a

lot of time with him, won't they?

A: I'm sure they will. You know, I think I'll just call

him. You have his phone number, ~~have~~ _don't_ you?

B: Yes, I do. Could you wait while I get it off my

phone? You're not in a hurry, ~~aren't~~ _are_ you?

UNIT 8

A 1. does   5. doesn't
    2. So   6. too
    3. hasn't either   7. either
    4. but

B 1. I speak Spanish, and so does my brother.
      or …my brother does too.
    2. I can't speak Russian, and neither can my brother.
      or …my brother can't either.
    3. Jaime lives in Chicago, but his brother doesn't.
    4. Chen doesn't play tennis, but his sister does.
    5. Diego doesn't eat meat, and neither does Lila.
      or …Lila doesn't either.

C   My friend Alicia and I have a lot in common. She

comes from Los Angeles, and so ~~I do~~ _do I_. She speaks

Spanish. I ~~speak~~ _do_ too. Her parents are both teachers,

and mine ~~do~~ _are_ too. She doesn't have any brothers or

sisters. ~~Either~~ _Neither_ do I. There are some differences, too.

Alicia is very reserved, but ~~I am~~ _I'm not_. I like to talk about

my feelings and say what's on my mind. Alicia doesn't

like sports, but I ~~don't~~ _do_. I'm on several school teams,

~~and~~ _but_ she isn't. I think our differences make things more

interesting, and so ~~do~~ _does_ Alicia!

UNIT 9

A 1. to use
    2. (in order) to save
    3. ordering
    4. to relax
    5. (to) study
    6. preparing
    7. Stopping
    8. to eat
    9. not to have **or** not having
   10. Cooking

B 1. doesn't **or** didn't remember going
    2. wants **or** wanted Al to take
    3. wonders **or** wondered about Chu's **or** Chu eating
    4. didn't stop to have
    5. forgot to mail

C A: I was happy to hear that the cafeteria is serving

salads now. I'm eager ~~trying~~ _to try_ them.

B: Me too. Someone recommended ~~to eat~~ _eating_ more salads

to lose weight.

A: It was that TV doctor, right? He's always urging ~~we~~ _us_

to exercise more, too.

B: That's the one. He's actually convinced me to stop

~~to eat~~ _eating_ meat.

A: Interesting! That would be a hard decision for us

~~making~~ _to make_, though. We love to barbecue.

UNIT 10

A 1. helped   4. let
    2. had   5. got
    3. made

B 1. didn't **or** wouldn't let me have
    2. got them to buy
    3. made me walk
    4. had me feed
    5. didn't **or** wouldn't help me take
    6. got him to give
    7. let them have

C   Lately, I've been thinking a lot about all the people

who helped me ~~adjusting~~ _adjust_ **or** _to adjust_ to moving here when I was

a kid. My parents got me ~~join~~ _to join_ some school clubs, so

I met other kids. Then my dad helped me ~~improved~~ _improve_ **or** _to improve_

my soccer game so that I could join the team. And my

mom never let me ~~to stay~~ _stay_ home. She made me ~~to get~~ _get_

out and do things. My parents also spoke to my new

teacher and had ~~she~~ _her_ call on me a lot, so the other kids

got to know me quickly. Our next-door neighbors

helped, too. They got ~~I~~ _me_ to walk their dog Red, and

Red introduced me to all her human friends! The fact

that so many people wanted to help me made me

~~to realize~~ _realize_ that I was not alone. Before long, I felt part

of my new school, my new neighborhood, and my

new life.

A 1. f   3. a   5. b   7. g
   2. e   4. c   6. d

B 1. get through with my work
   2. pick it up
   3. count on her
   4. call me back
   5. got off the phone
   6. put my pajamas on
   7. turned the lights off

C   I'm so tired of telemarketers ~~calling up me~~ *calling me up* as soon as I get back from work or just when I sit ~~up~~ *down* for a relaxing dinner! It's gotten to the point that I've stopped picking *up* the phone when it rings between 6:00 and 8:00 p.m. ~~up~~. I know I can count on it being a telemarketer who will try to talk me into spending money on something I don't want. But it's still annoying to hear the phone ring, so sometimes I ~~turn off it~~ *turn it off*. Then, of course, I worry that it may be someone important. So I end up checking caller ID to find out. I think the Do Not Call list is a great idea. Who ~~thought up it~~ *thought it up*? I'm going to ~~sign for it up~~ *sign up for it* tomorrow!

A 1. are   4. which
   2. whose   5. that
   3. thinks   6. who

B 1. who or that behave   5. that or which hurt
   2. who uses   6. which…upset
   3. which…convince   7. whose…is
   4. who or that…speaks

C   It's true that we are often attracted to people ~~which~~ *who or that* are very different from ourselves. An extrovert, ~~which~~ *whose* personality is very outgoing, will often connect with a romantic partner who ~~are~~ *is* an introvert. They are both attracted to someone that ~~have~~ *has* different strengths. My cousin Valerie, who is an extreme extrovert, recently married Bill, whose idea of a party is a Scrabble game on the Internet. Can this marriage succeed? Will Bill learn the salsa, ~~that~~ *which* is Valerie's favorite dance? Will Valerie start collecting unusual words? Their friends, ~~that~~ *who* care about both of them, are hoping for the best.

A 1. whose   4. who
   2. that   5. when
   3. where   6. who

B 1. where   5. whose
   2. that or which   6. who(m)
   3. that or which   7. when or that
   4. who(m) or that

C   I grew up in an apartment building ~~who~~ *that or which or no relative pronoun* my grandparents owned. There was a small dining room ~~when~~ *where* we had family meals and a kitchen in ~~that~~ *which* I ate my breakfast. My aunt, uncle, and cousin, in ~~who~~ *whose* home I spent a lot of my time, lived in an identical apartment on the fourth floor. I remember the time that my parents gave me a toy phone set that we used ~~it~~ so I could talk to my cousin. There weren't many children in the building, but I often visited the building manager, ~~who's~~ *whose* son I liked. I enjoyed living in the apartment, but for me the day ~~where~~ *when or that or no relative pronoun* we moved into our own house was the best day of my childhood.

A 1. get   6. to post
   2. may   7. must not
   3. 've got   8. be able to
   4. can't   9. might be
   5. help

B 1. 'd better not give or shouldn't give or ought not to give
   2. must register or 'd better register or 've got to register
   3. must not be
   4. must get or has to get or has got to get
   5. can't eat or must not eat
   6. may come or might come or could come

C 1. Could that ~~being~~ *be* Amelie in this photograph?
   2. With this site, I ~~must not~~ *don't have to* call to keep in touch with friends. It's just not necessary.

3. I don't know this person. I guess I'd ~~not better~~ *better not*

accept him as a friend on my Facebook page.

4. That doesn't look anything like Anton. It ~~doesn't~~ *can't*

~~have to~~ be him.

5. Were you able ~~remove~~ *to remove* that embarrassing photo?

UNIT 15

A
1. have
2. ought
3. could
4. given
5. shouldn't
6. should I

B
1. I should've studied for the math test.
2. You could have shown me your class notes.
3. I shouldn't have stayed up so late the night before the test.
4. He ought to have called you.
5. You might've invited me to join the study group.

C
I shouldn't have ~~stay~~ *stayed* up so late. I overslept and missed my bus. I ~~ought have~~ *ought to have* asked Erik for a ride. I got to the office late, and my boss said, "You might have ~~had~~ called." She was right. I ~~shouldn't have~~ *should've* called. At lunch, my co-workers went out together. They really could ~~of~~ *have* invited me to join them. Should ~~have I~~ *I have* said something to them? Then, after lunch, my mother called. She said, "Yesterday was Aunt Em's birthday. You could've ~~sending~~ *sent* her a card!" I really think my mother might ~~has~~ *have* reminded me. Not a good day! I ~~shouldn't have~~ *should've* just stayed in bed.

UNIT 16

A
1. must
2. might not have
3. have
4. taken
5. may
6. have
7. couldn't

B
1. might not have gotten my message **or** may not have gotten my message
2. must not have studied
3. couldn't have forgotten our date **or** can't have forgotten our date
4. may have been at the movies **or** might have been at the movies **or** could have been at the movies
5. must have forgotten
6. must not have seen me

C
Why did the Aztecs build their capital city in the middle of a lake? Could they ~~had~~ *have* wanted the protection of the water? They might have ~~been~~. Or the location may ~~has~~ *have* helped them to control nearby societies. At first, it must have ~~being~~ *been* an awful place, full of mosquitoes and fog. But it must ~~no~~ *not* have been a bad idea—the island city became the center of a very powerful empire. To succeed, the Aztecs had to have ~~became~~ *become* fantastic engineers quite quickly. When the Spanish arrived, they couldn't have ~~expect~~ *expected* the amazing palaces, floating gardens, and well-built canals. They must have been astounded.

UNIT 17

A
1. Spanish is spoken in Bolivia.
2. They play soccer in Bolivia.
3. Reza Deghati took the photo.
4. The articles were translated into Spanish.
5. Quinoa is grown in the mountains.
6. They named the main street El Prado.

B
1. was discovered
2. is spoken
3. is grown
4. is exported
5. are employed **or** have been employed
6. was made
7. has been performed
8. is attended

C
Photojournalist Alexandra Avakian was born and ~~raise~~ *raised* in New York. Since she began her career, she has covered many of the world's most important stories. Her work ~~have~~ *has* been published in many newspapers and magazines including *National Geographic*, and her photographs have ~~being~~ *been* exhibited around the world. Avakian has also written a book, *Window of the Soul: My Journey in the Muslim World*, which was ~~been~~ published in 2008. It has not yet been translated ~~by translators~~ into other languages, but the chapter titles appear in both English and Arabic. Avakian's book ~~have be~~ *has been* discussed on international TV, radio, and numerous websites.

UNIT 18

A
1. done
2. be replaced
3. could
4. had
5. be
6. won't
7. has
8. handled

B
1. should be trained
2. have to be given
3. must be tested
4. can be experienced
5. will be provided
6. may be sent
7. could…be developed

C   The new spacesuits are going to be ~~testing~~ *tested*
underwater today. They've got to ~~been~~ *be* improved
before they can be used on the Moon or Mars. Two
astronauts are going to be wearing them while they're
working, and they'll *be* watched by the engineers. This
morning, communication was lost with the Earth's
surface, and all decisions had to be ~~make~~ *made* by the
astronauts themselves. It was a very realistic situation.
This crew ~~will got~~ *will have or has got* to be very well prepared for space
travel. They're going to the Moon in a few years.

UNIT 19

A
1. have it cut
2. done
3. get
4. your house painted
5. by

B
1. get it repaired
2. have them cleaned
3. have them shortened
4. get it colored
5. get it fixed
6. had it removed
7. get it renewed
8. 'll have it checked **or** 'm going to have it checked
   or 'm having it checked

C   I'm going on vacation next week. I'd like to have
~~done some work~~ *some work done* in my office, and this seems like a
good time for it. Please have my carpet ~~clean~~ *cleaned* while
I'm gone. And could you have my computer and
printer looked at? It's been quite a while since they've
been serviced. Ted wants to have my office painted
~~by a painter~~ while I'm gone. Please tell him any color
is fine except pink! Last week, I ~~had designed some~~ *had some new brochures designed*
~~new brochures~~ by Perfect Print. Please call the printer

and have them delivered directly to the sales reps.
And could you also ~~get made up more business cards~~? *get more business cards made up*
When I get back, it'll be time to plan the holiday
party. I think we should have it catered this year ~~from~~ *by*
a professional. While I'm gone, why don't you call
around and get some estimates from caterers? ~~Has~~ *Have* the
estimates sent to Ted. Thanks.

UNIT 20

A
1. do…do
2. are
3. is
4. shop
5. happens
6. doesn't stay
7. closes
8. go
9. feel
10. think

B
1. When **or** If it's 7:00 a.m. in Honolulu, what time is
   it in Mumbai?
2. If you love jewelry, you should visit an
   international jewelry show.
3. A tourist may have more fun if she tries
   bargaining.
4. If **or** When you're shopping at an outdoor market,
   you can always bargain for a good price.
5. But don't try to bargain if **or** when you're shopping
   in a big department store.

C
1. If I don't like something I bought online, then I
   ~~returned~~ *return* it.
2. Don't buy from an online siteₓ if you don't know
   anything about the company.
3. When ~~he'll~~ *he* shops online, Frank always saves a lot
   of time.
4. I always ~~fell~~ *fall* asleep if I fly at night. It happens
   every time.
5. Isabel always has a wonderful timeₓ when she
   visits Istanbul.

UNIT 21

A
1. d
2. f
3. a
4. c
5. b
6. e

B
1. a. take
   b. 'll be **or** 'm going to be
2. a. will…do **or** are…going to do
   b. don't get
   c. 'll stay **or** 'm going to stay
   d. get

3. a. pass
  b. 'll celebrate **or** 'm going to celebrate

C It's been a hard week, and I'm looking forward to the weekend. If the weather ~~will be~~ *is* nice tomorrow, Marco and I are going to go to the beach. The ocean is usually too cold for swimming at this time of year, so I probably ~~don't~~ *won't* go in the water unless it's really hot outside. But I love walking along the beach and breathing in the fresh sea air.

  If Marco has time, he might ~~makes~~ *make* some sandwiches to bring along. Otherwise, we'll just get some pizza. I hope it'll be a nice day. I just listened to the weather report, and there may be some rain in the afternoon. ~~Unless~~ *If* it rains, ~~we~~ *we'll* probably go to the movies instead. That's our Plan B. But I really want to go to the beach, so I'm keeping my fingers crossed!

UNIT 22

A 1. I'd feel
2. were
3. could
4. you found
5. could
6. weren't
7. I'd

B 1. would…do
2. found
3. Would…take
4. knew
5. would become
6. put
7. made
8. would learn

C 1. Pablo wishes he ~~can~~ *could* speak German.
2. If he had the time, ~~he'll~~ *he'd* study in Germany. But he doesn't have the time right now.
3. He could get a promotion ~~when~~ *if* he spoke another language.
4. His company ~~may~~ *might* pay the tuition if he took a course.
5. What would you do if you ~~are~~ *were* in Pablo's situation?

UNIT 23

A 1. hadn't told
2. had
3. would have been
4. If
5. gone

B 1. **a.** would've been
  b. hadn't missed
  c. had been
  d. wouldn't have discovered
2. **a.** hadn't accepted
  b. had taken
  c. wouldn't have met
3. **a.** hadn't seen
  b. wouldn't have believed

C Tonight, we watched the movie *Back to the Future* starring Michael J. Fox. I might never ~~had~~ *have* seen it if I hadn't read his autobiography, *Lucky Man*. His book was so good that I wanted to see his most famous movie. Now, I wish I ~~saw~~ *had seen* it in the theater when it first came out, but I hadn't even been born yet! It would have been better if we ~~would have~~ *had* watched it on a big screen. Fox was great. He looked really young—just like a teenager. But I would have recognized him even ~~when~~ *if* I hadn't known he was in the film.

  In real life, when Fox was a teenager, he was too small to become a professional hockey player. But if he hadn't looked so young, he ~~can't~~ *couldn't* **or** *wouldn't* have gotten his role in the TV hit series *Family Ties*. In Hollywood, he had to sell his furniture to pay his bills, but he kept trying to find an acting job. If he ~~would have~~ *had* given up, he might never have become a star.

UNIT 24

A 1. says
2. "I'd love to."
3. planned
4. he
5. she'd cooked
6. told
7. had been
8. his

B 1. (that) she always gets up early **or** she always got up early.
2. (that) water boils at 100 degrees Celsius **or** water boiled at 100 degrees Celsius.
3. (that) he liked my haircut **or** he likes my haircut.
4. (that) she loved the pasta **or** she had loved the pasta.
5. (that) it was his own recipe **or** it is his own recipe.
6. (that) she mailed him the check **or** she had mailed him the check.
7. (that) his boss had liked his work **or** his boss liked his work.

C 1. A psychologist I know often tells me ×that people today tell hundreds of lies every day.×

2. Yesterday, Mia's boyfriend ~~said~~ [told] her that he liked her new dress.

3. When she heard that, Mia said she didn't really believe ~~you~~ [him].

4. I didn't think that was so bad. I said that her boyfriend ~~tells~~ [told or had told] her a little white lie.

5. But Mia hates lying. She said that to ~~me~~ [her], all lies were wrong.

UNIT 25

A 1. was   5. today
2. I   6. would
3. take   7. could
4. might   8. there

B 1. (that) it was going to rain
2. (that) it could be the worst storm this year
3. (that) it was going to start soon
4. (that) they should buy water
5. (that) they had to leave right then
6. (that) she would call me the next day

C What a storm! They said it ~~is~~ [was] going to be bad, but it was terrible. They said it ~~will~~ [would] last two days, but it lasted four. On the first day of the storm, my mother called and told me that we should ~~have left~~ [leave] the house right ~~now~~ [then]. (I still can hear her exact words: "You should leave the house *right now!*") We should have listened to her! We just didn't believe it was going to be so serious. I told her last night that if we had known, we would ~~had~~ [have] left right away. We're lucky we survived. I just listened to the weather forecast. Good news! They said tomorrow should ~~have been~~ [be] sunny.

UNIT 26

A 1. . (period)   5. say
2. give   6. told
3. "Please lie down."   7. advised
4. not to

B 1. He told **or** asked her to show him her license.
2. She advised **or** told him to get more exercise.

3. She invited **or** asked them to come to the English Department party.
4. He asked her to turn on the light.
5. She invited **or** asked them to hang out at her house.

C Too much stress is bad for your health. So, I asked my doctor ʌ[to] give me some tips on how to reduce everyday stress. First of all, she told me ~~exercising~~ [to exercise] every day. She also told me ~~to don't~~ [not to] work too long without taking a break. She advised me ~~doing~~ [to do] things to relax. For example, she said ~~that~~ [to do] to listen to music. She also ~~said~~ [told] me to sit with my eyes closed and to concentrate on my breathing. That helps lower blood pressure. She also advised me ~~no~~ [not to] drink too many beverages with caffeine. Finally, she said to ×get enough sleep×—at least seven hours a night!

UNIT 27

A 1. . (period)   4. I lived
2. if   5. I had
3. their office was

B 1. who the company had hired.
2. if **or** whether **or** whether or not I had taken the job.
3. if **or** whether **or** whether or not I liked my job.
4. how long I had worked there.
5. how many employees worked there.
6. why I wanted to work for them.
7. what the starting salary was.
8. if **or** whether **or** whether or not I could start soon.

C They asked me so many questions! They asked me where ~~did I work~~ [I worked]. They asked me who ~~was my boss~~ [my boss was]. They asked why I ~~did want~~ [wanted] to change jobs. They asked how much money I made. They ~~ask~~ [asked] me who I ~~have~~ [had] voted for in the last election. They even asked me what my favorite color ~~was?~~ [was.] Finally, I asked myself whether or ~~no~~ [not] I really wanted that job!

UNIT 28

A 1. we should   5. I should
2. our server is   6. ? (question mark)
3. . (period)   7. whether
4. to

B 1. where the restaurant is?
   2. if or whether the subway goes to the museum.
   3. if or whether we should tip the porter.
   4. why we didn't buy the book on tipping.
   5. how much we should tip the tour guide.
   6. if or whether you have any travel books.
   7. what this sign says?

C A: Hi. Is this a good time to call? I wasn't sure what

   time you have dinner?

   if or whether you were
   B: This is fine. I didn't know ~~were you~~ back from

   your trip.

A: We got back two days ago. I can't remember if I
   emailed
   ~~email~~ you some photographs.
                                                    you took
B: Yes. They were great. Can you tell me where ~~took~~

   ~~you~~ that picture of the lake? I want to go!
                              that was
A: Hmm. I'm not sure which one ~~was that~~. We saw a

   lot of lakes in Switzerland.

B: I'll show it to you. I'd really like to find out where
   it is
   ~~is it~~.

Information Gaps, Student B

EXERCISE 10 DR. EON'S CALENDAR

A INFORMATION GAP Work with a partner. Student B will follow the instructions below. Student A will follow the instructions on page 83.

STUDENT B

- Complete Dr. Eon's calendar. Get information from Student A. Ask questions and fill in the calendar. Answer Student A's questions.

  EXAMPLE: **A:** What will Dr. Eon be doing on Sunday the first?

  B: She'll be flying to Tokyo. What about on the second? Will she be taking the day off?

  A: No, she'll be meeting with Dr. Kato.

FEBRUARY 2077

SUNDAY	MONDAY	TUESDAY	WEDNESDAY	THURSDAY	FRIDAY	SATURDAY
1 fly to Tokyo	2 meet with Dr. Kato	3 attend World Future Conference	4 →→→→	5	6	7 →→→
8	9	10	11 ←→	12 fly to Denver	13 visit Mom and Dad	14 →→
15	16 give speech at Harvard University	17 meet with Dr. Rover	18	19 →→→	20 →→	21
22 relax!	23 work at home	24 →→→→	25	26	27 →→	28

B Now compare calendars with your partner. Are they the same?

EXERCISE 11 LONDON AND VANCOUVER

INFORMATION GAP Work with a partner. Student B will follow the instructions below.
Student A will follow the instructions on page 115.

STUDENT B

- Read about London and answer Student A's questions.

  EXAMPLE: A: London is the largest city in the United Kingdom, isn't it?
  B: Yes, it is.

LONDON

London is the capital and largest city of the
United Kingdom. It is also one of the oldest
and largest cities in the world. Located in
southeastern England, the city lies on the River
Thames, which links it to shipping routes
throughout the world. Because of its size, the
city is divided into thirty-two "boroughs" or
parts. With its many museums, palaces, parks,
and theaters, tourism is a major industry. In
fact, millions of tourists visit the city every
year to take advantage of its many cultural and
historical offerings. Unfortunately, like many
great urban centers, London has problems such
as traffic congestion, crime, and homelessness.

- Now look at the questions below. What do you know about Vancouver? Complete the
  questions by circling the correct words and writing the tags.

  1. Vancouver is / (isn't) the largest city in Canada, *is it* _____?

  2. It lies / doesn't lie on the Atlantic Coast, _____?

  3. It has / doesn't have a very large port, _____?

  4. It is / isn't a very beautiful city, _____?

  5. Many / Not many tourists visit the city, _____?

  6. You can / can't hear many different languages there, _____?

  7. Movie production is / isn't an important industry in Vancouver, _____?

- Ask Student A the questions. Student A will read a paragraph about Vancouver and tell
  you if your information is correct or not.

  EXAMPLE: B: Vancouver isn't the largest city in Canada, is it?
  A: No, it isn't. It's the third largest city.

EXERCISE 10 THE PHILIPPINES

A INFORMATION GAP Work with a partner. Student B will follow the instructions below. Student A will follow the instructions on page 283.

STUDENT B

- The Philippines consists of many islands and has many natural resources. Look at the map of Mindanao and complete the chart. Write *Y* for *Yes* if Mindanao has a particular resource and *N* for *No* if it does not.

- Student A has the map of Luzon. Ask Student A questions about Luzon and complete the chart for Luzon.

  EXAMPLE: **B:** Is tobacco grown in Luzon?
  A: Yes, it is. It's grown in the northern and central part of the island.

- Student A doesn't have the map of Mindanao. Answer Student A's questions about Mindanao.

  EXAMPLE: **A:** Is tobacco grown in Mindanao?
  B: No, it isn't.

		MINDANAO	LUZON
G R O W	tobacco	N	Y
	corn		
	bananas		
	coffee		
	pineapples		
	sugar		
R A I S E	cattle		
	pigs		
M I N E	gold		
	manganese		
P R O D U C E	cotton		
	rubber		
	lumber		

Mindanao

B When you are finished, compare charts. Are they the same?

Index

This index is for the full and split editions. All entries are in the full book. Entries for Volume A of the split edition are in black. Entries for Volume B are in blue.